Candiru

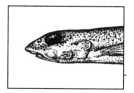

Other books by Stephen Spotte

Secrets of the Deep (essays)

Artificial Seawaters: Formulas and Methods (with Joseph P. Bidwell)

Captive Seawater Fishes: Science and Technology

Marine Aquarium Keeping (second edition)

An Optimist in Hell: Stories (fiction)

Home is the Sailor, Under the Sea: Mermaid Stories (fiction)

Whoever you are, be that person with all your might. Time goes by faster than we thought.

—Barry Hannah, "Get Some Young"

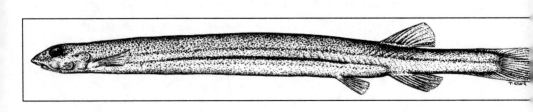

Candiru

LIFE AND LEGEND OF THE BLOODSUCKING CATFISHES

Stephen Spotte

CREATIVE ARTS BOOK COMPANY

Berkeley ∿ California

For information contact:
Creative Arts Book Company
833 Bancroft Way
Berkeley, California 94710

ISBN 088739-469-8

Library of Congress Catalog Number 2002105145

Printed in the United States of America

CONTENTS

ACKNOWLEDGEMENTS

I thank Naercio Aquino Menezes, Ramiro Barriga, João Batista Ferraz, Bruce B. Collette, Marion Conway, Stephen R. L. Farrar, John W. Fitzpatrick, Karsten E. Hartel, Gene S. Helfman, Colleen Hurter, Lois Jennings and the fourth-year Latin class of Fitch Senior High School (year 2001), William E. Kelley, Louis M. Kerr, Roosevelt McMillan Jr., Leslie K. Overstreet, Lynn Park, Patricio Ponce, Lúcia Rapp Py-Daniel, Ivan Sazima, Richard M. Segedi, Linnea Smith, Roxanna M. Smolowitz, Donald J. Stewart, Brad Stirn, Ricardo Y. Tsukamoto, and Jennifer Walton. For extended aid and tolerance, special thanks to the library staff of the Marine Biological Laboratory/Woods Hole Oceanographic Institution, James W. Atz, Ning Labbish Chao, Tamara L. Clark, R. Bruce Gillie, Erika Muschaweck, Paulo Petry, Robert E. Schmidt, Lucia S. Spotte, and Jansen A. S. Zuanon. The stanza from Theodore Roethke's poem "In a Dark Time" has been reproduced by permission of Doubleday, a division of Random House, Inc.

With two exceptions, passages from the foreign literature translated into English and published previously have been retranslated for this project. Much new material has also been included. Many of these sources are obscure and not easily found. In the interest of scholarship, the original foreign-language texts have been reproduced in the endnotes.

Introduction

Except for three species of vampire bats, certain small slender catfishes of the family Trichomycteridae (formerly family Pygidiidae)[1] are the only vertebrates believed to subsist solely on blood,[2] and they live exclusively in the tropical freshwaters of South America. Everything about them seems ambiguous, including the name. In Brazil they go by *candiru*, which supposedly means "pest," a term thought to be of Tupi origin.[3] In Spanish-speaking countries the terms used are *carnero* ("meat-eater") and *canero*. The origin and meaning of *canero* are uncertain.

I first heard about candirus on a late afternoon in January 1965 in Niagara Falls, New York. Bill Kelley, my boss at the time, was discussing South American rainforests in a setting that couldn't have been more antipodean. Outside the motel window lay a bleak, arctic landscape—snowdrifts mounded like sleeping bears, screes of dirty snow collapsed against buildings, glittering snowflakes turned sepia by the street lights.

Several of us were gathered in a room that served as a makeshift office while the new public aquarium was under construction. Bill had been discussing administrative matters, but lost interest. He held a kitchen match to his pipe while the rest of us waited impatiently. To me, this was all very exotic. I was 21 and just out of college. Charlie Beck, Charlie Radcliffe, and Win Brady were also present, along with Bill's wife, Ruthie. The aquarium itself consisted mostly of a cavernous hole in the ground and a roll of blueprints. Win had been hired as director; the two Charlies and I would take care of the animals and plants once the facility was built.

Bill blew smoke at the ceiling. "What we need," he said, "is a candiru exhibit." The rest of us looked at each other, except Ruthie, who grinned at the floor.

We passed the bottle of bourbon around. Having gotten our attention, Bill settled into his chair. "Candirus are little catfishes, very thin." He held up the blackened match. "Thicker than this and somewhat longer. In South America you hear stories about candirus swimming up somebody's pecker or asshole. Then they erect their gill spines so you can't pull them out. If you're the victim, that's a helluva problem."

Everyone laughed. "So how does this translate into an exhibit?" Win asked. "Do we have our visitors dangle their peckers in the water?"

Bill explained how candirus survive by sucking blood from the gills of other fishes. "They're like leeches. They latch on, suck blood for a few minutes, and drop off. You could use big carp to feed them. At the Cleveland Aquarium we had some candirus that sucked blood from goldfish. I've brought along copies of the published report." He nodded at a stack of reprints on the coffee table.

"Do candirus really attack people?" someone asked.

"I don't know." And he told us this story. A few years previously he and a colleague had been collecting fishes along the Rio Branco in what was then British Guiana. Nearby was a general store run by a Chinese national. Bill didn't recall having ever seen the proprietor. When they finished their work and returned to Georgetown, the airport manager told them he had recently visited this same man. They were friends and enjoyed taking a swim in the river on hot afternoons. One day the proprietor had taken off his bathing suit and was lolling naked in the water when a candiru swam into his rectum. Surgery had been necessary to remove it.

"Ever since," Bill said, "I've never waded in those waters without a swimsuit and a tight sphincter."

Even today candirus remain unknown outside ichthyological circles except for their peculiar and rare tendency to penetrate the urethra, vagina, or rectum of an unwary bather and lodge there. Most don't do this although, as lifestyles go, entering the gill chambers of large fishes to gorge vampirelike on their blood is hardly bourgeois.

That same year I began collecting information on candirus and filing it away in a cardboard box. Bill's report, coauthored with Jim Atz, was my first acquisition and remains among the best available. Years passed. I moved many times, but the box always went with me, and the stack of papers inside it grew thicker. Then in 1998 I decided to investigate the subject myself and attempt to answer the most basic and intriguing questions. Which sensory mechanisms might help candirus find prey in the murky rivers? How many species of candirus are there, and how can they be told apart? Are stories of attacks on human beings really true?

The answer to this last question is yes, but ferreting out the evidence wasn't easy. Despite numerous anecdotal accounts of candiru attacks, fully documented cases proved elusive. The 1829 report of Carl Friedrich Phillip von Martius, a German botanist who had traveled in Brazil, was the first to appear in the European literature. Typically, his words have the hollow ring of someone offering hearsay instead of proof. Based on such paltry evidence, what propelled his and similar tales into modern times? Where was the smoking gun? In Brazil, as things turned out, although by the time I arrived 2 years after the only confirmed attack, the odor of cordite was barely perceptible.

The candiru's story is kaleidoscopic, with elements imbedded in literature, language, exploration, science, philosophy, medicine, history, and legend. As I hope to show, what we know about the candiru is more than a compendium of ignorance and gruesome tales twice told. Candirus are very eventful creatures. They don't need our urethras to be interesting.

My narrative is neither wholly factual nor entirely fictitious, which is hardly surprising. The candiru hovers before us like a wraith, its biology no less elusive than its legend. Should I have strived for a more exacting separation of fact and fiction? Probably not. As Hemingway said, good books are truer than if they had really happened. There are stories to tell, so stick around. I'll take you on a wild ride down foggy rivers where truth and legend intersect and become, if just for a moment, indistinguishable.

Stephen Spotte
July 2001

It is a general rule that when the grain of truth cannot be found,
men will swallow great helpings of falsehood.

—Isaac Bashevis Singer, "Yentl the Yeshiva Boy"[1]

1.

Culmination of Evils

In Larry McMurtry's novel *Duane's Depressed*, the protagonist rents a room at a fleabag motel in west Texas called the Stingaree Courts where the hot water is cold, the cold water nonexistent, the mattress sags like a hammock, and the TV is stuck on the porno channel at high volume. He asks for a different room and is given the bridal suite. Everything works normally. The bed, however, smells fishy. That's because it's a waterbed, and living inside it is a catfish. No one knows how a catfish got in there or how it survives.

When the Stingaree eventually closes and someone comes to drain the bed, out flips the catfish, by then a local celebrity. An old man mopping the floor of the nearby Silver Slipper Bar demonstrates a certain grasp of proportion: "'No, it wasn't what you'd call big,' the old man said. 'How big could a catfish get, living in a damn water bed? But, like I said, it made the TV.'"

On hearing about a catfish inside a waterbed, Eugene Willis Gudger (Fig. 1) might have been on a train to Texas. Nobody had yet thought up waterbeds in Gudger's day, which is probably why he never wrote about them as possible living quarters for catfishes. A celibate, bookish man in the ichthyology department of the American Museum of Natural History in New York City between 1919 and 1953, Gudger was keenly interested in

Fɪɢ. 1 Eugene Willis Gudger, author of *The Candirú*. Source: Department of Library Services, American Museum of Natural History.

unusual interactions between fishes and people. Some of his publications dealt with rains of fishes during violent storms, migrating eels trapped in household water pipes, fishing dogs and fishing cormorants, the supposed predation of the giant European catfish (*Silurus glanus*) on humans, and attacks on boats by swordfish. He wrote about a shark found stuck in an automobile tire and about small fishes becoming entrapped in discarded "rubber bands," which he refused to accept were condom rings.[2]

The idea of a little South American catfish penetrating the orifice of an unwary bather fit well with the bizarre nature of these other subjects. In 1930, Gudger's investigation of candiru attacks on humankind appeared in two parts in *American Journal of Surgery*.[3] That same year the articles were combined and published as a short book called *The Candirú*.[4] Except for a brief preface written by Gudger and a foreword contributed by Aldred Scott Warthin, an ardent candiruphile himself, the text is a faithful reprinting of the two journal articles.

Gudger was, by most accounts, a competent biologist, but information for his writings came entirely from published sources. Although he lived a long life, his adventures were strictly of the armchair variety. The farthest he ever traveled beyond the continental United States was to Florida's Dry Tortugas, a scattering of tiny islands near Key West. In preparing his articles on the candiru he sought neither interviews nor firsthand experiences in the field, but merely solicited through correspondence the opinions of certain ichthyologists familiar with South American rivers.

The literature Gudger cites came from American and European books and journals. My own investigations indicate that he missed only C. H. Prodgers' *Adventures in Bolivia* and *Adventures in Peru*, which briefly mention candiru attacks but offer nothing Gudger did not already know, and the obscure work of a Swiss physician named Edwin Pfister on Egyptian penis coverings (see Chapter 8).

Gudger was accustomed to unearthing arcane sources because his principal duty at the museum was compiling bibliographies about fishes, although in this case much of the work had already been presented in Carl H. Eigenmann's 1918 monograph *The Pygidiidae, A Family of South American Catfishes*. Eigenmann was intensely interested in "urinophilous" catfishes, or those purportedly attracted to urine, and had tracked down most of the early references to candiru attacks. Gudger included these in his own work and added a few more, the most recent being Paul Le Cointe's 1922 report.

No one in Gudger's time or earlier could claim a completely credible eyewitness account of a candiru attack on a human being. In every case some critical observation or documentation was lacking, rendering the evidence circumstantial. Gudger was well aware of this. Having collected and studied all the information he could find on putative attacks, his objective was[5] ". . . to build up against the 'Candirú' a case which would stand up in court." His father had been a lawyer, and a suitable presentation of the evidence seemed good enough. It wasn't, of course. In science, it never is. As the anthropologist Braxton M. Alfred writes,[6] "Weight of evidence is adequate support for a decision only when it cannot be deferred, as in jurisprudence." Without actual proof of at least one attack, Gudger's final argument seems thin. His summation is well reasoned, even compelling, but no jury of modern scientists could find the candiru guilty beyond reasonable doubt.

Those early sources are still worth recounting. Usually Eigenmann or Gudger covers the information adequately; elsewhere, one of them leaves out something interesting or misinterprets the source material. My objective in this chapter is to retrace their steps, filling in where their coverage is sketchy. Gudger's effort, by incorporating Eigenmann's, has been the most complete summary to date, but good coverage can also be found elsewhere.[7]

Before proceeding, I need to mention the two major groups of candirus. This is necessary because many who have written about candiru attacks have also speculated about the fish responsible. By custom, *candiru, carnero,* and *canero* apply loosely to several species of the families Trichomycteridae (which includes the subfamilies Vandelliinae and Stegophilinae) and Cetopsidae (subfamily Cetopsinae) in the order of catfishes called Siluriformes. The relationships of these families are illustrated in Fig. 2.[8] The vandelliines are relatively small and slender, the stegophilines slightly more robust and less slender proportionately. Cetopsids are the largest, some species attaining 25 centimeters or more in length. Examples of a stegophiline and a cetopsid are shown in Fig. 3. Vandelliines are illustrated in Chapters 3 and 4. Ichthyologists who study these groups can easily distinguish one from the other, but they look the same to local inhabitants of South American river communities. Consequently, a term like *candiru* carries about the same recognition value as "bass" and "minnow" in North America.

For convenience, I restrict the definition of candiru and its Spanish synonyms to those trichomycterid catfishes known to suck blood from the gills of other fishes and thought to live on blood exclusively.[9] These also seem the most likely candidates to attack humans. To date, the confirmed bloodsucking catfishes have all been vandelliines. Participation of the stegophilines in bloodsucking is still unconfirmed, and no cetopsid indulges in such behavior. Lumping the cetopsids with the candirus is especially inappropriate.[10]

The trichomycterids include at least 30 genera and 200 species of small, mostly nondescript fishes.[11] Many inhabit the leaf litter of rainforest streams and live obscure, humble lives scavenging or feeding on aquatic insects and any terrestrial insects that happen along.[12] Within the family Trichomycteridae is the subfamily Vandelliinae (the vandelliines), consisting of six putative genera and perhaps 15 species, although no one

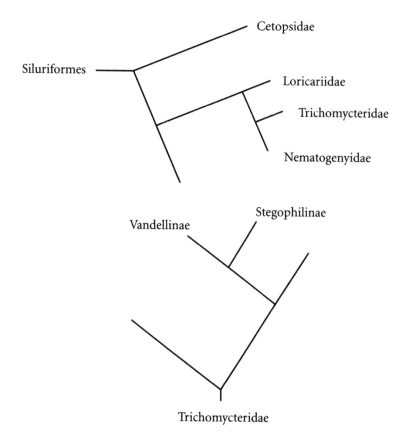

FIG. 2   Partial cladogram of the siluriform catfishes. *Top:* Families Trichomycteridae and Cetopsidae. *Bottom:* Trichomycterid subfamilies Vandelliinae and Stegophilinae. Source: After de Pinna (1998).

is really sure. So far as we know, all are bloodsuckers and therefore "true" candirus, assuming the limits of my definition. Their taxonomy is discussed in Chapters 3 and 4.

Species of another trichomycterid subfamily, the Stegophilinae, are believed to be scavengers[13] or to feed on the mucus[14] or scales[15] of other fishes. They comprise about four genera and 14 species.[16] Some authorities include certain stegophilines with the vandelliines as bloodsuckers based on three lines of evidence: (1) their occasional discovery in the gill chambers of larger fishes, (2) the collection of specimens containing what appears to be ingested blood, and (3) the belief by some that they attack human urogenital openings. *Stegophilus insidiosus* (Fig. 3, top), the first species of stegophiline described, was also the first fish of any kind ever obtained from the gill chambers of another, in this instance a pimelodid catfish (*Pseudoplatystoma* sp.).[17]

The Brazilian ichthyologist Agenor Couto de Magalhães adds to the circumstantial evidence of stegophilines as bloodsuckers with these stories:[18]

> Another fact. It was told to me that, one day, at a bend of the Rio Purús, in the vicinity of the great lake Ayapuá, a fisherman went to the place where repeated splashes of large fish could be heard, at the base of the *matupá* [floating masses of vegetation, mostly dead]. More out of curiosity than need of fish, the caboclo[19] gently came closer, and, standing in his dugout canoe, threw the net at the last air bubbles the fish had left behind.
>
> As he brought in the net, he found only one tambaquí[20] in it, a fact that startled the fisherman, who proceeded to try to find out what had caused the fish such distress. Examining it, he saw that the anus was eroded, and inside the rectum he found four Candirús that justified the tambaquí's distress.
>
> Some time ago it was recorded, in the vicinity of the waterfall of the Rio Mogí-Guaçú, in Pirassununga, [state of] São Paulo, the following: there often appeared dead, floating dourados[21] with large numbers of strange little fish inside their gills. Those unknown enemies of the dourados preferentially attacked the most sensitive organ of the fish, disabling it in a few minutes; it was not possible for me to obtain any of those hematophagous fish, but it was told to me that they were like a small cascudin,[22] of about an inch, with a dark-colored mouth, similar to that of the mandy;[23] it was known in that place by the name of "dourado-killer"; I believe it to be a variety of Stegophilus insidiosus [*sic*]. [S. Spotte, transl.]

The identity of these small fish was never determined.

According to the American ichthyologist Warren E. Burgess, another stegophiline of the species *Homodiaetus maculatus*[24] ". . . probably enters the gill chambers of the host, where it feeds on the blood of the gills." The

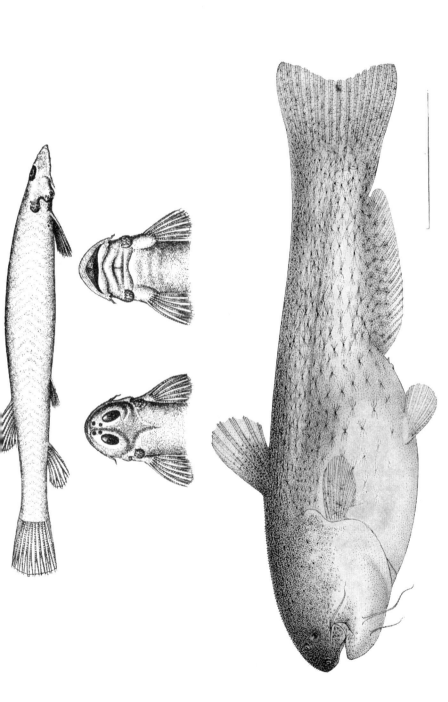

FIG. 3   Top: *Stegophilus insidiosus* Reinhardt, 1858 (lateral view). *Middle left:* Head and upper body (dorsal view). *Middle right:* Head and upper body (ventral view). *Bottom: Hemicetopsis macilentus* Eigenmann, 1912. Scale of bottom illustration = 1/2 inch. Source: After Eigenmann (1912, 1918a).

Uruguayan ichthyologists Garibaldi J. Devincenzi and Raúl Vaz-Ferreira call this fish by its common name, *chupa-chupa*, or "suck-suck." They obtained specimens from the side of a pimelodid catfish (*Luciopimelodus pati*) and speculate that it chews bits of flesh from the external surfaces of other fishes:[25]

> This small fish appears in nets stretched along river banks in the search for minnows for bait, where there is a sandy bottom; also found fastened to the sides of the big silurids [sic] such as the surubí,[26] the patí,[27] and also the armored [catfishes], usually in the months of March and April. For reference we have of the word of experienced fishermen that they attack [larger] fish leaving them moribund, bleeding, and with frayed skin.
>
> Given the smallness of the teeth and their position a little behind the labial border, how can lesions so extensive be explained? Dr. Couto de Magalhaes [sic], in his "Monograph of Brazilian Freshwater Fishes," recounts that when introducing some live specimens of *Trichomycterus brasiliensis* into an aquarium containing a layer of sand on the bottom, he noticed that these fish were able to hide completely beneath the sand, entering with great ease using the oscillatory movements of a propeller. Lately we have had the opportunity of observing the habits of another pygidiid [sic] (*Pygidium* [sic] *angustirostris*), and we also noticed that after a brief exit to search for tiny prey, [the fish] quickly buries itself in the sand again by using its head in an oscillatory movement. We postulate, therefore, that the chupa-chupa, when settling on the side of its victim, gnaws with the purpose of making it bleed by using the erectile opercular spines by means of the above-mentioned vibratory movement. It is difficult to attribute the lesions to the action of the interopercular spines because these are directed backwards and are concave towards the inside. To actually enter [the victim], the *Homodiaetus* would have to impart to their body a strong backwards movement. Examination of the body of an injured fish will possibly clarify this obscure point. [S. Spotte, transl.]

Pseudostegophilus scarificator, which Burgess suggests is perhaps a synonym of *H. maculatus*,[28] might be a facultative bloodsucker; in other words, blood is not its only food. The Brazilian ichthyologist José Ricardo Alves Guimarães has interesting things to say about this species, which is a nuisance to commercial fishermen near the Emas Rapids of the Rio Mogy-Gassú, where it attacks fish awaiting sale in traps or tethered to the riverbank, sometimes penetrating the anus of its victims and burrowing into the body cavity. According to Alves Guimarães:[29]

> Thus we learned that the predator fish did not attack the larger fish in the free state, as affirmed by the fishermen, but just those caught among the stones that were thrashing around, bleeding, unable to resist, and nearly dead.

> They also attacked the big fish caught in traps, a fact previously observed by von Ihering, showing no preference for any special location (anus) but attached mainly to the gills, the hindmost fins . . . and unprotected places where blood could be found in abundance. [S. Spotte, transl.]

Alves Guimarães implies that *P. scarificator* is exclusively hematophagous, but this seems doubtful in a species that feeds opportunistically. In addition, blood can be difficult to obtain from dead flesh. Alves Guimarães says:[30]

> We [*sic*] observed that this small nematognathan [catfish] attacks fish that have been dead for several hours and sucks them eagerly.
>
> Corumbatás[31] taken from the freezer of Messrs. Bianchini and Quilici were placed quietly by us in a backwater where these parasites were abundant, and they promptly attacked them.
>
> A similar attack was made by these fish on the legs of children . . . who were playing in the water, attaching to them without causing lesions.
>
> This fixation on their victims persists only in the river.
>
> If the host is removed from the water, the parasites detach and fall off almost immediately, which hindered us considerably in photographing them.
>
> It seems that water pressure aids in the maintenance of the animal on its prey during moments of suction.
>
> We noticed that this small fish in general swims belly up when searching for its host. This fact appears to us to be linked with the great amount of air existing inside its short intestinal tube when it lacks food, which is composed only of blood sucked from larger fish, which we have verified by microscopic examination.
>
> The intestine when replete resembles a black tube occupying the whole ventral part of the animal and is easily observable through the thin wall of the belly. [S. Spotte, transl.]

As to the possibility of stegophilines attacking humans, the Brazilian ichthyologist Mário C. C. de Pinna writes,[32] "Stegophilines and vandelliines are popularly known in the Brazilian Amazon as 'candirus' and their accidental penetration of the urethras of humans and other mammals have [*sic*] been reported several times. . ." In the case of stegophilines this behavior is unconfirmed.

Acanthopoma annectens might be the most likely stegophiline to attack the urethras of humans and other mammals, but the only evidence is a secondhand report described later in this chapter. I found no direct proof of obligate hematophagia in any species of stegophiline. Reports of their attacks on human urogenital openings are speculative too.

Another family of siluriform catfishes, the Cetopsidae, has about six genera and 14 species.[33] A representative is shown in Fig. 3, bottom. Almost since their discovery cetopsids have been wrongly accused of sucking blood from other fishes and of entering human urogenital openings; for this reason they appear frequently in my narrative. Much of the confusion arose because the original "candiru" described in 1829 was named *Cetopsis candiru*.[34] This fish is wrongly blamed for attacks on humans (see below). Its modern name is *Hemicetopsis candiru*.[35] Cetopsids feed on the flesh of dead and dying fishes and other animals[36] or prey on insects (terrestrial and aquatic) and aquatic invertebrates.[37] They are also fierce predators, gathering in schools and attacking larger fishes.[38]

In *Amazon: The Flooded Forest*, the American biologist Michael Goulding has this to say about certain cetopsids:[39]

> There are two notorious groups of fish in the Amazon and they are both called *candiru*. The larger *candiru* are sometimes called whale-catfish because they somewhat resemble cetaceans in general body form, though the largest species only reach about 25 centimetres in length. Like the *piracatinga* catfish [*Calophysus macropterus*, Pimelodidae], they are able to bite out pieces of flesh but, unlike the former, they also attack live animals, especially injured ones. Similar to red-bellied piranha behaviour, a school of these *candiru* can devour a victim very rapidly. The *piranhas* play this role in the floodplain waters whereas the *candiru* are mostly restricted to along river banks. The whale-catfish *candiru* become especially numerous near sites where fishermen are gutting their catches and throwing the innards into the water. At times the water seems to be boiling because of the voracious appetites of these fish. They will also attack large catfish that have been hooked on long lines. In this case the first individuals attack the anal area and, almost immediately, large numbers of others join in. The rapacious *candiru* eat their way through the intestines and stomach and devour the soft underside of the disadvantaged animal. They then eat the back muscles. If a catch is not brought aboard or ashore in time, all that is left is the head and a relatively clean skeleton.

Nor does Goulding exempt cetopsids from attacking human skin. In the same section of his book he tells us:

> The whale-catfish *candiru* . . . occasionally attack bathers. The wounds result in very distinctive scars. Once a *candiru* catfish bites its victim, it then rotates its body in a somewhat erratic fashion. The effect is almost that of a drill, that is, to cut deeper into the flesh. The scar resulting from these bites looks like it might have been caused by a large cigar that was extinguished on the skin.

These could be the "cupping-glass" wounds mentioned elsewhere in the literature (see below) and often blamed on stegophilines.

Ermanno Stradelli mentions the cetopsids in his 1929 Portuguese-Nheêmgatú dictionary, calling them candirus:[40]

> Candirú—Calopsis candirú—Small, very voracious fish . . . that perceives the odor of blood. They travel in shoals, and unfortunate [is] the wounded man or animal that falls among them. In a few moments it is devoured alive, leaving only a perfectly clean skeleton. Happily they only attack the wounded; were this not so, in many areas it would be impossible to take a bath. [S. Spotte, transl.]

Among Brazilians, the cetopsids are sometimes called *candiru-açu*, where *açu* represents, according to de Pinna,[41] ". . . an augmentative in the Tupi language, an allusion to the larger size of cetopsid candirus when compared to ordinary . . . candirus." In other words, "big candiru." Some specialists reserve it for a single species, *Hemicetopsis candiru*.[42]

Schools of the large species of cetopsids are often visible from shore. It is probably one of these to which Couto de Magalhães refers:[43]

> Speaking again of the Candirú-y, I remember hearing from somebody that their presence is felt when the rivers drop, a little before the beginning of the rainy season. They then appear in enormous shoals, approaching the margins of the great rivers and ascending the streams which, in that place, are called igarapés. On early evenings, with flashlights or lanterns, one can see the cordons they form, almost on the surface of the water, going towards the aforementioned streams of water that flow into the great rivers; fishermen interpret the ascent of the Candirús up the streams, as well as the ascent of smaller fishes, as a presage of imminent rising of the river. The Candirús gather at night along the margins of the great rivers or lakes they inhabit. [S. Spotte, transl.]

Jansen A. S. Zuanon, an ichthyologist at Instituto Nacional de Pesquisas da Amazônia in Manaus, told me three stories about cetopsids.[44] Once while aboard a houseboat anchored in the Rio Solimões at Ilha da Marchantaria he caught a redtail catfish (*Phractocephalus hemiliopterus*), or *pirarara* as it's called in Brazil, and tethered it to the boat. Soon a smaller catfish appeared, which he assumed was a cetopsid, and repeatedly attacked the anus of the larger fish.

Several times since, Jansen has come across strangely collapsed skins of the large armored catfish *Lithodoras dorsalis* (family Doradidae). This fish, true to its name, is covered by impervious bony plates and openly exposed only around its mouth and anus. Jansen suspects that cetopsids attack the anus and, having ripped it open, burrow into the catfish's abdomen and eat it alive from the inside, leaving only the skin undisturbed.

In the early 1990s, Jansen met a pathologist who showed him photographs of autopsies he had performed on human corpses retrieved from the Rio Solimões. When some of them were opened, cetopsids slithered out.

The earliest notation of candiru attacks on humans appears in the preface of Johann Baptist de [von] Spix and Louis Agassiz's text *Selecta genera et species piscium quos in itinere per Brasiliam annis MDCCCXVII-MDCCCXX*, published between 1829 and 1831.[45] The preface, written by Carl Friedrich Philippe de [von] Martius, includes this:[46]

> I should briefly mention another fish which is dangerous to man. The Brazilians call it *Candirú*; the Spaniards in Maynas [a state in Peru] call it *Canero*. It is impelled by a curious instinct to enter the excretory openings of the human body. Whenever it comes in contact with these openings of persons bathing in the stream, it violently forces its way in, and having entered, it causes constant pain, and even danger of life, by biting the flesh. These fishes are greatly attracted by the odor of urine. For this reason, those who dwell along the Amazon, when about to enter the stream, whose bays abound with this pest, tie a cord tightly around the prepuce and refrain from urinating. This fish belongs to Cetopsis [*sic*], a genus which I have already described. But I do not know whether it is the younger individuals of the two species which I have described (C. Candirú [C. Candiru in the original text] and C. Coecutiens), or whether a third species of smaller fishes has been given this cruel instinct by nature. [Transl. in Eigenmann 1918a: 263; the translation given by Gudger (1930c: 3) follows this one closely.]

According to von Martius, cetopsids might be guilty of attacking humans, although he recognizes that the cetopsids he has formally described to science are perhaps too large to enter human urogenital openings. The last phrase in his last sentence is prescient, anticipating discovery of the vandelliines, which occurred in 1846 (see Chapter 3). Von Martius is the first to mention the possibility of candirus being attracted to urine, a subject I take up in Chapter 7.

The next entry in the literature is by von Spix and von Martius in Volume 3 of their *Reise in Brasilien in den Jahren 1817–1820*, published between 1823 and 1831:[47]

> In *Pará* [now Belém], we not seldom heard talk about the dangers, which people bathing in the river were exposed to by the little fish *Candirú*, and what was told about this fish sounds so bizarre that I am almost afraid to repeat this here. *Cetopsis* is a genus belonging to the salmons [*sic*], which distinguish themselves by a single row of teeth, a flattened form of the head

and small eyes, which lie under the skin and almost do not shine through. One species of this genus, the *Candirú* of the natives, a little fish of the length and width of a finger, — I cannot say unfortunately whether it is one of the younger individuals of one of the two species illustrated by us (*Cetopsis Candirú Pisc. t.* 10. *f.* 1 and *C. coecutiens t.* 10. *f.* 2) or a third one, not yet described, because the samples collected by us were lost, — has the habit of slipping very aggressively and quickly into the external cavities of the human body. It causes here the most painful and dangerous incidents, and can only be taken out with great effort, because it spreads the fins. The odor of human excretions seems to attract the little fish, and the Indians suggest therefore to refrain from satisfying a certain urge when bathing, or to cover a certain part carefully. The Indians, which served us as rowers, reinforced their story about this strange behavior with several examples, but since we had generally noticed that the belief in the unlikely and extraordinary, together with a ridiculous fear of ghosts, was a curious trait of the character of these people, their reports did not register with us until we were educated about the truth of this by our friend Dr. Lacerda, as eyewitness. [E. Muschaweck, transl.]

Here again human excretions are identified as possible attractants. The fish's behavior of "slipping very aggressively and quickly" into its victims is repeated by later authors and confirmed by modern findings, lending unusual credibility to this report (see Chapter 11). Dr. Lacerda, unfortunately, disappears into history, and we learn nothing further about his unusual experiences.

At age 28 the Austrian botanist Eduard Friedrich von Poeppig traveled through Chile and Peru and down the Amazon. He describes his observations in a 1836 book titled *Reise in Chile, Peru und auf dem Amazonenstrome, Während der Jahre 1827–1832*. In a footnote, von Poeppig writes:[48]

In Maynas, under the name of *Canero*, in [the Rio] Solimoẽs [*sic*] under the name of *Candirú*, it is very well known and much feared. The attack of a fish in this way is so bizarre that one almost cannot believe in it at first. Also Mr. von Martius (Journey III, 955.) confesses to have regarded this tale of the Indians very skeptically, until the well known natural scientist and physician at Pará, Dr. Lacerda, declared it to be founded on truth. I myself have been an eyewitness of such a case in Yurimaguas [eastern Peru], when an Indian woman suffered such terrible pain and loss of blood after the penetration of a Canero into the vagina that everyone thought she was lost. After interior and exterior application of the Xagua [*jagua*],[49] the little fish was expelled at once, and the woman did not lose her life. The great superstition of the Indians kept me from getting this one [collecting this specimen], but I have owned a great number of Caneros, which were caught at Yurimaguas and which were all scarcely two inches long, and were so fully developed that they could not be evaluated as young individuals. Unfortunately they spoiled in the bad spirits [rum] of the country. So far as I can recall from memory, none of the illustrations of *Cetopsis* (Martius, *Pisces*, tab. 10. f. 1. 2.) seems to fit the Canero of Maynas. In some areas of the [Rio] Marañon, especially at Pebas, the Caneros were so extraordinarily common that it was sufficient to let some drops of blood of shot birds fall into the water to attract swarms of these very small and highly dangerous predators. [E. Muschaweck, transl.]

Gudger omitted the last sentence from his own translation. Von Poeppig's observation is the first of candirus being attracted to blood in the water. Moreover, he recognizes his specimens as something other than cetopsids, and as adults, not juveniles. Von Poeppig presents his eyewitness account of the attack in a straightforward manner without embellishment. His story seems credible.

In 1840, a note on the candiru titled "Remarkable Habit in a Fish" appeared in *Annals and Magazine of Natural History*, the authorship credited to "Schomburgk's MSS." A year later this article, translated anonymously into German and attributed simply to "Herr Schomburgk," was published in *Froriep's Notizen*.[50] Gudger believed the source to be Robert H. Schomburgk, the English naturalist and explorer.

Schomburgk tells us that while at San Joaquim on the Rio Bremeo,[51] the inhabitants warned him about bathing in the river. They told him about a small fish called the "cancliru" [*sic*] whose propensity it was to enter the urethra or rectum, especially if a careless bather should "satisfy nature" while in the water. Extraction was difficult and often accompanied by inflammation. Sometimes the victim died. Schomburgk discounted these warnings, but had second thoughts when he returned to Europe and read the passage of von Spix and von Martius quoted above.

Whether the people who warned Schomburgk could distinguish between the cetopsids and the candirus is unclear. Schomburgk writes:[52] "The fish was described to me to be about half an inch in length, and to be gregarious. MM. Spix and Martius consider it to be a species of *Cetopsis*." Even today no one can say if the vandelliines are "gregarious"— that is, whether individuals of the same species school or even hang around together. This might be another instance of attacks by vandelliines being blamed on cetopsids, which are larger, often seen during the day, and generally easier to observe.

Among the important early descriptions of candiru attacks is that of Francis de Castelnau, a French naturalist and diplomat. Later writers have often ridiculed it. However, as shown in Chapter 11, dis-

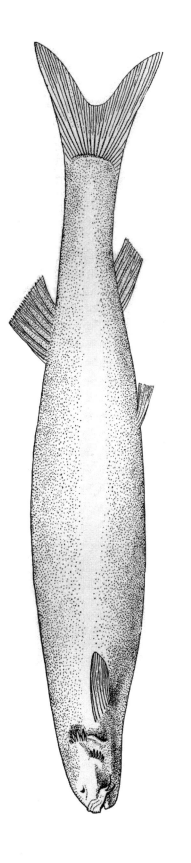

FIG. 4 *Pareiodon microps* Kner, 1855 (=*Trichomycterus pussillus* de Castelnau, 1855), a stegophiline reportedly able to leap out of the water and swim up urine streams to attack the urethras of human males. Lateral view. Source: Eigenmann (1918a).

missing de Castelnau's words too hastily might be unwise. Like most people, de Castelnau had no firsthand information. Writing in 1855, he tells us:[53]

> This species (*Trichomycterus pusillus*) is, on behalf of fishers of the [Rio] Araguay, the object of a most singular prejudice: they claim that it is very dangerous to urinate in the river, because, they say, this small animal springs out of water and penetrates into the urethra while going back up along the liquid column. [S. Spotte, transl.]

In his 1855 volume, de Castelnau describes *Vandellia plazai* as a new species (see Chapter 3), failing to associate the vandelliines with attacks on humans and blaming instead the species he has named *Trichomycterus pussillus*. This fish now bears the name *Pareiodon microps* and has been placed with the stegophilines. In Latin, *pusillus* means small, or insignificant, and *P. microps* is neither. As seen in Fig. 4, *P. microps* is actually large and robust, and its attacks on human urethras are doubtful. The specimen illustrated was thick and 145 millimeters long.[54]

Next in the chronology is a brief entry by the English ichthyologist Albert C. L. G. Günther. In his 1864 listing of fishes in the British Museum, Günther acknowledges the reports of attacks on humans, but points out the lack of firm evidence.[55] His comments are the earliest I found linking the vandelliines specifically with attacks on humans.

Karl von Müller's 1870 contribution is a secondhand report about a candiru collected by the German explorer Gustav Wallis in the Rio Huallaga. His recounting of Wallis' stories of attacks is especially interesting:[56]

> In these very little known waters, namely the [Rio] Huallaga, the traveler [or *our* traveler, Gustav Wallis] observed a fish, which I want to recommend especially to the attention of science. It is there called the Candirú and everyone is rightfully afraid of it with regard to the water, as one is afraid of mosquitoes and ants on land. The fish itself is small, not even 3/4 of a span,[57] built like a catfish, with a wide, round head, on which the two little eyes lie close to each other, the front fins spread like wings underneath it, and the rest of the body ends in a wedge. On its back the color is darker with indistinct spots, and so little [that] the creature itself is not very special in any way. But it is a terrible pest for a swimmer, namely a kind of leech, which [even] attacks [the] expert swimmer, causing wounds on him all over as with a cupping glass, and when it has succeeded in fastening itself to the body it spreads a bundle of needles in the wound, and is then attached like a barb and can only be taken off the body by painful surgery. This habit of the fish is all the more awful and dangerous, because it likes

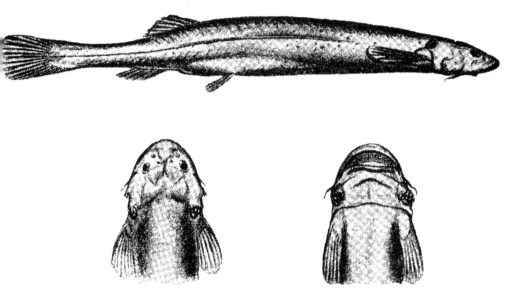

FIG. 5 *Acanthopoma annectens* Lütken, 1892. *Top*: Lateral view. *Bottom left*: Head and upper body (dorsal view). *Bottom right*: Head and upper body (ventral view). Source: After Eigenmann (1918a) and Lütken (1892).

> to seek out the most private body parts; there are stories about cases, which ended in death after the surgery. I will take care that this curious fish, which I have in front of me in alcohol, will come into the right scientific hands and will receive its own scientific name, which it does not yet have. [E. Muschaweck transl.]

The fish observed by Wallis attacks like a cetopsid, not a vandelliine, and vandelliines are probably incapable of producing "cupping-glass" wounds. However, it also seems to have characteristics of the candirus. Cetopsids attack the exterior body surfaces of large fishes and other animals and also scavenge on carcasses; it is the candirus that supposedly enter the urogenital openings of humans.

Von Müller's report is important because Wallis wisely kept the fish for later identification. It was described in 1892 by the Danish ichthyologist C. Lütken, who established a new genus and named the fish *Acanthopoma annectens* (Fig. 5). The species, which is not a cetopsid, has been placed in the trichomycterid subfamily Stegophilinae. As shown in this figure and Fig. 3 (top), a stegophiline's mouth might produce "cupping-glass" wounds.

Burgess writes:[58]

Fig. 6   The fish (a cetopsid) wrongly accused by Marcoy of attacking human urethras. Source: Marcoy (1875).

> *Acanthopoma annectens* is one of these fishes that have the name "candiru," and of course it has the familiar candiru habits. It attacks like a leech and produces wounds all over the fish. It spreads a bundle of opercular and interopercular spines into the wound and remains there, being very difficult to remove. They also invade the "private parts" of wading or swimming animals but apparently exist in these passages only a short time, as they quickly die from a lack of oxygen. *A. annectens* is of a dark color and has indistinct blotches.

Burgess cites no references to establish these startling claims, but I see similarities between his text and the translation of von Müller given above. The descriptions of the fish's coloration are similar, and both texts refer to "private parts" as sites of attack. Von Müller seems to have been Burgess' source. If so, we still have only von Müller's claim that *A. annectens* attacks the urogenital areas of human beings.

In 1867 the German engineer Franz Keller (or Franz Keller-Leuzinger) and his father were commissioned by the Minister of Public Works in Rio de Janeiro to explore the Rio Madeira and determine where a railroad could be built along its banks to circumnavigate the rapids. Keller spent 17 years in South America, and the account of his adventures was published in 1874. In it he describes the candiru as[59] ". . . an almost transparent, thin little fish, of less than a finger's length, which penetrates with eel-like nimbleness into the orifices of the bathers and causes many fatal accidents, according to the reports of the riverines."

Laurent Saint-Cricq also knew about the candiru. In his two-volume *Travels in South America*, written under the pseudonym Paul Marcoy, he distinguishes at least on a functional basis between the cetopsids and the vandelliines. Nonetheless, he considers them a single species: those "candirus" entering the urogenital openings of their victims are simply smaller members of the same species. He notes their facility for entering "into the secret parts of bathers" where they erect their fins (actually, their opercula). Marcoy's advice is to not urinate in the river when bathing.

Marcoy's illustration bearing the legend "The candiru" shows a cetopsid (Fig. 6). He describes the fish as having smooth skin, a brown back, zinc-colored sides, and a nearly white belly. The round head, tiny eyes, and microscopic teeth are characteristic of cetopsids. He tells us that the larger specimens[60] ". . . make a remorseless war on the calves of the natives who come within their reach: they dart impetuously at the fleshy mass, and rend a portion away before the owner of the calf has time to realize the loss."

A fellow Frenchman, the novelist Jules Verne, mentions "Paul Marcoy" (quotation marks his) several times in La Jangada. Huit cent lieues sur l'Amazone. He obviously had read Marcoy's report when he writes:[61]

> One also collected, by thousands, those "candirus," a sort of small silurid [sic], of which some are microscopic, and that made a pincushion [pelote] of the bather's calves if he carelessly ventured into their vicinity. [S. Spotte, transl.]

The context of this statement is interesting. In the preceding sentence the characters in the novel had been fishing from their raft and caught several fishes of "exquisite flesh" (chair exquise). Did they eat the "candirus" too?

As shown in Fig. 7, Marcoy and his companions captured "candirus" (cetopsids) using an unusual method. River turtles were a common source of protein in Marcoy's time and remain so today. Marcoy and his companions immersed the shell of a freshly killed and butchered turtle a few inches under the water. "Candirus" of all sizes appeared soon after to feed on remnants of flesh. The shell was then raised quickly, imprisoning them.

The American zoologist James Orton made two trips to equatorial South America and never encountered a venomous snake or dangerous mammal. Writing in the third edition of The Andes and the Amazon, published in 1876, he repeats the stories of candirus attacking the "nether openings" of people who bathe in the rivers, but failed to find evidence of their truth.

In his 1880 text An Introduction to the Study of Fishes, Günther revisits the

F<small>IG</small>. 7   Marcoy and companions catching cetopsids using a freshly cleaned turtle shell. The original figure legend is "Fishing the candiru." Source: Marcoy (1875).

subject of candiru attacks, noting of the genera *Stegophilus* and *Vandellia* that the natives of Brazil hold members of these genera responsible for attacks on humans, but emphasizes that confirmation has not been attained.

In a report that later generated considerable controversy, the Belgian ichthyologist and herpetologist George A. Boulenger exhibited preserved specimens of the candiru *Vandellia cirrhosa* before a meeting of the Zoological Society of London on 30 November 1897. J. Bach, a physician in La Plata on the Rio Jurua, had recently explored other locations along this river where he obtained the specimens displayed. Bach's information, presented by Boulenger:[62]

> The fish is attracted by the urine, and when once it has made its way into the urethra, cannot be pulled out again owing to the spines which arm its opercles. The only means of preventing it from reaching the bladder, where it causes inflammation and ultimately death, is to instantly amputate the penis; and at Tres Unidos, Dr. Bach had actually examined a man and three

boys with amputated penis [*sic*] as a result of this dreadful incident. Dr. Bach was therefore satisfied that the account given of this extraordinary habit of the 'Candyrú' is perfectly trustworthy.

Bach is not a credible source. As later pointed out by the French biologist Clément Jobert (see below), Bach never actually witnessed a candiru attack, nor had he ever treated a victim of an attack. In Jobert's opinion, piranhas probably bit off the penises Bach thought had been amputated by Indian medicine men.

Jobert, professor at the University of Dijon, collected fishes on the Amazon from Pará (now Belém) to Tabatinga in 1877. Not until 1898 did he write about it in a lengthy article published in *Archives de Parasitologie*. He knew of Boulenger's presentation and repeated some of his remarks about the supposed attraction of candirus to urine, the incidence of inflammation caused by attacks, and the likelihood of death unless the penis is amputated immediately. More interesting is Jobert's description of an attack on himself:[63]

> I had not been in the water for five minutes when I felt a rapid succession of what seemed like claws in the lumbar region, the belly, and the ribs. Seeing the water around me turn red I hurried back to shore and saw that in the areas where I had felt the sensation of being clawed, blood was flowing from parallel wounds, they could have been made by some instrument, so regular were they; groups of five or six lines, at least a centimetre long and very close together; I did not try to determine their depth, but the narrow wounds bled copiously. [V. Gill, transl.]

A physician known to us only as Dr. Castro treated Jobert's wounds and told him about a candiru he had once extracted from the urethra of a black woman attacked while she was bathing and urinating in the river. The fish had to be torn out, ripping her mucous membranes.

Jobert was attacked on his exterior surfaces. This would implicate cetopsids or possibly stegophilines except for the wounds, which were parallel scratches instead of "cupping-glass" bites. At least one ichthyologist later believed they had been inflicted by vandelliines, as I discuss in Chapter 3.

In his 1886 book *Durch Central-Brasilien Expedition zur Erforschung des Schingú im Jahre 1884*, the German ethnologist Karl von den Steinen lists the candiru along with other fishes from the headwaters of the Rio Xingu, an affluent of the Amazon, and also reports them from the Rio Batovy. About this second location, he writes:[64]

When bathing, we become careful. Candirus were found here, a transparent fish 2 cm long with a yellow iris which likes to penetrate into accessible body cavities. If this same [fish] slips into the urethra, which frequently occurs, it attaches by means of fin-hooks to the mucous membrane; if a warm bath does not succeed in driving out the troublemaker, only an operation remains. Then the Sertanejo himself does not hesitate, but goes into the urethra, and in many cases [the victim] will perish from this heroic procedure. [E. Muschaweck and S. Spotte, transl.]

Gudger noted that von den Steinen is unclear on what he meant by "operation," but presumed he was referring to amputation of the penis. The original text is indeed confusing, but I interpret the next sentence as "goes into the urethra," which could involve slicing open the penis to remove the fish (external urethrostomy). If so, this is the first mention of a surgical procedure used on men and boys other than amputation, and the first account of treating victims by having them soak in a warm bath.

Algot Lange, in his 1912 book *In the Amazon Jungle*, tells about the *candiroo-escrivão*,[65] obviously a cetopsid. At Remate de Males, a village at the junction of the Rio Itecoahy and the Rio Javary (or Javari), it fed on offal thrown into the water by the village butcher. Later we learn about the other candirus, which apparently are vandelliines:[66]

Before leaving the subject of fish, I will mention another species, smaller than the *piranha*, yet, although not as ferocious, the cause of much dread and annoyance to the natives living near the banks of the rivers. In fact, throughout the Amazon this little worm-like creature, called the *kandiroo*, is so omnipresent that a bath-house of a particular construction is necessary. The kandiroo is usually three to four inches long and one sixteenth in thickness. It belongs to the lampreys, and its particular group is the Myxinos or slime-fish. Its body is coated with a peculiar mucus. It is dangerous to human beings, because when they are taking a bath in the river it will approach and with a swift powerful movement penetrate one of the natural openings of the body whence it can be removed only by a difficult and dangerous operation.

Lange recounts a fatality suffered by one of the villagers who hemorrhaged and died following such an operation. The problem, he tells us, is the fish's stiff, pointed dorsal fin, which serves as a barb and hinders its removal.

Lange's reporting contains three serious mistakes, the first two noted by Eigenmann and Gudger. Candirus are not remotely related to the lampreys, and lampreys do not occur in South American freshwaters. As a resident of New York City, Lange could easily have checked this by asking someone at the American Museum of Natural History. Vandelliines lack spines on all their fins. The interopercular and opercular spines no doubt hinder the extraction of a live candiru from a human orifice. Finally, the fruit of the breadfruit tree, mentioned elsewhere by Lange, is soft and unsuitable for making into a dipper for bathing. Unless the fruit is picked while still unripe, it falls from the tree and splatters on the ground.

Some of Lange's descriptions sound right: the fish's size, its "worm-like" appearance, and the ferocity with which it penetrates into a human orifice. Nonetheless, it is doubtful that anyone at Remate de Males died from a candiru attack while Lange was staying there. Gudger is equally dubious of Lange's comments, calling them "entirely worthless."[67] Lange is prone to boasting and belongs in that genre of South American adventurers who see the tropical rainforest as evil and their own survival as an act of heroism.[68] He emphasizes that Remate de Males means "Culmination of Evils." To him, every creature in the village is an enemy. Becoming distressed at repeatedly failing to squash a large tarantula with a hammer, Lange describes the hunt's conclusion:[69] "When my hand grew steady again, I took my automatic pistol, used for big game, and, taking a steady aim on the fat body of the spider, I fired." The tarantula escaped unharmed.

Lange reports hearing a tale of an anaconda that, when killed, measured 52 feet 8 inches. Lange himself claims to have shot and killed a specimen 56 feet long and 2 feet 1 inch in diameter. When dried, the skin measured 54 feet 8 inches and when spread had a width of 5 feet 1 inch. Lange intended to take the skin back to New York, but after describing the skinning and drying episode he never mentions it again. Had it reached New York it would have been nearly 18 feet longer than any snake of any species ever recorded.

Joseph F. Woodroffe left England in October 1905 to work as a clerk for rubber buyers on the Amazon. His book called *The Upper Reaches of the Amazon* was published in 1914. Woodroffe had no particular interest in natural history, but mentions the candiru. He describes it as small (about 2 inches) with two barbs just behind its gills. As I discuss later, these barbs are numerous and found directly on the gill covers, or opercula. Woodroffe admits to never having seen evidence of candiru attacks, but is nonetheless convinced of their occurrence.

Eigenmann, in his 1918 monograph, addresses candiru attacks in more detail than anyone before. As an ichthyologist, Eigenmann notes that the term "candiru" means different things to different people, cetopsids in one case, vandelliines in another. He points out that this "habit" of entering the gills and possibly other organs of larger fishes had been attributed to members of the genera *Cetopsis, Pareiodon, Vandellia*, and *Acanthopoma*. He does not dismiss the possibility that the young of some of these larger fishes might be urinophilic, or that the Indians might consider such smaller species as *Vandellia* to be the young of the others.

In referring to Boulenger's report, Eigenmann emphasizes (as had Jobert) that Bach's evidence was circumstantial:[70] "Dr. Bach did not himself operate or help to operate to remove the Candirú and a much simpler operation than amputation would be sufficient to remove it."

After evaluating the available information, Eigenmann becomes convinced that in the Amazon basin fishes called candirus attack humans by penetrating the urethra:[71]

> Whether the widely prevalent belief that the Candirú is tropic to urine, and consequently has a tendency to enter the urethra, or whether the Candirú's tendency to burrow leads it accidentally to enter the urethra, are all matters that must for the present remain in debate. A very interesting subsidiary question is, whether, if Candirús are tropic to urine they do not also enter the urethræ of aquatic mammals and of large fishes. Further study may demonstrate that some species of Candirús have become parasitic in the bladders of large fishes and aquatic mammals.

The hypothesis that a fish could truly parasitize the interior milieu of a larger animal is astonishing. Here and in his other writings on the subject Eigenmann never confronts the formidable physiological difficulties of life inside a mammalian bladder (see Chapter 7).

In a 1920 article in the journal *Science*, Eigenmann describes how certain candirus are sanguinivorous and how some attack the urethras of unwary bathers, erecting their spines on the opercles once inside. Eigenmann then writes,[72] "If not excised they finally enter the bladder and cause death."

In a letter to Gudger, W. E. Pearson, a student of Eigenmann's, describes a candiru attack as recounted to him by an expatriate American. Pearson admits it is hearsay. The American was living at a rubber station on the Rio Madidi, an affluent of the Rio Beni. It was his Indian wife who witnessed the attack. She had gone to the river with the other women to wash clothes. As was the custom, they undressed and sat down in the water.

Suddenly, one of the women screamed and ran to the bank. Her companions examined her and found that a "candiru" had penetrated into her vagina. She was taken to a hut where the women extracted the fish, but not before its spines had torn the flesh and caused loss of blood. The victim survived. Pearson then says,[73] "It is certain that anything but the very young of the candirú (*Urinophilus erythrurus*) of the Beni basin would be too large to enter the urethra of a man." As will later be shown, this conclusion was premature.

G. H. H. Tate of the American Museum of Natural History told Gudger that the guilty fish[74] ". . . is said to be about 3 inches long, bluish, slimy, with spines which it erects after entering the orifice." According to Tate, an attack by a candiru causes considerable loss of blood. The fish can only be removed after its spines have been clipped off. From stories already recounted, candirus are often simply pulled out despite the consequences. Clipping the spines from a candiru lodged in a man's urethra would be nearly impossible with the primitive surgical tools then available in those river outposts.

Paul Le Cointe, writing in 1922, describes candiru attacks but confuses the cetopsids with the vandelliines. This is evident in his description of cetopsids attacking wounded animals and stripping the flesh from dead ones:[75]

> Very small, but solely preoccupied with doing harm, is the "*candiru*" (Cetopsis), which does not exceed 5 to 8 centimetres in length. It often becomes fastened [in] the mesh of sweep nets which are badly damaged by the sharp spurs of its fins [*sic*]: gathered in groups, they contend in ability with "piranhas" to strip a cadaver of its flesh, or even to devour alive a wounded animal which seeks refuge in the water. The worst is that it sometimes penetrates the anal or vaginal cavities of bathers and there, bristling its terrible spurs which resist all pulling out, can cause serious problems if it is not extracted as soon as possible with the necessary precautions. We personally know three cases of this curious mishap. [L. K. Overstreet, transl.]

Without further details, Le Cointe's account is questionable. Still, he claims knowledge of events in which candirus have specifically attacked humans.

Gudger wrote to Le Cointe in 1925 and received a detailed reply. In Le Cointe's experience, the vagina was the most frequent site of attack, although the rectum was likely to be penetrated as well. Attacks were always induced by urinating in the water while bathing. I shall quote Le

Cointe's story as told by Gudger because it represents only the second eye-witness account in the literature (von Poeppig's is the first):[76]

> During my very long sojourn in Amazonia (since 1891) I have been able to satisfy myself . . . that the candirú is really able to penetrate into the anal or vaginal cavities of men or women bathers. Its introduction into the vagina is the most frequent phenomenon, appearing moreover to be always provoked by the imprudence of the victim in urinating in the water where she is bathing.
>
> At the time of occurrence of one of the three accidents of this kind of which I have had full cognizance, it was incumbent on me to become a party in the matter. The thing happened on the upper Beni (in Bolivia). An Indian woman, belonging to a party engaged in the exploitation of rubber which I was directing at the that time (1891), took her bath in the river and feeling herself wounded tried to extract with her hand the candirú which had already penetrated almost entirely into the vaginal cavity and which spreading out its fins [Gudger interjects, gill-covers] armed with pointed spines resisted all her efforts, wounding her profoundly. Then they brought to me this woman who was bleeding profusely. Quickly recognizing what the trouble was, it was necessary for me to push the candirú forward in order to disengage the spines driven into the flesh, then to turn it in order to bring the head to the front. It goes without saying that such an operation, performed without appropriate instruments, provoked a violent hemorrhage. The Indian woman suffered greatly but she had the good fortune to recover completely in a month.

Gudger does not reveal the date of Le Cointe's letter or whether the original was written in French and translated. Assuming none of the meaning has been lost, Le Cointe's story is compelling and believable.

In 1929, Gudger once more wrote to Le Cointe asking if he had obtained additional information. He had not, but passed Gudger's letter to Americo Campos, a physician in Pará and a professor at the local medical school. Campos sent a reply (presumably to Gudger) telling him he had no personal observations to report. However, a lady whom he knew at Obidos (Doña J. S.) told him a candiru had attacked her vagina. A physician had subsequently removed the fish. Campos had heard other tales of candirus penetrating human ears, noses, and anuses.

Cecil Herbert Prodgers was an English adventurer who went to South America to earn his fortune. A large, fleshy man, Prodgers worked as a trainer and owner of racehorses, a gold prospector, a hunter of Inca treasure, a mine foreman, a dealer in chinchilla skins, an entrepreneur, an exporter—any enterprise that might make money. He traveled extensively, knew many people, and recounted his experiences in two books.

In *Adventures in Bolivia*, published in 1922, Prodgers admonishes against bathing in the tropical rivers and streams of South and Central America because of "kandiros," described as "a kind of slimy leech" with a barbed dorsal fin and capable of getting into the rectum. Candirus are not found in Central America, they aren't leeches, and the dorsal fin isn't barbed. In *Adventures in Peru*, published 3 years later, Prodgers again reports on the candiru using a name (presumably Spanish) that I found nowhere else:[77]

> The *canderos* is even a greater menace [than the piranha] to bathers. This veritable fiend measures but one and a half to three inches long, and is a shark in miniature. Its fins are similar, and so are its teeth. The former fold down at will on the back; then the *canderos* looks like a worm. Their favourite point of attack is the fundament. Directly they force an entrance they spread their fins and begin to burrow, and so to get rid of them then a serious operation is required.

Gudger tells of a letter he received from E. C. Starks, a professor at Stanford University. While collecting fishes in the Philippines in 1926, Starks met Charles C. Ammerman and told him of Gudger's interest in the candiru. Ammerman had been assigned to South America as a surgeon in the U.S. Navy and spent time during 1910 and 1911 on the Rio Madeira. He had performed "two or three" operations on victims of candiru attacks. He once attempted to pull a candiru out of a victim's penis. When the tail came off, he was forced to operate,[78] ". . . making a supra-pubic opening into the bladder to remove the fish which had penetrated into that organ."

At first reading this story seems incredible. A candiru that had reached all the way to the bladder and still had part of its tail within reach would be quite long. Too long for a vandelliine? In Chapter 11, I show that vandelliines at least 13 centimeters (5 inches) in length are perfectly capable of wriggling into the urethra of a grown man. The facts of Ammerman's story seem valid, and his account contains the first credible mention of a candiru reaching the human bladder.

Gudger also corresponded with Alfredo da Matta, a physician in Manaus, Brazil. According to him, candirus are attracted to blood and likely to attack women who are menstruating when they go to the river to wash clothes. He recounts two reports of attacks, one on a girl, the other on a fisherman working naked in the Rio Solimões at Boa Vista. The report about the girl is our third eyewitness account (da Matta attended her personally):[79]

> The first concerns a girl who, while menstruating, went naked to bathe herself in the Cambixe, Rio Solimões. The girls were in the habit of staying quietly in rather shallow water, only their heads out of water, and thus bathing themselves. This is what she was doing. The candirú introduced itself part way into the vagina, causing a hemorrhage when it was pulled out, and a subsequent severe inflammation. This operation requires some caution and skill because if, in order to withdraw it, the candirú is caught by its tail or by its body, it expands its dorsal and ventral spines [sic] into the tissues, which fix it there more firmly than ever. The girl had to stay in bed some days.

I believe da Matta's story even though he invented spines that candirus don't have. Physicians often fail to notice such things. He clearly saw his task as removing the fish, not identifying it, although a preserved specimen would have made him a hero to future candiruphiles.

The truth is this: the purest poetry isn't worth as much as one soft, sweet perversion.

—Edgard Telles Ribeiro, *I Would Have Loved Him If I Had Not Killed Him*[1]

2.

Urinary Misconduct

Here I review the recorded history of purported candiru attacks during the post-Gudger period, 1931 to the present. What surprises me is how little knowledge has been gained since von Martius' brief account, and how quickly urban humanity accepts unsupported tales of these events, even obvious embellishments. In an era of gorge and puke, the cost of titillation goes up daily, but nothing really changes. The eighteenth-century French fairy tale "Ma mère m'a mon père m'a managé" tells about a mother who chops her son into small pieces and makes a casserole, which her daughter then serves to the father. Two centuries later, television news cameras took us live to the contents of Jeffrey Dahmer's refrigerator. As the American novelist E. L. Doctorow reminds us,[2] "You may think you are living in modern times, here and now, but that is the necessary illusion of every age."

In 1931, Konrad Guenther published his English edition of *A Naturalist in Brazil*. Guenther states that piranhas and not "crocodiles" are the most dangerous animals in Brazilian rivers. He also mentions candirus, which can force their way into the urethra where they are difficult to extract because of their spines. Guenther recognizes that these spines are located on the gill covers and not the fins. He claims no personal knowledge of any candiru attacks.

Also in 1931 the Brazilian ichthyologist Agenor Couto de Magalhães published his *Monographia Brazileira de Peixes Fluviaes* in which he tells us:[3]

> Much has been written about the peculiarity of these fishes for penetrating with incredible ease into the urethra, vagina and even the anus of persons bathing in rivers where they are plentiful. Women are especially vulnerable, mainly if they enter the water while menstruating and fail to protect themselves with bathing suits; large shoals of candirús, attracted by the blood, become excited, and, ordinarily thrust themselves at the mucous membrane inside. It is said that the candirú penetrates the man's urethra when, unaware, he urinates where they live. With urination, the canal [literally, channel] opens up and they [the candirus], aided by the odor of urine or for some other reason, make for the opening. Even if they do not fully penetrate, the operation of removing [them] is difficult and very painful, because it is known that their opercula expand inside the urethra and the little spines with which they are provided nail them to the mucous membrane. [S. Spotte, transl.]

This is an interesting contribution. Couto de Magalhães is among the first to suggest women are attacked more often than men. Like some of his predecessors, he equates these events with blood in the water. The fishes responsible are obviously visible (presumably in daylight) and travel in shoals, or schools. Vandelliines are thought to be mainly nocturnal (a subject I take up later), and whether they form schools is not known. Superficially at least, Couto de Magalhães seems to be describing cetopsids. However, when the subject switches to attacks on men, he clearly means vandelliines. Couto de Magalhães is the first author to mention that expansion of the urethra during urination might make entry easier. As an ichthyologist, he recognizes that attachment of the spines to the mucous membranes also involves expansion of the opercula.

The Brazilian writer Osvaldo Orico, in *Vocabulario de Crendices Amazonicas*, his 1937 book on Amazonian superstitions, tells us that the candiru, which he recognizes to be a vandelliine, lives in groups along the margins of rivers. It takes advantage of any human orifice. In the town of Pinheiro, where he grew up, mothers advised their children not to urinate when bathing in the rivers and streams because these fish, attracted to the urine, would invade their bladders.

In his *Dicionário de Animais do Brasil*, published in 1940, the Brazilian naturalist Rudolpho von Ihering begins his characterization of the candirus by noting that the name is nonspecific:[4]

This common name, Amazonian, applies to two kinds of small skin fishes,[5] some of the family *Trichomycteridae*, genera *Vandellia* and *Stegophilus*, that, with the "Cambevas"[6] of the same family, have opercular and preopercular [actually, interopercular] spines; others, of the family *Cetopsidae*, do not have these spines; the barbels are small, 6 in number [*sic*]. These last fish (genera *Cetopsis* and *Hemicetopsis*) reach a length of 30 cms. and bear the appropriate name of "candiru-açu"[7] . . . . To representatives of the first-mentioned family, *Vandellia cirrhosa* and *Stegophilus intermedius* and *insidiosus* (this last of the Rio S[ão] Francisco), have been imputed several injuries, ones which, however, had always been questioned . . .

To species of a genus of the same family, and also known as "Candirus", [are attributed] similar exploits. Already as Castelnau [*sic*] reiterated, on the [Rio] Araguaia, *Pareiodon pusillus* is feared by the fishermen, to the point where they do not dare urinate directly into the water, because they fear that this small fish, in going up the liquid column, will penetrate into the urethra. Miranda Ribeiro [*sic*], in Manaus, verified that *Pareiodon microps* is a carnivorous fish, that it pulls circular pieces of skin from live catfishes. What in fact enables it to do this is the dentition, hidden in a pleat of mucous membrane, but that, once exposed, gives the impression of miniature shark teeth (*Galeocerdus maculatus*),[8] simplified and with the larger curved tip outside.

Gathered in legions, as if they were small piranhas, they [seek] flesh not only of dead animals, but hunt the wounded as well, that come to seek refuge in the water.

Much more dangerous is the habit of the candiru *Vandellia cirrhosa* that tries to penetrate into the swimmer's urogenital opening. The maximum size that this fish reaches is 70–80 mms., but specimens of 40 mms. are only 4 mms. in diameter and this is why it is easy for them to insinuate, and to penetrate, completely into the cavity [urethral canal]. And the worst is that the fish of this family, as also noticed in the "Cambevas", their close relatives, have numerous spines in the opercular area and these, if one tries an extraction, become more and more imbedded in the flesh, provoking serious hemorrhage. This fact, testified to several times by an Amazonian doctor, calls for a difficult extraction, and for the riverine population to proceed, fearing the candiru, it takes providence to avoid accidents of this nature, to which mainly the women are subject. With evident exaggeration the men fear to release a direct jet [of urine] into rivers inhabited by candirus because, they say, they might be able to rise up and penetrate. [S. Spotte, transl.]

Von Ihering clearly differentiates between the cetopsids and the vandellines even to the point of describing anatomical distinctions.

In 1941, Kenneth W. Vinton and W. Hugh Stickler followed up Gudger's articles in *American Journal of Surgery* with their own. Vinton had first heard about the *carnero* from Charley Lamott, a radio announcer and former purser. Lamott once led a party of gold miners over the Andes and down the Amazon. In 1936, while returning from South America, Vinton and he shared a stateroom. Lamott was a raconteur, and the story of a little fish that swims into human orifices was one of many he told. Vinton discounted it completely until Indians later told him about a small fish that attacks people in the manner Lamott had described. The Indians became very excited in recounting these tales, although the method of attack was never made clear.

Vinton later met the Rev. Edgar J. Burns, an American missionary living in Yurimaguas, a town on the Rio Huallaga in eastern Peru. Burns possessed some medical knowledge. When questioned about these putative attacks, he responded:[9]

> Oh yes! You mean the *carnero*. It is true that they attack people by entering the body orifices and feeding inside the body. They have spines on the head, and once one starts into an opening the spines prevent if from being withdrawn.

The pharmacognosist H. H. Rusby had traveled extensively in tropical South America. In a letter to Vinton and Stickler he wrote that attacks on both women and men were well established:[10] "Feather-bed explorers and theoretical researchers have disputed the facts, but the evidence is abundant and confirmed." Rusby himself did not supply any evidence. Vinton and Stickler refer to Gudger's work as confirmation of Rusby's comments, which actually adds nothing in the way of proof.

At the time of their visit, Vinton and Stickler report, Burns had lived in the Amazon region for 7 years, the last three in Yurimaguas where one of his duties was providing medical aid to the Indians. During his total tenure he had known 10 cases of people attacked by *carneros*. In half of these he had personally treated the victims; in the other five he had treated the victims after someone else removed the fish. Once he treated three people within a week.

The 10 victims comprised four women, three girls aged 10–16, one man, and two boys of 12 and 13. Burns knew of many other attacks and in some instances had talked to the victim afterwards. Most were women, and in his experience women were attacked far more often than men. According to rumor, *carneros* sometimes entered the ears, nostrils, or anus, but he could not verify this.

The amount of bleeding was variable, Burns reports. In some cases victims bled so profusely that emergency medical procedures were necessary to stop the hemorrhaging. He had never heard of anyone bleeding to death, but thought it possible. He states,[11] "The natives speak vaguely of such deaths, but here again there is no real proof."

Vinton and Stickler asked Burns if urination might have triggered *carnero* attacks in the victims he had treated. Burns replied that in every case attacks occurred while the victim was immersed and urinating. As Vinton and Stickler point out, whether candirus are attracted to urine can be determined only by experimentation, although they were inclined to believe it.

Burns is still another eyewitness, and I find him credible. He expresses knowledge of the *carnero* from the start and apparently had records (or excellent recall) because he knew the sex and age of most of the victims he had treated. He modestly describes his medical intervention after these attacks and politely discounts the belief of the Indians that victims might bleed to death, raising the question of proof.

The American ichthyologist William Ray Allen summarizes what was known in *Fishes of Western South America*, published in 1942. Eigenmann, who died in 1927, is listed as coauthor. Allen acknowledges Gudger's publications for much of his source material on candiru attacks. Like Gudger, he never found evidence of an authentic attack on a human being. In a pre-1930 letter to Gudger that Gudger included in his two articles and book, Allen writes:[12]

> I was told of numerous cases of the Candirú's entering the urethra, but they were always some distance downstream, and when I arrived downstream I was told of many such cases upstream. At Iquitos I got on the trail of some cases and followed as far as there was a clue, or a hope, or a shred of a name to inquire about. The most hopeful of these cases turned out to be a real human being. But alas when I got to his home he had just departed by the last launch.

Allen was reluctant to blame candiru attacks on any species in particular.

The Colombian ichthyologist Cecil W. Miles, writing in 1943, echoes Eigenmann's opinion that the "habit" of entering the opercular chambers of fishes (and human urethras) is[13] ". . . merely an extension of the family instinct for hiding among rocks and holes along the river banks . . ." He considers urine to be the stimulus prompting attacks on humans.

The American ichthyologist George S. Myers states in 1944 that cases of attacks by candirus on both men and women have been confirmed, but cites no sources of evidence. In his opinion, the offending species are the same ones that attack the gills of large fishes and suck their blood.

The American ichthyologists Leonard P. Schultz and Edith M. Stern, in their 1948 edition of *The Ways of Fishes*, write that to urinate in waters where candirus are present "is tempting fate," and in his 1949 edition of *The Life Story of the Fish*, Brian Curtis tells us that natives in regions where candirus occur dread to go into the water.

Lewis Cotlow was a New York insurance executive, but his hobby was tramping around in remote South American rainforests hanging out with the Indians and making films of their daily activities. In *Amazon Head-hunters*, published in 1953, he recounts his experiences among the Jívaro and other tribes of Ecuador and Peru, including having witnessed a candiru attack. Cotlow seems to have been an unpretentious man able to poke fun at himself. The elements of danger are stated as part of his narrative, but nowhere does he dwell on them. In my opinion, Cotlow was not a man to exaggerate, and I trust his observations. The attack occurred when everyone in the *jivaria* gathered in a nearby stream.

The stream had been poisoned, and Cotlow was carrying stones to shore up the temporary dam. Gasping fish lay on the surface, and some of the women busily tossing them into baskets were standing in water nearly to their waists. Then one of the women screamed and ran for the shore. She lay down, still screaming, while the others gathered around her.

A young man ran to the *jivaria* and returned with the witch doctor and an older woman. Cotlow asked, by means of crude sign language, what had happened. The men made "wriggling motions" with their hands and pointed to their genitals. By this time the medicine man had taken over. Cotlow's view was obscured, but the woman gave a piercing scream. He noticed a good deal of blood on the ground beside her, then she was carried to the *jivaria*.

When Cotlow's guide appeared and could translate the stream of events from Jívaro into Spanish, Cotlow learned the truth. "Canero," his guide had said simply. Cotlow writes:[14]

> The poor girl in the river had felt the canero dart into her vagina. She screamed and ran to shore. The young man had brought from the *jivaria* a kind of bamboo forceps with which the canero was removed, the spines clutching at the tender flesh and ripping it. The *wishinu* [witch doctor] had placed medications in the wound to stop the bleeding. The girl recovered, but she was unable to walk for several days and was quite weak from loss of blood.

In 1959 the American novelist William S. Burroughs—jailbird, heroin addict, Beat writer, Harvard graduate, fugitive, drunk, misogynist, marijuana farmer, and murderer—published his most famous work, a dark, frantic, drugged-out tale of homosexual and scatological fantasy that fellow writer Jack Kerouac suggested calling *The Naked Lunch*.

Burroughs liked Kerouac's idea, but no one else liked anything about his book until a Paris publisher took a chance. Burroughs had traveled to South America searching for *yagé*, which fellow addicts told him was the ultimate high, and he knew the story of the candiru. It seemed to fit perfectly with his literary plans. He mentions the fish in one hallucinatory passage in which "adolescent hoodlums" of all nations take to the streets. In their rampage they release the inmates of zoos, insane asylums, and prisons, destroy priceless art, and[15] ". . . throw sharks and sting rays, electric eels and candiru into swimming pools . . ." Parenthetically, he adds, ". . . the candiru is a small eel-like fish or worm about one-quarter inch through and two inches long patronizing certain rivers of ill repute in the Greater Amazon Basin, will dart up your prick or your asshole or a woman's cunt *faute de mieux*, and hold himself there by sharp spines with precisely what motives is not known since no one has stepped forward to observe the candiru's life cycle *in situ* . . ." On this last point Burroughs is dead on, and the candiru's "motives" are still a mystery.

Beginning in 1943, Helmut Sick, a German, served as chief naturalist on an expedition into central Brazil that lasted 7 years. His book *Tukani* recounts those years. Sick was a superb naturalist, a specialist in birds who also had broad knowledge of other organisms. Only when discussing fishes does he seem to falter. He describes some of the fishes of the Rio das Mortes and includes the candiru among those measuring 6 feet or more.

The prospect of a 6-foot candiru is stupefying, and this statement could be attributed to a translating error of the original German text were it not for Sick's subsequent description of the "sheat-fish." This minute animal, covered with tiny barbs, was liable to insinuate itself into the urethra of any man who urinated while in the water, and then only a surgical operation could remove it. By this he clearly means the candiru, although the sheat-fishes are members of a different family of catfishes, the Siluridae.

In the second edition of *Peixes da Água Doce*, published in 1962, the Brazilian naturalist Eurico Santos claims that despite their size candirus are as bloodthirsty as piranhas. The candiru, he continues, has neither the piranha's terrifying dentition nor its strength, and an animal of sufficient size should be able to defend itself. However, the candiru's mode of attack is different. People bathing in rivers risk the possibility of a candiru penetrating the urethra or vagina. Human beings and domestic animals are susceptible to attack when they attempt to cross rivers. Women are supposedly attacked more often because their vulnerable parts are more accessible. Candirus are most likely to attack when the victim urinates in the water. However,[16]

> It has even been said that it is not necessary to urinate under the water, it is sufficient to urinate some distance above the river, because the *candiru* rises to the jet.
> This is still unproven and seems improbable. [S. Spotte, transl.]

The English ichthyologist Rosemary McConnell, writing in 1967 about dangerous fishes of the Rupununi savanna region of Guyana, mentions the stingray, electric eel, and candiru. Writing in 1975 as Lowe-McConnell, she tells us that[17] ". . . the candiru (*Vandellia cirrhosa*), is reputedly attracted to urine and widely believed to enter the orifices of unwary bathers."

David St. Clair's 1968 travel book *The Mighty, Mighty Amazon* repeats the litany of candirus being attracted to urine and swimming up urine streams even if a man is standing above the water.

An anonymous author, writing in *Environment Southwest* in 1969, calls the candiru the "vampire fish" and tells us of its attraction to human urine. Once inside the body it pierces the skin and gorges on blood. Death from inflammation ensues when the fish reaches the bladder. Woman are more vulnerable to attack, ". . . but males suffer more." It isn't known for certain whether a candiru, once inside its human victim, makes its way deep into the body, nor do we know that candirus, having gained access, feed inside their human victims.

Helen and Frank Schreider wrote a book called *Exploring the Amazon*, published in 1970. Their guide advised that candirus were dangerous only in sluggish waters, and that[18] ". . . trousers were the best protection against carnero . . ."

Walter Armbrust, writing in 1971 for the German aquarium hobbyist magazine *Aquarien und Terrarien*, tells us how a candiru penetrates the urethra of the unsuspecting bather, then spreads its gill covers. According to Armbrust, certain native tribes induce this to happen, regarding it as a test of courage and a lesson in enduring pain. Russian roulette played with candirus would seem more like a test of natural selection. Armbrust fails to mention which tribe plays this game. He makes no claim of having witnessed such a ritual.[19]

The American physician John R. Herman published an article on the candiru in a 1973 issue of *Urology*. He states:[20] "Although Gudger found proof that this fish was attracted by the body secretions of man, especially flesh and blood [*sic*], he was unable to prove urinophilia." Gudger never intended to prove that candirus are attracted to anything. He simply set forth the different claims and evaluated them.

The American ichthyologist Karl R. Lagler and coauthors, in their 1977 text *Ichthyology*, state that candirus can lodge in the urethra of human males or in the bladder of human females, and that other body openings are also entered. They might have been first to distinguish (if indirectly) between candiru attacks on men and women based on comparative length of the urethra. The authors do not say this, but the urethra of a human female is shorter, presumably making the bladder easier to reach. Of course we have only one believable report of a candiru having entered the bladder of a human being (see Chapter 1).

The German zoologist Bernhard Grzimek, writing in 1973, tells us that candiru attacks have "repeatedly caused death." Furthermore,[21] "If the afflicted individual does not want to have blood poisoning he must undergo amputation." These statements have no factual basis.

Goulding spent several years in Brazil studying the indigenous fishes, mainly those of commercial value. He traveled widely and knew about candirus, but apparently never came across evidence of attacks. In *The Fishes and the Forest*, published in 1980, he writes of the vandelliines:[22] "Some species evidently insinuate themselves into the ears, noses, anuses, and perhaps vaginas of bathers, but the exact culprits have not been identified."

In *Amazon: The Flooded Forest*, Goulding discusses the trichomycterids that purportedly attack humans, emphasizing that such incidents are difficult to verify. Women are particularly reluctant to display the wounds. In his experience, candirus are little feared, although menstruating women sometimes avoid bathing where candirus are known to be common. Goulding then says:[23] "One motif in native folklore is of a candiru entering the penis by swimming up the stream of water of a urinating male. Fortunately this is highly improbable!"

Goulding agrees with the general belief that women are attacked more often than men. However, he stands alone in not considering the urethra a principal site of attack, and he relegates to folklore the notion of candirus being attracted to urine.

Unlike other writers, Goulding found little indication that the fear of candirus is widespread. My own evidence, although much more limited, is similar. Many people who live along the rivers, including fishermen, seem never to have heard of the candiru, or if they have know little about it. On the Rio Jauaperi, at the very location where the Brazilian ichthyologist Paulo Petry and I caught candirus at night, naked children splashed during the day while their mothers washed clothes. The candiru seems to be unknown. On the Rio Tiputini, an affluent of the Rio Napo in Ecuador, local boatmen have never heard of the *carnero*, although at least one species (*V. wieneri*) inhabits this drainage system (see Chapter 3).

Burgess, in his 1989 *An Atlas of Freshwater and Marine Catfishes*, says:[24] "Although other fishes have similar habits and may be included in the collective term 'candiru,' *Vandellia cirrhosa* is probably the species most commonly meant when referring to the candiru." He recounts the story of how other "candirus" can be captured using a bloody cow's lung as bait.[25]

Burgess continues:[26]

> Perhaps the most notoriety that the candiru has received is by its habit of at times entering the urogenital openings of mammals, including human bathers, especially if they happen to urinate while in the water. . . . The fish is said to possibly follow the flow of urine as it would the flow of water from the exhalent gill chambers of a fish. After penetrating as far as the slender but powerful fish can manage, it locks its opercular and interopercular spines into position, resulting in excruciating pain for the victim, possible massive hemorrhage, probable infection, and commonly the need for surgical procedures for removal of the offending fish.

In a 1991 article, J. L. Breault states that the candiru is called "urethra fish" in English, giving Grzimek as his source. Breault then cites Herman's statement that, once inside the urethra, the candiru spreads its opercula in an attempt to obtain oxygen. Neither author explains how Herman could know this.

The American physician Bruce W. Halstead published a book in 1992 called *Dangerous Aquatic Animals of the World*, which contains a chapter on the candiru.[27] However, Halstead's careless scholarship, outdated references, unsubstantiated comments, and numerous errors render his text untrustworthy. His most recent sources of information appear to have been Eigenmann's 1918 monograph and the 1942 book by Eigenmann and Allen, *Fishes of Western South America*. Halstead refers to the family of catfishes containing the candirus as the Pygidiidae (the modern name is Trichomycteridae) and considers *Urinophilus* a valid genus (see Chapter 3). Like many others, he confuses the vandelliines with the cetopsids. Halstead also tells us that among the effects of candiru attacks are "secondary infections." Perhaps so, but the comment is unsubstantiated. He calls these fishes "culprits capable of urinary misconduct."

Also in 1992 the Brazilian zoologists Alpina Begossi and Francisco Manoel de Souza Braga published an article on food taboos and folk medicine among fishermen living along the Rio Tocantins. They write:[28]

> There are two kinds of candirú of common occurrence in Amazon [*sic*]: one type has few inches of length [*sic*] and is a gill parasite and people are afraid of it because it can go inside the uretra [*sic*] and other body cavities (family Trichomycteridae); the other, which is the one referred to in our study, is bigger and necrophagous (Cetopsidae).

In 1994 the English journal *New Scientist* published a note about a fierce candiru purported to be an undescribed species, smaller (1 centimeter long) and "more voracious" than the others and having two teeth in the back of its mouth. Wilson Costa, a biologist from an unnamed Rio de Janeiro university, discovered the fish in the Rio Araguaia. According to Costa,[29] "On one occasion . . . one of the tiny candiru slipped into a cut on a researcher's hand and could be seen wriggling under the skin towards a vein." Costa offers no evidence of attacks on humans, but assumes they occur.

This report is extraordinary in three respects. First, an adult candiru of only 1 centimeter would be among the smallest fishes in the world. Second, having two teeth at the back of its mouth would make it unique among candirus, perhaps even disqualifying it as a member of the group. Third, its behavior when attacking the researcher is remarkable. I somehow can't picture a fish—even a very tiny fish—slipping into a cut on the hand and then "wriggling under the skin towards a vein." How could it know the location of a vein on a human hand? Success would be assured nonetheless: movement in any direction would lead eventually to a blood vessel. Separating the layers of skin isn't an easy task, especially for a fish out of water, and progress would be very slow.

The American ichthyologist Gene S. Helfman and coauthors make passing mention of the candiru in their 1997 text *The Diversity of Fishes*, and Carolyn Shea later contributes to the misinformation about candiru attacks in the January-February 1999 issue of *Audubon* magazine. Despite no evidence, she identifies the guilty species as *V. cirrhosa*. According to Shea, a "jokester" once named the fish *Urinophilus diabolicus*. Although now invalid (see Chapter 3), this name was never intended as a joke, nor was it ever applied to the fish called *V. cirrhosa*.

My own queries via the Internet on candiru attacks yielded four worthwhile responses, none an eyewitness account. The first is from Paulo Petry and seems to reinforce Costa's observation:[30]

> I have talked to several physicians that work at the public hospital in Manaus, and they tell me that they have seen cases where *Vandellia* penetrates under the skin of people, but have never had the chance to document the fact myself; there might be medical records available, but it will take some time to find them.

In the second, the American ornithologist John W. Fitzpatrick says:[31]

> I have your inquiry about candiru. I know of one case, which occurred in southeastern Peru in the mid-1970's (Manu National Park). I was not present, but heard about it later in the same year from park guards who were. As I remember it, the man (a Lima bureaucrat, visiting the fledgling park) had to be helicoptered out of the Manu area and flown to Cuzco for surgical removal of the fish.

FIG. 8   Undated clipping from the Manaus newspaper *Popular da Tarde*. Courtesy of João Batista Ferraz, Instituto Nacional de Pesquisas da Amazônia.

In the third, Linnea Smith, an American physician in charge of a remote clinic in the lowlands of eastern Peru, writes:[32]

> I am afraid that you are right, the mythical reputation of the candirus greatly outshines their actual dangers. I have never seen a case. My assistant once reported that when I was in the city some folks had brought in their 5 year old son, who had had one in his rectum. They had removed it, and were concerned about a little bleeding. End of story.

The fourth is an undated and very smudged letter in Spanish written by Jean-Luc Sanchez, a resident of France, to Señor Mago-Leccia (location unknown). I received a copy from the American ichthyologist Jonathan N. Baskin by way Paulo Petry on 24 February 2001. The letter is brief, just five short paragraphs. Sanchez apologizes for his tardy response, briefly discusses candirus, then states in the third paragraph:[33]

> As for these Trichomycteridae, they were caught with a net and peccary blood in Ecuador during a month in 1995, while making an expedition to the river Rio Curaray and [its] affluents. An Ecuadorian soldier died the previous year in the Rio Curaray because of the penetration of a "canero" (or "candirú) [sic] into his ear. [S. Spotte, transl.]

My final entry is part of a news report of a candiru attack that appeared in a Manaus newspaper called *Popular da Tarde*. The paper ceased publication sometime in the 1980s and left no archives that anyone can find. On 13 November 1999, João Batista Ferraz, a forestry scientist at Instituto Nacional de Pesquisas da Amazônia, handed me a photograph of the news clipping (Fig. 8). The headline reads, "Peixe Tardo Ataca Banhista" ("Horny Fish Attacks Bather"). A stevedore named João Costa Lira was swimming at *na escadaria da Panair* (the staircase at PanAir)[34] when he felt something *liso e roliço* (slippery and round) penetrate his anus. The last line of the article states that the doctors are trying to remove the fish from his bowels. Regrettably, Batista had thrown away that issue of the newspaper along with the rest of the article, leaving us to ponder Costa's fate and speculate if he still might be sitting on a pillow.

This chapter and the previous one have dealt with the history of candiru attacks. I now offer a synopsis of whose reports seem believable and whose do not. We can start by jettisoning the fictional statement of the novelist William S. Burroughs. In fairness to Burroughs he merely advocates releasing candirus into swimming pools, and he never claims to have seen a candiru attack, not even while stoned.

Von Martius' contribution can be dismissed as hearsay, but von Poeppig's account is highly credible. He claims to have witnessed a candiru attack, but relegates his observations to a footnote. Clearly, he wasn't seeking accolades.

Schomburgk's account can be thrown out as hearsay too. He bases the credibility of candiru attacks on secondhand reports, as does de Castelnau. So does von Müller in his recounting of events told to him by Wallis. Neither Keller nor Marcoy has an original observation, Orten dismisses rumors of attacks out of hand, and Günther, from the comfort of England (and no doubt safely encased in tweed trousers), simply reports what others have told him, interjecting a healthy dose of doubt.

Bach's account, relayed by Boulenger, is not credible, and Jobert offers nothing new in terms of candiru attacks on the human urogenital system. Von den Steinen gives us more rumors. Lange's account of a death following a candiru attack seems preposterous considering the many errors in his book and its general tone of exaggeration and gothic horror.

Allen traveled widely in lowland South America. Along the way he sought evidence of candiru attacks without finding any. Eigenmann took reports of candiru attacks seriously, but never found conclusive evidence either. Pearson's story, told to Gudger in a letter, is hearsay (which Pearson acknowledges). Tate's information is also secondhand. Le Cointe, in his correspondence with Gudger, reveals his direct observations and seems credible. Also believable are the accounts of Campos, Ammerman, and da Matta. Prodger's stories can be dismissed, and Couto de Magalhães merely summarizes everyone else's hearsay. I thought Burns' accounts, as related by Vinton and Stickler, ring true, and Cotlow's tale is told directly, and, I believe, truthfully.

Depending on how you count, the tally to this point is approximately 65 entries in the literature dealing with candiru attacks, nearly all of them hearsay or recitations of the hearsay of others. Typically, we have only the words of an explorer or physician, often translated from another language or told to a second party. In many cases there is no source, simply a tale everyone accepts as true.

In my opinion, only seven of these accounts are credible: von Poeppig (1836); Le Cointe, Campos, Ammerman, and da Matta (all in Gudger 1930c); Burns (in Vinton and Stickler 1941); and Cotlow (1953). Still, no exemption can be granted from the vicissitudes of story telling. None of these witnesses presents hard evidence. In no case was the fish, after extraction from its victim, preserved and later identified, nor are there affidavits, photographs or illustrations, or any other manifestation of a smoking gun. In only one instance—that involving Doña J. S.—do we hear from the victim, but through a physician who was not in attendance. Her account of the attack, which Campos casually exhumed from memory, was presumably translated into English and later given to us by Gudger.

If, as some explorers tell us, candirus are feared throughout the Amazon basin, why is it some travelers mention them and others don't? Among those silent on the subject have been outstanding naturalists whose observations are beyond reproach. They lived with the river people, spoke their languages, knew their legends and cultures, and never mention the candiru.

We can account for these omissions in several ways starting with the immense size of the Amazon basin and the relative rarity of candiru attacks. Perhaps candirus are dangerous only in certain regions, although the areas traveled by many explorers of the past two centuries have often overlapped. Maybe the unverified stories of candiru attacks were simply not worth mentioning, strange as this seems.

Alexander von Humboldt's protean knowledge was unmatched in his time. Nothing seems to have eluded his keen gaze during tramps through tropical South America with the botanist Aime Bonpland, as reported in his three-volume *Personal Narrative of Travels to the Equinoctial Regions of America During the Years 1799–1804*, published originally in French. Von Humboldt certainly would have repeated any secondhand stories of candiru attacks, considering his unconcealed disdain of undocumented evidence and belief in unproven phenomena:[35] "Nature has the appearance of greatness to man in proportion as she is veiled in mystery; and the ignorant are prone to put faith in everything that borders on the marvelous."

Two of the greatest naturalists of the nineteenth century—Henry Walter Bates and Alfred Russel Wallace—do not mention the candiru in their writings. Wallace had proposed to Bates a joint trip to the Amazon. Their purpose was to gather facts towards solving the origin of species. They would earn their living by collecting specimens and shipping them back to England for sale to museums and private collectors.

They arrived in Brazil in 1848 and stayed together for 2 years, then Bates went up the Rio Solimões and Wallace up the Rio Negro. Wallace remained another 2 years; Bates stayed a total of 11 years, collecting 14,712 species of animals, of which some 8,000 were previously unknown to science.[36] Upon returning to England, he wrote *The Naturalist on the River Amazons*, an account of his stay in South America that was published in 1864. Several species of fishes are discussed, and some are even illustrated, but the candiru is not among them.

Wallace's *A Narrative of Travels on the Amazon and Rio Negro* was published in 1855. Although Wallace collected many species of animals, including numerous fishes, he makes no mention of the candiru.

The American ichthyologist Louis Agassiz, who at age 20 was given the task of organizing and describing von Spix's collection of freshwater fishes from Brazil, later spent a year in the Amazon basin, leaving New York by steamer on 1 April 1865. He made numerous collections and was conversant with many people in the interior. *A Journey in Brazil*, coauthored with his wife, describes in detail the more interesting fishes. While at Teffé, Agassiz[37] ". . . has a corps of little boys engaged in catching the tiniest fishes, so insignificant in size that the regular fishermen, who can never be made to understand that a fish which is not good to eat can serve any useful purpose, always throw them away." The collections evidently did not include any candirus.

In 1913 and 1914, Theodore Roosevelt and the Brazilian explorer Colonel Candido Rondon led an expedition through the Brazilian rainforest and down the River of Doubt. Roosevelt told their story in *Through the Brazilian Wilderness*, published in 1920. Adventure was their mission, and their personal firearms were more than weapons; they were lovely, well-greased companions. Many passages are devoted to encounters (or tales of the encounters of others) with venomous snakes, jaguars, cougars, fire ants, fever, gigantic man-eating catfishes, caimans, and piranhas. Roosevelt sought out the bizarre and the dangerous, and had he come across stories of candiru attacks he surely would have mentioned them.

Leo E. Miller, an American naturalist and collector of mammals for the American Museum of Natural History in New York City, accompanied Roosevelt and Rondon. He later published a book titled *In the Wilds of South America* that summarizes his experiences during 6 years in Colombia, Venezuela, British Guiana, Peru, Bolivia, Paraguay, and Brazil. He mentions the piranha (called *caribe* in Spanish-speaking countries of South America), but never the candiru. Miller was an experienced field naturalist whose text indicates a deep knowledge of the plants and animals he encountered.

G. M. Dyott was a young English engineer hired by the Peruvian government to investigate the feasibility of air transport into remote regions of the rainforest where railroads were still many years away. Starting from Yurimaguas on the Rio Huallaga, he made his way up the Rio Marañon and through the Pongo de Manseriche. His guides later deserted him. Starving, he found his way back to the Rio Marañon, was taken in by a tribe of Aguarunas, and held captive for several weeks. He had brought along a Spanish edition of Conan Doyle's *The Hound of the Baskervilles*, and reading it endlessly was his principal source of amusement. This is all recounted in *Silent Highways of the Jungle*, published in 1922. Nowhere does he mention the candiru.

We also have Gordon MacCreagh's fascinating journal about aiding a group of American scientists deep in the rainforest. MacCreagh was not a naturalist, although he had considerable field experience. His job was to procure food, map routes, hire and manage the help, oversee pitching camp, and so forth. In *White Waters and Black*, published in 1926, he announces his intentions at the start:[38]

> For nobody has ever been sacrilegious enough to keep a running record of the intimate doings of a party of eminent professors loose in the wild woods. I, one of the eight white men, propose to keep such a record; and I propose, if possible, not to encumber it with a single item of scientific value.

For MacCreagh the trip is one of uninterrupted hilarity. The scientists bicker continuously, become ill, complain about the rain and mosquitoes, and generally behave like swine. Instead of discussing important issues with his men, the director of the expedition issues memorandums from his tent. In "Bulletin Number One," he informs them that they have just crossed the Andes. Later, when the statistician suffers several personal setbacks including loss of his false teeth, he issues his own memos from an adjacent tent castigating the director's inept leadership. MacCreagh records every absurdity. Nothing bothers him, certainly not the discomfort. Mac-Creagh is most upset when a pack mule carrying his bagpipes tumbles over a precipice in the Andes. The pipes are retrieved, but not the mule.

One day a scientist referred to as the Respectable Member returns from his tramp in the woods with a baby tapir. The little beast is soon obnoxiously tame:[39]

> Its name is Nebuchadnezzar Ben Ibrahim, Benny for short, and it lives on bananas and rice and blotting-paper and botanical specimens and socks. Its innocent life has been threatened, up to date, by every member of the party at least once, and by the Botanist and the cook a dozen times each. So it waxes fat and thrives amazingly.

MacCreagh and Benny spend much time frolicking together in tropical rivers, their orifices conspicuously free of candirus. The party travels down the Rio Beni, Rio Madeira, and Rio Solimões, then up the Rio Negro. Along the way they stay with the local residents and hire Indians to help them. Although the Ichthyologist catches many interesting fishes, MacCreagh mentions just the piranha as being dangerous. Everyone bathes regularly, wary only of piranhas and caimans.

Kenneth Good, an American anthropologist, entered the rainforest as a graduate student in 1975 and did not emerge permanently until 1986. During those years he studied the Yanomamo, a primitive people on the Rio Orinoco in Venezuela near the Brazilian border. He was adopted into the tribe he was studying, learned its language, and married a Yanomamo woman. *Into the Heart,* published in 1991 with coauthor David Chanoff, tells his story. The Yanomamo bathe every day, apparently without knowledge of candirus.

What can we make of all this? The returns so far are confusing. If the legend of the candiru is a melody, which section of it forms the tessitura? From such eminent naturalists as von Humboldt, Wallace, and Bates comes a resounding silence at least as forceful as any secondhand story of a candiru attack. That any of them elided tales about the candiru in his travelogue seems improbable. Candirus, if would appear, are either dangerous to human beings or they aren't, depending on the source. Or perhaps they simply are not worth mentioning.

Not to be dismissed are the few credible eyewitnesses whose accounts we have just examined. Their voices can scarcely be heard through the din of hearsay. In later chapters I discuss which chemical components of human blood, perspiration, or urine might be attractive to candirus and whether certain articles of clothing are worn by native South Americans for the purpose of repelling candirus. No matter if the perspective is direct or oblique, the truth remains elusive. Still later, I describe how I risked (sort of) my own urethra in the interest of science before coming upon evidence that should assuage even confirmed doubters. These subjects are coming soon, but candiru taxonomy consumes the next two chapters: what do candirus look like, how many species are there, and how can they be told apart?

Yes, we had a great-uncle who was a fish, on my paternal grandmother's side, to be precise, of the Coelacanthus family of the Devonian period (the fresh-water branch: who are, for that matter, cousins of the others—but I don't want to go into all these questions of kinship, nobody can ever follow them anyhow).

—Italo Calvino, "The Aquatic Uncle"[1]

3.

A Very Singular Fish

On my bookshelf is a tattered little volume called *Sports Afield Collection of Know Your Fish*, written by Tom Dolan. I've had it since 1960, the year it was published, when it cost me 50 cents. Inside are color illustrations of North American freshwater fishes arranged by family, along with information on their habits. Dolan presents only the most prominent families. This is obvious because each has its own coat of arms, something lesser families probably couldn't afford. Across the coat of arms of the Ictaluridae is written, "Any Damn Fool Knows a Catfish."

But don't be taken in. Nobody can claim complete expertise in identifying the various kinds of catfishes, and certainly this is true of candirus. Still, I feel an obligation to try. After all, those little creatures responsible for the legends do exist, and taxonomists have names for at least some of them.

The naming of a fish begins when a taxonomist examines it and notices something different. After comparing its features with those of the fish's closest relatives and deciding the differences are substantial enough, the taxonomist gives it a scientific name of its own. The specimens used in the description—the type specimens—are deposited in museum collections and assigned identification numbers. When a description is morpholog-ical, species differences can be based on such features, or characters, as position and shape of the fins, dentition (arrangement, number, size, and shape of teeth), proportional relationships of body parts, coloration, and positions of the fins and the number of fin rays and fin spines on each. The fin rays function to stiffen the fins, and their number is sometimes diag-nostic of a species. The extent to which characters vary is often subjective, and later taxonomists might combine two species having minimal differ-ences. In cases of synonymy, the older scientific name takes precedence; the newer name passes into history.

Eigenmann's 1918 monograph is the most recent review of trichomyc-terid taxonomy. Much new information and many additional museum specimens have accumulated since, but contemporary ichthyologists have yet to review the material and bring everything together. Because the nomenclature of this group is outdated and in disarray, existing ichthy-ological keys are useful only as general guides.[2]

Trichomycterids are smooth and scaleless and shaped like eels, with the dorsal, pelvic, and anal fins set back towards the tail. On the gill covers are usually two or more patches of spines; at the corners of the mouth are bar-bels, or "whiskers." One pair of these (the lower, or rictal, barbels) is shorter than the other (the maxillary barbels) and sometimes barely visible. Tri-chomycterids also lack two structures possessed by most catfishes, an adi-pose fin (a small fatty fin between the dorsal and caudal fins) and mental barbels (barbels underneath the chin). In addition, they generally lack the well-developed spines on the pectoral and dorsal fins found on most cat-fishes. Salient features are labeled in Fig. 9.

Now comes the technical part. Notable are the integumentary teeth, or odontodes (sometimes called denticles, denticulations, barbs, spines, prickles, or dermal teeth), on the gill covers (Fig. 10), although not all species of trichomycterids have them. These are the two or more patches of spines mentioned in the previous paragraph, unique to this group and occurring solely on the opercular and interopercular bones.[3]

As mentioned previously, within the family Trichomycteridae is the sub-family Vandelliinae (the vandelliines), consisting of six putative genera and perhaps 15 species (Table 1). So far as we can tell, all are confirmed bloodsuckers and therefore true candirus, assuming the acceptance of my

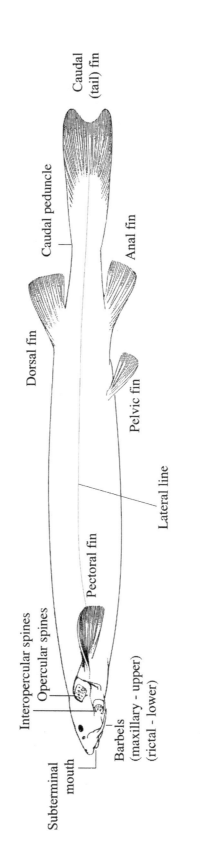

Fig. 9 Some external structures of trichomycterids as represented by a candiru. Lateral view. Source: Stephen Spotte.

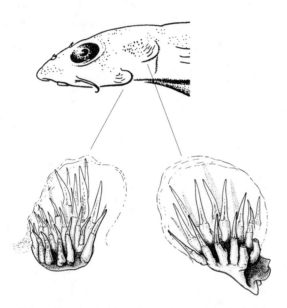

FIG. 10 Interopercular spines, or odontodes (left) and opercular spines, or odontodes (right) of a representative vandelliine, *Vandellia beccari*. Courtesy of Robert E. Schmidt and American Society of Ichthyologists and Herpetologists. Source: After Schmidt (1987).

definition in Chapter 1. (To repeat, candirus are those trichomycterids known to suck blood from the gills of other fishes and thought to live on blood exclusively.) The American ichthyologist Robert E. Schmidt, writing in 1993, describes the vandelliines as having (1) teeth reduced in number, (2) rami of the lower jaw not meeting in the middle (Fig. 11, top), (3) median vomerine (or premaxillary) tooth patch (Fig. 11, bottom),[4] (4) ethmoid[5] forked distally and articulated with the maxilla, and (5) 2–4 "claw-teeth" on the distal end of the maxilla.[6] The "claw-teeth" of the van-delliines are enigmatic characters, appearing ghostlike to some specialists while remaining invisible to others, sort of like dandruff on a light-colored suit (Plate 1).

Formal descriptions of candirus have been published since 1846, but the question of how many species exist has no clear answer. Some are probably synonyms of others. If so, names outnumber valid species. Here, I divide the existing genera into two groups, the first comprising *Vandellia* and *Plectrochilus*, the second consisting of *Paravandellia*, *Branchioica*, *Parabranchioica*, and *Paracanthopoma* (see the next chapter). The logic serves merely as a flimsy crutch on which I can lean while discussing van-delliine taxonomy. No evolutionary implications are intended.[7] Disposition of type specimens of the species discussed in this chapter is summarized in Table 2.

TABLE 1. Numbers of specimens used to describe the existing genera and species of candirus.

Genera	Species	Number of specimens examined in the original descriptions
Vandellia		3
	V. cirrhosa	3
	V. plazai	1
	V. wieneri	1
	V. balzani	1
	V. hasemani	3
	V. hematophaga	?
	V. beccari	1
Plectrochilus		1
	P. machadoi	1
	P. sanguineus	1
	P. erythrurus	10
Paravandellia		1
	P. oxyptera	1
Branchioica		2
	B. bertoni	2
	B. phaneronema	4
Parabranchioica		1
	P. teaguei	1
Paracanthopoma		2
	P. parva	2

Source: Stephen Spotte

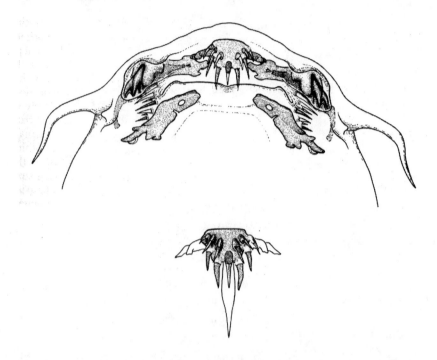

FIG. 11   *Top:* Upper and lower jaw bones (ventral view). *Bottom:* Vomer, or premaxilla, of a cleared and alizarin-stained specimen of *Vandellia beccari.* Courtesy of Robert E. Schmidt and American Society of Ichthyologists and Herpetologists. Source: After Schmidt (1987).

Genus *Vandellia* Cuvier and Valenciennes, 1846
Vandellia cirrhosa Cuvier and Valenciennes, 1846

In establishing the new genus *Vandellia* in 1846 and placing within it the species *V. cirrhosa*, the French naturalists Georges Cuvier and Achille Valenciennes described the first candiru.[8] Their specimens, three total, had been sent to Paris in 1808 by the botanist Domingos Vandelli, professor of natural history at Lisbon, mixed in with some other catfishes and addressed to the attention of Lacépède at the Muséum National d'Histoire Naturelle. There they remained unnoticed for 38 years. When finally described, the genus was named *Vandellia* in Vandelli's honor. According to the Brazilian ichthyologist Alípio de Miranda Ribeiro:[9]

> These [specimens] assuredly were obtained from Alexandre Rodrigues Ferreira, who gives a good illustration of this species in his drawings of fishes [and] which we [*sic*] have reproduced here. [S. Spotte, transl.]

TABLE 2. Disposition of type specimens.

Species	Museum	Type	Number	Origin	Collector	Collected
Vandellia cirrhosa	MNHN	Syntype (2)	A6308	"America"	Vandelli	1808
Vandellia plazai	MNHN	Holotype	A6309	Rio Ucayali, Peru	de Castelnau	1846
Vandellia balzani				Bolivia		
Vandellia wieneri	MNHN	Holotype	A9934	Rio Napo, Ecuador	Wiener	1881
Vandellia hasemani	FMNH	Holotype	58523	Rio Mamoré, Bolivia?	Haseman	1909
	FMNH	Paratype (2)	58524	Rio Mamoré, Bolivia?	Haseman	1909
Vandellia beccari				Essequibo River, Guyana		1932
Vandellia hematophaga	CAS	Lectotype	116766	Rio Tietê, Brazil	—	—
(Urinophilus) diabolicus	CAS	Holotype	59940	Iquitos, Peru	Allen	1920
Plectrochilus machadoi	MNRJ	Holotype	978	Rio Solimões, Brazil	Machado da Silva	—
(Vandellia) sanguinea	FMNH	Holotype	58086	São Antonio de Rio Madeira	Haseman	1909
(Urinophilus) erythrurus	CAS	Holotype	64599	Rio Morona, Peru	Allen	1920
	CAS	Paratypes (6)	64600	Rio Morona, Peru	Allen	1920

CAS = California Academy of Sciences (San Francisco), FMNH = Field Museum of Natural History (Chicago), MNHN = Muséum National d'Histoire Naturelle (Paris), MNRJ = Museu Nacional, Rio de Janeiro. Source: Stephen Spotte.

FIG. 12   Reproduction of the first known illustration of a candiru. It depicts one of the specimens used by Cuvier and Valenciennes to describe the genus *Vandellia* and species *V. cirrhosa* in 1846, but predates their work. Source: de Miranda Ribeiro (1911).

I show this illustration as Fig. 12. If I understand de Miranda Ribeiro correctly, Rodrigues Ferreira, who died in 1815, possessed these specimens initially and prepared a drawing before sending them to Vandelli. Cuvier and Valenciennes subsequently published an ichthyological description of *V. cirrhosa* 31 years after Rodrigues Ferreira's death, but their accompanying illustration (shown here as Fig. 13) was not the first to depict a candiru. A much later drawing by an uncredited illustrator is shown in Fig. 14. Nothing is known about the specimen that served as the model.

Cuvier and Valenciennes had no knowledge of their fish's eclectic feeding behavior, and certainly did not suspect it of attacking the urogenital openings of human beings. Valenciennes, who wrote the brief descrip-

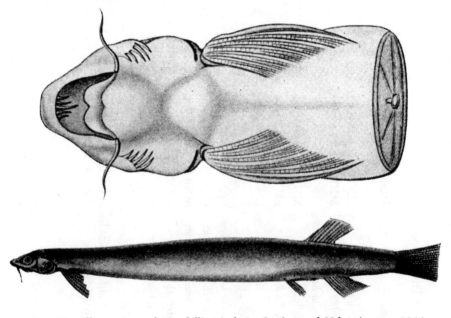

FIG. 13   Illustration of *Vandellia cirrhosa* Cuvier and Valenciennes, 1846. Also redrawn with extra barbels and questionable color by de Castelnau (see Plate 2, middle illustration). Source: Cuvier and Valenciennes (1846).

TABLE 3. Fin ray counts for species of *Vandellia*.

Species	Dorsal	Anal	Caudal	Pectoral	Pelvic	Source
V. cirrhosa	8	10	24	8	6	Cuvier and Valenciennes (1846)
	8–9	9–10	—	6	6	Pellegrin (1909b)
V. plazai	9	8	—	7	5	Pellegrin (1909b)
V. balzani	8	8	—	8	6	Perugia (1897)
V. wieneri	—	—	—	—	—	Pellegrin (1909a)
V. hasemani	11	10	—	6	—	Eigenmann (1918a)
V. beccari	8	6	—	6	5	di Caporiacco (1935)
V. hematophaga	—	—	—	—	—	Alves Guimarães (1935)

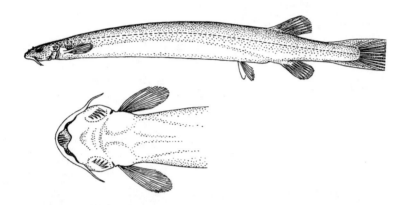

FIG. 14   *Vandellia cirrhosa* Cuvier and Valenciennes, 1846. Source: Norman and Greenwood (1975).

tion, was uncertain even of the origin of his specimens, remarking in his opening sentence that the species before him was[10] ". . . a very singular fish, which is probably from America." He mentions the rounded, elongated body compressed towards the tail, the depressed head and snout. He observed the small inferior mouth (a mouth in which the lower jaw is shorter than the upper and opens entirely underneath the head), the lower jaw that was "notched in the middle,"[11] the thick lips and fleshy barbels at the corners of the mouth, the fins set far back on the body, the absence of scales on the skin, and the preopercular spines (these are actually located on the interopercle). Table 3 depicts his fin ray counts and also the counts of other species discussed in this chapter. Valenciennes tells us the eye is very small, although the eye shown in his illustration (Fig. 13) is quite large. Of the size of his fish, he writes:[12] "The length of our specimens is 2 inches 9 lines," or 68.7 millimeters.

Years later the French ichthyologist Jacques Pellegrin disputed several elements of Valenciennes' work.[13] Valenciennes' illustration of *V. cirrhosa* (Fig. 13) depicts a truncate caudal fin (one that is square on the end), and so does the illustration in Fig. 14. In Pellegrin's opinion the caudal is not truncated, but very slightly notched with lobes that are rounded and equal. Pellegrin noted that the opercular spines had been overlooked in the original description, and he counted only 6 rays on the pectoral fin, not 8 (Table 3).

Valenciennes recognized the uniqueness of his fish and regretted the cursory description. My translation:[14] "I know that this description is incomplete, but as it is, one finds there the proof that this fish does not fit into any of the known genera." Nobody knew then—or now—anything about the reproductive biology of *V. cirrhosa*. During a literature search, I found only one mention of the reproductive status of any candiru. In 1912, de Miranda Ribeiro reported that a specimen of *V. cirrhosa* captured in December (date and location not recorded) and measuring 94 millimeters in length had ripe ovaries (*ovarios repletos*).[15]

In earlier literature the range of *V. cirrhosa* is said to be the Amazon and Orinoco basins, Rio Jurua, Rio Hyavary, Manáos [Manaus: Rio Negro, Rio Solimões?], Rio Apure, and Rio Mamoré.[16] Through 2000, NEODAT[17] listed 53 entries (369 specimens) for *V. cirrhosa*. Collection locations include Brazil (Rio Janauari, "Manaus," Rio Javari [or Javary], Rio Cotingo), Venezuela (Rio Suripa, Rio Caparo, Rio Tucupido, Rio Orinoco, Rio Sarare, Rio Arriba, Rio Apure, Rio Portuguesa, Rio Arriba Guanarit, Rio Masparo, Rio Bocono, Rio Las Mari, Rio La Pena [La Piña?]), and Bolivia (Rio Itenez, Rio Baures, Rio Curiraba).

Vandellia plazai Castelnau, 1855

The first specimen of the next new species of *Vandellia* was collected in 1846 in the Rio Ucayale (or Ucayali), Peru, by de Castelnau, the French explorer and diplomat mentioned in the first chapter, and described by him in 1855 (Plate 2, top illustration).[18]

De Castelnau's description:[19]

Genus *Vandellia*

This curious genus has been established by M. Valenciennes (*Hist. des Poissons*, t. XVIII, p. 386); he places it temporarily in the family of the *Ésoces*, but it seems to me to have strong connections with the *Trichomyc-terus*, which one places among the *Siluroïdes*, and I decided to make it follow these fish.

One has not described still again a species, *Vandellia cirrhosa*, for which one does not know the homeland precisely, but that comes certainly from one of the streams of Brazil, and probably of the Amazon. We [*sic*] are going to make known a second one.

No. 4. VANDELLIA PLAZAII, nov. sp.

(Plate XXVIII, fig. 1.) [shown here as Plate 2, top]

This species differs from the one that was known up to now by its more stretched out body, and whose height is contained thirteen times in the length [and whose height is one-thirteenth of the total? length],[20] while it is only ten in *cirrhosa*. The head is more widened, more rounded forward; the tail is truncated obliquely. The body is entirely of a bluish white, uniform, becoming a little yellow underneath; the head is the color of Siena;[21] the caudal fin has its upper half red, the lower black.

I took this species in the Rio Ucayale (Peru), 13 September 1846.

I dedicate this species to the venerable Father Plaza,[22] prefect of the missions of the Pampa del Sacramento, who received us with much kindliness and humanity, when after extraordinary sufferings, we finally arrived in Sarayacu, in a state that made this worthy missionary shed some tears.

Note.—As a point of comparison, I represent *Vandellia cirrhosa* in pl. 28, fig. 2. [Shown here as Plate 2, middle illustration.] [S. Spotte, transl.]

Eigenmann's illustration is shown as Fig. 15. The shape of the tail is different from that of de Castelnau's fish. The coloration of *V. plazai*, as described by de Castelnau, is unlike any other vandelliine. Were these colors still vivid after 9 years in a preservative, or did de Castelnau reproduce them from memory?

Pellegrin examined de Castelnau's specimen of *V. plazai* and compared it with the three type specimens of *V. cirrhosa*, stating:[23]

> This species is easily distinguished from those previous by its elongated shape, the height of the body being contained about 13 times in the total length [the height of the body about one-thirteenth of the total length]; the head more rounded, the barbels composing less than half the length of the head, the pectoral as long as the head. The caudal is notched to pointed lobes. [S. Spotte, transl.]

He assumed de Castelnau meant total length and not standard length (SL), which is length minus the caudal fin (de Castelnau was not specific).[24] He thought that fin ray counts in the species were similar (Table 3). Pellegrin counted 8 or 9 hooked teeth in the upper jaw, 7 or 8 interopercular spines, and a dozen opercular spines in 3 or 4 rows. In ending this part of his report, he says,[25] "Another beautiful specimen of this species caught by Dr. [C.] Jobert at Calderão, in the Rio Solimões (upper Amazon), also exists in collections of the Museum of Paris."

Shown in Plate 3 are some hard tissues of specimens that Paulo Petry and I caught in the Rio Jauaperi, Brazil, in late October and early November 1999. They were identified tentatively as *V.* cf. *plazai*. In life, our specimens were translucent tan with silver abdomens, containing none of the rich colors of de Castelnau's fish (Plate 2).

FIG. 15 *Vandellia plazai* de Castelnau, 1855. Lateral view. Scale bar = 1/4 inch. Source: After Eigenmann (1918a).

Eigenmann enumerates 12–16 opercular spines in 3 or 4 rows and 7 or 8 interopercular spines. By his estimation the head is[26] ". . . more rounded than in *cirrhosa*; barbel less than half the length of the head; pectoral as long as the head; 8 or 9 teeth in the upper jaw."

Specimens of *Vandellia plaizae* [*sic*] caught in the Rio Huallaga near Yurimaguas, Peru, by Vinton and Stickler were 5–6 inches long with a diameter slightly less than a pencil. Their photographs of the fish in life are reproduced elsewhere (Fig. 42, Chapter 7). The specimens are doubtfully *V. plazai* (notice the strongly forked tails and compare with *V. wieneri* described below).

The ichthyologist George Dahl published notes on three specimens of *Vandellia plazai* caught in 1959 in the Rio Guayabero, Colombia, part of the Rio Orinoco system. He writes:[27]

> This species is apparently not . . . limited to the gills of their hosts, but may fasten to their outer surfaces. The specimen captured on January 17th was caught in a casting-net; when hauled ashore, it was biting the twine of the net. When taken up, it immediately fastened to the author's hand. Allowed to remain for a short while, it succeeded in drawing blood, apparently using its mouth as a sucking apparatus and rasping with the long teeth in the middle part of its upper jaw. It seemed to be utterly avid for a meal of blood and had to be forcibly removed. When held in tweezers, its long body wriggled in eel-like curves, and it even tried to bite the metal.

How Dahl knew—or suspected—that *V. plazai* attaches to fishes at locations other than the gills is left unanswered. Modern ichthyologists consider all species of *Vandellia* to be hematophagous,[28] although gill tissue might not be the only source of nourishment. In a 1947 publication the Brazilian ichthyologist Paulo de Miranda Ribeiro lists three specimens of *V. plazai* archived at the Museu Nacional, Rio de Janeiro, as having been collected by Benjamin Rondon[29] "From the wound of a caiman."

Along with Paulo Petry and Jansen Zuanon, I studied captive candirus in Brazil in 1999. At least one fish was ovigerous (not all were examined afterwards). Our specimens of *V.* cf. *plazai* came from the Rio Jauaperi, an affluent of the Rio Negro, and from the Rio Solimões near Manaus.[30] Eigenmann records *V. plazai* from British Guiana (now Guyana).[31] He later gives its range as the "Middle and Upper Amazon basin; [Rio] Ucayale, [Rio] Calderon; Lake Hyanuary," saying,[32] "It is principally distinguished by its more elongate form." De Miranda Ribeiro caught a specimen at Manaus, which means it probably came from the Rio Negro or

Rio Solimões.[33] Through 2000, NEODAT listed specimens from Peru (Rio Napo, Rio Yaguas, Rio Madre de Dios, Rio Manu, Rio Ucayali). A specimen from the Rio Yaguas is listed as "taken from hook wound in a catfish (*Brachyplatystoma*)." Other specimens are listed from Brazil (Rio Amazonas, Rio Javari [or Javary]), Venezuela (Rio Guanare, Rio Portuguesa, Rio Siapa), and Bolivia (Rio Beni, Rio Mamoré). Three fish labeled *V. plazai* were collected in the Essequibo River, Guyana, in 1997.[34] If these specimens indeed belong to *V. plazai*, the range of the species has been extended to another drainage system.[35]

Vandellia balzani Perugia, 1897

Next in the chronology is a species described In 1897 by the Italian ichthyologist Alberto Perugia, who named it in honor of its collector, Prof. Luigi Balzan.[36] There appears to have been only one specimen, captured in the Rio Beni at Mission Mosetenes, Bolivia. Perugia's fish was never illustrated, but from its description seems similar to *V. cirrhosa* and *V. plazai*. The fin ray counts are shown in Table 3.

The complete description:[37]

> Head very flattened, as wide as long, a little longer than the height of the body, and one-fourteenth the total length (excluding the caudal). The eye, round with free edge, is placed forward on the face; its diameter is contained 5 times in the length of the head and $2^1/_3$ in the interorbital space [its diameter is one-fifth the length of the head and about 43 percent of the interorbital space]. The corner of the operculum is armed with a few relatively robust, curved hooks placed in two groups, one on the subopercle [actually, the interopercle] and a more numerous [group] on the upper angle of the opercle. The barbels are thick and short, half as long as the head. The small pectoral, a little shorter than the head, has 8 rays. The nostrils are oval and very close to the anterior edge of the eye; they measure half its diameter. The mouth is a special shape, well represented in the figure given by Cuvier and Valenciennes, Plate 547, for *Vandellia cirrhosa*; it is inferior, totally devoid of teeth, the lower lip introduces an inlet to its anterior edge [is "notched"]. On the inclined vomer are 8 teeth bent towards the inside, of which the two middle ones are the longest and strongest, measuring about 1 mm., and the other ones gradually decrease [in size], the two outside [teeth] being very small. The branchial opening is narrow and immediately in front of the pectorals. The body is depressed towards the head, rounded off up to the front of the dorsal fin and to the end of the anal fin, and then flattened up to the base of the caudal. The ventral [pelvic] fins are shorter and narrower than the pectorals, and situated at the posterior end of the body a little distant from the anal fin. This [the anal fin] starts halfway underneath the dorsal fin and has 8 articulated rays,

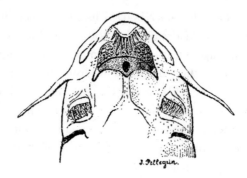

FIG. 16   Head (ventral view) of *Vandellia wieneri* Pellegrin, 1909. Source: Pellegrin (1909b).

as long as those of the dorsal fin and a third of the length of the head. The caudal is notched, with the external rays slightly elongated and equal.

The general color (in alcohol) is brown on the back and yellowish on the abdomen. On the back can be seen a tiny black spot that is also extended onto the rays of all the fins. The caudal is yellow.

Rio Beni. Mission Mosetenes.

According to what Günther says in Introduction to the Study of Fishes, these fishes live parasitically in the branchial chamber of the large silurids [*sic*].[38] [S. Spotte, transl.]

Vandellia wieneri Pellegrin, 1909

Pellegrin described the species *Vandellia wieneri* from a single specimen caught in 1881 by Charles Wiener in the Rio Napo, Ecuador.[39] Pellegrin's description is more thorough than those of Valenciennes and de Castelnau, but contains no illustrations. That same year he illustrated the underside of the head in a different publication (Fig. 16), and 2 years later provided a drawing of the whole fish (Plate 4, illustration 2). In external appearance,[40] "The general coloration is olive, the fins grayish." The mouth and teeth are typical of the genus *Vandellia*:[41]

> The mouth is small, inferior, flattened. The upper jaw is very prominent; it is shaped like a half-crown composed of nine sharp teeth, in the shape of hooks, inward-curving; these teeth are normally laid down, but capable of being raised to a certain degree; the middle ones are much longer than the lateral ones. [S. Spotte, transl.]

Pellegrin lists 15 opercular spines in 4 rows. As in all members of the genus *Vandellia* they are toothlike and sharp with the tips directed upward and back. Below them is another group of interopercular spines numbering 7 or 8 in 2 rows. The intestine is described as simple, without convolutions.

Pellegrin, who apparently was unaware of Perugia's description of *V. balzani*, considered this new species closest to *V. cirrhosa*. To make his comparison, Pellegrin had examined the type specimens of *V. cirrhosa* and *V. plazai*. From those results, he provides a key to the other three species of *Vandellia*. The barbel referred to is probably the maxillary barbel. My translation:[42]

> Height of body 7 times in length [one-seventh its length] without the caudal. Barbel extending one-third the length of the head. Pectoral shorter than the head. Caudal forked, [leading] to pointed lobes.
>
> *Vandellia Wieneri* sp. nov.

> Height of body 9 times in length [one-ninth its length] without the caudal. Barbel extending half the length of the head. Pectoral longer than the head. Caudal very slightly notched, [leading] to rounded, equal lobes.
>
> *Vandellia cirrhosa* C. V. [Cuvier and Valenciennes]

> Height of body 12 times in length [one-twelfth its length] without the caudal. Barbel extending less than half the length [of] the head. Pectoral as long as the head. Caudal notched, [leading] to pointed lobes.
>
> *Vandellia Plazai* [de] Castelnau

In this report, Pellegrin also discusses candiru attacks on humans, citing the writings of de [von] Spix and Agassiz, de Castelnau, Günther, Boulenger, and Jobert (see Chapter 1). He begins by stating:[43]

> It has long been a widespread belief among Indians of Brazil that bathers can be attacked by a small fish known as the *Candiru* which, attracted by the odor of urine, penetrates into the urethra and there causes some serious disorders, generally followed by death. [S. Spotte, transl.]

Pellegrin goes on to blame the attack described by Jobert not on cetopsids but a vandelliine, specifically *V. wieneri*:[44]

> The fishes that attacked Dr Jobert belong, in my opinion, incontestably to the genus *Vandellia*, species *Vandellia Wieneri* . . . If one refers to the above description of the mouth and opercular apparatus, one will easily understand the working of these various organs; one will easily understand that the half-crown of hooked teeth placed forward in the mouth, teeth *capable of being raised to a certain degree and numbering 5 or 6, principally produce these parallel, regular wounds, and in a group of 5 or 6 lines* [Pelle-

grin's emphasis]. Interopercular spines on the underside of the head, also a few [of which are] erectile, can also, to a certain extent, tear teguments, but they are usually used for holding on. As for the opercular spines . . . they seem to me, given the direction of their tips, destined to facilitate [forward] progression of the animal and to prevent it from backing out after it enters a narrow duct, for example between the branchial lamellae of the platystomes. [S. Spotte, transl.]

In a footnote, Pellegrin remarks that the attacking species could also have been *Vandellia plazai*. Other evidence that vandelliines (in this case, *V. cirrhosa*) occasionally attach to humans comes from Santos. In the 1981 edition of *Peixes da Água Doce*, he writes:[45]

At times these fish, like leeches, also hold onto the legs of whomever enters the river, but without causing damage.
When they hold onto the legs it is enough to leave the water so that they soon fall off and die. [S. Spotte, transl.]

Pellegrin performs a unique service by describing the mouth and associated structures of *V. wieneri* and then assessing their functions. He says:[46]

The ensemble of these diverse features indicates great specialization: the teeth and the opercular and interopercular spines permit attachment to a host and erosion of the teguments; the disposition of the buccal cavity seems to facilitate ingestion of sanguine liquids drawn from wounds inflicted this way. [S. Spotte, transl.]

Elsewhere he writes:[47] "The very peculiar disposition of the buccal apparatus and distinctly conspicuous operculum of *Vandellia Wieneri* indicate great specialization and appear to establish a strongly advanced parasitism."

Although Pellegrin speculates no further, it is here and in part of his formal description that we find the first—and still the only—supposition of how candirus might actually suck blood from the gills of their victims. In describing the buccal apparatus, he states:[48]

Behind the teeth, the buccal cavity is covered with numerous papillae, then restricted by a pronounced fold. The sides of the lips are quite thick. The lower jaw, greatly notched in the middle, is completely devoid of teeth; behind is a large membranous veil, pierced in its center by a small opening that does not appear to be accidental; this veil, as it approaches the upper fold, closes all the anterior portion of the buccal cavity; at rest it folds back posteriorly. [S. Spotte, transl.]

Furthermore, Pellegrin writes of this membrane,[49] ". . . when in a state of rest it subsequently recedes."

Pellegrin seems to be talking about a buccal pump. If so, an explanation of how candirus can ingest such large volumes of blood so quickly becomes apparent. My description of this process is conjectural.

The candiru slips under the operculum of its victim, anchors itself in place by its odontodes, and bites down on a gill filament, puncturing the thin tissue with its vomerine teeth. Simultaneously, the joints of the vomerine teeth contract and draw inward, pulling the upper jaw over and towards the site of attachment (see Plate 3, bottom two illustrations). Bleeding starts. The lips form a seal that perhaps aided by the flexible mandible (separated in the middle) shuts off any hiatus remaining from the forward projection of the upper jaw. Pellegrin's *voile membraneux* completes the seal when it "closes all the anterior part of the buccal cavity." Accordingly, a candiru creates and sustains a partial vacuum between its point of attachment to the prey and the anterior side of the membrane by rapidly expanding and contracting its buccal muscles, opening and closing the opercula in synchrony. This causes the membrane to oscillate back and forth, drawing in blood through the opening in the veil as if through a syringe each time the opercula close and the buccal cavity expands. The seal could be broken during each half-cycle when the opercula open, allowing the membrane to re-form in preparation for the impending vacuum and intake of blood. Or perhaps by some other means a seal is retained through the cycle. By either mechanism a candiru could literally *pump* blood rapidly into its gut while minimizing the amount of incidental water ingested. When satiated, a candiru relaxes the joints of its vomerine teeth (in effect, erecting them) and opens its gills and mouth, breaking the seal (assuming there is a seal). Next it darts forward to disengage the teeth and odontodes before folding the odontodes and dropping away.

Through 2000, NEODAT listed only one specimen of *V. wieneri*, archived at the Royal Ontario Museum, Ottawa (ROM 50260). Its origin is the Rio Solimões 30 kilometers west of Manaus, Brazil. The specimen is large (148 millimeters in total length).

Vandellia hasemani Eigenmann, 1918

Eigenmann illustrated and described the new species *Vandellia hasemani*, which he named in honor of its collector (also his former student and sometime antagonist), John D. Haseman.[50] The three type specimens came from the Rio Mamoré.[51] The fin ray counts are given in Table 3. Another specimen is listed in the collections of the Muséum National d'Histoire Naturelle, Paris.[52]

Eigenmann considered his new species similar to *V. wieneri* despite having never seen Pellegrin's type specimen archived in Paris, which is larger than the type of *V. hasemani* (92 millimeters compared to 72 millimeters). Eigenmann counted 5 or 6 teeth on the premaxilla (or the vomer) of *V. hasemani* and states that the caudal fin is forked for about two-ninths its length (Fig. 17), making it substantially less forked than the caudal of *V. wieneri* (Plate 4, illustration 2), which appears to be forked for nearly half its length. These species names might be synonyms. If so, *V. wieneri*, being the older, has precedence.

Eigenmann mentions the eyes almost as an afterthought, but notes their location (the anterior half of the head) and size (only a little larger than the posterior nares). Their tiny diameter might be one of this specimen's most distinctive features. Whether the eyes of *V. wieneri* are larger is unknown, but from Pellegrin's illustrations they seem so. From my reading, Pellegrin says only,[53] "The eyes are small, oval, their largest diameter a little less than the interorbital space and twice the distance from the end of the snout."

Vandellia beccari di Caporiacco, 1935

The Italian ichthyologist Lodovico di Caporiacco described *Vandellia beccari* as a new species based on one specimen captured in January 1932 near Rockstone in the Essequibo River, British Guiana (now Guyana).[54] The ichthyological description itself, written in Latin, is brief and not illustrated. In 1987, Schmidt published a well-illustrated redescription based on specimens he had collected in Guyana; I have reproduced one drawing as Fig. 18. All specimens listed by NEODAT through 2000 were caught in the Essequibo; one specimen is listed simply as "Guyana."

Di Caporiacco's description begins:[55]

> Total body length (without the tail) 57 mm.; maximum body height 5,5 mm.; head length 6 mm.; maximum head height 5,5 mm.
>   Length of the head almost ten times, and the height of the body more than ten times, contained in the length of the body. [Head length about one-tenth, body height less than one-tenth, of body length.]

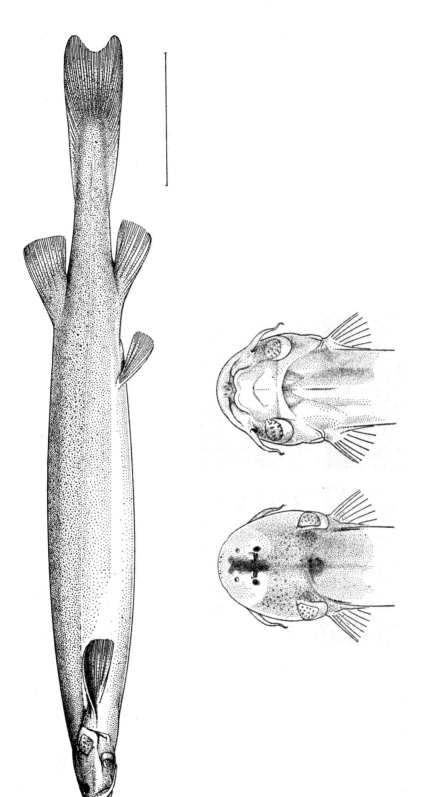

FIG. 17 *Vandellia hasemani* Eigenmann, 1918. *Top*: Lateral view (scale bar = 1/2 inch). *Bottom left*: Dorsal view of head and upper body. *Bottom right*: Ventral view of head and upper body. Source: After Eigenmann (1918a).

Rostrum round. Preorbital distance one-third as large as the eye; interorbital distance equal to diameter of eye (1,5 mm.). Maxillary barbel 2,5 mm. long, thus not reaching to half the length of the head. [S. Spotte, transl.]

The genus *Plectrochilus* (discussed in this chapter in a later subsection), which had been established in 1917, is distinguished from *Vandellia* by the presence of teeth on the mandible. Evidently unaware of this, di Caporiacco continues,[56] "Premaxillary armed with 9 robust, long teeth; mandible armed with minute teeth." Di Caporiacco recognized the absence of mandibular teeth as a distinguishing character of the genus *Vandellia*, but evidently felt it was not very important. He writes:[57]

Mandible armed with minute teeth distinguishing it from *V. plazai* Castelnau [*sic*] and *V. hasemani* Eigenm[ann] (and also from *V. cirrhosa* C. V. [Cuvier and Valenciennes] and *V. wieneri* Pellegrin?); equipped with nine premaxillary teeth and number of rays on dorsal and anal fin like *V. sanguinea* Eigenm[ann]; number of rays on dorsal and anal fin like *V. wieneri* Pellegrin, but caudal not forked; number of rays on anal and pectoral fins and shorter head distinguish it from *V. cirrhosa* C. V. [Cuvier and Valenciennes]. [S. Spotte, transl.]

M. L. Azzaroli later examined di Caporiacco's specimen without finding mandibular teeth.[58] Schmidt saw none in his own specimens and counted 7 vomerine (or premaxillary) teeth instead of 9.

Some of di Caporiacco's counts and measurements:[59]

Opercular spines 10 in two rows; interopercular spines 9. . .
Dorsal fin starting 42 mm. from tip of rostrum; its base 3,5 mm. in length; anal fin beginning just after start of dorsal, at that point 44 mm. from tip of the rostrum; its base 3,5 mm. in length. Pectoral fin 5,75 mm. in length. Ventral [pelvic] fin starting 36 mm. from tip of rostrum, 5 mm. in length at its base. Caudal fin barely emarginate. [S. Spotte, transl.]

An accurate color description was impossible because di Caporiacco's specimen had been preserved:[60]

Color white: chromatophores present on upper sides, a few small obscure spots can be distinguished, [being] especially visible on the head and upper caudal peduncle. Caudal fin darkened. [S. Spotte, transl.]

If the preservative is alcohol, most fishes eventually turn white. According to Schmidt, live specimens of *V. beccari* are transparent. Two bands of chromatophores traverse the caudal peduncle, extending onto

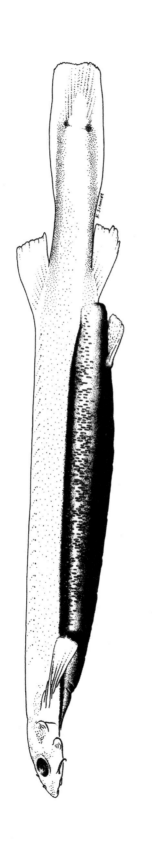

Fig. 18 *Vandellia beccari* di Caporiacco, 1935 (lateral view). The gut is dark, distended, and probably filled with blood. Courtesy of Robert E. Schmidt and American Society of Ichthyologists and Herpetologists. Source: Schmidt (1987).

Fig. 19 *Vandellia hematophaga* Alves Guimarães, 1935.
Source: Alves Guimarães (1935b).

the caudal fin. The upper band starts at the base of the dorsal fin; the lower originates a little in front of the anal fin. The two bands converge slightly as they emerge onto the caudal fin. Schmidt writes,[61] "The bands are connected by a vertical line of melanophores on the caudal fin (visible only under a microscope)."

According to Schmidt, *V. beccari* can be distinguished by the shape of its caudal fin (either truncate or slightly emarginate), distinctive color pattern, 6 or 7 anal fin rays, and 6 pectoral fin rays.

Vandellia hematophaga Alves Guimarães, 1935

Alves Guimarães described the species *V. hematophaga* (Fig. 19) from an unstated number of specimens, but never designated a holotype.[62] The American ichthyologist James E. Böhlke obtained one of Alves Guimarães' specimens, entered it into the collection at Stanford University, and in 1953 designated it the lectotype.[63] This is the only specimen of *V. hematophaga* known to exist. I have not seen it, but its inclusion in the genus *Vandellia* seems questionable. My reasons are given at the end of this subsection.

Alves Guimarães received his fish at the start of the rainy season from the city of Salto, state of São Paulo, Brazil. They came from the Rio Tietê, having been picked from the gills of *dourados* (*Salminus* sp.)[64] and *piracamjubas* (*Brycon* sp.).[65] His description is brief and unremarkable. My translation:[66]

Height of the body 6 times in the length [one-sixth of the length] (without the tail). Eyes 1/4 the size of the head. Barbel originating from a pleat at the corner of the upper lip and extending for 1/3 the length of the head. Pectorals a little shorter than the head, with 6 to 7 rays. End of tail truncated, slightly oblique with the upper rays a little longer . . . Operculum and preoperculum [actually, interoperculum] covered with bristles [rijas]. Occiptal shield wedge-shaped, anterior end with a series of spines on each side, [extending] a third of the way to the base. Snout with extremity terminating in an inferior, thick lip. Mouth inferior.

Average size of 6 measured specimens:

Head: 4 m/m in length
Occipital: 4 m/m in height (mx. of the body)
Body: 24 m/m (without caudal)
Eyes: 1,1 m/m [diameter?]
Pectoral: 3,³/₄ m/m with 6–7 rays
Dorsal: 20 m/m from base of head
Ventral [pelvic]: 21 m/m from base of head

Following his description, Alves Guimarães makes some important observations:[67]

The species just described by us [sic] is a parasite of large *Characidae*. It does not attack healthy and free fish, but just those that are tied off in the fisheries [literally, nurseries]. For this reason our informants judge it to be a specific parasite of *Salminus* sp. and *Brycon* sp., but only fish that are confined at Salto.

These fish, which are suspended from a line strung through the branchial cavity, are immersed in the river to await eventual buyers. The candirús, the common name of the species, swim along the sides of the captive fish until near the opercula. When these open during a breathing movement, the parasites quickly penetrate into the branchial cavity, where they fasten onto the gills, changing in such a way that, when they abandon the prey, their bodies are expanded 3 to 5 times in thickness from the volume of ingested blood. You can see then the short intestine dyed red, through the thin, very distended abdominal wall.

They attack their victims in shoals, producing fatal hemorrhages. They are, however, parasites exclusively of the branchial area, thus differing biologically from the fish described by von Ihering that preferentially parasitizes the anal area and the lower intestine of the host, according to [that] author.

These fish were observed for the first time in Salto this year and after fifteen to twenty days had disappeared as suddenly as they had appeared. [S. Spotte, transl.]

The fish Alves Guimarães describes has much in common with a candiru of a different genus, *Branchioica bertoni* (see Chapter 4). Like *B. bertoni* it is very small (less than 25 millimeters), has a more southern range than *Vandellia* spp., and attacks tethered fishes during daylight and in schools that are readily visible.

Genus *Plectrochilus* de Miranda Ribeiro, 1912 (=*Urinophilus* Eigenmann, 1918)

Plectrochilus machadoi de Miranda Ribeiro, 1912 (=*Urinophilus diabolicus* Myers, 1927)

Plectrochilus is an enigmatic genus plagued by the worst sort of identity crisis, that of possible nonexistence. Fishes of this name reposing in museum collections most likely are specimens of *Vandellia* wearing transparent disguises.[68] How the name *Plectrochilus* came to persist is a tortuous—even diabolical—story.

In 1917, Alípio de Miranda Ribeiro described a new genus and species of trichomycterid he named *Plectrochilus machadoi*. The collection location was not identified.[69]

Eigenmann, unaware of de Miranda Ribeiro's work, independently described a similar fish based on 10 specimens collected by Allen from the Rio Morona, Peru (?),[70] and placed it in the genus *Urinophilus* for its presumed attraction to human urine.[71] He called the species *Urinophilus erythrurus*.

Still puzzled about the identity of his new fish, Eigenmann writes:[72]

> This species differs from the others of the genus *Vandellia* in having concealed teeth on the ends of the mandibles. It resembles them so much in other points that it naturally raises the question whether these structures have not been overlooked in *V. cirrhosa* and *wieneri*. They cannot be seen without considerable effort.

He wondered whether Valenciennes and Pellegrin might have missed seeing mandibular teeth when preparing their descriptions of *V. cirrhosa* and *V. wieneri*. As mentioned before, the absence of teeth on the lower jaw is an important diagnostic character of the genus *Vandellia*. Both men say they looked. Valenciennes states clearly:[73]

> I do not believe that there are teeth in the jaws, but on the roof of the

vomer, that advances . . . until the side of the intermaxillaries, there is a small group of five pointed teeth-like hooks, of which the center is longest; then come the two lateral, a little shorter, and shortest are the external, the smallest. [S. Spotte, transl.]

And Pellegrin tells us,[74] "The lower jaw, greatly notched in its middle, is completely devoid of teeth . . ."

Eigenmann's justification for establishing the genus *Urinophilus* was peculiar. He had available two groups of vandelliines, one with and the other without mandibular teeth. Uncertain of which group *Vandellia* represented, he provisionally left it intact and established *Urinophilus* for whichever group turned out *not* to be *Vandellia*. He states:[75] "When we know which one can legitimately lay claim to the name Vandellia [*sic*] the other one can be baptized as Urinophilus [*sic*]." I suppose this is similar to naming a star or planet you've never seen but suspect might exist.

Myers subsequently described another putative urine-lover in 1927, assigning it the specific name *diabolicus*. Myers believed it to be the true candiru, that scourge of human urethras and anuses up and down the Amazon, although without supporting evidence this was wishful thinking. During a stay in Rio de Janeiro, Myers examined the type specimen of *Plectrochilus machadoi* and in 1944 declared its synonymy with *Urinophilus diabolicus*. By the rules of zoological nomenclature the genus *Plectrochilus*, being older, takes precedence over *Urinophilus*.

Although Eigenmann had first proposed establishing the genus *Urinophilus* in 1918, his confusion about it and *Vandellia* was not resolved in print for another 2 years. The validity of *Urinophilus* depended on whether the original specimens of *Vandellia cirrhosa*, described in 1846 by Cuvier and Valenciennes, possessed mandibular teeth. Those specimens have always been archived at the Muséum National d'Histoire Naturelle in Paris. Eigenmann never personally saw a specimen of Valenciennes' *très-singulier poisson*. Instead, he wrote to Pellegrin asking him to look at them and examine once again the type specimen of *V. wieneri*, which Pellegrin himself had described in 1909. Pellegrin reported back that none had teeth on the lower jaw, prompting Eigenmann to state in a 1920 publication,[76] "The name *Urinophilus* becomes, thereby, restricted to the only known species with teeth on the tips of the mandibular rami, *Urinophilus sanguineus* (E.)." (I discuss this fish on p. 75.)

Not that it mattered in the end. *Urinophilus* officially dates from 1920, or 3 years after de Miranda Ribeiro's description of *Plectrochilus* was published, rendering it an invalid genus. Fetching though it is, the name *Urinophilus diabolicus* was dumped on the taxonomic scrap heap. Eigenmann's argument nonetheless died a slow death (Eigenmann and Allen include it in their 1942 book *Fishes of Western South America*).

A patch of tiny concealed teeth on the end of each mandibular ramus is apparently the sole character distinguishing *Plectrochilus* from *Vandellia* (Plate 5). The teeth in my figure are conspicuous because of the high magnification and because much of the overlying tissue concealing them had been removed with a strong oxidizing solution. Such structures might exist within the range of individual variation of other vandelliines, in which case their taxonomic utility would be lessened considerably. Burgess states:[77] "The presence or absence of a patch of minute teeth on each ramus of the mandible depends on the condition of the museum specimens, as well as there being intermediates between the two genera." Although likely, this statement is speculative until confirmed. Since the 1930s, some have discounted the uniqueness of mandibular teeth. In their key to the subfamily Vandelliinae, Devincenzi and Vaz-Ferreira do not mention *Plectrochilus*, stating in a description of the genus *Vandellia*[78] ". . . mandible inferior without teeth, or with some exceedingly small teeth in the end of the rami . . ."

Even if present, these near-mythical teeth constitute a flimsy descriptor, comparing with a redoubtable character about as closely as a sheer negligée compares with a ski parka. Their presence might be inadequate even to establish a new species, much less a new genus.

I had difficulty translating de Miranda Ribeiro's descriptions in Latin. Some effort was necessary because the genus and species characters are pivotal in sorting out the candirus. Maybe this attempt will spare future scholars and candiruphiles the heartburn I experienced:[79]

Plectrochilus gen. nov.

In shape, like *Stegophilus*. Head small, flattened, wedge-shaped anteriorly, mouth inferior, consequently gape is oblique [?], teeth incurving, radiating in the shape of a crown from the vomer, in the manner of *Vandellia*: intermaxillaries with three erect subtriangular spines, curved at the base along their length, emerging from a small pocket at the lip near the base of the barbel; there is a small barbel attached to the jaw; nostrils recessed in front of the eyes; the eyes subcutaneous, superior; opercle and preopercle [actually, the interopercle] densely provided with spines; gill opening large and exposed, with branchiostegal membrane surmounting the isthmus. Body flattened with dorsal and anal fins one after another, positioned posteriorly, pectorals and ventrals [pelvics] free [?]. A line runs along the side.

Plectrochilus machadoi, sp. nov.

Length of head 7,5; maximum height 6,8. [Length of head 13 percent of [total?] body length; maximum height [of body] 16 percent of [total?] body length.] Mouth as [in genus description] above, [maxillary] barbel reaching halfway to preopercle. Eye small, placed in front half of the head. Pectoral fin shorter than [subequal to] length of head, first ray elongated, the rest truncate; ventrals [pelvics] originating halfway between pectoral fin and base of tail; ventrals small, reaching to anus. Dorsal posterior of ventral and having about three dorsal rays, rear ones subtruncate [almost square but slightly notched], moderately flat after first ones. Peduncle slender. Caudal forked, lobes subequal, numerous accessory rays. Color reddish-brown sprinkled with a little black on the back. Maximum length—65 millim. Called "*little candirú*" by local inhabitants. [S. Spotte, transl.]

Through 2000, NEODAT listed only the type specimen.

Plectrochilus sanguineus (= *Vandellia sanguinea* Eigenmann, 1918; = *Urinophilus sanguineus* Eigenmann, 1920)

In his 1918 monograph, Eigenmann describes *Vandellia sanguinea* as a new species (Fig. 20).[80] His brief account is based on a single specimen of 62 millimeters collected at Santo Antonio do Rio Madeira, Brazil, by Haseman on 3 November 1909.[81] In a 1920 publication, Eigenmann places this fish in the genus *Urinophilus* and without comment changes its specific name from *sanguinea* to *sanguineus*.

The original description presents the head as 1/11.66[th], or 8.6 percent, of the (total?) length. This fish is apparently long and sinuous, similar to *V. plazai*. The eye, Eigenmann reports, is located in the anterior half of the head[82] ". . . a little more than four in the length of the head to the tip of the opercular spines [a little more than one-fourth of the distance between the tip of the snout and the end of the opercular spines]."

The rest of the description:

Maxillary barbel extending to the tip of the interopercular spines, two in the head [one-half the length of the head]; the lower barbel minute, only about half a millimeter long as compared with the 2.5 mm. of the maxillary barbel; two, flat, recurved teeth on the end of the maxillary concealed just in front of the barbel; five premaxillary [or vomerine] teeth graduated from the long middle one to the minute lateral ones; the mandibles widely separated from each other, each with about five minute teeth; the teeth concealed by the lip; five spines in the main row of the interopercle, the middle ones very strong, directed backwards, about five spines in supplementary rows; five spines in the main row of the opercle, about ten in supplementary rows; distance between origin of ventrals [pelvics] and base of middle caudal rays two in its distance form [sic] the snout [half the distance?]; origin of anal behind the origin of the dorsal, the last dorsal ray over the middle of the anal, distance between anal and base of middle caudal rays five and five tenths in the length [about 18 percent]; distance between origin of dorsal and base of middle caudal rays two and eight tenths in its distance from the snout [about 37 percent]; caudal truncate, with numerous accessory rays. Translucent, the eyes black.

Through 2000, NEODAT lists other Brazilian specimens (upper Rio Catrimani, Rio Negro, Rio Jurua, Rio Amazonas).

Plectrochilus (=*Urinophilus*) *erythrurus* (Eigenmann, 1922)

Eigenmann described this species as *Urinophilus erythrurus* (Fig. 21) after examining 10 specimens measuring 120–145 millimeters in length.[83] It was the second species placed in the genus *Urinophilus*, which Eigenmann had proposed earlier,[84] the first having been *U. sanguineus*.

The description consists of a cursory text accompanied by good illustrations. It reads in part:[85]

Body compressed; head depressed, flat below, arched above, depth of head equals distance between centers of eye; distance between eyes equal to snout; eye about 5 in the head [diameter of eye about one-fifth the length of the head]; 5 to 9 teeth in a crescent (on the premaxillary?) below the snout; a series of about four, claw-like teeth on the maxillaries, the teeth concealed in a fleshy pocket . . . very few recurved teeth at the ends of the mandible . . . the tips of the mandible widely separated; outer [maxillary] barbel extending to the end of the interopercular spines; interopercular spines numerous (about ten) their tips curved . . . opercular spines more numerous, about twenty-five, curved at the tip . . . pectorals about equal to the head less half the snout, distance between origin of ventrals [pelvics] and base of the caudal about equal to a third of the length, origin of dorsal forward of the vertical from the origin of the anal; depth of caudal

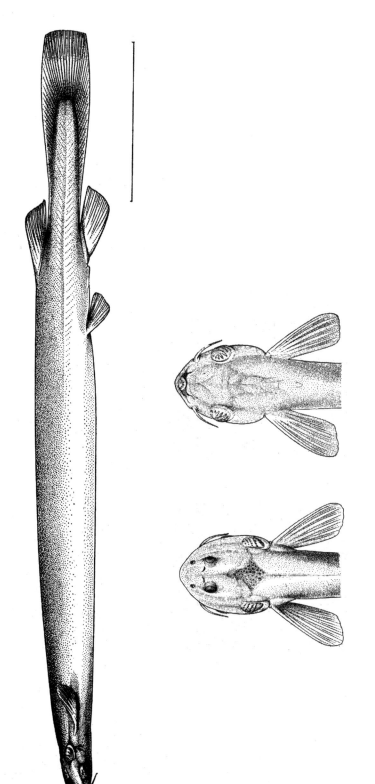

FIG. 20 *Plectrochilus sanguineus* (Eigenmann, 1918). *Top:* Lateral view (scale bar = 1/2 inch). *Bottom left:* Dorsal view of head and upper body. *Bottom right:* Ventral view of head and upper body. Source: After Eigenmann (1918a).

peduncle three or more in its length [one-third or less of its length]; caudal emarginate.

This fish has no unusual features to distinguish it from some of the other vandelliines, except perhaps the numerous opercular spines (about 25) and greater length. "Claw-teeth" on the premaxillae are certainly not unique.[86]

A fish supposedly of this species is shown in a color photograph by Burgess.[87] Assuming its identification is correct, *P. erythrurus* has a truncate caudal fin with a longitudinal black line through its center, larger and more distinct than depicted in Eigenmann's illustration, although his fish had been preserved.[88] Eigenmann's fish has a forked tail. In the photograph the rest of the fish looks pale brown and translucent. Eigenmann describes its coloration as[89] "Plumbeous [plumbous] above, white below, the middle of the caudal dark, the outer parts pink in life."

Eigenmann and Allen give the range as Peru (Rio Morona, Rio Paranapura, Rio Ucayali) and Bolivia (Rurrenabaque).[90] Through 2000, NEODAT lists a specimen of *Vandellia erythrurus* from Colombia ("Lake or stream 50 miles upriver from Leticia)," and additional specimens of *P. erythrurus* from Peru (Rio Ampiyacu, Rio Amazonas at Iquitos).

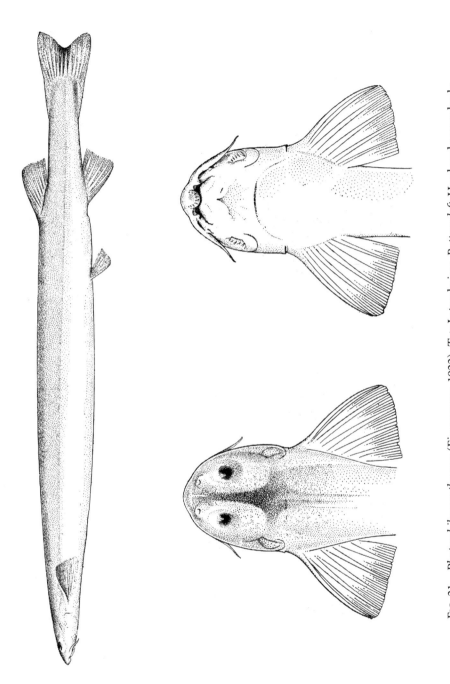

FIG. 21 *Plectrochilus erythrurus* (Eigenmann, 1922). *Top:* Lateral view. *Bottom left:* Head and upper body (dorsal view). *Bottom right:* Head and upper body (ventral view). Source: After Eigenmann (1922).

We would look at them, trying to bring our eyes up to the glass, touching it with our noses, annoying the old women who sell them, as they go about with their nets to hunt aquatic butterflies, and we understood less and less what a fish is.

—Julio Cortázar, *Hopscotch*[1]

4.

And Four Not So Singular

Members of the other four genera of the vandelliines—*Paravandellia, Branchioica, Parabranchioica, Paracanthopoma*—are smaller than the species of *Vandellia* and *Plectrochilus*. To my knowledge, none has ever been implicated in an attack on a human being, although as bloodsuckers they too qualify as candirus. Disposition of type specimens of the species discussed is summarized in Table 4.

Genus *Paravandellia* de Miranda Ribeiro, 1912
Paravandellia oxyptera de Miranda Ribeiro, 1912

In 1912, Alípio de Miranda Ribeiro described *Paravandellia* as a new genus and placed within it the species *P. oxyptera*. No illustration was included, but in 1947 Paulo de Miranda Ribeiro provided one (Fig. 22, bottom). Although the genus and species descriptions are short, I spent lots of time translating them. The vocabulary and phrasing of de Miranda Ribeiro's Portuguese seem idiomatic (perhaps anachronistic); some statements are contradictory, others redundant.[2] Eigenmann's translation

TABLE 4. Disposition of type specimens.

Species	Museum	Type	Number	Origin	Collector	Collected
Paravandellia oxyptera	MNRJ	Holotype	790	Rio Paraguai, Brazil	de Mirando Ribeiro	—
Branchioica bertoni	CAS	Holotype	63840	Asunción, Paraguay	de W. Bertoni	—
	CAS	Paratype	77288	Asunción, Paraguay	de W. Bertoni	—
Branchioica phaneronema	MCZ	Paratype	35874	upper Cauca, Colombia	Miles	1942
	USNM	Paratype	120141	upper Cauca, Colombia	Miles	1942
Parabranchioica teaguei	MNRJ	Cotype	3606	Payssandú, Uruguay	Teague	1941
Paracanthopoma parva	—	—	—	Rio Catrimani, Brazil	Lako and Salathé	—

CAS = California Academy of Sciences (San Francisco), Museum of Comparative Zoology (Boston), MNRJ = Museu Nacional, Rio de Janeiro, USNM = U.S. National Museum (Washington, D.C.). Source: Stephen Spotte.

omits part of the original and occasionally alters its meaning (see below). My attempt:[3]

Paravandellia, *gen. nov.*

This genus should be considered between *Stegophilus* and *Vandellia*, its general characteristics being closer to the first group. Dorsal [fin] posterior to the ventrals [pelvics] and semi-anterior [?] to the anal; both posterior to the middle of the body. Head triangular, nostrils separate, without barbels, eyes without free margin; mouth inferior, teeth in a series in the maxillaries and in a band [*facho*: literally, beam] in the intermaxillaries; a barbel at the angle of the mouth; preopercle [interopercle] and opercle separate, having needlelike teeth [*facho acicular*, literally, needlelike beam].

Paravandellia oxyptera, *sp. nov.*

D. 12; Ps. 1 + 6; Vs. 6; A. 10

[Fin rays: D = dorsal, P = pectoral, V = pelvic, A = anal]

Larval characteristics; body depressed anteriorly, compressed posteriorly. Head triangular, or heart-shaped, 1/8th of the total length, including the caudal that is its equivalent in length; eyes large (capable of seeing with the entire globe because of transparency of the teguments), approximately 2 and 1/2 times in the head [comparable in diameter to approximately 40 percent of the length of the head] and about one diameter from the tip of the snout; mouth inferior, with carved [?] [*entalhado*] mandible not containing teeth; barbel barely reaching half the distance from preopercle *facho acicular* [literally, needlelike beam]. Pectorals large, forked, 1/4th larger than the head, with the first ray spiny, stiff, and the largest in extension; from it the others decrease abruptly until the fourth, then increase again up to the last internal one. Dorsal beginning a little behind the distance between [?] the base of the pectorals and the tip of the caudal. The ventrals [pelvics] are very small and are located anteriorly [?]; the anal under the last rays of the dorsal and of the same shape as the dorsal, although lower [?]; tail forked, with the upper lobe a little larger. Uniformly white [in alcohol?], black retina. A specimen measuring 0,022 m.

Eigenmann's description of the genus based on de Miranda Ribeiro's:[4]

No nasal or mental barbels, one (probably two) barbels at the angle of the mouth, first pectoral ray not continued as a filament; gill-opening small, mouth inferior, with a band of teeth in the middle of the upper jaw and a single series laterally; no teeth on the mandible; ventrals [pelvics] much nearer tip of caudal than snout; opercular and interopercular spines separate from each other. Caudal forked ("furcada"). Ribeiro [*sic*] says that this genus may be considered between *Stegophilus* and *Vandellia*, having the general appearance of the former.

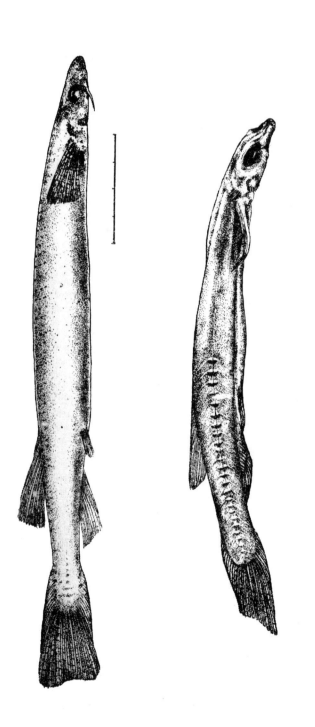

FIG. 22 *Top*: Unidentified fish of Otto Schubart (lateral view, scale bar = 4 millimeters?). *Bottom*: The "mummified" type specimen of *Paravandellia oxyptera* de Miranda Ribeiro, 1912 (lateral view). Source: de Miranda Ribeiro (1947).

Eigenmann's version of de Miranda Ribeiro's species description:[5]

Head triangular, eight times in the length [one-eighth of the length] including the caudal; D. 12, A. 10, P. 7; dorsal behind the ventrals [pelvics], partly over anal, both [both what?] behind the middle of the body; origin of dorsal nearer tip of caudal than base of pectorals; eyes without a free margin, large, two and one-half times in head [diameter of eye 40 percent of the length of the head], equal to [length of] snout; maxillary barbel reaching at most to tip of interopercular spines; pectorals large, falcate, one-fourth longer than head, the first ray longest, the next rapidly graduate, the outer rays longer again; caudal forked, the upper lobe a little the longer; anal similar to the dorsal, under the last rays of the latter.
White, the eyes black.

As to the fish's habitat, I understand de Miranda Ribeiro to say[6] ". . . I found this curious fish among pseudo-rhyzomes of the *agua-pé*, in Caceres, at the edges of the Rio Paraguay, in October of 1908."

According to Eigenmann, the single known specimen of *P. oxyptera* was obtained[7] ". . . among the water-weeds of the stream near San Luis de Caceres, in the Upper Paraguay basin." Later in the same publication Eigenmann repeats part of de Miranda Ribeiro's description of the collection site as[8] ". . . among the 'pseudo-rhyzomas de Agua-pé' *Eichornea* [*Eichhornia*] *azurea*, in the margin of the Paraguay River near San Luis de Caceres."

De Miranda Ribeiro did not mention the name of the plant he found in association with his fish, and its identity is uncertain. The botanical name in the above quotation is Eigenmann's addition, inserted without evidence. In Brazil, the common name *aguapé* refers to several species of *Eichhornia*; for example, *E. azurea* is called *aguapé de cordão*.[9] Much later, Paulo de Miranda Ribeiro, in reference to this same specimen, lists the location as[10] ". . . Caceres—Mato-Grosso—Rio Paraguay . . ."

Burgess writes:[11] "*P. oxyptera* was collected from under the scales of a characin, and one specimen of *Paravandellia* was collected from an electric eel." He does not cite a source for these statements; if valid, they indicate that *P. oxyptera* might feed on mucus, as does another species of trichomycterid, the stegophiline *Ochmacanthus alternus*.[12]

In his introductory sentences, Paulo de Miranda Ribeiro states that a specimen belonging to the subfamily Vandelliinae was received from the biologist Otto Schubart.[13] Its arrival offered an opportunity to compare this fish with vandelliines in the ichthyological collection of the Museu Nacional, Rio de Janeiro, including the type specimen of *Paravandellia oxyptera*. Oddly, de Miranda Ribeiro gives only a cursory description of

Schubart's fish and avoids any mention of its possible taxonomic affiliation. He focuses instead on other genera and species—notably *P. oxyptera*—and possible synonymy of *P. oxyptera* with some of these. Schubart's unidentified vandelliine is shown here as Fig. 22 (top illustration). De Miranda Ribeiro's description of it:[14]

> The specimen sent by Dr. Otto Schubart, No. 4684 of the ichthyological collection of the National Museum, features the following characteristics: — Total length — 0,023 m and standard length 0,020 m; head — to the opercular opening — 0,003 m; eyes relatively large; interorbital space — 0,001 m; greatest height — 0,002 m; mouth inferior, having two barbels at each corner, the internal ones smaller; a grouping of teeth larger than the others, arranged in three series, bounded on each side by a series of much smaller teeth, in the anterior part of the upper maxillary; teeth in the shape of a claw ("claw-teeth") present; jaw with teeth in the extremities of its rami. No nasal or mental [chin] barbels. Opercular membrane linked closely to the isthmus without, however, forming a fold over it. Opercular and preopercular [actually, interopercular] spines relatively robust and curved — 12–13; distance from the first dorsal ray to the tip of the snout, 0,014 m, and from that same point to the base of the median caudal rays — 0,007 m. The first anal ray is placed corresponding, more or less, to the middle of the base of the dorsal. Distance from the first ventral [pelvic] ray to the tip of the snout — 0,014 m, and of that same point to the base of the median caudal rays — 0,065 m. Pectorals — 6, truncate; anal — 7; dorsal — 8; caudal subtruncate with few accessory rays evident. The color is *isabelino* [literally, Elizabethan] with scattered light stippling, set in parallel series along the dorsal median line to the sides — as it can be seen in the print — stippling that repeats on the rays of the fins. (Material preserved in alcohol). According to information provided by Dr. Otto Schubart — this specimen was collected among the scales of a [specimen of] *Prochilodus* fished from the Rio Mogi-Guaçu. [S. Spotte, transl.]

Unable to find *dentes em forma de garra* ("claw-teeth") on the type specimen of *Paravandellia oxyptera* (Fig. 22, bottom), de Miranda Ribeiro places blame on the specimen's poor condition:[15] "Today it is an old relic; a specimen of tiny dimensions, and has been transformed into a true mummy." He succeeds in finding mandibular teeth, and by their presence is inclined to agree with Eigenmann that the genera *Branchioica* and *Paravandellia* could be synonyms. In Eigenmann's opinion, closer examination of specimens of *Paravandellia* might reveal teeth[16] ". . . at the end of the maxillary (premaxillary?) and on the mandibles when they are examined minutely." If true, *Branchioica* could be merged with *Paravandellia*.

This much is clear, but the subsequent text in Portuguese contains a puzzling redundancy:[17]

> Justification for the present note is, in our [sic] view, the specimen of *Paravandellia oxyptera*.
>   Despite this, we [sic] could not verify — given the poor condition of the specimen, the presence of "claw-teeth" in the type [specimen] of *Paravandellia oxyptera*, — the verification of teeth in the jaw leaves no doubt, in agreement with Professor Eigenmann, as to the possibility of the synonymy of this genus with *Paravandellia*. [S. Spotte, transl.]

Synonymy with itself? Logically, the last-mentioned genus in the above quotation should be *Branchioica*. This is not simply a misprint because de Miranda Ribeiro continues:[18]

> The caudal of the type [specimen] of the last-mentioned genus [*Paravandellia*] was said to be "forked" (whereas the one of *Branchioica* is described as subtruncate) — it might have been judged as such by virtue of the drying of its rays, which did not permit us [sic] to open some of them, and make a perfect judgement of their shape . . . [S. Spotte, transl.]

On this point, the English summary is inconsistent with the body of the text.

Although he did not examine any specimens of *Paravandellia*, Baskin is skeptical about possible synonymy:[19]

> It is unlikely . . . that these two genera are the same, because the mandibular teeth of *Branchioica* are large, well developed and easily seen. The small size (22 mm.) however, of the only specimen of *Paravandellia* reported (Miranda-Ribeiro, 1912) is characteristic of *Branchioica*.

As to their possible distinction, Eigenmann had written that *Branchioica* is found in the lower portion of the Rio Paraguay and *Paravandellia* in the upper portion and, as just mentioned, that *Paravandellia* purportedly has a forked tail, whereas the caudal fin of *Branchioica* is subtruncate.[20]

Having found "claw-teeth" in specimens of *Parabranchioica* (discussed here in a later section), de Miranda Ribeiro suggests merging this genus into *Paravandellia*, so long as "claw-teeth" could also be verified in the type specimen of *Parabranchioica teaguei*.[21] In his view, this would eliminate the species *Parabranchioica teaguei* and *Branchioica bertoni* (see the next section), leaving only *Paravandellia oxyptera*. The fate of *Branchioica phaneronema* (also discussed later) is not mentioned; presumably its name would change to *Paravandellia phaneronema*. Baskin, however, found "claw-teeth" on the premaxillae of all vandelliines he examined.[22] In addition, a "co-type" of the type specimen of *Parabranchioica* he looked at proved indistinguishable from *Branchioica*, which provides a tentative reason to consider dropping *Parabranchioica* from the list of valid genera.

Attempting to explain any real or perceived differences between *Branchioica* and *Paravandellia*, Eigenmann states:[23]

> With fishes as rare as these and as small as these, the question arises whether two species are really different, or whether the described differences are due to the fact that one worker uses a hand lens, and the other a binocular dissecting microscope with an arc spot-light.

It was probably this statement that irritated Alípio de Miranda Ribeiro, although I find nothing insulting in Eigenmann's remarks. Thinking Eigenmann had denigrated his description of *Paravandellia*, de Miranda Ribeiro defends his methods:[24]

> In *Paravandellia*, Prof. Eigenmann feels poor and short sighted my methods—But there I gave a generical [*sic*] diagnosis of 5 lines and about 40 words, followed by specific [*sic*] diagnosis on [*sic*] 17 lines.

NEODAT through 2000 listed additional Brazilian specimens collected from the Rio Paraná and Rio Taquari. Two other specimens collected by Schubart comprise collection MNRJ 4684 (collection date unknown, Rio Mogi-Guaçu, Mato Grosso) in the Museu Nacional, Rio de Janeiro; the specimen shown in Fig. 22 (top) is one of these. Still another (MNRJ 8914) was captured by Schubart at Curimata, state of São Paulo, on 9 June 1954.

Genus *Branchioica* Eigenmann, 1918
Branchioica bertoni (=*B. bertonii*) Eigenmann, 1918

Eigenmann tells of having received a preserved specimen of an undescribed fish from A. de W. Bertoni of Puerto Bertoni, Paraguay, collected from the Rio Paraguay.[25] He prepared a description, which was then set aside along with the specimen—and forgotten. Eigenmann writes,[26] "Later he [de W. Bertoni] sent me two more specimens, all three having been taken from the gills of a large characin, *Piaractus brachypomus*." The formal description of the genus *Branchioica* and species *B. bertoni* was published twice. One includes no illustrations,[27] but Eigenmann provides them in the other (Fig. 23).[28]

The species of *Branchioica* are distinguished superficially from those of *Vandellia* by their smaller size (about 24 millimeters) and by having teeth in the lower jaw. The presence of "claw-teeth" on the premaxilla is not diagnostic of the genus *Branchioica*.[29] In life, the eyes are black, the fish itself translucent, although not without pigment. According to Eigenmann, *B. bertoni* has[30] ". . . chromatophores on the snout, along the back, along the base of the anal, on the base of the caudal, along the side of the abdominal cavity, and a few on the pectoral."

A color photograph in Burgess' *An Atlas of Freshwater and Marine Catfishes* shows a specimen of *B. bertoni* on the gills of a pimelodid catfish (*Pseudoplatystoma* sp.).[31] It apparently attacks both characins and larger catfishes.

The Brazilian zoologists Francisco A. Machado and Ivan Sazima observed the feeding behavior of specimens of *Branchioica bertoni* at Porto São Benedito and Volta Grande, Rio Cuiabá Antônio de Leverger, Mato Grosso, after tethering large catfishes of the species *Pseudoplatystoma corruscans* (or *P. coruscans*) and *P. fasciatum* to the riverbank. Candirus approached in 4–10 minutes, and attacks on the tethered catfishes took place without noticeable differences both day and night (Fig. 24):[32]

> The feeding activity of *B. bertonii* occurred as a stream of dozens to hundreds of individuals moving along the body of the host, from its tail to its head . . . The movements were eel-like, interrupted occasionally with stops of 2 to 3 seconds. During these interruptions, the animal adopted an oblique position, its mouth seeming to scrape the surface of the host as the rest of its body undulated. The concentration of blood-feeders was greatest in the branchial area of the host; numerous individuals entered the branchial chamber, and others emerged when the opercula were opened during breathing movements of the catfish. The time spent by blood-feeders in the branchial chamber was, at most, 1 to 3 minutes; upon emerging, their abdomens were red and greatly dilated . . . . Dilated individuals usually abandoned the host and swam towards the bottom (some of these satiated individuals moved without definite direction towards the body of the prey without, however, returning to the branchial chamber). On one occasion, intense activity was observed by *B. bertonii* near the anal opening of one of the *Pseudoplatystoma fasciatum*; it was impossible to confirm whether they penetrated into the intestinal cavity.
>
> The succession of numerous individuals of *B. bertonii* heading for the branchial chamber of the same host was once observed over a period of 6 h and involved thousands of blood-feeders. The blood-feeders readily abandoned the branchial chamber when the host was removed from the water. However, on two occasions some specimens were removed directly

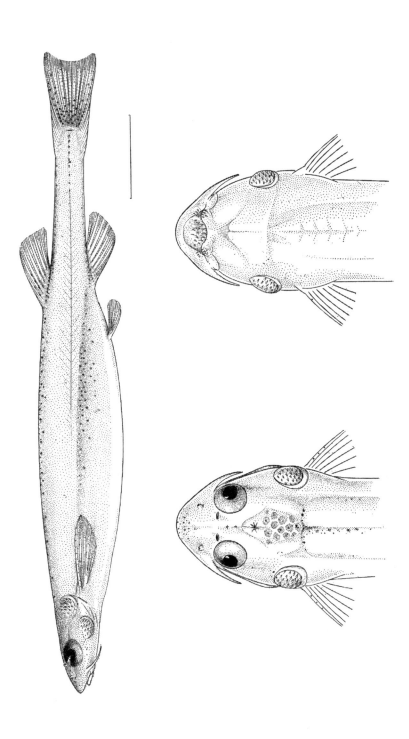

FIG. 23 *Branchioica bertoni* Eigenmann, 1918. *Top:* Lateral view. *Bottom left:* Head and upper body (ventral view). *Bottom right:* Head and upper body (dorsal view). Two scale bars are shown on the original of this plate. The top one is 1/8 inch. The bottom bar, which is underneath the illustration of *B. bertoni*, gives no indication of length, but is measurably shorter than the first (a real measurement of 2.3 vs. 2.6 centimeters). Source: After Eigenmann (1918a).

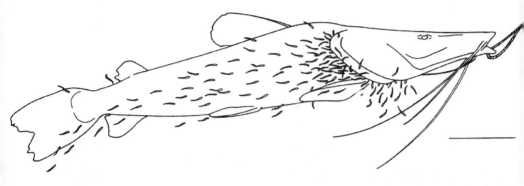

F<small>IG</small>. 24   Groups of the vandelliine *Branchioica bertoni* Eigenmann, 1918 approaching a tethered pimelodid catfish (*Pseudoplatystoma* sp.) to feed on its gills. Scale bar = 10 centimeters. Source: Machado and Sazima (1983).

> from the [branchial] chamber . . . after the host had been exposed to the air. The death of a captive *P. fasciatum* was observed once, about 1 h after *B. bertonii* began their activities. After the death of this specimen, activity of the blood-feeders ceased. The gills of the fish attacked by *B. bertonii* bled at several locations, mainly in the area proximal and medial to filaments of the first branchial arch. [S. Spotte, transl.]

The American ichthyologists Stanley H. Wietzman and Richard P. Vari call this species "*Paravandellia bertonii* (Eigenmann, 1918)" without justifying the name change.[33] If the genera *Paravandellia* and *Branchioica* eventually prove synonymous, as suggested previously, then *Paravandellia* has precedence.[34]

Through 2000, NEODAT listed records from Brazil (Rio Cuiabá, Rio Paraguay, Rio Taquari, upper Paraná) and Paraguay (Rio Paraguay, Rio Apa, Rio Paraná).

Branchioica phaneronema Miles, 1943
Branchioica phaneronema Miles, 1943 (=*B. magdalenae* Miles, 1943)

In two 1943 publications—the first in Spanish, the second in English— Miles describes *Branchioica phaneronema* from four specimens collected in the upper Rio Cauca, Colombia, ranging in length from 24–27 millimeters.

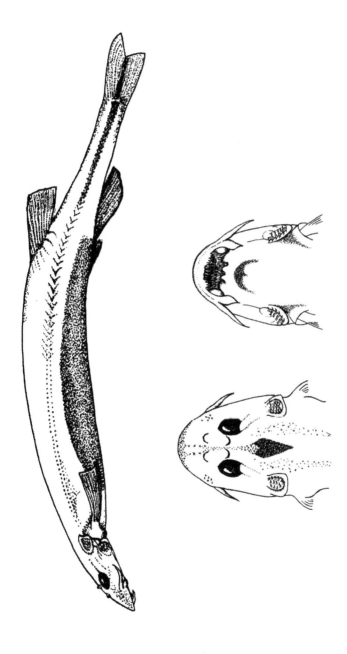

FIG. 25 *Branchioica phaneronema* Miles, 1943. *Top:* Lateral view. The gut is dark, distended, and probably filled with blood. The specimen shown is 27 millimeters long. *Bottom left:* Dorsal view of head. *Bottom right:* Ventral view of head. Source: After Miles (1943a, 1943b).

Three of the four accompanying illustrations, which appeared in both reports, are reproduced here (Fig. 25). The original description:[35]

Branchioica phaneronema, new species.

Height, 6 to 7 [one-sixth to one-seventh of total? length], head 5.33–6.0 [head about 17–19 percent of total? length], eye 4 in the head [diameter of eye one-fourth the length of the head], 1 to 1.5 in the interorbital distance [diameter of eye three-fourths of the interorbital distance or equal to it]. An oval group of spines on the operculum, directed upwards, and another on the interoperculum in a sense posteroinferior. Two series of long thin teeth on the premaxillary [or vomer], with an irregular series of shorter teeth to each side. A small group of teeth at the interior termination of each mandibular element, hidden in the flesh of the lower lip, their curved tips at right angles.

Distance between the origin of the dorsal fin and that of the tail is some-what less than the predorsal distance. Distance between anal and caudal, 6 into the total length. [Distance between anal and caudal one-sixth of total length.] The origin of the ventrals [pelvics] is closer to the tip of the caudal than to the origin of the pectorals. The anal [fin] originates under the last dorsal rays, and the first dorsal ray is above a point forward of the ventrals. Caudal emarginate, its upper lobe longer. Caudal with few accessory rays. Pectoral fins 1,6, the first ray curved, longer and thicker than the rest, its length, measured from the end of the opercular spines, longer than the head. Humeral process prominent.

Differs from the genotype of *Br. bertonii* in that the upper maxillary barbel [*sic*] is shorter, and it ends at the level of the center of the eye, whereas the lower one is larger and visible —the specific name, from the Greek, *phaneros*, visible, and *nema*, thread. Also differs in the shape of the mouth and in the curved mandibular teeth. It is distinguished from *Br. magdalenae* Miles in coloration, in the pectoral fins, in the size of the barbels, in the more prominent humeral process, and in the less outstanding accessory radii.

Color is translucent in life, the underside red, a dark lateral band that orig-inates after the operculum becomes successively darker and extends onto the central radii of the caudal fin. The upper lip and the barbels pigmented.

Type. A specimen that measures 27 mm. Upper School of Tropical Agri-culture, Cali. Collectors, [Cecil] Miles and [Luis] Olaya.

Paratypes. Three specimens of 24 mm., 25 mm. and 26 mm. distributed as follows: Museum of Comparative Zoology, Cambridge, Mass., EE. UU., National Museum, Washington, EE. UU., and Institute of Natural Sciences, Bogotá, Colombia. [S. Spotte, transl.]

In distinguishing this fish from *B. bertoni*, Miles cites the rictal (lower) barbel as being[36] ". . . considerably larger and broader . . . almost half as long as the upper." This upper, or maxillary, barbel is shorter than in *B. bertoni*, extending to the center of the eye. Otherwise, the characters Miles lists differ little from those describing *B. bertoni*.[37]

Cesar Román-Valencia redescribed *P. phaneronema* based on new specimens collected from the Rio La Vieja and Rio La Miel, affluents of the Rio Magdalena, Colombia.[38] He had been unable to find the types archived in Colombia by Miles some 55 years earlier. The specimen of *B. phaneronema* sent by Miles to the National Museum of Natural History (Washington, D.C.) had arrived without preservative and was in poor condition. In Román-Valencia's opinion, data obtained from it were of doubtful value. Vari, who took the measurements, concurred.[39] Román-Valencia evidently did not examine the Cambridge specimen. Oddly, he does not mention the size of his sample or how *B. phaneronema* compares with *B. bertoni*.

Miles described *Branchioica magdalenae* as a new species based on 12 specimens collected in the Rio Magdalena, Colombia, from gills of a pimelodid catfish (*Pseudoplatystoma fasciatum*).[40] In his opinion, they could be distinguished from *B. phaneronema* by their smaller size (all less than 24 millimeters in length), a few minor anatomical differences, and the near absence of pigment. Miles considered this species closer to *B. bertoni* than to *B. phaneronema*, differing from *B. bertoni*[41] ". . . in the shape of the mouth, and principally in the mandibular teeth, the tips of which are abruptly curved outwards at a right-angle." The original description appears as a footnote in the Spanish publication:[42]

> *Branchioica magdalenæ*, new species. The Magdalena's Branchioica [*sic*] is very similar to the form from the upper Cauca, but each of the many studied specimens is smaller than those from the Valley. They lack pigmentation, except for a poorly defined lateral band that does not extend onto the radii of the caudal fin. The first ray of the pectoral fin is not notably stronger than the others and is shorter than the cephalic length. The upper barbel extends to the posterior border of the eye, whereas the lower is insignificant; in this detail each [of the specimens] resembles the genotype, but the maxillary teeth are similar to those of *Br. phaneronema*. All specimens of *Br. magdalenæ* were found in the gills of the Tiger Catfish, *Pseudoplatystoma fasciatum*, whereas those of *Br. phaneronema* were discovered buried in the bottom mud. *Type*, 1 specimen of skeletal length 22 mm., collected in Honda by Luis Olaya and deposited at the Institute of Natural Sciences, in Bogotá, Colombia. Paratypes were also dispatched to the M. C. Z. at Harvard and to the National Museum in Washington. [S. Spotte, transl.]

A paratype of *P. magdalenae* sent by Miles to the National Museum of Natural History had, like the specimen of *P. phaneronema*, arrived dry, having lost its preservative in transit. Nonetheless, Román-Valencia claims it does not differ from his specimens of *P. phaneronema*. How he obtained confirmation is unstated and especially puzzling if the specimen in Washington is in poor condition. He seems not to have examined the specimen sent by Miles to the Museum of Comparative Zoology.

Román-Valencia treats *B. phaneronema* and *B. magdalenae* as synonyms without explaining how he decided which name has precedence. Perhaps the reason can be traced to Miles, who described both putative species in his 1943 publications but listed *B. phaneronema* first. Román-Valencia also gives *Paravandellia magdalenae* as a synonym and cites Weitzman and Vari as the source, but these authors merely presume *P. magdalenae* to be a valid name and list it without any redescription.[43] Dahl had also considered these species as one.[44]

Specimens of *Branchioica phaneronema* have been found on the gills of the characin *Ichthyoelephas longirostris*.[45]

Through 2000, NEODAT listed only Miles' Colombian specimens: two of *B. phaneronema* and a single specimen of *B. magdalenae*.

Genus *Parabranchioica* Devincenzi and Vaz-Ferreira, 1939
Parabranchioica teaguei Devincenzi and Vaz-Ferreira, 1939

Devincenzi and Vaz-Ferreira established the genus *Parabranchioica* in 1939, placing within it the species *P. teaguei*. Their article is illustrated by a small photograph of the specimen and three photomicrographs, two of the mouth, the third depicting a transverse section of the gut. Better illustrations were published later (Fig. 26). The description is based on a single specimen collected by Gerard W. Teague, British vice-consul in Paysandú, Uruguay, from the gills of a "river palometa," *Pygocentrus* (=*Rooseveltiella*) *nattereri*.[46] According to the authors, Teague,[47]

> ... cultured amateur in natural sciences and honorary collaborator of the Museum of Natural History —and at that time very fond of fishing — brought to the Museum a lot [collection] of fish that he found of interest, with special attention on a small specimen that had been stuck to the gills of a "river palometa" (*Rooseveltiella nattereri* Kner [*sic*]). [S. Spotte, transl.]

Devincenzi and Vaz-Ferreira continue:[48]

> When trying to remove it, he [Teague] encountered great resistance and was forced to pry it off with a knife, observing then that the small fish's stomach was filled with blood, and that the gills of the palometa continued to bleed. [S. Spotte, transl.]

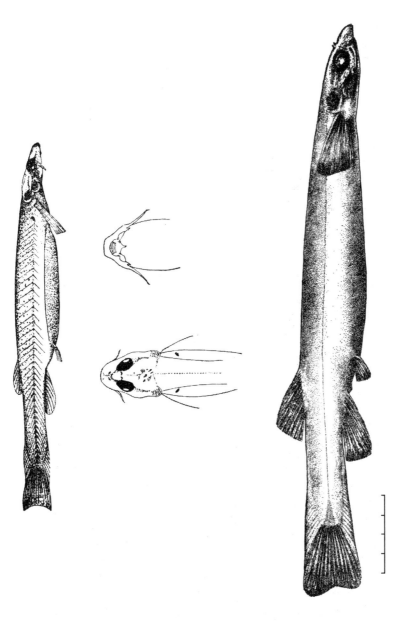

Fig. 26 *Parabranchioica teaguei* Devincenzi and Vaz-Ferreira, 1939. *Top:* Lateral view. *Middle left:* Head and upper body (dorsal view). *Middle right:* Head (ventral view). *Bottom:* Lateral view of specimen MNRJ 3606 (Museu Nacional, Rio de Janeiro, scale bar = 4 millimeters?). Sources: Top and middle illustrations from Devincenzi and Vaz-Ferreira (1926–1940); bottom illustration from de Miranda Ribeiro (1947).

Devincenzi and Vaz-Ferreira recognized that their fish fed on other fishes, but were less certain how permanently it attached to its prey. To obtain more specimens, one of them went twice to the Rio Uruguay near the city of Paysandú:[49]

> We [sic] went there to find this fish, well-known by the common name of "leech", and considered by the fishermen to be a true plague, because, according to them, at certain times of the year they "bleed" the [other] fishes, leaving them "colorless" and unfit for consumption. [S. Spotte, transl.]

They go on to say:[50]

> The information we were given on the habits [of this fish] was contra-dictory: while some assured us that the fish live permanently attached to their host, others insisted that the attachment is temporary [literally, acci-dental] and the host is abandoned once the needs of the *huésped* [literally, guest] have been satisfied. Nonetheless, all the specimens obtained —eight so far —were extracted from the gills of two different species, and the fact that they did not fall off after the host was removed from the water lends credence to the first hypothesis. [S. Spotte, transl.]

The abbreviated description consists of a few measurements embedded in four lines of text:[51]

> Total length, 19.9 mm.; length without caudal, 17.7; head, 6.7 in length without caudal [head about 15 percent of length without caudal]; eye 3.8 in head [diameter of eye about 26 percent of the length of the head]; snout 3.3 [snout about 30 percent of the length of the head]. [Tip of] snout to start of dorsal fin, 12.05 mm.; [tip of] snout to start of anal fin, 12.85 mm. D. 8. A. 7. [S. Spotte, transl.]

The authors describe in a key how, in their opinion, *P. teaguei* differs from the other vandelliines (see the key near the end of this chapter). Burgess claims that *Branchioica* now contains, in addition to its own species, those formerly placed in the genus *Parabranchioica*, but without explaining how *Parabranchioica* came to be eliminated.[52]

Raúl Vaz-Ferreira also reports *P. teaguei* to be sanguinivorous:[53]

> The "leech [fish]" feeds exclusively on blood of other fishes that it obtains after introducing itself into the branchial cavities and provoking lacerations of the thin sheets [of branchial tissue]; after being satiated, their alimentary canal, nearly straight, appears dilated, spherical [*globuloso*, but probably *globoso*], and red, similar to that of a true "leech." [S. Spotte, transl.]

According to Devincenzi and Teague,[54] only big siluriform fishes are attacked. In the middle portion of the Rio Uruguay the species is most prevalent from February to April, then diminishes steadily until disappearing in (austral) winter.

Through 2000, NEODAT listed another specimen of *P. teaguei*, also caught by Teague in Uruguay.[55] Still another specimen is listed as *Paravandellia teaguei*.[56]

Genus *Paracanthopoma* Giltay, 1935
Paracanthopoma parva Giltay, 1935

Paracanthopoma parva is a monotypic genus (i.e., contains only one species) that Louis Giltay described in 1935 from two specimens collected by Kalo and Salathé (given names unstated) in the upper Rio Catrimani, Brazil. Distinguishing characters include two rows of teeth in the upper jaw (Fig. 27, bottom), teeth on the mandible (Fig. 27, bottom), large branchial opening, and branchiostegal membranes united at the midline and free of the isthmus. Of the vandelliines, only *Paracanthopoma* is known to possess this last character.[57] As Schmidt correctly points out, Eigenmann's key misleads by implying that all vandelliines are included.[58]

In this same publication, Schmidt reports on two specimens of *P. parva* collected by K. and R. Schmidt at the confluence of the Mazaruni and Cuyuni Rivers, Kartabo Point, Guyana, and examined a third specimen collected by C. Laks from the upper Rio Catrimani, Roraima, Brazil, in the collection of the California Academy of Sciences in San Francisco. One specimen from Guyana was taken from the gills of a pimelodid catfish (*Brachyplatystoma vaillanti*); the second was found dead in a bucket containing other catfish (*Doras micropoeus*). It might have been feeding on one of these potential prey fish.

Through 2000, NEODAT listed these records and one for Bolivia (Madre de Dios, *P.* cf. *parva*).

Key to the Genera—subfamily Vandelliinae

In Burgess' key to the trichomycterid genera, *Plectrochilus* is distinguished from *Vandellia* by having teeth on its mandibular rami.[59] Devincenzi and Vaz Ferreira produced a key to the genera of the subfamily Vandelliinae by translating Eigenmann's key into Spanish and adding a fourth entry (mmmm) to show the position of *Parabranchioica*. Below is my translation from their Spanish back into English.[60] Not surprisingly, the phrasing differs slightly from Eigenmann's original. I give their version because Eigenmann's key is more available to readers of English.

Key to the Genera of the Subfam. Vandelliinae

Narrow mouth; weak mandibular arches not meeting in the midline; scarce, weak, pointed teeth (*Vandelliinae*).

m.—Some depressible teeth in a simple series in the middle of the upper jaw; lower jaw without teeth, or with some exceedingly small teeth in the end of the rami; caudal rounded or emarginate.
Vandellia Cuv. & Val. [Cuvier and Valenciennes, 1846]

mm.—A row of depressible teeth in the middle of the upper jaw; a simple series of much smaller teeth to the sides of the middle row; without teeth in the lower jaw; forked caudal fin with longer upper lobe.
Paravandellia Mir. Rib. [de Miranda Ribeiro, 1912]

mmm.—Two series of depressible teeth in the middle of the upper jaw; a much smaller simple series of teeth beside the middle series, and a tooth in [the form of a] claw (*claw-like tooth*) in the end of the middle series; two short series of teeth in the end of the mandibular rami; caudal fin subtruncate.
Branchioica Eigenmann [1918a]

mmmm.—Several series of teeth, numerous in the front series, in the middle of the upper jaw; simple series of lateral teeth without intermediate claw-like tooth; small series of teeth in each end of the mandibular rami; caudal fin emarginate.
Parabranchioica Devincenzi [and Vaz-Ferreira, 1939]

How many species of candirus are there? This chapter and the previous one give evidence of more species names than valid occupants.[61] The first candiru to be named was described from three specimens. Consider how few specimens have served to describe the other vandelliines (Table 1). Early ichthyologists have left a legacy of six presumed genera and 15 putative species described from slightly more than 30 specimens.[62] When modern specialists get around to studying the subfamily Vandelliinae, the outcome might be one or two species of *Vandellia*, no species of *Plectrochilus* (this genus is merged into *Vandellia*), fewer species of *Branchioica* (probably just *B. bertoni*), and elimination of *Parabranchioica*. If the genera *Paravandellia* and *Branchioica* are merged, the name *Paravandellia* takes precedence by having existed first.

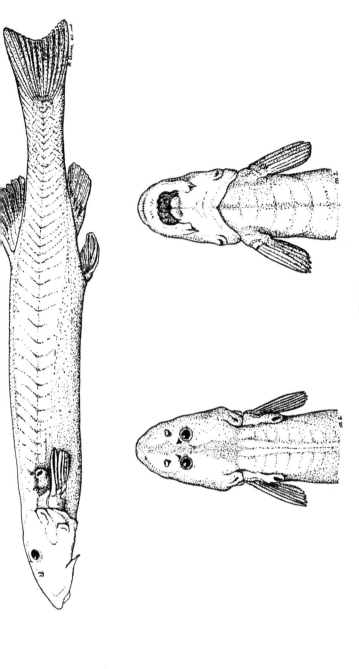

Fig. 27 *Paracanthopoma parva* Giltay, 1935. *Top:* Lateral view. *Middle left:* Head and upper body (ventral view). *Middle right:* Head and upper body (dorsal view). *Bottom:* Mouth showing upper and lower jaw teeth and denture bones (ventral view). Courtesy of l'Institut Royal des Sciences Naturelles de Belgique, Robert E. Schmidt, and Verlag Dr. Friedrich Pfeil. Sources: Top three illustrations from Giltay (1935); bottom illustration from Schmidt (1993).

Epigraphs in an undecipherable language, half their letters rubbed away by the sand-laden wind: this is what you will be, O parfumeries, for the noseless man of the future.

—Italo Calvino, "The Name, The Nose"[1]

5.

Good Smells, Good Vibrations

The American philosopher Thomas Nagel once published an article titled "What is it Like to Be a Bat?" His conclusion: who knows? One species can never understand what it's like to be another, so don't even bother trying. Having stated a basic truth—that of universal remoteness among species—I shall now violate it by discussing how a candiru *might* perceive its world, finding sustenance and romance, and maybe even happiness.

Sight is the most important sense, you say? Never! The sensory world is driven, directed—and in the end controlled—by smell. Surely there can be no doubt. Proof is all around, not excepting the personal effluvia often repellent to others but rendered impalpable to us by the need to detect odors besides our own. If you doubt me, consider this simple thought experiment. It's a hot summer day and you are riding a stifling, crowded bus. At the next stop two people get on and take the remaining empty seats, which happen to be on each side of you. One is a kid with purple spiked hair and enough lip studs and eyebrow rings to set off an airport metal detector. His clothes came straight from a Salvation Army bin and once belonged to someone twice his size. This kid is visually unappealing, but clean. The other guy, although dressed in slacks and sportshirt, emits the mingled odors of unwashed armpit, old gym socks, mundungus, and garlic and anchovy pizza. Which one gets most of your attention?

At times the failure of our olfactory sense can be excruciating. Monsieur de Saint-Caliste, Cavino's anguished protagonist in "The Name, The Nose," is left no choice except to consult Madame Odile in her *parfumerie* and hope she can reveal the identity of a mysterious woman with whom he danced the previous night at a masquerade ball. He remembers his nostrils pressed into the soft white angle of a neck and shoulder, his moustaches twitching like the joined vibrissae of some crazed, rutting beast. Her unusual perfume is his single clue, if only he can describe it. Madame Odile pores over her list of clients, checking off each special scent: a heliotrope used by only four women in all of Paris, including the wife of Cou-

Location Fish	Taste buds /cm²		
	1	2	3
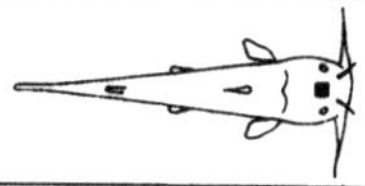	675	549	409
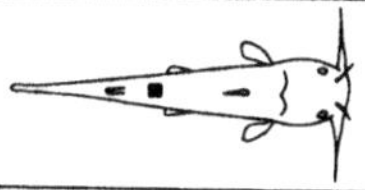	474	318	171
	411*	415*	269*
	408	285	284
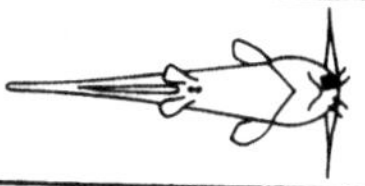	?	?	531

FIG. 28   Number of taste buds at specification locations (black) in a North American siluriform catfish, the brown bullhead (*Ictalurus nebulosus*). * = left side. Counts are from three fish. Source: Peters et al. (1974).

lommiers (the cheese manufacturer) and his mistress, a blend prepared exclusively for Carole (the courtesan), finally an exotic aroma that has a "depressant" effect on men and is never purchased twice.... Sadly it is none of these, although its essence lingers on the edge of memory. As Calvino tells us,[2] "... everything is first perceived by the nose, everything is within the nose, the world is the nose."

Spoken from a human's point of view, of course. Had our distraught M. de Saint-Caliste been born a catfish he not only would have smelled this lovely perfume, but also tasted it. Moustaches aroused to bristling astonishment, taste buds hastening the flavor of perfumed clavicle directly to the brain ... but why torture ourselves over such inexplicable matters as accidents of birth? We should ask instead whether a catfish in love could suffer this much.[3]

In water, the distinction between olfaction and gustation is less certain than it is in air, the resolution far more intimate. To a catfish a nose is much more than a nose. Practically speaking, a catfish *is* a nose—not to mention a mouth—a creature that "sniffs in" the environment by pumping water continuously through its olfactory capsules, and whose external surfaces are blanketed with thousands of taste buds (Fig. 28).[4]

No one has ever measured the limits of a candiru's powers of taste and smell, but one of its relatives, the channel catfish (*Ictalurus punctatus*), can detect individual amino acids at the nanomolar level, or one molecule of amino acid among a billion molecules of water. Amino acids betray the presence of food, but because fishes excrete them they might also serve as social cues.[5]

Imagine yourself impossibly freckled. Every bit of you, including the palms of your hands and the soles of your feet, is peppered with tiny lentigos, each of them a sensitive cluster of taste cells. Now imagine yourself as a candiru so equipped and drifting down a river, your whole body sensitized to taste and odor, the very stream a colossal *parfumerie*—a protean caldron hinting of food, lust, nausea, fear, birth, death.

Out of this disquieting smorgasbord an intriguing molecule tumbles against one of your thousands of olfactory pits, having arrived through that endless pipeline, your nose. Molecules of this same chemical roll along your sides like miniature ball-bearings, ducking into gustatory pits on your head and along your sides to the very end of your tail, and all the while you smell them, taste them, again and again like a single bite of chocolate that melts repeatedly on the tongue, its sweetness wafted into the nostrils. Meanwhile, a different molecule touches you somewhere else, a different odor and taste, noxious perhaps, but interesting . . .

Oh my! What was that? You pause by a cleft in the riverbank and wallow momentarily in the unmistakable fragrance (or is it taste?) of candiru in heat (or the piscine equivalent), maybe male, maybe female. Candiru sex lives are unknown to us, so take your choice. It's like joining a love partner in a hot tub, except in this situation the water alone will do.

You've encountered this scent trail, or odorant plume, by skulking along the riverbank. Finding it was no accident. Candirus, like beagles, keep their noses close to the ground, probably because good smells are concentrated there. In some marine environments, odorant plumes released by prey animals become attached to particles of the substratum; this augments their detection by bottom-dwelling predators.[6] The males of still other animals use odorant plumes to find mates.[7] In both cases, detection is obfuscated by increased current flow and turbulence, which disperse molecules of taste and smell and make their sources difficult to locate.[8] In the complete absence of current flow, odorant plumes stagnate. Without a chemical trail to follow, a predator's odds of finding prey are greatly diminished.[9] Assuming they use chemoreception to find food or mates, candirus probably operate most effectively at some optimal current flow.

In the race among the senses, the nose wins hands down. Coming in second is vision, right? Probably not. In the race of all things, nothing is faster than light. But underwater, sound travels farther. In the dark, turbid rivers of lowland South America where light penetration is severely restricted, sound reception is likely to be more important than vision,[10] especially to a bottom-dwelling catfish.

Riverine fishes are surrounded by all kinds of sounds. Noise, which is sound devoid of any relevance, includes rain hammering the surface, eddies sucking and slurping away the riverbanks, the slap of wind-generated waves, the tumbling of rocks and the swash of floating vegetation, the continuous rush of the water, and the chirps, grunts, splashes, and squeaks of animals. For a fish to separate a relevant sound—that is, the signal—requires circumventing the noise. This can be accomplished by possessing a sound reception system that receives important signals at a special frequency, or by not sensing the noise at all because most of it falls outside the receptive range.[11]

Fishes themselves make myriad sounds. Depending on the species, a fish might grind its teeth, clap its gill covers, rub certain fin rays and spines together, or even beat its sides with its pectoral fins, causing the swimbladder to resonate like a drum.[12] Sounds received and interpreted by individuals of the same species fall within the purview of communication. Some big catfishes on which candirus prey might communicate using sound. Whether candirus can intercept these messages and use the information to track individuals transmitting them is unknown. Fishes mostly use sound to communicate with others of their species, not to hunt prey.[13] However, the possibility remains that the sounds made by big catfishes might attract hungry candirus.

Fishes disrupt the water through which they swim, leaving behind physical disturbances as involuntary evidence of their passing. Whether the effect constitutes "sound" is open to interpretation. Subjectively, sound is what the ears receive and "hear." Objectively, sound is a vibration or mechanical disturbance in an elastic medium, such as air or water, that resumes equilibrium after the disturbance has passed. Underwater, these distinctions are anything but straightforward.

When an elastic medium like water vibrates, its particles begin to oscillate, or deviate from equilibrium. In physics, particles are volumes of gas or liquid of very small dimensions, although larger than molecules. Shouting underwater disturbs the equilibrium of the particles in front of your mouth, creating acoustic pressure that moves outward as a series of

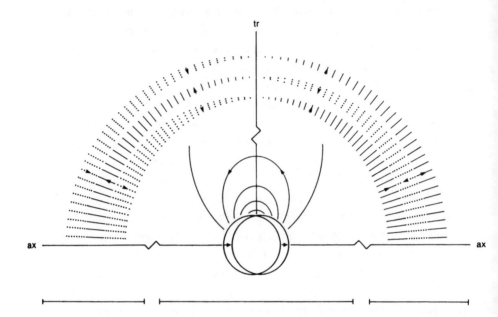

FIG. 29   Dipole field of a vibrating sphere. *Left and right:* Dipolar local flow. *Middle:* Radial propagating sound wave. Arrowheads = particle velocities, dashes = compression, dots = rarefaction; ax = axis of vibration, tr = transverse plane. Source: Kalmijn (1989).

concentric waves. Particles in the way are displaced from their normal state because the momentary change in pressure exceeds the pressure at equilibrium.

Sound traveling through air comprises periodic pressure waves detectable by the human ear, but acoustic energy underwater exists in two forms: distant pressure waves called far-field effects (those that have traveled some distance from the source) and particle displacements close to the source known as near-field effects. The two effects occur simultaneously, making it very difficult to define which of them—if not both—constitutes "sound."

A swimming fish, as just mentioned, disrupts the water around it. Water pushed away by the head streams along the sides and fills voids left by the tail. From a distance the effect resembles a dipole source (Fig. 29).[14] Wherever it goes, a moving fish drags this configuration along like an acoustic shadow, and the outward-flowing pattern gives other fishes— including predators—such information as whether they (the potential prey) are swimming steadily or accelerating. The signal is undampened and thus unforgiving, available to friend and foe.[15] From the figure it would seem that the hydrodynamic flow around the fish and the propagated sound wave are different phenomena, although both are described by the same equation;[16] any distinction rests in how predators receive them.

The wake produced by a swimming fish leaves a characteristic flow pattern—a piscine footprint—that can last for many minutes.[17] Fish wakes take the form of three-dimensional vortex chains[18] and contain information of potential use to predators, including the direction of the moving prey and the interval of time since its passing. As shown in Fig. 30, water pushed away from the head of a swimming fish is accelerated. Because a fish undulates as it swims, the wave passing along its body is subjected to alternating pressure and suction at the convex and concave bends. The speed of the wave accelerates, peaking at the tail, which throws off vortices with each lateral sweep. The alternating strokes of the tail generate mirror-image vortices that swirl in opposite directions. The effect is a dynamic plume of trailing concentric eddies.

As a fish swims, the displacement of particles caused by its movement falls off quickly with distance from the source; in other words, with distance from the fish. What prevails is a series of pressure waves moving quickly outward, and this defines the far-field. Both a pressure wave and disturbances caused by particle displacement prevail near a swimming fish, thus defining the near-field. We can expect that a predator senses its

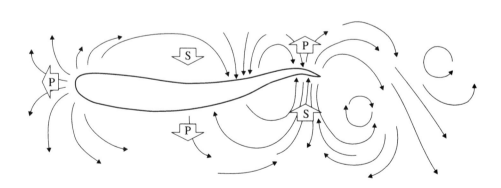

FIG. 30   Schematic illustration in plan view of the flow pattern near a swimming fish. S = a suction zone beside a concave bend in the body; P = a pressure zone near a convex bend in the body. Arrows show the main directions of flow. Scale bar = 50 millimeters. Courtesy of Ulrike K. Müller and Company of Biologists Ltd. Source: Müller et al. (1997).

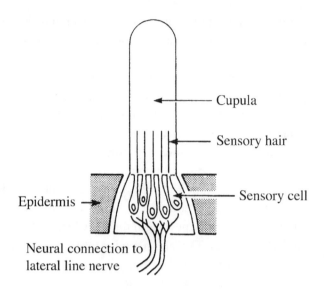

FIG. 31   Diagrammatic cross section through an ordinary lateral line canal organ, or free neuromast. The neuromast consists of a cluster of pear-shaped sensory cells surrounded by long, slender supporting cells (not shown). Sensory hairs on top of the sensory cells project into a gelatinous cupula, which is secreted by the free neuromast and projects into the water. Source: Spotte (1992) after Dijkgraaf (1952).

prey mainly in the near-field. Hypothetically, a predator swimming in its prey's wake (or zig-zagging through it) remains in the near-field even though the other fish is still some distance away. Far-field detection might be limited to special sounds used to communicate,[19] or to track the prey's general direction.[20]

Some fishes hear better than others, and those with the best hearing belong to the group called otophysans. The otophysans account for more than 60 percent of all species of freshwater fishes, including the siluriform catfishes. On this basis we might surmise that candirus have excellent hearing.

Otophysans hear well because they possess both a swimbladder and Weberian ossicles.[21] The Weberian ossicles are small bones—actually, modified vertebrae—connecting the front end of the swimbladder with the inner ear. A sound received from the far-field must be amplified, which requires a transducer, or a mechanism that transforms energy but can also serve as both a source and receiver of sound. A swimbladder fulfills this function.[22] Pressure waves arriving from the far-field are transformed to near-field displacement energy before transmission to the inner ear via the swimbladder.[23]

In addition to the inner ear, fishes have one or more lateral lines along each side (Fig. 9, Chapter 3) that are used as acoustic receptors. The lateral line extends onto the head. Its function is similar to the ear's, and the two organs have a common embryologic origin and morphology. The lateral line detects changes in displacement, meaning disturbances in the near-field.[24] It achieves this through special organs embedded in the lateral line canal (Fig. 31).

A candiru's lateral line might detect a big catfish swimming past in the near-field, but not until it comes within a few candiru body lengths;[25] that is, unless it happens to be following in its prey's wake. Having detected the prey, a predator's response can be lightning quick. Because the lateral line organs are stretched out from head to tail, a predator can monitor changes in displacement along its whole body, gaining some idea of its prey's location. This works if the spatial interval is mostly free of such interfering factors as vortices and turbulence.[26] Then, the Dutch-American acoustician A. J. Kalmijn writes:[27] "From the shape of the field, the animal may, by proper data processing, extrapolate the position of the target and strike at it in one fast, well-aimed move." Additionally, the lateral line appears to be insensitive to sounds from the far-field, including falling rain, wave-generated noise, and noise from shipping.[28]

If a rock falls from an underwater bluff and no fish is present to hear it, can there be sound? Of course, says the physicist. After all, sound is a vibration or mechanical disturbance in an elastic medium. The notion that something has to hear it seems irrelevant. The biologist disagrees. In the life sciences, the concept of sound is based on its reception. But even if a fish were present when the rock fell, did it "hear" anything? Does the inner ear of a fish qualify as a suitable organ of hearing?

I've explained how fishes presumably hear in the far-field, and that this is accomplished with the inner ear. However, some scientists, notably Kalmijn, think a fish's inner ear is used most often to detect near-field effects.[29] In this respect it functions like the lateral line. Near-field disturbances aren't "sound" by most definitions used in biology, creating the dilemma of a hearing organ the principal purpose of which is not hearing. Kalmijn, who raised this problem, also proposed a solution: simply consider near-field effects as sound too.[30] In some ways this attempt to solve the problem by amalgamation merely blurs the edges of how we think of sound, leaving us no more enlightened.

But back to our story. After lying quietly in a shallow sandpit until after dark, you pick up a signal, the sounds of big catfishes vocalizing. They arrive as pressure waves from the far-field, are transformed to near-field displacement energy, and transmitted to your inner ear via the swim-bladder. Dinner! This scene is conjectural, of course. As a human being I can only infer your sensory capabilities. I don't know if the catfishes on which you prey ordinarily vocalize, or communicate using sound, and I'm guessing you can hear them and intercept their signals.

Being hungry, you start moving. Far-field detection has let you know the prey is out there, but not its location. It might be only a few meters away, but in which direction? By assuming a path similar to that shown in Fig. 32, you arrive within your prey's near-field.[31] Catfishes seldom study geometry, so you now rely on me to explain it. Once inside the far-field disturbance generated by the prey, any direction taken that intersects the outward-flowing lines of pressure waves at an unchanging angle leads to the source of the disturbance;[32] in other words, to that big fat catfish rooting in the mud.

Having penetrated your victim's near-field, latching on is no problem, but whether you use smell (or taste), the lateral line directly, "hearing," or one of the senses we haven't yet discussed, is still a mystery. Whatever

FIG. 32   Functions of the lateral line and inner ear in detecting moving objects. (1) Near the source the local-flow field is complicated: the lateral line detects spatial differences in the particle acceleration field along the length of the body (hydrodynamic detection). (2) Farther from the source the local-flow field is mainly dipolar: the inner ear detects the particle acceleration field averaged over the volume of the body (near-field hearing). (3) At large distances from the source the propagating sound wave dominates: the inner ear detects the radial particle acceleration field (far-field hearing). Source: (Kalmijn 1989).

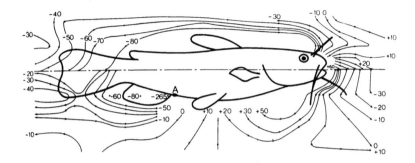

FIG. 33   Equipotential lines (in microvolts) of the bioelectric fields of an anesthetized catfish, the brown bullhead (*Ictalurus nebulosus*). Source: Peters et al. (1974).

works for lunch probably works for love too. Candirus perhaps use the lateral line or inner ear (or both) to find mates, but who knows?

I suppose things could happen like that, but consider the possibility of the love or hunger spark being electric, not chemical or auditory. This spark idea is worth pursuing.

Every living thing moves or stands still in the midst of its personal electric field. Each time a muscle contracts, the electric field it produces fluctuates.[33] In animals, working muscles and the activation of nerves are powered by chemically generated electricity, miniscule currents slipping between cells, racing across synaptic grids. The resultant modulations are a manifestation of life.[34]

A swimming, breathing fish moves through the water surrounded by an electric field the strength and polarity of which stream outward, ebb, and retract like the Northern Lights. The outer epithelia at the boundaries of the skin and gills have electric potentials and therefore are sources of electric current. When it breathes, a fish exposes the epithelial layers of its mouth and gills to the water, producing an electric signal. The strongest electric fields are concentrated around the gills and mouth, but also the anus, which is evidence that the alimentary tract—which connects the mouth and anus—is electrogenic (Fig. 33).[35] When a catfish opens its mouth, an electric field emanates from the mouth and gill slits and comes together just behind the anus.[36] Bruises or lesions also generate noticeably more electricity than undamaged portions of the body.[37]

Many—perhaps all—siluriform catfishes possess electroreceptors in the skin (Fig. 34).[38] These are also called pit organs, small pit organs, and teleost ampullary organs. They take the form of microscopic ampullary

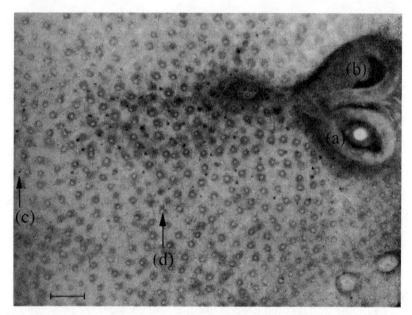

FIG. 34 Photograph of the skin of the brown bullhead (*Ictalurus nebulosus*): (a) base of barbel (cut off), (b) opening of nasal sac, (c) small pit organ, (d) taste bud. Scale bar = 1 centimeter. Source: Peters et al. (1974).

organs connected to ampullary canals barely longer than the thickness of the skin (Fig. 35). They sometimes are visible to the unaided eye as tiny dots. The canals, which are part of the lateral line system, are filled with fluid or a gelatinous substance and transmit electric stimuli received at the skin to appropriate subdermal locations where a neurotransmitter takes over, initiating a response.[39] These structures allow catfishes to passively detect the electric fields of other organisms in the same manner as sharks and rays.[40]

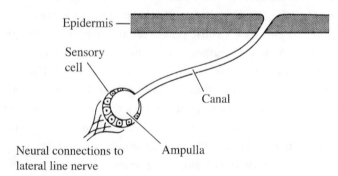

FIG. 35 Diagrammatic cross section through a specialized (ampullary) lateral line organ (sensory hairs, or kinocilia, not shown). Source: Spotte (1992) after Szabo (1974).

Whether such signals emanating from a big fish are perceptible to a hungry candiru is conjectural, but some catfishes have electroreceptors all over their bodies (Fig. 36), and candirus also appear to have them (Fig. 37). To suggest that candirus might detect prey from a distance great enough to be useful piles on additional conjecture, and whether any such signals are within a candiru's range of detectable frequencies adds still another element of uncertainty. We can say only that a hungry candiru *might* be capable of detecting its prey's electric field.

Location \ Fish	Small pits / cm²		
	1	2	3
	114	137	54
	53	56	23
	35* / 42	28* / 28	101* / 33
	?	125	24
Total	2500	?	4000

FIG. 36 Number of small pit organs at specific locations (black) in the brown bullhead (*Ictalurus nebulosus*). * = left side. Counts are from three fish. Source: Peters et al. (1974).

It's a very dark night, but since when does a light bulb need light to make it work? As you drift along, tasting and smelling the water, you're

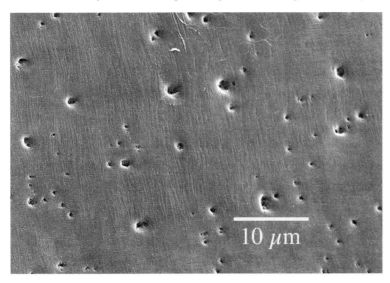

FIG. 37 Scanning electron photomicrograph of skin on the posterior dorsal surface of the head of a candiru (*Vandellia* cf. *plazai*). Some of these pores are probably openings into canals of small pit organs. μm = micrometers. Source: Stephen Spotte.

also poised to receive electric signals. Some of these are uniform fields emanating from the environment, but being a candiru your interest is in electric fields of biological origin and usually labeled "love," "lunch," or something equally utilitarian.

The discerning catfish, upon receiving one of these impulses, deciphers the message and makes a decision. For example, prey organisms typically betray themselves as dipole electric fields, specifically direct current (DC), but they can also be portrayed as low-frequency fields. Once inside the prey's electric field, the predator's response depends on interpreting differences in electric potential across its own skin.[41] Electric potential is the sum of electric charges between two points, which in this situation appears almost simultaneously at the electroreceptor organs. Stimulation of the electroreceptors requires an adequate voltage gradient across them.[42] Human beings, of course, lack electroreceptors comparable with those of catfishes.[43] The only analogy I can think of is to be in contact with a source of electricity low enough that you feel only a slight tingling.[44] A catfish sensing lunch or love must feel a buzz too, after its own fashion, although not being catfishes we can't possibly anticipate the sensation.

A catfish's electroreceptor system is enhanced by the high resistivity of its skin. Being resistive to electricity is the same as being a poor conductor or a good insulator. It allows detection of nearly the full potential differences.[45]

Sharks and rays are the champions of electroreception, but nearly all of them live in saline waters. High concentrations of ions, or the dissolved components of salts, greatly increase the electric conductivity of water.[46] Pure water is a very poor conductor of electricity because it lacks calcium, sodium, chloride, and other ions. Freshwater therefore has greater resistivity than seawater, and the rivers and streams of tropical South American lowlands, with their extremely low ionic concentrations, are among the most resistive natural waters in the world. Not surprisingly, the skin resistance of most freshwater fishes is comparatively greater than in sharks and rays. It forms a high-impedance barrier between the high-ionic tissues underneath and the low-ionic water outside.[47] Similarly, dry human skin has high resistivity, which can be lowered radically by a little sweat and its complement of ions. If you insist in sticking your finger into an empty lamp socket, at least wipe off the sweat first.

I'm uncertain of the form taken by "potential" love, although in engineering terms we might define it as the sum of electric potentials at the skin of the recipient. Noticeable differences no doubt exist among species and even among individuals of a single species, but we understand very little about how it works. Maybe such abstractions hold true only for poets and catfishes. We know that passive reception is ineffective unless the prey is quite close, ordinarily within a distance perhaps equal to the predator's body length,[48] and the same would also be true of prospective mates.[49] Unless your electric fields overlap, there can be no spark of love.

Whether electroreception is involved in candiru reproduction is unknown, although other aquatic animals use it. The round stingray (*Urolophus halleri*) lives on sandy bottoms and spends much of its life buried underneath the sand. During the mating season, males cruise just above the bottom using electroreception to search for buried females. Upon finding one, a male checks her out by administering a thorough scan, sight unseen. If he likes her electric signals, he digs her up and mates with her.[50]

Electroreception would seem more useful to a conventional trichomycterid catfish—one that feeds on insects—than to a bloodsucking candiru. Invertebrates generate weak electric fields.[51] An insectivorous trichomycterid cruising the bottom might use electroreception to detect an aquatic insect attached to a rock or hiding under a soggy leaf.

What about candirus? Because no one has ever followed a candiru around underwater at night and observed its behavior, we can only guess how it uses electroreception to find prey—if indeed it uses this sense at all. A candiru could station itself where large prey fishes are likely to swim past. Other catfishes constitute the principal prey. Most are nocturnal, becoming active at twilight or after dark. Alternatively, a candiru might go cruising and eventually bump into its prey. Either situation is possible, but the first is more probable. We can be fairly certain that candirus are most susceptible to capture at night. In Chapter 9, I describe how Paulo Petry and I, wading in the Cachoeira do Travessão of the Rio Jauaperi, Brazil, consistently caught candirus at night but never during the day. Paulo, Jansen Zuanon, and I later seined candirus from the Rio Solimões at midday (Chapter 10), but they were probably buried in the sand. Haseman writes:[52]

> The fishes belonging to the genus *Vandellia*, as well as to other genera of the *Pygidiidae* [*sic*], lie buried in sand-bars, and I have often seen them when disturbed rise like a flash and bury themselves again in an instant, leaving a small round hole where they re-entered the sand.

From what we know—or rather suspect we know—candirus stay quietly hidden during the day, emerging at night to feed and look for mates.

You were drifting down the river when last I checked, smelling and tasting the great wide world, receiving sounds and dragging around your acoustic shadow, buzzing and being buzzed electrically by all manner of living things. Suddenly, there's a pulse recognizable as food. It's the electric field of a big catfish. Every time this monster breathes you receive a blast of DC current. The big guy must be close because a candiru's receptive range is limited to probably no more than a few centimeters. What I haven't mentioned is that you've been trailing him for some time, swimming behind in his wake, tasting and smelling him as he roots around in the mud using his own electroreceptors to find food. You tasted him long before detecting him electrically, but once nearby his electric fields are huge.[53]

He's headed into the current. You swim up from behind, sensing the strong pulse around his anus, but that's not the objective so you keep moving along his flank. The pulse of DC current is evident each time his gill covers open. Easy timing. You make a final dash and slip inside when he breathes. Latching onto a gill filament is easy. It's probably safe to assume that more than one mechanism led you here, and vision might have been one of them.[54]

Notice I've placed vision at the end, not because it's unimportant but because I can't imagine how useful it could be to a catfish active mainly at night in waters either stained the color of dark tea or having the transparency of *café au lait*. Then again, not being a candiru, what do I know? I can't see images clearly underwater unless I wear a dive mask, which retains a permanent air space between the water and my corneas. Without this space everything is badly out of focus: the human cornea has a refractive index nearly identical to that of water, causing a loss in optical power of about 80 percent.[55] Even the most visually challenged candiru is better adapted than this. The large eyes of some candirus offer indirect evidence of adequate vision: large eyes perform more effectively than small eyes simply because the lenses are bigger.[56]

Light entering water is reflected, refracted, scattered, and absorbed, phenomena that reduce its intensity, alter its spectral qualities, and, overall, exert a negative effect on vision. To obtain clear images a fish's eye must gather sufficient light from the environment to focus on the retina then resolve that light into images.[57] However, images can't be formed until the light has been refracted sequentially through the cornea, aqueous humor, and finally the lens. To overcome the handicap of image resolution that plagues the human eye underwater, fishes have evolved spherical lenses of considerable refractive power. This helps them surmount the refraction problem, but others just as formidable remain.

Light entering water is both absorbed and scattered, but scattered light has the greater effect on vision.[58] The scattering of light, caused mainly by its reflection off suspended particles, reduces the contrast of images on the retina; absorption of light by dissolved and particulate matter reduces their brightness.[59] The English biologist John N. Lythgoe compared the effect of scattered light underwater to looking through fog.[60] This "underwater fog," or veiling light, which reduces contrast and therefore visibility, limits daylight vision more than any other factor.

Water absorbs the different wavelengths of light selectively. The purest waters (those containing the fewest contaminants) absorb red light most strongly. They appear blue under daylight illumination because the water molecules themselves scatter blue light. Ordinarily, natural waters contain enough impurities to affect the properties of light, tending to redden the environment. Gilvin (also called yellow substance, humus, and *Gelbstoffe* in German) is a pigmented suite of compounds resulting from plant decay. It absorbs light strongest in the blue region of the spectrum and weakest in the red end. The tea-colored blackwater streams of lowland South America are characterized by pigmented organic compounds, mainly humic and fulvic acids.[61] Although they look black, their spectral composition is dominated by red, and perhaps we should call them red-water streams instead. Suspended particles from surface runoff and erosion, such as sand and silt, also influence the color of water, but mainly through the scattering of light rather than its absorption.

The vertebrate eye contains rods and cones. These photoreceptor cells are, respectively, low-light and high-light receptors. Cones make possible the discrimination of specific wavelengths of light, which is synonymous with color vision; the effect is to greatly enhance contrast perception. Many fishes inhabiting deep or murky waters, or that are active at night, have only rod-mediated vision. Compared with cones, rods need fewer photons to "excite" them into producing a neural signal and therefore make optimal use of the little light available. This is accomplished at the expense of contrast perception and, therefore, visual acuity.

Visual acuity underwater depends on two relative characteristics of the photoreceptor cells: their adeptness at gathering photons from the surrounding dimness, and their capacity to distinguish objects against the diffuse background illumination known as the background spacelight. These characteristics define, respectively, the limits of photosensitivity (the capacity to see in dim light) and contrast perception (the capacity to form retinal images).

Vision is restricted in dim light because fewer photons are available to be captured. Each white dot in Fig. 38 represents a captured photon. In the top illustration, no image is possible because the photons are scattered into the eye by suspended particles in the water. The presence of particulate matter between the object and the eye enhances the effect of veiling light, preventing an image from taking form.[62]

The clarity with which an object can be detected underwater depends on its radiance, or degree of contrast against the background spacelight. It also depends on whether the object is moving or stationary. The page on which you read these words is motionless. Human thoughts transferred to printed words don't move, but information is still transmitted. In the animal world, movement is often a prerequisite to action, important in the detection of prey by predators and vice versa.[63]

If the veiling light between object and observer simply attenuated, or fell off, the object would get darker with increasing distance, but contrast would not change and the image would appear the same. In fact, the veiling light causes a loss of contrast with increasing distance as the radiance of the object begins to equal that of the background spacelight (Fig. 39).[64]

In fishes having both rods and cones, visual acuity and perhaps color vision might be the equal of ours. I say this with a caveat: in biology, light is defined as that portion of the optical spectrum that imparts visual sensation *in human beings*. We timidly extend this definition to nonhuman animals without real evidence of its accuracy. Despite similarities in eye anatomy, we can't know what a fish actually sees, or whether it perceives color.[65]

What to make of all this? We can assuredly state that fishes, as a group, possess the capacity to see very well in what are typically low-light photic environments. I can understand how vision might be important to fishes living in the clear waters of a coral sea, but what about those that inhabit the muddy Rio Amazonas or the tea-colored Rio Negro? In clear oceanic waters an object might conceivably be visible 100 meters away, compared with only a few centimeters in the Amazon.

Many freshwater fishes can see far into the red end of the spectrum, some species even into the infrared, which is invisible to humans. To date, no marine species is known to possess infrared vision. Being able to see red and infrared is naturally a great advantage in blackwater streams where most of the transmitted light is red. In fact, most light absorbance in these waters occurs in the blue region of the spectrum, and transparency to red light explains the red coloration.[66] We don't know what a candiru's world

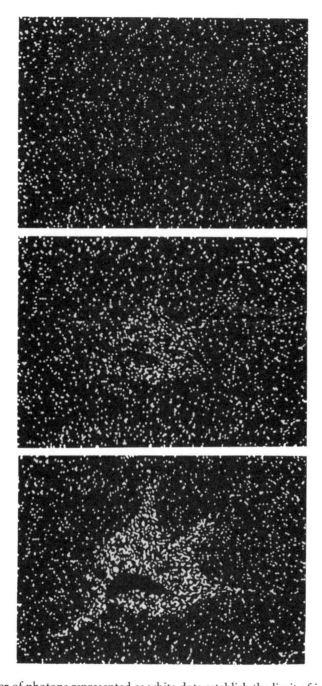

FIG. 38 Number of photons represented as white dots establish the limit of information contained in an image. The shark is swimming towards the observer. *Top:* The shark is invisible because the image-forming light it reflects is absorbed by the water and only the background spacelight is visible. *Middle:* Veiling light is reduced because the thickness of the water between the shark and observer is also reduced. *Bottom:* The shark is so close that the little image-forming light has been lost, and the amount of veiling light is negligible. Brightness of the light is proportional to the number of photons. Brightness of the background spacelight stays constant; what changes is the brightness of the image. Source: Lythgoe (1988).

looks like, but to those living in the Rio Negro and other blackwater streams it probably looks red, as if they were wearing rose-colored glasses.

At least one observer claims that the reflective eyes of candirus might be used in communication, although he never tested his assertion. The German naturalist Karl Heinz Lüling writes:[67]

> I could keep several of the *Vandellia* catfish, which I caught, in small aquariums with mud on the bottom, for up to three days. The little animals dug themselves in close to the surface [of the mud], in a way that the top parts of their eyeballs, shining strongly from guanim cilium, were clearly visible on the surface of the mud. When the fish swam around rapidly, their eyeballs flashed. They would probably be able to notice these characteristic "luminous traces" even in cloudy waters and so — especially at spawning time — stay in contact with each other. [E. Muschaweck and S. Spotte, transl.]

When last seen, you were dining on the gill filaments of a big catfish, but back up a minute. I see a little starlight, very little, maybe sufficient to cough up a few photons. Adequate to form a visual image on your retinas? Perhaps. They come streaming through the surface, running a gauntlet of suspended particles (which reflect them) and dissolved organic molecules (which absorb them). Not many reach the bottom where you hang out.

We can simplify here and combine dinner and a mate. (It's all food.) Veiling light, that "underwater fog" between your eye and the object of your desire, isn't an interfering factor in the absence of light. We could say the same for background spacelight, which illuminates the background behind the object. Put plainly, no light is no light. If you happen to be in the muddy Amazon with its uncountable trillions of suspended particles all reflecting and absorbing light, then scatter is a big problem. The Scots biologist W. R. A. Muntz calculated that vision would be impossible below 2.3 meters in the Rio Solimões, a whitewater affluent of the Rio Amazonas.[68]

If you're moseying down the Rio Negro, which is clearer than the Amazon but more highly pigmented, absorption might be the principal interfering factor. Fortunately, you probably have lenses that let you see red. Assuming enough photons could be mustered, contrast perception would be adequate to form an image. It's tough to say. Your eyes are fully formed and functional. I can tell by examining them. No doubt they're used to see something. As for me, I can't see much at all in your world even while wearing a dive mask.

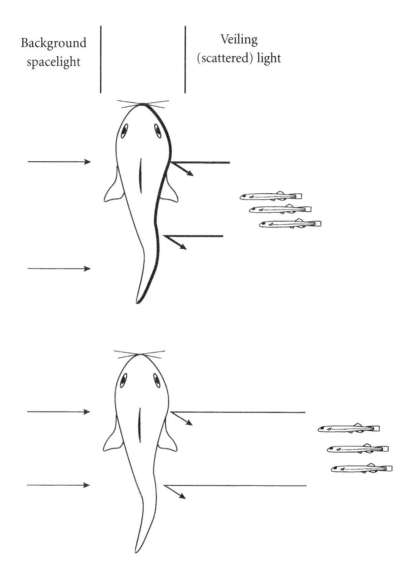

FIG. 39   Candirus approaching prey. The scene and conclusions are hypothetical. *Top:* Up close, the prey looks brighter to the candirus because the thickness of the veiling light, now reduced, exceeds the radiance of the background spacelight. *Bottom:* From a distance, veiling light causes a loss of contrast as the radiance of the object begins to equal that of the background spacelight. Source: Stephen Spotte.

Ah, it is the fault of our science that it wants to explain all; and if it explain not, then it says there is nothing to explain.

—Bram Stoker, *Dracula*[1]

6.

A Bloodsucking Life

Jonathan Harker was a young attorney from London who found himself imprisoned in Count Dracula's castle deep in the Transylvanian wilderness. The castle was a very strange place, but nothing about it was stranger than the proprietor, among whose many peculiarities was his habit of leaving the castle only after sunset. The regularity of the Count's nocturnal travels puzzled Harker less than his method of egress. Not content to use the front door, the Count left through his window high above the ground. Moving head-down, toes and fingers gripping slight crevices among the stones of the castle wall, he scooted along with the speed of a harried lizard, his black cape billowing like wings. Harker didn't realize at the time that here was a vampire on its way to dinner.

Being a vampire of any kind is difficult, requiring special adaptations. A case can be made for Count Dracula's hands. Based on Harker's description, they seem particularly suited for scaling castle walls:[3]

> Hitherto I had noticed the backs of his hands as they lay on his knees in the firelight, and they seemed rather white and fine; but seeing them now close to me I could not but notice they were rather coarse—broad, with squat fingers. Strange to say, there were hairs in the centre of the palm. The nails were long and fine, and cut to a sharp point.

Candirus suck the blood of other fishes, and we could just as easily call them vampire fishes. In Chapter 3, I discussed the unusual shape and arrangement of vandelliine teeth, apparently an adaptation for gripping and puncturing gill tissue, and the notion that rapid ingestion of large volumes of blood might be enhanced by a buccal pump. I emphasized that both possibilities are conjectural.

A very real problem, one never before considered, is how candirus are able to digest blood. Without the right physiological adaptations, trying to live exclusively on blood and nothing else can be fatal. And what about bloodsucking from a philosophical perspective? Are vampires parasites or predators? These are the topics I take up here.

THE BLOODSUCKING PROBLEM

Blood is 80 percent water, but the remainder is almost pure protein, containing negligible concentrations of fats and carbohydrates. Thus a diet of blood presents the difficult physiological challenge of maintaining consistent internal water balance while quickly excreting excess nitrogen from the breakdown of protein before it can rise to toxic concentrations. If certain forms of nitrogen accumulate to critical levels in the brain of a fish or a human being, death follows quickly.

Blood and other proteins are composed of amino acids linked by peptides. Nitrogen is a basic constituent of amino acids. The digestion of fats and carbohydrates produces carbon dioxide and water as the only end products. The digestion of proteins and their component amino acids also yields carbon dioxide and water, in addition to nitrogen. Deamination is one process that occurs when amino acids are digested. During deamination, nitrogen as amino groups (NH_2) is separated from the rest of the amino acid molecule and either incorporated into the tissues in some other form or expelled into the environment. Ammonia (NH_3), the nitrogenous end product of deamination, is highly toxic to internal tissues and fatal if not flushed away promptly or converted to urea or uric acid, which are far less toxic.[3]

Animals excrete amino groups as ammonia, urea, uric acid, or some combination of these. Freshwater fishes expel excess nitrogen from the gills directly as ammonia.[4] The fact that fishes are immersed in water ordinarily makes this convenient. As a small, highly soluble molecule, ammonia diffuses quickly from blood to water through the extremely thin

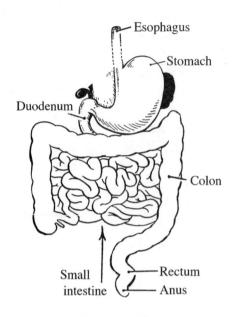

Esophagus

Stomach

Duodenum

Colon

Small
intestine

Rectum

Anus

FIG. 40   The human digestive system.
Modified from various sources.

gill tissues. Mammals are less fortunate. The ammonia produced by deamination must be transformed into urea, which is not only less toxic but conserves water. To dissolve and dispose of 1 gram of nitrogen as ammonia takes 300–500 milliliters of water; to flush away 1 gram of urea nitrogen takes only about 50 milliliters.[5] Birds and reptiles excrete excess nitrogen mainly as uric acid. Although fishes and mammals can excrete uric acid too, they do so in lesser quantities.

What we know about subsisting on a diet of blood comes from studying the anatomy and physiology of a vampire bat, *Desmodus rotundus*. In the more conventional mammalian digestive system food passes sequentially through the esophagus, stomach, small intestine, and large intestine, or colon (Fig. 40). Vampire bats lack a large intestine,[6] and at the end of the esophagus is a T-shaped junction leading to a tubular stomach on one side and a small intestine on the other (Fig. 41). By this unusual arrangement ingested blood first enters the intestine before overflowing into the stomach.[7] Instead of protein digestion, the principal function of a vampire bat's stomach is to rapidly remove water from the ingested blood. Augmenting this process is a rich network of blood vessels, and the stomach itself is the cecal type (i.e., a closed pouch).

Vampire bats are sometimes unable to get airborne after ingesting almost 50 percent of their body weight in blood.[8] A satiated bat's immediate problems are to lessen its weight so it can fly back to the roost and to rid itself of huge amounts of excess nitrogen, the consequence of having swallowed almost pure protein.

As a weight-reducing measure, water separated from the ingested blood is converted immediately to urine and excreted. To conquer the nitrogen overload problem, feeding vampire bats quickly convert the ammonia produced by deamination of blood protein to urea before it becomes fatal. (Terrestrial animals are unable to excrete ammonia directly, and converting it is their only choice.[9]) To then rid itself of the urea, a vampire bat begins urinating copiously within 2–3 minutes of the onset of feeding; the amount of urine discharged is proportional to the volume of blood consumed.[10] Despite blood's high protein composition, no protein appears in the urine.[11] Urine flow peaks about 10 minutes after cessation of feeding, then declines to a low after 6 hours.[12] In the experiments of the American zoologists William N. McFarland and William A. Wimsatt, 62 percent of the total urine excreted over 7 hours was obtained in the first hour.

A vampire bat's own blood becomes more viscous as feeding proceeds

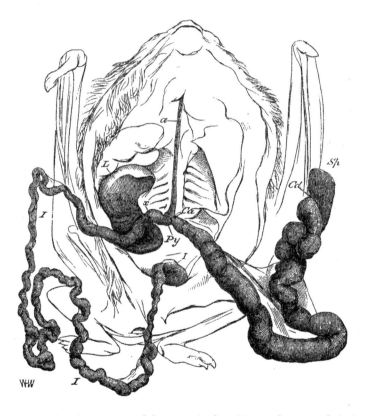

FIG. 41   Digestive system of the vampire bat (*Desmodus rotundus*). Symbols: œ = esophagus, Ca = start of cardiac sac of the stomach, Cd = fundic cecum, Py = pyloric division of stomach, Sp = spleen, L = liver (x is where bile duct opens into alimentary canal), I = intestine. Scale = approximately natural size. Source: Huxley (1865).

because of the explosive increase in plasma urea,[13] which the kidneys rapidly assimilate. Simultaneously, the urine, which starts out dilute, becomes more concentrated over time, thereby conserving internal water. The astonishing volume of urine required to flush out urea at the start of feeding dangerously depletes a vampire bat's reservoir of physiological water.[14] Several hours after most of the excess nitrogen has been dumped, the kidneys shift to a water conservation mode to protect the tissues from dehydration. Surprisingly, vampire bats drink no water at all, only blood, and low relative humidity in the air can cause them to lose critical amounts of tissue moisture, especially when flying. As McFarland and Wimsatt put it:[15]

> In a very real sense the vampire bat can be considered to inhabit a "desert" in the midst of the tropics. But the desert is delimited not by environmental aridity, but rather by the unusual nutrition and behavior of the vampire.

With this knowledge we can now turn to candirus, where problems of water conservation and nitrogen overload ought to be simpler.[16] Despite having no information on candiru digestion, we can examine certain facts and make some assumptions. Below are four reasons why, in my opinion, candirus are likely to be ordinary ammonia excreters despite their unusual diet.

First, ammonia excretion is typical of fishes. Nearly all freshwater species, including catfishes, excrete waste nitrogen predominately as ammonia.[17] This is advantageous because it takes less energy to produce ammonia than to produce urea.[18] Animals eat to acquire energy, and the source of animal energy is adenosine triphosphate, or ATP. Without ATP, muscle contraction is impossible, including involuntary movements that keep hearts pumping, fins moving, and vital organ functions stable and rhythmic. But ATP isn't free. After each muscle contraction the amount used up must be replenished, and its manufacture comes at a metabolic price. The production of urea is costly, requiring two units of ATP for each unit of urea produced.

Second, candirus breathe water exclusively. Certain air-breathing fishes emerge from water periodically and at such times excrete urea, although they excrete ammonia when fully submerged and breathing water.[19] Given a physiological "choice," ammonia is the preferred chemical form.

Third, candirus live in very soft waters of low pH. Under such conditions the diffusion of ammonia from the gills into the environment is enhanced rather than restricted.[20] Certain other fully aquatic fishes living in strongly alkaline freshwaters excrete only urea,[21] the result of not being able to expel ammonia into environments of high pH.

Fourth, the candiru has at its disposal abundant physiological water. As stated previously, compared with flushing urea from the tissues, flushing away the same amount of nitrogen as ammonia requires perhaps 10 times more water. Although freshwater fishes actually drink very little water they are nonetheless permeable, and the excess absorbed at the skin and other sites is voided by frequent urination.[22]

Both vampire bats and candirus feed rapidly and swell noticeably with blood.[23] Vampire bats produce a pungent, semi-liquid feces,[24] and very little of it.[25] As mentioned above, the fundic cecum contains a rich vascular network, evidently augmenting the rapid removal of water.[26] This structure is also remarkably distensible. In bats that have recently fed, the fundic cecum unfolds to accommodate large volumes of blood.[27] A feeding vampire bat is unlikely to suffer osmotic stress. Before feeding, the osmotic concentration of its blood averages about 325 milliosmoles per liter, only 8 percent hyperosmotic to beef blood (296–300 milliosmoles per liter).[28]

I've never seen captive candirus defecate, despite having watched them intermittently over several hours. The gut of vandelliines is a straight tube. The connective tissue of its walls is lined with loosely-spaced fibers indicating elasticity, perhaps to accommodate rapid expansion during feeding (Plate 6, top). The candiru could easily offset osmotic stress simply by imbibing water along with blood, although doing so would take up volume and dilute the blood's total nutrient value. In either case, osmotic stress is an unlikely problem: the candiru feeds on other freshwater fishes, and the ionic concentration of its own blood is no doubt similar to that of its prey, ordinarily between 200 and 300 milliosmoles per liter.[29] This range considerably exceeds the ionic concentration of soft freshwaters, which can be as low as 1 milliosmole per liter.[30]

PARASITE OR PREDATOR?

Gudger's book *The Candirú* bears the provocative subtitle, *The Only Vertebrate Parasite of Man*. Gudger believed this, and so do lots of people today. Gudger never actually presented a case for candirus being parasites of humankind, but simply assumed it was true. Here I address four questions: (1) What exactly is a parasite? (2) What distinctions can be drawn between parasitism and predation? (3) Is the candiru a parasite or a predator? (4) Can Gudger's statement be correct?

It isn't always obvious when one organism is parasitic on another or just along for the ride. Like beauty, parasitism's attributes are sometimes unique to the observer. Being nonspecific and overlapping, both beauty and parasitism are amenable to multiple definitions, none satisfactory to everyone. I shall start by comparing parasitism with other types of associations among plants and animals.

In his 1879 booklet *Die Erscheinung der Symbiose* the German botanist Heinrich Anton de Bary's defines symbiosis as[31] ". . . the living together of dissimilarly named organisms." In other words, organisms of different species. Note that de Bary says nothing about the biological "motives" for these associations or how any real or imagined "benefits" might be distributed. As emphasized by the American biologist Mary Beth Saffo,[32] "From the conceptual perspective of de Bary . . . symbiosis is an association defined by intimacy of interaction, rather than by the consequences of that interaction." Symbiosis, in other words, is just what de Bary says it is: the cohabitation of dissimilar organisms. Nothing else is stated or implied. From this pure beginning the term soon acquired added conditions of mutual beneficence. In this context, symbiosis became a synonym of mutualism, an intimate association between dissimilar organisms in which both parties benefit measurably.[33] "Mutualistic symbiosis" is a synonym.

The Belgian zoologist Pierre-Joseph van Beneden first used the term commensalism in 1876, invoking a relationship in which one dissimilarly named organism gained nutritional benefit from its partner without causing harm. They were, in a sense, at table together, and van Beneden made this clear by titling his book *Animal Parasites and Messmates*.[34] Some observers later allowed a certain amount of harm to creep into van Beneden's definition; others discarded the criterion of a feeding association and let the relationship stand as mere togetherness.

Parasitism has often been defined as a relationship between dissimilar organisms in which one lives at the expense of the other, deriving nutritional benefits from the blood or tissues of its associate. By this definition, foxes are parasitic on rabbits, an obvious fallacy. Some earlier observers decreed that the host must be severely injured, or even die, before parasitism could be invoked. In direct contradiction, others saw the parasite as deriving some benefit from its host, but not killing it. Still others visualized a sort of equilibrium assuring continuity of the association without harm to the host. Sometimes the demarcation separating parasitism from predation was the death of the aggrieved party. The English zoologist N. A. Croll writes:[35] "There are cases of parasites killing their hosts outright, notably among the leeches; it would perhaps be valid to consider such a leech as a predator rather than a parasite."

Modern biologists, by showing parasitism to be subtler, have shifted its meaning away from overt harm to the host. According to the English parasitologist Philip J. Whitfield:[36]

> A parasite is seen, in this new light, as an organism showing varying degrees of metabolic dependence on its host. This metabolic dependence can occur in the areas of nutritional materials, developmental stimuli or the control of maturation.

At the same time, parasites must evade a host's natural tendency to reject them.[37] As the English immunologist B. A. Askonas puts it:[38]

> [Parasites] have developed various means of evading immune control, which include antigen mimicry or uptake, anti-complementary activity, antigenic variation of the parasite's surface protein coat, replication within cells at an immunologically privileged site and/or induction of immuno-suppression in some infections that can affect responses to the invading organisms specifically, or depress most immune responses in others.

By modern definitions, the mammalian embryo is unquestionably parasitic. The English immunologist Peter B. Medawar likened pregnancy to a tissue transplant from a genetically different (allogeneic) individual and wondered how human beings could procreate.[39]

Population biologists provide still another perspective by considering parasitism in terms of host-parasite populations and ignoring interactions at the level of the individual. In fact, the principal effects of parasitism are believed by some to be felt in populations.[40] According to the English parasitologist H. D. Crofton:[41]

> The term *parasitism* refers to an ecological relationship between the populations of two different species of organism; one of these is referred to as the parasite and the other the host species. The features of this ecological relationship are: (*a*) the parasite is physiologically dependent on the host, (*b*) the infection process produces or tends to produce an overdispersed distribution of parasites within the host population;[42] (*c*) the parasite kills heavily infected hosts; (*d*) the parasite species has a higher reproductive potential than the host species.

Crofton's criteria set provocative standards. Candirus fail to meet the first, but easily qualify for the second. As to the third, a tethered fish observed by Machado and Sazima died about an hour after candirus began to feed on it. However:[43]

> One of the most notable characteristics observed in the feeding behavior of *B. bertonii* is the large number of individuals gathered in a same host fish, sometimes reaching thousands of individuals. This number is probably related to the host [having been] captive, unable to move and avoid the stream of blood-feeders. We do not believe that a healthy individual of an active species such as *P. fasciatum* [would] be attacked with such intensity in normal circumstances. It is probable that *B. bertonii*, other Vandelliinae, and some Stegophilinae notice when a potential host is wounded, captive, or otherwise at a disadvantage. . . . In normal circumstances the number of blood-feeders exploiting the same prey should be considerably smaller, although this is difficult to observe because of the habits of the fishes used as hosts. [S. Spotte, transl.]

As to Crofton's fourth criterion, no data exist on the reproductive biology of any species of candiru. Comparison with the other fishes on which they prey is impossible.

The special adaptations common in parasitism are rare in simple predator-prey relationships.[44] For many biologists, a key component must be the inevitable death of the prey.[45] Accordingly, if a rabbit pursued by a fox isn't killed and eaten, predation has not occurred. The prey, in other words, has "escaped" predation. Actually, it has escaped one of the last events in a *predation sequence*. As preludes to making a kill, the fox must first find and then pursue a rabbit successfully. In my view, nuances that together comprise the behavioral and ecological content of predation—its biological "intent"—define predator-prey associations, not the outcome between individuals. Just as modern definitions of parasitism allow the host to survive, so should this option be extended to the prey in any predator-prey relationship.

Questions about whether candirus are parasites of humankind or other species has a long history. Confusion on this point, upon leaking into the large puddle of doubt, seems simply to have stirred the mud around. Is the candiru ever a parasite? Certain characteristics of candirus are sometimes presented as evidence of adaptation to a parasitic life. Stated in a teleological format, these include: (1) fins set far back on body, presumably to be out of the way when darting underneath a gill cover; (2) small size and sinuous shape to assist entry; (3) capacity to produce copious skin mucus, possibly to act as a lubricant when entering small openings;[46] (4) soft skin to facilitate entry; (5) spines on the gill covers, supposedly for anchoring in place while feeding; and (6) astonishing agility. The unusual buccal apparatus might serve as a pump to ingest blood rapidly, an idea developed more fully in Chapter 3. Whether any of these constitutes a true adaptation for parasitism (or even bloodsucking) is conjectural.

Implied in most definitions of parasitism is the notion of permanent association through one or more parts of the life cycle, and here the candiru fails. If a parasite has no intention of sticking around, heroic measures like antigen mimicry are unnecessary. Crofton's conditions must be held in abeyance until we understand candiru population biology, although whether any species of candiru could meet them all seems doubtful.

Bloodsucking does not always define an obligate form of parasitism nor, in my view, is death the necessary culmination of a predator's attack. What seems important is the degree of intimacy of any such association. I consider candirus to be predators, not parasites, relying on their prey for nutrition and nothing else. Taken alone, Whitfield's allowance for dependence on "nutritional materials" makes a weak case for defining a parasite. So far as we know, candirus have no specialized metabolic, developmental, or maturational needs requiring association with another species of fish, nor must they evade a host's immune response. In my experience, candirus attack their prey, suck blood violently for a few seconds or minutes, and drop away. A candiru's life, except when feeding, is completely independent, no different in this respect from any other predator's.

Are vampire bats, leeches, ticks, and mosquitoes predators too?[47] I believe so, although the same can't be said of the diseases they carry. The mosquito-borne sporozoans known collectively as malaria are unquestionably parasitic.[48] Unique anatomical features ascribed to parasitism (e.g., the vampire bat's stomach, the mosquito's mouthparts, the candiru's buccal apparatus) can just as easily be the adaptations of predators. The same can be said of an anticlotting factor called draculin in vampire bat saliva that prolongs blood flow,[49] the sensitivity of mosquitoes to lactic acid and carbon dioxide emitted by their prey (see below), and certain spines thought to be used by candirus for gripping gill tissue (see Chapter 3). Such "adaptations" are merely observational categories devised by human beings to make nature seem logical. Like candirus, vampire bats and mosquitoes often attack prey nonselectively and live apart or sometimes temporarily on the external surfaces of their victims. Insects that depend on a diet of blood throughout their life cycle—for example, the bedbug (*Cimex lectularius*) and the conenose, or kissing bugs (*Triatoma* spp., *Paratriatoma* spp.)—contain symbiotic bacteria that presumably aid in digestion. Insects that feed on blood during only part of the life cycle lack these bacteria; in other words, the metabolic association is less intimate.[50] Included in this second group are lice, fleas, mosquitoes, and biting flies, all of which I think of as predators.

The candiru has always been considered a parasite. Even so, the nature of its parasitic association has been unclear. Lüling writes of candirus:[51]

> The whole group of these tiny, weakly pigmented small catfish is phylogenetically very conspicuous in its effort to penetrate into the abdominal and gill cavities of other large fish and in its urinophilic behavior: They are "occasional parasites and semi-parasites", but when they actively injure the abdominal walls, gill filaments, and the walls of urinary and sexual organs of mammals and humans, they are real parasitic vertebrates. [E. Muschaweck, transl.]

Lüling confuses the cetopsids with the vandelliines. The former sometimes burrow into the abdominal cavities of large fishes; the latter might be exclusively hematophagous. He considers both to be parasitic or "semi-parasitic," whatever that is.

Until early in the last century there was still some question as to whether vandelliines attack the gills of other fishes. It was Pellegrin who recognized the candirus as true bloodsuckers:[52] "The vandelliines therefore represent, in the silurids [*sic*], the final state of specialization, characterized by parasitism."

In the second edition of *Ichthyology*, Lagler and coauthors consider the candiru to be parasitic:[53] "One fish that can perhaps be regarded as a true parasite is the small candiru, a South American catfish of the family Trichomycteridae, which lives naturally on the gills of larger fishes and sucks blood from them." What constitutes a "true parasite" is not discussed, and neither is the implication that candirus are permanent occupants of the gill cavities of their "hosts." In *Fishes of the World*, Joseph S. Nelson includes the entire family Trichomycteridae in the "pencil catfishes or parasitic catfishes" because of the "habits" of certain members of the subfamilies Vandelliinae and Stegophilinae.[54]

According to Grzimek,[55] "Since the parasitic catfishes feed on the gill elements and probably the blood of the host as well, they can quite correctly be designated as parasites, living at the expense of another animal without killing that animal." True enough to satisfy the classic definition, but not modern ones stipulating metabolic dependency.

Writing about candirus in 1880, Günther concludes[56] "... there is no doubt that they live parasitically in the gill-cavity of larger fishes (*Platystoma*), but probably they enter these cavities only for places of safety, without drawing any nourishment from their hosts." Even in Günther's day, parasitism was understood to be an adaptation in which nourishment is indeed drawn from the host. Günther implies that candirus enter the gills of larger fishes because they offer convenient hiding places. The association, in other words, is harmless, detrimental to neither party.

Pellegrin disagreed, writing in 1909:[57]

> In the vandelliines, the development of opercular and interopercular spines, the specialization of the buccal apparatus of *Vandellia Wieneri*, are indications not of simple commensals, but of parasites, living certainly at the expense of their host. [S. Spotte, transl.]

Eigenmann quotes Pellegrin extensively[58] while leaving unstated his conclusion that the vandelliines—presumably all of them—feed exclusively on blood.[59] Eigenmann mentions *Stegophilus insidiosus* and the vandelliine *Branchioica bertoni* as inhabiting the gill cavities of larger fishes, but without suggesting whether they might be predatory or parasitic.[60] This is especially odd considering Pellegrin's belief that the teeth of vandelliines are specifically adapted to hematophagia whereas those of the stegophilines are not:[61]

> In closing it is noteworthy that the few voluminous teeth, in the shape of sharp hooks in the upper jaw, are peculiar to the genus *Vandellia*, that they are absent in the neighboring genera *Stegophilus* Reinhardt and *Acanthopoma* Lütken, where they are replaced by a strip of very numerous small, sharp teeth. [S. Spotte, transl.]

Like Lagler and coauthors, Curtis implies that candirus are permanent residents in the gills of larger fishes:[62]

> One tiny inhabitant of Brazilian fresh waters actually lives inside other fishes. It is so small that it can slip into the chamber which houses the gills, presumably doing this when the gill cover is open to let the water escape, and in this extraordinary spot it makes its home.

Burgess draws a peculiar distinction between the "candirus"—which purportedly are urinophilic, attack humans, and are known with certainty to attack the gills of larger fishes—and other "parasitic" species:[63]

Not as well known, but perhaps just as dangerous to their intended victims, are the scale-eaters *and the parasitic species* [emphasis added]. Among the latter are small species of no more than 50 mm that are said to live as parasites in the gill chambers of larger fishes, including larger catfishes, eating the gill filaments and drinking the blood and body juices of the host.

This statement also implies that "parasitic" forms live permanently within the host's gill chambers, which is unlikely. Of the known hematophagous species, all enter the gill chambers of their hosts to feed, leaving immediately when satiated. None, so far as we know, resides there.

Are candirus, as Gudger tells us, the only vertebrate parasites of humankind? Not according to modern criteria of parasitism. Furthermore, if candirus are parasites, so are vampire bats. Gudger never mentions them, but vampire bats often attack sleeping humans, and they are also vertebrates. Gudger uses "parasite" without ever defining it. To him, the penetration of a candiru into a human urethra seems sufficiently "parasitic."

The idea that candirus are parasites of human beings is especially attractive to physicians, two of whom I shall quote. In *Dangerous Aquatic Animals of the World*, Halstead says:[64]

Although there are many unknowns regarding the biology and medical aspects of the candirú problem, there appears to be sufficient scientific evidence to justify their reputation as a "human vertebrate parasite" in a rather general sense of the term.

And of course we have *The Candirú*. In his foreword to Gudger's little book, Warthin recounts how he became fascinated by tales of candirus told to him by Eigenmann. Warthin writes:[65] "This story of his made a great impression upon my pathological imagination [*sic*], for here was the *first and only vertebrate parasite of man* [Warthin's emphasis] known to parasitology."

Text continued on page 141.

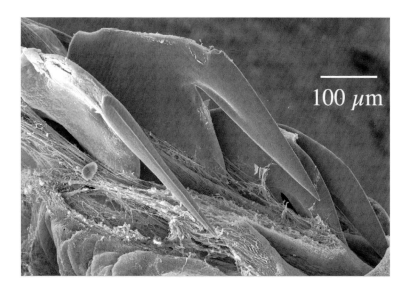

100 μm

PLATE 1   Left "claw-teeth" of a specimen of *Vandellia* cf. *plazai* (60.9 millimeters SL) from the Rio Jauaperi, Brazil, as seen through a scanning electron microscope. μm = micrometers. Source: Stephen Spotte.

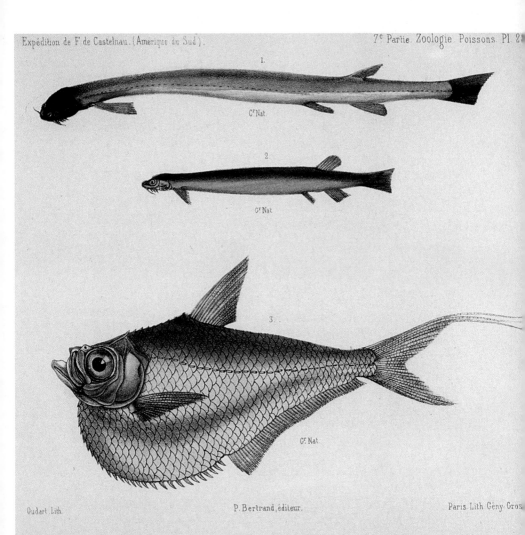

Plate 2 *Vandellia plazai* de Castelnau, 1855. Top figure (lateral view). Courtesy of the Smithsonian Institution. Source: de Castelnau (1855).

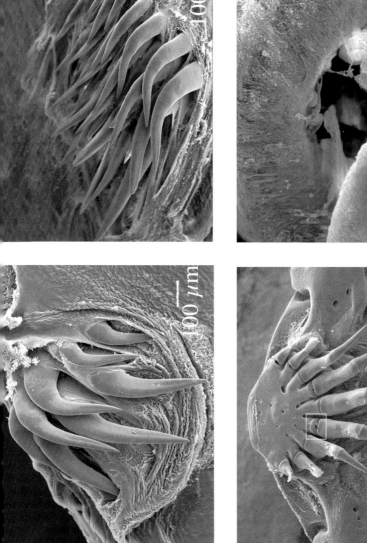

PLATE 3 Some hard structures of *Vandellia* cf. *plazaii* (60.9 millimeters SL) from the Rio Jauaperi, Brazil, as seen through a scanning electron microscope. *Top left*: Right interopercular spines. *Top right*: vomerine teeth. *Bottom left*: Right opercular spines. *Bottom right*: Moveable joint (enlargement of enclosed area of figure to the left). In life, the conduit contained nerves, blood vessels, and muscles, enabling movement. Same specimen as Plate 1. μm = micrometers. Source: Stephen Spotte.

1. Tetragonopterus Riveti Pellegrin.   3. Chaetostomus aequinoctialis Pellegrin.
2. Vandellia Wieneri Pellegrin.   4. Arges Vaillanti Regan.
5. _ Arges Regani Pellegrin.

PLATE 4 *Vandellia wieneri* Pellegrin, 1909. Lateral view (Illustration 2).
Courtesy of the Smithsonian Institution. Source: Pellegrin (1911).

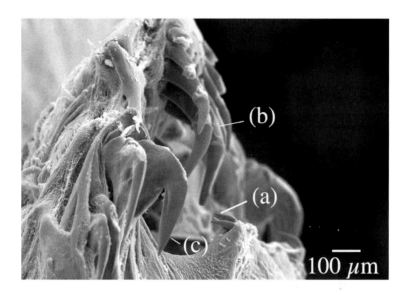

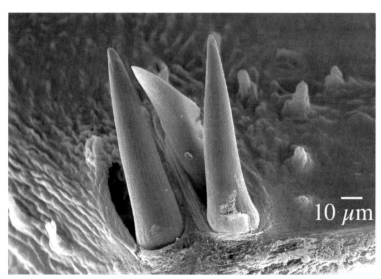

PLATE 5   *Top:* Scanning electron photomicrograph of the jaws of a candiru (*Vandellia* cf. *plazai*) showing (a) the three teeth on the right mandibular ramus, (b) vomerine teeth, and (c) "claw-teeth." *Bottom:* Enlargement of the same three teeth on the mandibular ramus. Same specimen as Plates 1 and 3. μm = micrometers. Source: Stephen Spotte.

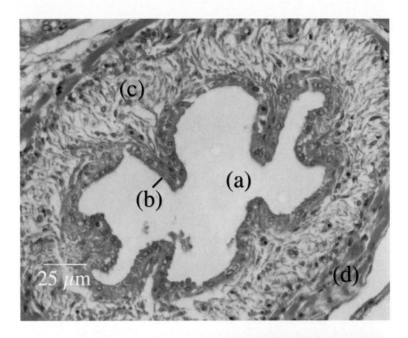

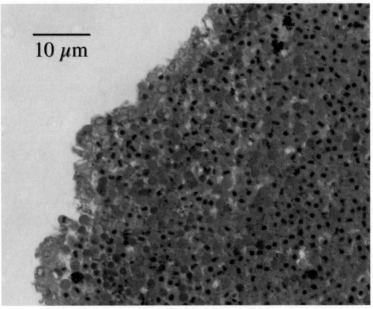

PLATE 6   Cross sections through the gut of two candirus (*Vandellia* cf. *plazai*) of similar size. *Top:* Empty gut of a candiru (57.1 millimeters SL). Note the folds extending into the lumen and the large amount of space among the fibers of connective tissue. (a) Lumen of gut, (b) epithelial cells, (c) connective tissue, (d) striated muscle. *Bottom:* Full gut of another candiru (57.2 millimeters SL). As the connective tissue (not shown) expands, the folds of epithelium flatten out. The gut is filled with nucleated red blood cells. μm = micrometers. Source: Stephen Spotte.

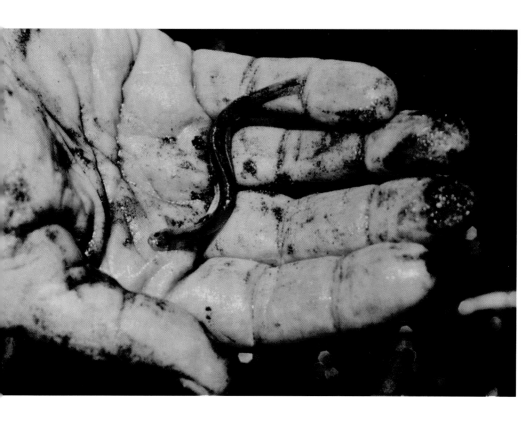

PLATE 7 A candiru (*Vandellia* cf. *plazai*) captured 6 November 1999 in the Rio Solimões near Manaus and photographed in the muddy hand of Jansen Zuanon. Source: Stephen Spotte.

PLATE 8   Ventral view of an unidentified candiru removed from the urethra of FBC, a 23-year-old man attacked while swimming in the Rio Amazonas, photographed beside Steve Spotte's left index finger. Ruler = 3 centimeters. The fish is 133.5 millimeters SL. Source: Stephen Spotte.

When you wet the bed first it is warm then it gets cold.

—James Joyce, *A Portrait of the Artist as a Young Man*[1]

7.

Embracing Urine

Certain rodents are adept at following old urine trails, and the candiru historian needs a similar skill, figuratively speaking. In the first chapter I took up the scent starting with von Martius, pointing out various landmarks in candiru history along the way. Here I discuss the putative attraction of candirus to urine and investigate certain lesser hypotheses about why they might attack humans. In assessing the reasons candirus could have for embracing urine—or for us to embrace it on their behalf—it becomes necessary to discuss what urine is.

Urinalysis didn't always take place in air-conditioned laboratories filled with humming equipment, and only recently have those who performed the tests worn white coats and sheathed their hands in plastic gloves. The Canadian medieval historian Ruth Harvey tells of a time when urinalysis was an art, and urine was best judged in a glass flask shaped like the human bladder. Held to the light, the physician studied a specimen's density. If he could see his finger joints pressed against the back of the flask the urine was "thin;" otherwise it was "thick." Gauging the color and noting any suspended matter were important too. Of the four elements, fire and air rose, water and earth sank. If the urine foamed, the patient's source of trouble was his head; if particles settled to the bottom of the flask, this indicated problems with the kidneys or gout in the feet. A conscientious physician might taste the specimen. Was it sweet? If so, his patient's internal fire had undercooked the sample, rendering it pale and thin, evidence of "the pissing evil," the malady we recognize today as diabetes.

When it comes to a discerning palate, even the most skilled medieval physician was no match for the humblest catfish. Writers on the candiru have suggested as much by describing how those who urinate in South American rivers place themselves in immediate danger despite an obvious and enormous dilution factor. However, the capacity to perceive trace concentrations of urine and any positive tropism towards it are separate phenomena. Stated differently, a substance that is neither interesting nor useful to a candiru falls into the category of "chemical noise" and most likely will be ignored. Perhaps urine, blood, and sweat, which share many chemical constituents, are linked as attractants. This intriguing possibility will now be discussed.

THE URINE-LOVING HYPOTHESIS

As previous chapters attest, many who have written about candirus are convinced of their attraction to mammalian urine, with blood a distant second. Belief in the urine-loving hypothesis is immensely popular for reasons not entirely clear. Perhaps we're titillated by the notion of a fish being lured to our delicate and very private genitalia. Maybe it's disgust at the thought of some exotic creature discovering extraordinary properties in our personal effluvia. Explorers from von Martius to our own time have been anxious to gain favor for their exploits. What better way than by announcing a remarkable new observation, even if it seems preposterous? As the American historian Robert Darnton tells us,[2] "Common sense itself is a social construction of reality, which varies from culture to culture." There you have it. A belief already embedded in the social order of certain South American Indians wormed its way into the intellectual ecosystem of eighteenth-century Europe and promptly faded into the background. Sheltered in this welcoming environment, evolutionary transformation from legend, and doubtful observation to basic truth, was both natural and rapid.

Keep in mind that everything about candiru attacks so far has been hearsay, including the factors inducing them. Women who are menstruating are thought to be in greater danger than women who aren't. By consensus, women are attacked more often than men, according to some because of their anatomy: women have an additional orifice, the vagina, which is also larger—and presumably more accessible—than the urethral or anal openings of both women and men. However, descriptions of attacks on men seem far more terrifying because of the threat of penectomy. (And because the reports have mostly been written by men instead of by women.)

Historically, the urine-loving hypothesis has assumed that candirus follow "urine trails" for the purpose of entering the mammalian urethra. What they do upon achieving this objective is less clear, although some writers are convinced the bladder is the ultimate destination. An inherent attraction to urine explains how candirus end up in the urethra, neatly linking cause and effect, or so it seems. Actually, the hypothesis has some crippling deficiencies.

The most obvious is lack of evidence that candirus find urine attractive. Hypotheses must be testable to fall within the purview of science. Although the urine-loving hypothesis qualifies, only three tests have ever been made, and those crudely. Most recently, Paulo Petry, Jansen Zuanon, and I performed an experiment in Brazil using human urine and other potential attractants that yielded completely negative results.[3] I describe this work in Chapters 9 and 10.

In a scientific experiment there must be, at minimum, two groups: a control group not exposed to the treatment, and a treated group that is. In our tests, the control group was given a tiny dose of plain water while the treated group received equal volumes of other substances, one being urine. Predictably, the behavior of the candirus used as controls did not change when a little water was emptied into their aquariums. However, urine added to aquariums containing the treated candirus elicited no response either. In other words, results from the test group were negative, or not different from the controls, forcing acceptance of the null hypothesis—the hypothesis of no difference. Do the results demonstrate that candirus are *not* attracted to urine? No. They show only that under the conditions of our experiments, human urine induced no visible change in the behavior of these candirus when compared with the behavior of the controls.

The next most recent attempt was Lüling's in 1965. In discussing a trip he made to the Peruvian Amazon and the lower Rio Ucayali, he offers the only direct evidence I found that candirus might be urinophilic. Unfortunately, he fails to mention which "caneros" his test fish might have been, and their ostensive attraction to urine is merely an offhand comment. Nonetheless, part of his report is worth quoting:[4]

> I am a little surprised that the two fishers, in this heat, are going into the water in what seem to me quite thick and close-fitting [bathing] trunks, and I turn to my companions. They try to explain, but I hardly

understand them in their broad, almost singing tongue, and hear only the word "canero" several times. Now I can understand the connection because I know that here in the clayey mud lives a very interesting, tiny fish that is so named. They are species of *Plectrochilus* and *Vandellia*, which belong to the Schmerlenwelsens. They are only a few centimeters long, narrow and bandlike, quite whitish because they are almost colorless except for some pigmented stripes. On the gill covers these creatures have a tiny area of pointed spines. These dwarf catfish (called "candiru" in Brazil) are supposedly attracted by traces of urine and so get, if even only occasionally, into the urinary organs of amphibious mammals, and, extremely rarely, into the urinary and sex organs of bathing people. This results in ugly secondary inflammations. So one of these species is accordingly named *Urinophilus diabolicus* . . . ingeniously proving what is called the "devilish lover of urine". In the wide Amazon there supposedly live Indian tribes who, during certain rites of passage, using strings of raffia, strongly bind together or leave untied the glans penis or vagina as a test of courage. One originally attributes this ritual to the fear of these urinophilic little catfishes. Therefore the fear of the fishers to go into the water wearing nothing, or only light, inadequate bathing trunks!

With tweezers I pick the tiny fish from the mud in the net and look at them in detail. Some are then preserved in alcohol; others go still alive into a separate small container. For 3–4 days I can keep the delicate dwarf fish in a small glass container with a little mud on the bottom, into which they immediately dig beneath the surface. When I put some urine into one side of the aquarium, two of them actually come out and swim around excitedly. [E. Muschaweck, transl.]

In an article published 4 years later, Lüling again mentions the attraction of this same group of fish to urine. He repeats much of his earlier story, but gives it a slightly different ending:[5]

> When I introduced a little urine with tweezers [*sic*] into one side of the aquarium, an increase in activity could be noted, but in the narrow aquarium it only led to aimless swimming around. [E. Muschaweck, transl.]

Urine would be difficult to pick up using tweezers (*Pinzette*). Lüling evidently meant *Pipette*. In this same publication he claims to know which species are urinophilic:[6]

> Most of the *Vandellia* and *Plectrochilus* species are very surely strongly urinophilic, whereas this is in no way certain about the "fish with the fine-sounding name" "*Urinophilus diabolicus*", as mentioned before. [E. Muschaweck, transl.]

He provides drawings of these fishes, but their identity is uncertain.

How credible is Lüling? Not very. He was unaware that the name

Urinophilus diabolicus had been changed to *Plectrochilus machadoi*, that *Vandellia sanguinea* had become *Plectrochilus sanguineus*. Do I think his candirus were actually attracted to urine? No. In my experience, captive candirus get up from the bottom and swim around for various reasons or no reason (at least none obvious to me). Okay, I admit it. I'm envious of Lüling because he can pick up urine with tweezers, but I still don't believe his results.

Allen's is the only other attempt to test the attractant qualities of urine. Writing in 1921, he states:[7]

> An effort was made by the expedition to confirm the widespread urinophilous reputation of the *candirú* (*carnero* of Peru). A Briggs' lead-in trap properly baited was frequently placed in rivers in the hope that it might demonstrate such a tropism. This was never successful.

Recounting his effort 21 years later in *Fishes of Western South America*, Allen says:[8]

> Eigenmann was greatly interested in establishing the truth as to the alleged tropism toward urine . . . . He was sufficiently convinced to attach the opprobrium [?] of it to a new genus of Vandelliinae, *Urinophilus*. At his suggestion I made repeated efforts to collect these minute fishes by means of their attraction to urine. This was done by saturating cotton and cheesecloth with urine and using it as bait in a glass-jar type of lead-in trap, with a small funnel opening. The experiment had only negative results.

Allen concludes that the case for urinotropism ". . . is very weak indeed."[9]

Having read Allen's 1921 article, Gudger contacted him:

> Seeking for details of this baiting, I wrote Professor Allen suggesting that to make an absolute test of the matter it would be necessary to have a reservoir of urine discharging into the trap a steady stream, and that this urine would have to flow out of the mouth of the trap with the current, and so attract fishes facing upstream. He kindly answered that: "I merely saturated with urine rather tightly rolled pledglets of cotton and cheesecloth. These were used for bait. It may not have been as good a method as a steadily feeding reservoir of urine, but I believe that it should have answered the purpose." Whether or not candirús are known to abound in the streams where the traps were set is not stated.

Gudger's last point is well taken: if Allen knew candirus were in the vicinity during his tests he never mentioned it. The Swiss zoologist Volker Mahnert indirectly notes Allen's futile attempts at capturing candirus using urine as bait:[10]

How do candirus find their human hosts? For a long time one spoke of an attraction by the presence of urine in the water, and it is only after experiences of an American researcher that one began to doubt the supposed urinophilic behavior of these fishes. But this problem has not been resolved in a satisfactory manner: the researcher in question had apparently not verified the presence of candirus in the river where he had immersed his trap containing a rag impregnated with urine. More likely, vandelliines are attracted by the perspiration of bathers, or by the presence of blood in the water. [S. Spotte, transl.]

What we have to date are three feeble efforts to test the urine-loving hypothesis. Thorough experiments are needed before any conclusions can be drawn. The candirus my colleagues and I tested were apathetic in the presence of fresh urine. In Lüling's attempts, the test subjects were doubtfully candirus. In Allen's efforts, candirus were doubtfully available.

I ought to mention still one other attempt, hardly an experiment. In 1998, while working along the Rio Tiputini, Ecuador, I baited two wire minnow traps with cotton balls soaked in my own urine and set them in the river at sunset. Results were negative. I was never able to determine if vandelliines were present in the area, and you can't catch a fish if it isn't there.[11]

The urine of domestic animals might also be an attractant, although we have scant evidence. The Rev. Burns, a missionary in Yurimaguas, Peru, told Vinton and Stickler this story:[12]

A neighbor of mine rushed a cow to his balsa or raft to embark it. The animal did not wish to go on to the craft. As it was urinating, it slipped into the river and came up bleeding profusely—decidedly from the urinary vent. I understand the cow died the same day from loss of blood.

No one knew how long the cow had been in the water, but it must have been quite a long time to die of blood loss from candiru attacks. I doubt this story. Why would the owner have abandoned his cow if the objective was to move it across the river?

The urine-loving hypothesis fails to explain how candirus become lodged in the ears, nose, and anus (assuming this happens) unless they are attracted initially by the urine, become excited, and enter the first orifice they find. Most of all, the conceptual basis for embracing urine as an attractant ignores a certain evolutionary cohesiveness. The act of swimming into a human orifice and becoming stuck there has negative survivorship because any candiru this foolish is soon dead. And after identifying a potential victim by its urine stream and attacking, what does a candiru gain in terms of nourishment? Urine is not listed among the major food groups except for bacteria and fungi, and it would make an improbably ascetic diet for a fish. To a candiru the prospects of dining on vaginal or urethral tissue, or even blood derived from abraded tissue, might be less satisfying if escape afterwards is impossible.

What did a starving urinophilic catfish do if no human beings were bathing nearby? Wait for an unwary tapir or dolphin, or maybe a caiman? Except for offhand mention of candirus attacking domestic animals, there have never been reports of "urinophilic" candirus attacking the urogenital openings of any species except humankind. Most naturalists or travelers have ignored this dilemma. If certain candirus aren't obligate urinotrophs, what are they?

Even among scientists, few have looked beyond the obvious problem of how candirus survive when there's no "urine trail" to follow and no ure-thra to enter. In his musings, Eigenmann apparently didn't consider that "urinophilic" candirus might also be gill parasites. He ignored the physio-logical dilemma of how a free-living aerobic creature like a trichomycterid catfish could enter the urethra of a larger animal, migrate to the bladder, and survive. And having arrived, did it stop requiring oxygen, and was urine its only food? Eigenmann never explained how a fish supposedly dependent on urine managed to persist as a species, except obliquely:[13]

> A very interesting subsidiary question is, whether, if Candirús are tropic to urine they do not also enter the urethrae of aquatic mammals and of large fishes. Further study may demonstrate that some species of Candirús have become parasitic in the bladders of large fishes and aquatic mammals.

Implied in the above passage is an imaginary equilibrium between "par-asitic" candirus and their "hosts," an arrangement that presumably did not extend to humans: in a later publication Eigenmann writes,[14] ". . . if not excised they [candirus] finally enter the bladder and cause death." All this, of course, was speculation. Eigenmann had not a scrap of evidence to sup-port his advocacy of either urinophilic behavior or internal parasitism.

The environment inside a mammalian bladder is no place for a fish, especially a freshwater fish. The physiological hazards are considerable. Oxygen is in doubtful supply, and the temperature of 37°C (human body temperature) exceeds by perhaps 7°C the temperature typical of open river waters in the lowlands of tropical South America. Add to this the high ionic strength of fluid inside the bladder, which contrasts with the very low ionic strength of South American tropical rivers and streams. Human urine is salty. At about 20°C its specific gravity is 1.005 to 1.030,[15] or comparable to that of offshore seawater, which at 20°C is about 1.025.[16] If candirus can survive in the mammalian bladder they should be able to survive in seawater, or in urine heated to human body temperature. A simple test using live candirus, a couple of volunteers with full bladders, a camp stove, a thermometer, a hydrometer, and a bucket would resolve the issue quickly.

What could Eigenmann have been thinking? Parasites either reproduce while inside a host or metamorphose into a different form in preparation for seeking another host. At least one parasitic worm sheds its eggs in human urine.[17] Did Eigenmann believe candirus did this too? He never mentions any role for human beings in the reproduction of urinophilic fishes.

Although the South American lowlands support several species of aquatic and semi-aquatic mammals, there probably aren't enough individuals to maintain a population of strictly urinophilic fishes. To my knowledge, no one has ever dissected a capybara, tapir, dolphin, or manatee and recovered candirus from its bladder. Except for dolphins, these other mammals are hunted and butchered for food throughout their range. Surely someone would have noticed a bladderful of little fish. The same is true of large fishes, which are routinely caught and butchered. If candirus invade these other animals too, why haven't they been reported?

Unlike Eigenmann, Santos wondered how, once inside their human victims, candirus managed to obtain oxygen. He questioned whether the victim could be abandoned at will and whether candirus were actually attracted by urine. He was curious to know if candirus feed on blood from the lesions they inflict or if the damage might simply be mechanical. Without suggesting parasitism, he also raises the question of whether candirus attack fully aquatic mammals:[18] "If candirus attack man and domestic animals and other 'warm-blooded' animals, will they not attack the *manatee* and *common dolphin* [Santos' emphasis] of Amazonia?"

I've commented on how hard it might be for organisms other than internal parasites to survive inside a mammalian bladder. Most general statements are refutable, and this one too comes with a caveat. In an 1811 article titled "Case in Which the Larvae of an Insect Were Voided in the Urine," the physician William Henry begins by describing his patient,[19] "Mr F. aged about 62, of a robust make, and plethoric habit . . ." Henry discusses the patient's urinary symptoms and discomfort, then says:

But the most remarkable circumstance in Mr F.'s case is, that, for five or six weeks past, there have been voided, along with his urine, the larvae of an insect, pretty exactly resembling the common maggot. They are not only alive but vivacious; and besides those which are entire, the heads and bodies of several others may be observed, detached from each other. Of the entire insects, he has frequently discharged three or four at once; and they appear in the urine . . .

The little creatures were turned over to a local naturalist who pronounced them "coleopterous larvae;" in other words, the larvae of a beetle, perhaps *Curculio nucum*. Henry was an Englishman, and I presume Mr. F. was too.[20] The nationality of his beetles is uncertain.[21]

THE MUDDLED MENU HYPOTHESIS

I'm bothered by why candirus are said to find urine so compelling when they make their living sucking blood. Suppose a component of urine is the same substance given off by the large fishes on which candirus prey, and further suppose that this substance is a feeding stimulus. Then penetration into a mammalian urethra is *not* a candiru's final objective, and if urine is indeed an attractant this is not by revealing cues to the mammalian urethra or bladder but because one or more of its constituents triggers an ancestral memory of something else. Such a substance (or substances), if sensed through taste or smell, leads me to suspect that human urine might have factors in common with the exudates of large catfishes. Stated differently, a candiru might follow a "trail" of something specific in human urine, a physiological signal given off by its natural prey.

Ammonia is a likely candidate. Fishes excrete the majority of waste nitrogen directly as ammonia. In contrast, humans excrete very little ammonia in urine, and the amount produced in the liver from amino acid metabolism is converted to urea, which is far less toxic. In air, ammonia at concentrations of a few parts per billion attracts bloodsucking insects that prey on humans, including the conenose, or kissing bug,[22] horsefly (*Hybomitra lasiophtalma*),[23] and human body louse (*Pediculus humanus*).[24] Human breath contains ammonia at 120–3170 parts per billion, far above the detection limits of these predators.[25]

Human urine also contains inorganic ions that vary in amount by how much we have sweated, drunk, or lost in the feces. Of the cations (positively charged ions), sodium, potassium, calcium, and magnesium account for 99 percent.[26] I mentioned in Chapter 1 a letter to Gudger from

E. C. Starks. Included is an unusual observation noted by Starks in the context of his conversation with Charles C. Ammerman, the naval surgeon assigned to the Rio Madeira from 1910–1911:[27]

> Dr. Ammerman then said that it was the belief on the river that the fish entered the urethra or vagina only when urine was passed while in the water. Prof. Starks wrote me that: "He said that if one urinated into the water, these fishes would come to the top and act as if crazy for the urine, the salt water."

We don't know if Ammerman's "candirus" were the same as those he excised from victims along the river. The fish he observed could have been vandelliines, but more likely were cetopsids. Candirus are less conspicuous. Some of the literature I found on cetopsids suggests an affinity for blood.[28] Like urine, blood is salty. A sudden influx of inorganic ions (dissociated "salts") might excite cetopsids and perhaps even candirus only because some of the same compounds occur in blood (assuming blood is an attractant).

The sum of inorganic ions plus urea and creatinine account for 70–90 percent of the density and total solid content of normal human urine.[29] If urea and creatinine are disregarded, organic acids (uric, hippuric, and citric acids) account for 33–50 percent of the organic fraction; most of the rest consists of low-molecular weight substances.[30]

Aside from water, urea is the principal constituent in human urine. Its origin is the blood, which obviously contains urea too. Small molecules (i.e., those of low molecular weight) are usually the most biologically active, and urea stands out as a possible attractant. Except for albumin, the urine of a healthy person is relatively free of proteins.[31] Those present bear a strong similarity to blood proteins, although their proportions are different.[32] The exception is again albumin, which exists in blood and urine at similar concentrations.[33] Albumin is the smallest of the simple proteins in blood and very stable, and its form in urine is identical. Either albumin or creatinine could possibly attract candirus.

Eigenmann and Allen suggest that the "warmth" of urine might be the defining signal.[34] Certainly the higher temperature of fresh urine compared with that of the surrounding water might signal a mammal in the vicinity, but whether candirus can make use of such a stimulus has not been shown. The urine of large reptiles and prey fishes would be nearly the same temperature as the environment.

Amino acids are confirmed attractants. The channel catfish of North American freshwaters is sensitive to incredibly small concentrations of amino and bile acids in the environment.[35] Threshold levels of detection for some amino acids are within the range of 10^{-11}–10^{-9} molar,[36] making the taste and olfactory cells of the channel catfish among the most discerning on Earth, at least among vertebrates. Although the kidney reabsorbs most of the urinary amino acids, trace concentrations are still excreted in the urine. We can assume that taste and smell are important to trichomycterid catfishes, but how important has not been tested.

Blood and urine are linked in other ways. Urine contains the waste products of cellular metabolism. In the act of urination, we also lose water. If we happen to be dehydrated, the water necessary to keep proper fluid balance is derived from the plasma. As mentioned, most useful substances (e.g., glucose, amino acids) are reabsorbed in the kidney and seldom appear in substantial concentrations in urine. Several large molecules are common to both blood and urine, although at least two-thirds of those in urine with a molecular weight greater than 30,000 have no known counterpart in blood.[37]

What about blood itself as an attractant? Eigenmann had been eager to confirm the urine-loving hypothesis, and in *Fishes of Western South America* Eigenmann and Allen summarize what was known or suspected about candiru attacks:[38] "That it [the candiru] is strongly tropic to flesh or blood has been demonstrated." Actually, this behavior has been demonstrated in the cetopsids, as mentioned above, but rarely in the vandelliines. An event that occurred in the Rio Beni basin is described in a letter to Gudger from "Mr. Pearson" (presumably W. E. Pearson, one of Eigenmann's students):[39]

> A single specimen of *Urinophilus erythrurus* was captured one evening as I was using fresh meat to attract fish that might be near the river's edge. The meat was permitted to float down stream a short distance and there was picked up in a seine. The fish had fastened itself into the flesh by means of the retrorse hooks on its operculum.

Eigenmann and Allen acknowledge this event, then add:[40] "Marcoy described a similar episode in which a turtle shell with the meat cut away was both bait and trap for swarms of *carnero*." Marcoy's "carneros" (Figs. 6 and 7, Chapter 1) were obviously cetopsids. Eigenmann and

Allen correctly recognize them as a such, but somehow confuse them with the species that attack human urogenital openings. They also mention a vandelliine captured by Allen while it was feeding in the abdominal cavity of a large catfish. Myers, in his 1927 publication, named the fish *Urinophilus diabolicus* (now *Plectrochilus machadoi*) and states in his description:[41]

> Dr. Allen found this specimen (called "Carnero" in Peru) halfway buried in the belly of a large river catfish, "Doncella" (*Pseudoplatystoma*). It had burrowed directly through the body-wall and was distended with blood.

The circumstances imply that at least one species of candiru is not an obligate gill predator. As further evidence, five fish captured in 1958 and identified as *Vandellia plazai* were[42] ". . . taken from [a] hook wound in a catfish (*Brachyplatystoma*)." Whether blood attracted them is unknown.

More compelling are the stories of Vinton and Stickler, published in 1941. They fished for candirus in the Rio Huallaga at Yurimaguas:[43]

> Upon learning that the carneros could be caught by using a large piece of bloody meat, we spent two long afternoons fishing for them. The first time we used a cow's lung, which we repeatedly sopped in blood, and captured two nice specimens. . .
> When the slithery carneros found the bloody meat, the dip net was not necessary to capture them for they writhed about and literally wormed their way into the flesh. When the lung was lifted from the

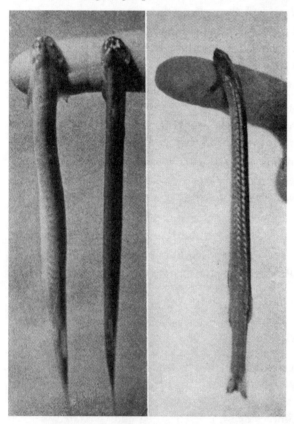

FIG. 42   Specimens identified as *Vandellia plazai* de Castelnau, 1855 holding on by their odontodes. Note the forked tail of the specimen on the right, which is characteristic of *V. wieneri*. Source: Vinton and Stickler (1941).

water they clung to it with their spines and were removed only with some difficulty. In the same way they clung to the finger of their captor . . . . These specimens have since been identified at the American Museum of Natural History by Mr. John S. Robas as *Vandellia plaizae* [*sic*], one of the specimens [*sic*] known to attack man. . .

The little fish are extremely bloodthirsty. Even after the lung was lifted from the water, the vicious little creatures continued to crawl about the bloody surface biting and chewing as they went. One of the specimens found an opening in the lung and almost disappeared by rapidly wriggling its way inside. When an attempt was made to pick up the live specimens, their instant reaction was to turn and bite the offending fingers. The bite of these fish was like the rasping of a coarse file . . . and, like a file, would draw blood if applied too often in the same spot.

The authors' photographs are reproduced here as Fig. 42. The fish is clearly a vandelliine, and it seems to have been attracted to blood in the water.

Human sweat has received only token recognition in the candiru literature. In the previous section I quoted Mahnert, who suggests that sweat might be a more effective attractant than urine. Mahnert gives no reasons for this assertion, but his idea has merit.

As derivatives of the plasma, urine and sweat contain many of the same substances, including high concentrations of sodium and chloride and lesser amounts of potassium, calcium, and magnesium.[44] Two other prominent compounds in sweat are ammonia and urea. Sweat produced by the ocarina glands contains 0.7–25 millimoles per liter (12–425 milligrams per liter) of ammonia and 3.9–67.7 millimoles per liter (235–4,000 milligrams per liter) of urea.[45] The urea is quickly converted to ammonia by resident bacteria on the skin. These are numerous and varied.[46] Human sweat also contains considerable amounts of lactic acid (27–37 millimoles per liter).[47]

In air the combination of lactic acid, carbon dioxide, and ammonia is irresistible to female yellow fever mosquitoes (*Aedes aegypti*).[48] Taste receptors in the legs of tsetse flies (*Glossina* spp.) respond positively to specific components of human sweat, including uric acid, several amino acids (e.g., phenylalanine, tyrosine, leucine, valine), and lactic acid.[49] The malaria mosquitoes *Anopheles atroparvus* and *A. gambiae* are particularly attracted to human feet, and washing the feet reduces this preference substantially.[50] The offensive odor of moist, dirty feet is caused by certain lipids.[51] Fittingly, one group of researchers found that a synthetic mixture of 12 aliphatic fatty acids identified from Limburger cheese is also attractive to females of *A. gambiae*.[52] Do candirus have similar preferences? Possibly.

If any detail of the picture just painted applies to the candiru, then consider this before immersing your sweaty, grungy body in a lowland South American river. Once submerged, your clothes and skin initiate a drifting chumline of ammonia, urea, amino acids, lactic acid, aliphatic fatty acids, inorganic ions, and who knows what else. Urination increases the concentrations of some of these substances and adds others, and the overall flavor is enhanced by any blood oozing from scratches and cuts. You might indeed pose an inviting target for nearby candirus, but there's no need to worry if you're wearing tight underwear. So rest for a time with your head out of the water. Expect squadrons of mosquitoes to appear, attracted in part by the ammonia on your breath. Anyone with a body in this condition surely has teeth to match.

THE FATAL STREAM HYPOTHESIS

Another favorite hypothesis involves the natural tendency of most fishes to swim into currents, a behavior called rheotropism. A candiru presumably senses a stream of urine, which it mistakes for a natural current of water. Orienting into it, the candiru soon becomes entrapped inside someone's urethra. According to this "fatal stream hypothesis," taste and smell, if they have any influence at all, are of secondary importance. Rheotropism as applied to urine streams might function effectively only in sluggish waters. In strong currents, the rushing of water around and over stones and debris would overwhelm a tiny stream produced by someone urinating. Candirus occur in both still and rushing waters. As Armbrust colorfully explains:[53]

> The head of the animal is covered with fine sensory cells, which react to streaming water. They dare not swim into the mouths of big fishes because that is too dangerous and they might be swallowed. They take the side exit, which they use as an entrance. At the precise moment when the big fish expels exhalent water through its gills, the catfish senses this stream, swims into it, and in a flash hooks onto the gills. It is this stream of water that misleads the little fellow. If a mammal urinates in the water, it senses the stream, swims into it, and finds the situation fatal. Naturally this is true only if people are not wearing bathing trunks. [S. Spotte and E. Muschaweck, transl.]

In the third edition of J. R. Norman's *A History of Fishes* is a brief discussion of how the candiru might be induced to enter a human urethra. P. H. Greenwood, author of this edition, notes that attacks commonly occur while the victim is urinating, but discounts an attraction to urine as the enticing factor, telling us instead,[54] "It seems more probable . . . that the flow of urine is merely mistaken by the fish for the respiratory current coming from the gill-opening of a fish."

THE WRONG TURN HYPOTHESIS

Have you ever made a wrong turn onto a freeway and seen a sign saying the next exit was 5 miles away? What choice did you have except to continue on? In such situations stopping and turning around, or backing up, would be suicidal. Some think this is how candirus find themselves trapped in human orifices. How, you ask, can a creature so highly adapted to sucking blood from fish gills make such a stupid mistake? Easy. Not every move in life is the right one, and certain moves can be fatal. Life itself is peripatetic; it's just that some stopovers last longer than others. Evolution allows more slack than we think, and not every adaptation is perfect. In this case, even if a candiru detects the mistake, the backwards curve of its spines permits no directional changes. The only choice? Continue moving forward. We know from aquarium observations that after a candiru has located its victim, the attack occurs with blinding speed. At some juncture in the sequence, movement towards the prey becomes non-reversible.

In *The Life Story of the Fish*, Curtis mentions that candirus are believed to attack human beings by entering the "excretory openings." He then says:[55]

> It may be assumed that this is an error on the part of the fish. Entry into the organ is supposed to occur during urination by the human under water, when the outgoing stream presumably resembles, to the candiru, the expiratory current from the gill chamber of a fish. Certainly no fish would deliberately enter a hole from which there was no way of emerging, and to be stuck in the human urethra must be most unpleasant for the candiru, but it is even more unpleasant for the human, and the only way to prevent the intruder from reaching the bladder and causing death is to perform an immediate operation.

Breault suggests that the candiru might not be attracted to urine, but nonetheless swims into a urinating person's urethra[56] ". . . simply because its normal instinct is to swim upstream into the water streaming out of a larger fish's gill cavity." With appropriate drama (and some confusion about female anatomy), Schultz and Stern state:[57]

> Entering the penis or vagina they [candirus] may penetrate well into the urethra. There, unable to turn, in the throes of suffocation, they erect their fishhook-like spines.

Armbrust, writing in a 1971 issue of the aquarium hobbyist magazine *Aquarien und Terrarien*, tells about the candiru's own hobby:[58]

> These eccentric animals have thought of a very special hobby, which seems to normally end with their own death. Therefore it cannot be intentional but only a mistake that makes them behave like this. [E. Muschaweck, transl.]

Armbrust is among the few to suggest that swimming up a human urethra might not be typical in a candiru's daily life, referring to it as an error. He wonders why such attacks happen and speculates that they can't occur during searches for food because too few mammals are available. Moreover, being unable to back out, the candiru would soon die.

Surely a burst and even an orgy of dressing up is a sign of vigour and of something to console any man for the declining age in which we live, and the collapse of culture and taste.

—Hilaire Belloc, "On Dressing Up"[1]

8.

On Dressing Down

Did the indigenous people of South America ever wear protective devices over their genitals as a precaution against candiru attacks? Does drinking the hot juice of a certain tropical fruit or its external application dissolve or cause the expulsion of a candiru lodged in the urethra? These remain open questions.

After evaluating the evidence, Gudger correctly concludes that certain South American tribes indeed wear genital coverings, but no one knows why. Ever since, Gudger's statements and those of the German ethnologists he quotes have been wrongly interpreted to mean that such devices have been worn specifically to protect against candiru attacks. Humankind is an oddly stubborn species much given to belief in fallacies, and for this reason the subject is worth revisiting.

The notion of protecting oneself against candiru attacks while bathing in rivers started with von Martius:[2]

> These fishes are greatly attracted by the odor of urine. For this reason, those who dwell along the Amazon, when about to enter the stream, whose bays abound with this pest, tie a cord tightly around the prepuce and refrain from urinating. [Translation in Eigenmann (1918a: 263); the translation given by Gudger (1930c: 3) follows this one closely.]

This says something about the men but not the women, suggesting cultural reasons for binding the foreskin. Gudger points out von Martius' statement before referring to Jobert, who had been warned by residents of Pará to follow the example of the Indians and wear a protective device as they did. Jobert writes:[3]

> Not twenty-four hours had I been at Pará [now Belém] when I was warned about the Candirŭs: *"Cuidado com o Candirŭ, ô homen!"* Be very careful, *"com este biche temivel"*; do not go swimming (they said) and do not urinate in the water, or do as the Tapuyos do, and use protective binding, which we shall show you how to tie.
>
> At first I thought this was one of those far-fetched cautionary tales always told to newcomers. Later, I had to admit that what I had thought of as tittle-tattle deserved a certain amount of consideration. When I saw the Tapuyos, with the melancholy gravity characteristic of the Indian, tying their protective knots, I believed, if not in the possibility of attack by the Candirŭ, at least in the serious fear of such an attack. Certainly these fishermen at the water's edge engaged in their precautionary binding offered an odd spectacle: there could be nothing pleasant about tying oneself up in this way. Yet their profound conviction of having avoided peril, and their good-hearted astonishment at my refusal to do the same, lent a seriousness to this bizarre operation that banished all hilarity. They must have attributed my immunity from attack to some preparation, some mysterious maneuver customary to white people.
>
> For the rest, the fear inspired by the Candirŭ is not as widespread as one might think; even if belief in its existence and the damage it can do are strongly held by all, many fishermen took no precautions and practiced no constrictive knotting. And I never heard of any accidents. [V. Gill, transl.]

Gudger misreads Jobert's meaning:[4] "Later on some of the men, emboldened by his [Jobert's] immunity [to attack], left off the ligature, but Jobert never heard of any accidents." Jobert did not attribute the fishermen's later behavior to his own.

Boulenger, again quoting the mysterious Dr. Bach, tells us:[5]

> The 'Candyrú,' as the fish is called, is much dreaded by the natives of the Jurua district, who, in order to protect themselves, rarely enter the river without covering their genitalia by means of a sheath formed of a small coconut-shell, with a minute perforation to let out urine, maintained in a sort of bag of palm-fibres suspended from a belt of the same material. . .
>
> Mr. Boulenger further showed a photograph, taken by Dr. Bach, of two nude Indians wearing the protective purse.

The photograph, unfortunately, did not accompany the article, and we have only Boulenger's description of this "protective purse." Gudger tried unsuccessfully to track it down.

Jobert evidently thought candirus were a serious problem elsewhere if not in the vicinity of Pará. He repeats Boulenger's description, obtained secondhand from Bach, of the coconut-shell purse as a preventive measure against candiru attacks:[6]

> No precautions seem too great given the gravity of the danger: thus the indigenous men of the Jurua are careful to protect the precious organ with a coconut shell pierced at the end with a hole just large enough to permit urine to pass through. The shell is held in place by a net attached to a belt, both made of palm fibers. [V. Gill, transl.]

Karl von den Steinen's accounts of travels in South America between 1827 and 1832 contain brief mention of the candiru. In his 1886 book *Durch Central-Brasilien*, he illustrates and describes a pudendal covering worn by women of the Bakaïri (Fig. 43), but ascribes to it no particular function. It consists of a triangular piece of bark raffia, supposedly from the schischá tree, folded to the dimensions of 1–1.5 by 4 centimeters. Later von den Steinen comes across another tribe, the Kustenaú, and saw women wearing an identical device. Only in a passing remark does von den Steinen mention the candiru in reference to another tribe, the Trumaí, but the idea of protection against the candiru is apparently his own, little more than musing:[7]

> In a very strange and very primitive way they are protecting themselves against penetrating insects, — with a red cotton thread they bind the foreskin together in front of the glans, like a sausage. This device should also be of good use in the water against the inquisitive little Kandirú-fish. [E. Muschaweck, transl.]

As to the men of the Yuruna:[8]

> The Yuruna slip a little "cap" (a case in the form of a cone, horizontal on the top, but off-slanted on the bottom) made of dried palm leaves over the penis, which corresponds approximately in size and diameter to the two lower sections of the little

FIG. 43   Pudendal covering (*uluri*) worn by Bakaïri women at the headwaters of the Rio Xingu. Source: von den Steinen (1894).

FIG. 44   *Penisstulp.* Source: von den Steinen (1894).

finger. By this little cap, which sticks out straight from the scrotum, the erectile tissue is pressed back into the scrotum, so that it looks like a growth. But no part of the outer penis is visible on the outside of the little cap. And since the urethra is totally closed, insects cannot penetrate. [E. Muschaweck, transl.]

In *Unter den Naturvölkern Zentral-Brasiliens*, published in 1894, von den Steinen writes about the need of such protection and describes once again a penis covering, or (in German) *Penisstulp*, made of palm leaves (Fig. 44), and pudendal coverings made of bark. He could find no function for the penis coverings worn by men of the Trumaí except to guard against brush, thorns, and ticks, or perhaps to protect the tip of the glans penis during erections. Although unsure why such protection should be necessary, he offers several possibilities, one predicated on whether the Trumaí are subhuman:[9]

Is it possible that the young men reaching adulthood might wish to protect the glans, which becomes permanently uncovered by erections and sexual intercourse? Much can be said in favor of this. But brush and thorns might be the least reason for this wish for protection. More serious are the insults of the animal world. If the Trumaí were animals, as is said about them, which live in water and sleep on the bottom of rivers, they would urgently need to close the urethra against the little Kandirú-fish (*Cetopsis Candiru*) [*Hemicetopsis candiru*].[10] This transparent little pest, a span long, the appearance of which we have documented in 1884 on the Batovy, has the curious habit to penetrate into the accessible orifices of the body of a person in the water; it slips into the urethra, cannot go back because of its fins [*sic*] and easily causes the death of the unhappy person, whose last resort is only to perform the external urethrostomy with his knife. [E. Muschaweck, transl.]

The suggestion is for the victim to perform the surgery on himself, although the prospects of survival after such a crude excision are dubious. Continuing, von den Steinen tells us:[11]

Since the amphibious nature of the Trumaí is really doubtful, and the stay in the water of a fisherman or somebody portaging a boat through the cataracts is only of little importance, it is not necessary to fall back upon the occasional danger caused by the Kandirú. On the other side, though, the pest of the "Carapatos" (Ixodidae), ticks which are shaken down from the trees and stripped off the leaves, might make the protection of the glans very desirable for the inhabitants of the woods. These very small parasites attach themselves to the skin, suck themselves full of blood, with their elastic body walls swelling up to pea size, and are so fixed to the skin with their barblike jaws, they are torn apart if one tries to pull them off, and painful inflammation develops from the parts remaining. The Brazilian, who sometimes comes out of the woods covered with ticks, takes off his clothes as fast as possible and shakes out shirt and pants over the camp fire; if one of the pests has attached itself to the glans, he holds a burning cigarette as close as he can possibly stand it, in order for the creature to give up voluntarily and draw back from the mucous membrane without being torn to pieces. All of us have had to perform this procedure and the experience is one of the worst before reaching the solution. I am also of the opinion that the protection of the Indians is more effective than to be covered by clothing. [E. Muschaweck, transl.]

Note what von den Steinen says: *if* the Trumaí slept on river bottoms *then* they would need protection against candirus. He dismisses any real danger, telling us that because the amphibious nature of the Trumaí is doubtful, any attracks from candirus would only occur occasionally when fishing or portaging boats through rapids. In von den Steinen's opinion, men wear penis coverings for protection against hazards *other than* candiru attacks (he says little about the women). In his experience, ticks are particularly troublesome.

Fritz Krause, another German ethnologist, describes a penis covering worn by men of the Kanapó and Tapirapé tribes along the Rio Araguana, Brazil. It too is made of palm leaves, but has a slightly different design than the one described by von den Steinen (Fig. 45). Krause writes:[12]

> Clothing is almost nonexistent. The women go totally naked since early youth. The men, from puberty on, wear the penis cover made from strips of leaves (imudjé) . . . . Mostly it is pulled over the glans so that the foreskin is protruding like the end of a sausage; the edge of the cover is on the bottom . . . . Furthermore, they have leather sandals held by strings and braided straw hats, both stemming from the influence of Brazil. [E. Muschaweck, transl.]

FIG. 45 *Penisstulp*. Source: Krause (1911).

Krause doesn't speculate on why the penis covering is worn. This seems to have been left to later writers who misinterpreted his and von den Steinen's work.

A contradictory statement occurs in Gudger's book, and although Gudger was not directly responsible he allowed it to slip through. Gudger emphasizes that various devices worn over the genitals do not have any known function. It therefore seems strange that Warthin would begin his foreword to *The Candirú* by describing how coconut shells are worn as protection against candirus:[13]

> Some thirteen or fourteen years ago, the late Professor C. H. Eigenmann, of Indiana University, related to me an interesting tale concerning a minute South American catfish, which, attracted by the odor of urine, would enter the human urethra, where by erecting spines on its gill covers it could so firmly establish itself, that its removal could be accomplished only through amputation of the penis. As a matter of precaution against such an unhappy occurrence the natives protected themselves by tying coconut shells over their organs, when bathing in the rivers in which these urinophilous fish abound. Professor Eigenmann assured me of his belief in this story, for he had seen with his own eyes the natives wearing these protective codpieces, and had heard many tales of the human parasitism of these fish.

Warthin's words weigh on Eigenmann's veracity. Eigenmann indeed spent time in South America collecting fishes, but was he given to hyperbole? If he personally witnessed the "natives" wearing coconut shells, he apparently never ascertained the purpose, nor did he write about having seen these devices in use. We know he was enthusiastic about the urine-loving hypothesis, even to the point of establishing a new genus and naming it *Urinophilus*. Having failed to find evidence of urinophilic behavior by any species of trichomycterid catfish, touting the use of coconut shells to repel candiru attacks might seem enormously compelling.

I doubt that Eigenmann actually saw indigenous people wearing these devices. However, it's conceivable he told this to Warthin. How else would Warthin have drawn the association? Warthin never attributed to Eigenmann evidence of a direct link between the wearing of coconut shells and candiru attacks, but the implication of such a connection is strong. After all, Eigenmann was the expert, and Warthin deferred to him. For his part, Warthin's contribution to the candiru literature comprises the few paragraphs at the start of Gudger's book. He was a medical school professor, not an ichthyologist, and he had nothing to gain by issuing inexpert opinions.

In *Dicionário de Animais do Brasil*, published in 1940, von Ihering tells us:[14]

> The fact is that ethnographers have noted that in several regions of Amazonia and the Guianas, the Indians protect the pudendal parts, in a way to avoid accidents, the [candirus] provoking in them more fear than the piranhas. [S. Spotte, transl.]

He cites no references, nor does he tell us what sorts of coverings are used. His statement suggests only women wear such devices.

Lüling, contributing to the general misunderstanding about penis coverings in a 1969 publication, combines three figures from *The Candirú* that Gudger had taken from von den Steinen and Krause.[15] The legend to Lüling's figure begins,[16] "Protective devices of Brazilian Indian tribes against penetration of urinophilic catfish into the sexual organs . . ."

As mentioned above, none of these authors claims that the penis coverings they depicted were devised specifically to protect against candiru attacks. Like von den Steinen, Krause certainly knew about candirus. He describes how when pitching camp the thermometers were hung up, the barometers put out, and then a decision was made about whether to go swimming. He lists the dangers as piranhas, crocodiles, stingrays, and candirus:[17] "The candiru-fish, which penetrates only too gladly into all body-openings, hunts in the flat water around."

Vinton and Stickler cite the use of genital guards worn by Indians when bathing in the Rio Araguana, and in one of their figures reproduce an illustration of such an apparatus from Gudger, who had taken it from Krause. Once again, Gudger never attributes these items to protection against candiru attacks.

Eugenio Estellita Lins plagiarizes Boulenger (see above) without adding anything new:[18]

> This little creature [the candiru] is much dreaded by the Amazonian natives who, in order to protect themselves, rarely enter the river without first covering their genital organs by means of a sheath formed of a small coconut shell, with a minute perforation to let out urine. This is maintained in a sort of bag of palm fibers which is suspended from a belt of the same material.

Gastão Cruls, in the third edition of his *Hiléia Amazônica*, published in 1958, writes:[19]

> Despite its insignificant size, only about three centimeters, the candirus [*sic*] are quite fearsome, with the singular habit of introducing themselves into people's natural openings when they take a bath in waters infested by them. There were already those who deduced that it was for no other reason that the Parintintins and some other Indians keep the tip of the foreskin constantly tied. [S. Spotte, transl.]

In this case the actual motive for tying the foreskin has never been confirmed, nor does Cruls cite his source.

An anonymous writer in a 1969 issue of *Environment Southwest* provides this questionable information:[20] "Although both men and women wear special sheaths made of palm fibers to prevent the entrance of the candiru, they are not foolproof, and one must still be careful when in the water." How the relative safety of these devices was assessed isn't mentioned. The coverings for women could hardly be called "sheaths." Were they "foolproof" against candiru attacks? That's difficult to answer, considering this is not their apparent function.

Herman refers to these coverings as "cod pieces" and attributes to Gudger the claim that their use is circumstantial evidence as protection against candirus. Grzimek relates how warily the South American Indians protect against candiru attacks:[21] "For this reason some Indian tribes put some covering about the lower torso when they go swimming in these waters, something which they do not normally do." Grzimek gives no hint about where he got this information.

Jan Kinzer, writing in a 1959 issue of *Aquarien und Terrien*, describes once again the ubiquitous coconut shell and its putative function:[22]

> The up to 9 cm long pygidiid [*sic*] *Vandellia cirrhosa* Cuv. & Val. [Cuvier and Valenciennes] shows a very uncommon behavior. It is only found in the Amazon and is named Candirú by the native Indians. (The name Candirú is also used by the Indians of the Amazon area for similar genera and species.) This catfish has the highly unpleasant characteristic to penetrate into the urethra of bathing humans or also animals, and the Indians try to protect themselves against this by different protective covers of coconut shells and palm fibers. [E. Muschaweck, transl.]

Norman and Greenwood continue the tradition:[23]

> In some parts of Brazil another species of Candiru (*Vandellia*) is very much dreaded by the natives, owing to its unpleasant habit of entering the urethra of persons bathing in the rivers, and both men and women are in the habit of wearing special sheaths made of palm fibres to protect the external genitalia, when obliged to enter the water.

And Burgess writes:[24] "Natives are known to protect themselves from this fish by wearing tight-fitting clothing or even coconut shell guards over their private parts." Halstead also tells the story of the perforated coconut shell. He perpetuates the unproved use of genital coverings against candiru attacks and describes the "pudendal belt" made of bark (the *uluri*) and the *imudjé* made of palm leaves, before stating:[25] "Although the penis sheaths are used by primitive tribes the world over, it is believed by some scholars that the candirú and the piranha had a stimulating influence in their development in the Amazon region." This seems doubtful. Nonetheless, as late as 1996 I found an article by two American physicians once again citing the coconut-shell-with-a-hole story.[26]

Maybe the purpose of these devices is merely decorative, or lost to history. Speculation that requires no proof, the filling of psychological vacuums, we call fiction. In "Green Hell," a short story by the American writer T. Coraghessan Boyle, a plane goes down in a South American rainforest. One survivor, the most hated, deserts to join a tribe of Indians. Members of the tribe later kill his former companions, sparing only the unnamed protagonist. Having lost consciousness during the attack, he awakes in the Indian village and sees the deserter:[27]

> I am on the verge of bolting. But at that moment I become aware of a new figure in the group—pasty white skin, red boils and blotches, a fallen, purplish mask. . . . Naked and flabby. His penis wrapped in bark, pubic hair plucked. . . . Barefooted, he hobbles over to me, and the others turn back to their meal. "How are you feeling?" he says, squatting beside me.

R. Blanchard refers to the candiru and the wearing of protective devices along the Amazon:[28]

> We [sic] have already drawn attention to the Candiru,[29] a small fish of the freshwaters of Brazil, which evidently has the reputation for entering the urethra of bathers. Along streams where it lives, the natives and often individuals of the white race avoid entering the water without wearing a protective string around their foreskins or without having placed on their penises a condom made of indigenous materials. [S. Spotte, transl.]

Blanchard then adds:[30]

> A similar belief and practice occurs in southern Africa, where bilharzian hematuria exists. It is acknowledged that this illness is caused by a parasite that lives in water and that penetrates the urethra during bathing. The natives also have the habit of covering the glans or binding the penis when they enter the water . . .
>
> Opposite, we [sic] show the condom used by the Zulus of Rhodesia. This interesting object, very cleverly plaited, has been brought recently from Buluwayo [now Zimbabwe] by Dr A. Loir, to whom we are indebted for it. [S. Spotte, transl.]

Blanchard offers this assertion authoritatively, but without evidence (his illustration is shown here as Fig. 46). These few sentences are all he says

FIG. 46 Plaited condom worn by Zulus of Rhodesia (Zimbabwe), supposedly as protection against schistosomiasis. Source: Blanchard (1904).

about the device, but they generated much subsequent speculation, some of it passed off as fact.

Gudger tells us that the American Museum of Natural History had several of these artifacts in its ethnological collections. He had written to the Museu Nacional in Rio de Janeiro asking for photographs of any similar devices that might have been used in South America, but received no reply. Oddly, Gudger seems to capitulate, accepting without proof the presumed function of South American penis coverings to protect against candiru attacks:[31]

Finally, it is interesting here to note that, in these two far distant and absolutely unrelated regions, we have an excellent illustration of the saying of Alexander von Humboldt that different peoples in distant countries under stress of similar necessities devise similar apparatuses or processes to attain similar ends.

Blanchard's speculation has led us here. In seeking information about whether penis coverings of this sort might have been worn in Africa as protection against schistosomiasis (also called bilharziasis), I looked into ancient and modern Egyptian customs. Schistosomiasis is a parasitic disease caused by the blood fluke *Schistosoma haematobium*, a tiny worm that plagues people who live along the Nile and elsewhere in Africa and Asia.[32] The parasite was unknown to science until 1851 when a young German physician and naturalist named Theodore Bilharz found specimens while performing autopsies on Egyptian field workers.

Contrary to Blanchard's implication, the larvae of *S. haematobium* do not enter the urethra preferentially,[33] although no one knew otherwise in 1904, the year his note was published, and the discovery that schistosomes must pass the first stage of the life cycle in an aquatic snail did not happen until the first World War.[34]

The cercaria represents the infective stage. It burrows into human skin at any location.[35] After traveling through the heart and lungs by way of the bloodstream, cercariae eventually lodge and develop into adults in veins of the pelvis, lower colon, and rectum. Females deposit eggs in the walls of the bladder, urethra, or ureters.[36] Other sites of deposition are the pelvic organs (e.g., seminal vesicles, prostate, urethra, penis, uterus, vagina, and vulva). If cutaneous veins are invaded, eggs can break through the skin leaving lesions, and these sometimes erupt on the penis, perhaps giving the wrong impression that the penis is a principal site of infestation. The eggs develop quickly into embryos, which secrete an enzyme inducing abscesses in the host's tissues, allowing them to break free and be voided in the urine. The most serious consequence of a heavy infestation of *S. haematobia* is tissue fibrosis of the urinary tract, which obstructs urine flow and leads ultimately to renal parenchymal failure.[37]

In *A History of Urology in Egypt*, privately printed in 1956, J. Bitschai and M. Leopold Brodny write:[38]

> Since prehistoric times in Egypt, certain tribes practiced the wearing of a sort of case hiding the penis (as exists today among the Caffres [Kaffirs]). Rupestral drawings in Upper Egypt clearly show this custom. . . . Also the Egyptian god Bes is sometimes represented wearing a penile case. The Egyptologist E. de Naville found such cases on a very ancient statue and in the tombs of the 19th dynasty. Dr. Pfister . . . a Swiss urologist who spent a long time in Egypt, theorized that this device was believed to protect Egyptians working in water against Bilharzia disease, which so often manifested itself in the penile canal.

Bitschai and Brodny add that penis sheaths were also worn because of social customs.

The theory to which Bitschai and Brodny refer is contained in an article by Edwin Pfister published in 1913 in *Archiv für Geschichte der Medizin*. Gudger was apparently unaware of it. Although cited by Bitschai and Brodny as a principal source of original information, Pfister merely perpetuates the contemporary speculation. He had no proof of penis coverings being worn to prevent schistosomiasis, having based his assertion on Blanchard's 1904 publication. At the beginning of his article, he says:[39]

> When I had to write a short overview . . . about the last ten years of bilharzia research for Folia Urologica at the request of the editor, I came upon a note by R. Blanchard, that the Zulus of Rhodesia used to apply a sort of condom as prophylaxis against haematuria parasitaria, i.e., bilharzia, and always, then entering the river, where according to their assumption the distomes [cercariae] slip into the urethra, which these condoms are supposed to prevent. R. Blanchard also shows such an instrument, brought to him from Buluwayo by Dr. Loir; it consists of tightly plaited straw and has the form of a bottle pumpkin [squash] — and is called "Préservatif contre la Bilharzie, utilisé par les Zulus de la Rhodesia". [E. Muschaweck, transl.]

Pfister then cites Blanchard's mention in 1903 of penis coverings worn in South America to prevent candiru attacks, and brings von den Steinen back into the picture:[40]

> At the same time it is noted, that the Indians of central Brazil also use such [penis] cases, following a similar way of thought, i.e., against the penetration of candirus, transparent little fish, 2 ccm long with a yellow iris. These little animals are supposed to like to penetrate into body cavities accessible to them and also bore themselves into the mucous membrane of the urethra with their fins [sic]. Such a case — a case in the form of a cone made of palm leaves, at the top cut off horizontally, at the bottom cut off at a slant — is depicted by K. von den Steinen. [E. Muschaweck, transl.]

The belief that the Zulus, Kaffirs, and early Egyptians wore condoms to prevent schistosomiasis is unsubstantiated, requiring evidence that people afflicted by the disease associated it with polluted water. The link between a candiru and a candiru attack is obvious. Linking the blood fluke with symptoms of disease produced by schistosomiasis is far more difficult. The blood fluke's life cycle is complex and secretive, the infective stage microscopic.

The bond between *Schistosoma haematobium* and humankind is very old. Sir Armand Ruffer once examined the kidneys left in a mummy from the Twentieth Dynasty (roughly 3000 years ago) and found ova of *Schistosoma* in the right ureter.[41] Embalmers were supposed to remove all internal organs, but sometimes one or two got overlooked. Even in ancient Egypt good help was hard to find.

In Pfister's opinion, having a homely penis distorted by schistosomiasis and wanting to hide it from view is another possible reason for wearing a penis case. Pfister notes that statues and paintings depicting the Egyptian god Bes show him wearing such a condom. Bes is a homely little deity, short of stature with bandy legs, a wild beard, and a "rickety curvature" (*rachitische Kurvaturen*). Maybe Bes' penis is as ugly as the rest of him.

In the ninth edition of Asa Chandler's *Introduction to Parasitology* is this statement:[42] "The natives of some parts of Africa where *S. haematobium* occurs realize that infection may result from bathing, but from the nature of the disease they believe that infection takes place by way of the urinary passages, and therefore vainly employ mechanical devices to prevent infection in this manner." The implications are intriguing. What exactly are these "mechanical devices," and who wore them? Chandler does not say, nor does he cite any sources. No such devices were used in Egypt during the late nineteenth and early twentieth centuries. Pfister, who lived there for many years as a practicing physician, had never seen one.

How recent is knowledge of the causal relationship between *S. haematobium* and schistosomiasis? Could it have existed before the parasite's life cycle was deciphered? According to the American parasitologist Clark P. Read, the Ebers Papyrus, an Egyptian book of medicine written about 1600 years ago, clearly discusses roundworm and tapeworm infestations and methods of treatment. Read says,[43] "Schistosomiasis was described as a disease but without convincing evidence that the role of a trematode worm was known."

Perhaps the reason for any protection at all is simple aversion to water and a disinclination to get the private parts wet. Fiction hints at this. In *The Narrative of Jacobus Coetzee*, a novella by the South African writer J. M. Coetzee, the narrator states:[44] "Hottentots know nothing of soap and shun water to the extent of tying their prepuces shut while swimming."

Schistosomiasis causes scarring and thickening of the bladder wall. The eggs themselves often become calcified, turning into calculi. These mineral concretions form around an organic matrix, producing bladder and urethral stones ranging in size from smaller than a sand grain to slightly larger than an olive. Bilharz recognized blood flukes as the cause of inordinately high incidences of calculi among Egyptians by demonstrating how the eggs were at the centers of these concretions. In later years, attempts to dissolve calculi *in vitro* have an interesting connection with similar attempts to expel candirus from human victims.

Writing in 1945 in *Journal of Urology*, Estellita Lins offers a simple chemical recipe for dissolving bladder calculi based on a brew devised by South American Indians. This concoction, which Estellita Lins claims capable of dissolving a candiru lodged in the urethra, is a hot tea made from *jagua* juice. *Jagua* is the fruit of the tropical tree *Genipa americana*.[45] Von Poeppig first mentions this remedy in his 1836 book *Reise in Chile, Peru und auf dem Amazonenstrome, Während der Jahre 1827–1832*, but says nothing about drinking the brew. I quote von Poeppig's account in Chapter 1. For purposes here, the relevant parts state:[46]

> The fresh juice of the Xagua [*jagua*] is rightfully valued as the safest way to kill and expel that two-inch-long fish, which slips into the exterior cavities of the human body of careless bathers, and which can cause the most terrible incidents. . . . I myself have been an eyewitness of such a case in Yurimaguas [eastern Peru], when an Indian woman suffered such terrible

pain and loss of blood after the penetration of a Canero into the vagina that everyone thought she was lost. After interior and exterior application of the Xagua [*jagua*], the little fish was expelled at once, and the woman did not lose her life. [E. Muschaweck, transl.]

Santos repeats the story in his 1962 edition of *Peixes da Água Doce*, saying that in parts of the Peruvian Amazon natives skilled in medicine use a tisane made of the green fruit of the *jagua*, or *jenipapo*, and administer it both internally and externally. An anonymous source writing in 1969 tells us,[47] "It has been reported that swallowing the acrid juice from the green fruit of a local tree sometimes drives the fish out of the tract within two hours." This is an obvious reference to the fruit of *G. americana*, but no evidence to back its efficacy was provided.

Only Vinton and Stickler have performed a direct test:[48]

Since we had two live specimens [of candirus], this seemed an excellent opportunity to test the effect of the jagua juice on them. Although the water in the large container in which the fish were kept was changed several times during the night, one of the fish was nearly dead and the other quite sluggish the following morning. The jagua was collected and the juice prepared as quickly as possible. Then the livelier specimen was placed in the dilute mixture. The little fish became suddenly active and, after swimming around rapidly and showing other signs of discomfort for about two minutes, turned over on its back and remained motionless. The fish was not dead, however, for upon being placed in fresh water it revived. It was unfortunate that we did not have more live specimens with which to experiment for the vitality of this one was at low ebb, and the reaction may not have been normal.

Vinton and Stickler examined the anecdotal evidence carefully during their stay in Peru. They were aware of von Poeppig's statement and quote Marcoy from Gudger's text:[49]

To the horrible sufferings which the introduction of this living needle may occasion, the Ucayali doctors know of but one remedy which consists of a *tisane* made with the *genipa* or *huitach* apple, and which, taken very hot, act [sic], they pretend, on the urinary passages, and dissolves the animal which obstructs them.

Marcoy's belief is that *jagua* juice can dissolve a candiru trapped in the urethra, not merely drive it out.[50] This had interesting consequences that

I shall explain shortly. As to its intended purpose, Vinton and Stickler tell us that[51]

> ... the unripe jagua fruit ... is the standard treatment for dislodging the carnero once it has attacked. The centers of the smaller green fruits are scraped out, mashed and squeezed and mixed with water, the strength of the preparation varying considerably. The potion has a bitter taste and the puckering effect of a fairly strong astringent. The preparation is taken by mouth. In a comparatively short time, varying from a few minutes to about two hours, according to the natives, the fish is dislodged. Mr. Burns states that, although this cure sometimes causes the patients to become quite nauseated, he has never known the treatment to fail, nor can he learn of a failure from the natives. Neither has he ever known the fish to be dislodged without this form of treatment.

Before describing some case histories, Vinton and Stickler write:[52]

> The fish is reported to have been successfully driven out of the host's body so frequently that it is difficult to believe that the desired results have occurred as timely accidents in such a large number of cases. But in the absence of scientific proof the best we can do is to speculate in the matter.

Unaware of Vinton and Stickler's publication, Estellita Lins assumes *a priori* that *jagua* juice is a proven remedy. He begins by paraphrasing Marcoy:[53]

> For the horrible suffering which the introduction of this living needle [the candiru] may occasion, the natives know of but one remedy—the buitach apple (Genipa americana L.) [*sic*], which grows in the Amazon Basin and looks much like the breadfruit. Made into a brew and drunk very hot, it has the magic property of dissolving the skeleton of the fish. . . . Bladder incrustations present a parallel problem to the presence in the bladder and urethra of the Candiru, and they respond in similar fashion to the native remedy which dissolves the incrustations as it dissolves the skeleton of the fish, eliminating the need for surgery.

The problem, of course, is that no one has ever tested whether such a brew, even before cooling and dilution with urine (as would occur in the bladder), can kill a candiru even *in vitro*, much less dissolve it. Estellita Lins consequently devised a formula having a pH of 4.0 (Table 5). Instructions for its preparation are not included, but earlier recipes of similar composition were boiled, probably to dissolve the magnesium oxide, which is only slightly soluble except in strong acids (citric and tannic acids are weak). However, boiling would likely destroy the enzyme. The recipe's reproducibility is limited by not being volumetric; that is, the ingredients are added to 1 liter of water, rendering their concentrations uncertain. Properly, the dissolved ingredients are diluted to 1 liter of water.

Estellita Lins reported his formula cured 12 patients with small bladder calculi. Others have reported success with similar recipes. H. I. Suby and colleagues show radiographs of calculi before and after lavage to demonstrate their reduction in size.[54]

Is there a tisane that could dissolve the skeleton of a candiru in the urethra? Probably not. Before the skeleton could be reached, the flesh around it would have to be dissolved or separated from the bones, and none of the chemical solutions described effectively dissolves organic matter. This is just as well because the urethra is organic too. In my opinion, no concoction known, including hot *jagua* juice, is capable of dissolving a candiru lodged in a human urethra. And how could anything ingested reach a candiru lodged in the vagina? "Driving out" a candiru is also problematic, although anything hastening its demise could only help the victim.

TABLE 5. Estellita Lins' formula for dissolving calculi.

Compound	Amount
Methenamine	10 grams
Proteolytic enzyme (pepsin)	1 gram
Citric acid	32 grams
Tannic acid	32 grams
Magnesium oxide	4 grams
Sodium carbonate	4 grams
Water	1 liter

Source: Estellita Lins (1945).

"Redmond," he said, "there's no comradeship. There's no wine and no women and no song and nowhere sensible to shit."

—Redmond O'Hanlon,
In Trouble Again: A Journey Between the Orinoco and the Amazon[1]

9.

Down By The Riverside

I spread the mesh apart and eased myself down as if onto a nettle-covered, two-legged stool. The sunlight filtered through the blue tarpaulin overhead had a doomed, abyssal quality. Nearby the slick surface of the Rio Jauaperi slid past, its eddies writhing like scalded brown snakes just before the Cachoeira do Travessão dropped away. A mosquito landed on my wrist and clomped morosely around in the sweat. "This is it!" I shouted, but the hammock dumped me out for the second time.

"I'll get it," I said. "It's only a goddamn hammock."

Paulo, who was leaning against the side of the truck, looked doubtful. "There's some things a gringo can't learn."

I got up from the ground and changed the subject. "Let's go catch candirus." We were certainly prepared. The campsite was littered with nets, jars, specimen bottles, vials of chemicals, fishing gear, clothing, a camp stove, cameras, notebooks, flashlights, and medicines. Except for the nonlinear arrangement of these articles, the scene resembled the usual assortment of trash left by a receding tide.

That day we had driven 450 kilometers north from Manaus into Roraima, the northernmost state of Brazil sandwiched between Guyana and Venezuela. Paulo had been here before and had caught candirus along the edge of the rapids. But his specimens were now dead and preserved at Instituto Nacional de Pesquisas da Amazônia, or INPA, the multifaceted research facility in Manaus. Paulo had recently resigned his position there as collections manager in the ichthyology section and would soon return to the U.S. to complete work on a doctorate at Oregon State University. For our purposes, dead candirus wouldn't do. We needed live specimens to test the effectiveness of certain chemical attractants—more accurately, *potential* attractants. There was no evidence any of them would work, just guesses and hearsay.

We had left Manaus at seven-thirty and reached the outskirts before discovering the truck's registration was not in the glove box. It was a Russian four-wheel-drive Lada borrowed from Roberto Stieger Leite, a colleague of Paulo's at INPA.

"Why do we need papers?" I asked.

"Because we're sure to get stopped by the cops in some little town, and they'll ask us for proof we didn't steal the car. Then we'll need to explain who *we* are, and you'll have to show them identification, like a driver's license or something."

"I didn't bring any I.D. along. I didn't think I'd need it."

Paulo downshifted and wheeled the Lada into a U-turn. "You see?" he said crossly. "We'd have to go back to the house anyway. Man, nobody travels around Brazil without I.D." He seemed nervous and distracted, like someone with lots of items on his checklist.

"Relax," I told him. "You've been spending too much time in the U.S." I was feeling very Brazilian.

After picking up my wallet we went to Stieger's house and got the paperwork, and at nine-fifteen pulled into the village of Presidente Figueiredo for gas and to pick up two frozen chickens to use as bait. We hoped to catch some large catfishes by hook and line, tether them to the shore, and see if they would attract candirus. Paulo had also packed one of INPA's gill nets in case baitfishing didn't work.

At noon when we stopped for gas in Porto Fiscal the cops asked to see our identification and the Lada's papers. A half-hour later we crossed the Equator and entered the Northern Hemisphere.

The road, which is good in most places, connects eventually with the Venezuelan highway system and ends at the Caribbean Sea. The section we were traveling had been carved out of dense rainforest starting in the 1960s, although most of it had been paved only in the last few years. Marching towards the shoulders were gray parapets aligned in ranks like frozen waves where the macadam, softened by the intense heat, was being slowly shunted aside under the weight of passing vehicles. The road was sliding into the forest, a problem stemming partly from the subsurface layer, which is soil instead of the crushed stone ordinarily used in roadbeds. This roadbed had simply been graded and paved.

Land along the highway was being burned and cleared for subsistence farming and ranching. Trees lay strewn across the smoldering ground like charred matchsticks. In older pastures the blackness was softened by brilliant green Kikuyu grass, an African import planted widely in the Amazon basin as cattle forage. Nothing grew where the land had been stripped completely, not even the coarse vegetation expected in such places, and the earth was red and eroded as if exsanguinated and left to die.

We stopped for gas twice more, arriving eventually at a rutted turnoff leading directly into the forest. We followed this track for about 5 kilometers, swerving to avoid bogs and fallen trees, and then, at two-thirty, we saw the Rio Jauaperi, an affluent of the Rio Negro.

Others knew about the turnoff, and at least four groups of people were camped at the head of the rapids. It was hard to distinguish one from another because the campsites overlapped and the occupants were visiting back and forth. Litter was everywhere, and the air stank of human feces and rotting garbage. We drove a short distance upriver and found a spot on part of the broad sandstone floor of the riverbed, exposed now in the dry season (Fig. 47). After chopping a campsite at the edge of the woods, Paulo backed up the Lada and strung our hammocks between the roof rack and two trees. The tarpaulin was then pulled across a rope stretched from a tree to the front of the vehicle.

After watching my trials with the hammock, Paulo unfolded a camp chair and sat down to repair the gill net. I took my dip net and waded into the river to sweep the aquatic vegetation, catching only a few small tetras.

The river was tea-colored, dark, and swift. The bottom, scoured by the current, dropped steeply away. Downstream about 75 meters the rapids began, but here, where the riverbed climbed abruptly to meet them, ricocheting eddies boiled to the surface and spread in all directions. Standing was difficult, swimming impossible. These places of strong currents and the edges of the rapids were where we hoped to find candirus, although we would be looking for them mostly at night. Daytime searches might be fruitful too, but from what little we knew about candirus the odds of success seemed better after sunset.

Paulo joined me in the water. The air temperature was 35°C; the warm temperature of the river (30°C) and its deep reddish color were reminiscent of hematuric piss. We waded in to our necks and swept the shallows near the campsite with dip nets, then squelched down a path to the rapids

FIG. 47   Paulo Petry (left) and Steve Spotte (right) at the campsite on the Rio Jauaperi, 1 November 1999. Source: Stephen Spotte.

and swept along the upper crest, catching mainly tetras and small loricariid catfishes (Fig. 48). These last-mentioned are fishes with large
underslung, or subterminal, mouths. The jaws are shaped like suction
cups, and indeed function as such, enabling a loricariid to grip rocks in
strong currents to keep from being swept away. Loricariids have even been
seen moving up the vertical faces of waterfalls. They can do this by
relaxing their grip momentarily, slithering forward, and clamping down
again. For many species the diet consists of algae growing on the surfaces
of submerged rocks and sunken trees. A few of these comprise the "algae-
eating" catfishes kept in home aquariums.

Some of the people were packing their belongings and preparing to
leave, evidently anxious to navigate the road while there was daylight. One
group of *caboclos*, obviously intent on staying, had trucked in a diesel generator for powering a string of weak electric lights and a large refrigerator.
Several canoes with outboards were tied to the river's edge. The dwellings
were tarps stretched between trees with hammocks slung underneath.
Women washed clothes in the river while naked children splashed nearby.
What little wind remained died completely by four o'clock, its disappear-
ance a signal for the gnats and mosquitoes to emerge. Mercifully, black-
flies were scarce.

We continued scouting the river, wading through astonishing masses of
an aquatic plant, probably of the genus *Ceratopteris* (family Parkeriaceae).
Some of the leaves, which were brilliant green and looked like romaine
lettuce, were more than a meter long. Beer cans and other debris bobbed
in the verdant mats. "These are my countrymen," Paulo muttered.
"Fucking pigs." Just then a man walked to the river and threw in a plastic
bag filled with garbage. We watched it float briefly before disappearing
into the rapids.

Back at the campsite we heated up some canned food, and I determined our position.[2] Darkness approached, a deepening mauve that crept
skyward from behind the river and trees. Suddenly, bats were in the air,
and the evening grew stale and caliginous. Supper was chocolate cookies
and bottled water. We lay in our hammocks underneath mosquito netting
listening to the frogs and the generator's faint hum mingled with the roar
of the rapids.

In a 1911 article, Haseman warns that fishing in South America is the
riskiest of all scientific endeavors. He tells us:[3] "In addition to the dangers

besetting the collector on land the fisherman is in danger of drowning, stepping on a sting-ray, getting into contact with an electric eel, getting bitten by Piranhas, *Palometes*, and Candirus, or being carried off by either a large anaconda, or caiman."

As to personal health and hygiene, Haseman advises the fish collector to eat everything, especially fruits, vegetables, and lean meats, but to avoid fats. Work hard, he says. Go to bed early, sleep under mosquito netting, drink coffee instead of alcohol, and remain calm in the face of danger and hardship. Haseman confides that he bathed frequently, but didn't shave. He kept his stomach acidic and took a calomel purge at the first sign of indigestion. Finally,[4] "I learned to smoke and think I was the better for it, because tobacco soothes the mind and drives away many of the annoying insects."

FIG. 48   Paulo Petry dip-netting fishes in the Cachoeira do Travessão, Rio Jauaperi, 1 November 1999. Source: Stephen Spotte.

By seven-fifteen darkness was complete. Only a few stars flickered weakly through some high thin clouds. Wearing wet shorts and soggy sneakers and carrying our dip nets and large plastic bags, we took the path down to the rapids and waded in. The *caboclos* camped on the shore eyed us curiously through the smoke of their cooking fires. Paulo was wearing a headlamp, obviously a good idea when trying to stay balanced in the current and wield a net. I was carrying an underwater flashlight that could survive a dunking, but I needed two hands to push the net through the current. Much of the time I fished in total darkness, the useless flashlight stuffed in a back pocket.

The river was inky black, and we had to shout to hear each other above the rushing water. We probed through submerged vegetation along the top of the rapids and caught several interesting loricariids, knifefishes with pointed tails that can swim both backwards and forwards, and specimens of the genus *Leporinus*, some species of which reach edible size. We moved closer to the bank where Paulo, using my net with a mesh size of 1 millimeter, caught four candirus in a single sweep. We examined them under the lights. The water, little more than calf-deep, swirled madly around the boulders.

"They're the same as the ones I caught before," Paulo said. "I don't know what they are—which species—but they're candirus."

"They must lie waiting for a large fish to come by, then dart out and attack its gills," I mused. This was speculation. Nobody has any idea how candirus spend their time when not sucking blood. And besides, what large species of fishes would—or could—swim through such places? Probably more than I might imagine.

"Maybe that's how they do it," Paulo answered. "Of course, this section of the river just about disappears in the rainy season. You still see the rapids, but these shallow parts get flooded. After the rains start this particular habitat will be gone."

It was seven forty-five. Paulo handed back my dip net, and 15 minutes later I caught two candirus. Between us we eventually caught nine using my net. All were taken in very swift water not deeper than 30 centimeters, either over coarse sand or bare rock. We didn't catch any in quiet waters or in the rooted vegetation growing along the lip of the rapids. We also learned that a net of fine mesh is necessary.[5] Paulo's dip net was the type used in trout hatcheries and had a larger mesh size than mine. Candirus could easily escape through its openings. And it is, after all, the openings that matter most. As the English novelist Julian Barnes writes in *Flaubert's Parrot*:[6]

> You can define a net in one of two ways, depending on your point of view. Normally, you would say that it is a meshed instrument designed to catch fish. But you could, with no great injury to logic, reverse the image and define a net [as] . . . a collection of holes tied together with string.

We placed the candirus in two plastic bags along with a little river water. They were extremely slender—wormlike—and had been completely invisible in the dark turbid water of the river. Held to the light they were a translucent sandy color with iridescent silver bellies and coal-black eyes. Their movements were fast and sinuous.

The algae-covered rocks were slippery and treacherous. I took three bad spills during our forays into the upper rapids, and Paulo one. A misstep near the center of the river would have resulted in a very bumpy ride. We quit at eight-fifteen, exhausted from fighting the current, and trudged back to camp. I had brought along a portable aerator used for bait buckets, powered by two flashlight batteries. We transferred the candirus to a large plastic tray and set an airstone bubbling. Paulo kept some of the other fishes for his aquariums in Manaus. We left these in their bags but set the bags in buckets to keep them from tipping over. No aeration was necessary.

Bats fluttered silently around underneath the tarp; frogs croaked from the trees. Paulo changed into dry clothes and climbed into his hammock. I dried off on a dirty t-shirt before putting it on along with dry shorts, socks, and a long-sleeved shirt. Nights in the tropics can be cold, especially near dawn. I had forgotten to bring long pants and the blanket from my bed in Manaus, but neither would be necessary. The feeling of being chilled near the Equator is partly a response of acclimation, and my physiology was still in a cold-weather mode. Of his travels in South America, von Humboldt writes:[7]

> Though we had yet scarcely been two months in the torrid zone we had already become so sensible [*sic*] to the smallest variation of temperature that the cold prevented us from sleeping; while, to our surprise, we saw that the centigrade thermometer was as high as 21.8°.

Humboldt went on to say that during their stay at Guayaquil, Ecuador, in January 1808, he and Bonpland[8] ". . . observed that the natives covered themselves, and complained of the cold, when the thermometer sunk to 23.8°[C], whilst they felt the heat suffocating at 30.5°[C]."

I disembarked warily from my hammock at dawn. Paulo was walking back from the river. Behind him pale dreadlocks of mist rose off the surface. He reported that the smallest candiru had died. I mixed some 10 percent formalin using river water and popped it into a specimen bottle. We sat in the camp chairs and scarfed instant oatmeal and a peculiar Brazilian blend of orange juice and yogurt. There were also bananas and grapes and a fresh pineapple, and enough hot water for one cup of coffee each. We made them last by doubling the amount of instant coffee.

While Paulo stretched his gill net in the river, I mixed up the chemical solutions brought along to test as attractants. Our preliminary experiments would be done right on the riverbank, the first such tests ever attempted using candirus.

To lessen the possibility of an unknown organic compound in the river interfering with the test solutions and perhaps lessening their effectiveness, I filtered some river water by passing it several times through activated carbon granules sandwiched between layers of new quilt batting. Activated carbon adsorbs dissolved organic compounds from water nonselectively; the quilt batting removes any suspended particulate matter. The treated water was clear and colorless, unlike the original river water that in small volumes was pale brown and slightly turbid.

Using this water as the solvent, I mixed stock solutions of ammonium chloride and amino acids. A stock solution of a chemical is one in which a predetermined weight of solute (or volume of solution) is dissolved in a predetermined volume of solvent (filtered river water in this case) to yield a known concentration. Stock solutions ordinarily are concocted to be highly concentrated so that small amounts can be dispensed to larger volumes, yielding known dilutions.

When the experiments started, I would dispense predetermined amounts in with the candirus from an automatic pipettor that measures tiny volumes very accurately. Two containers would serve as test aquariums, receiving a test solution (ammonia or the amino acid mix) from the stock solutions; the other two would serve as controls, receiving equal volumes of filtered river water. We would measure any effect on the candirus by monitoring their behavior. According to our hypothesis, the test candirus should become excited after detecting a putative attractant and start to swim wildly around. We would recognize this "appetitive" response, I from having seen videos of captive candirus detecting and then attacking live goldfish (*Carassius auratus*) in aquariums, Paulo from having witnessed such attacks in aquariums firsthand. The behavior of the controls, in contrast, would not change.

Several problems were apparent. For one, we didn't know the recent history of our candirus. Their guts appeared to be empty—in other words, not distended with blood—suggesting that they hadn't fed immediately prior to capture the previous night. But we could not know this for certain. If they failed to respond to the test conditions, one reason might be satiation. In human terms, a pizza is far less appealing if you've just eaten a pizza. How often did candirus feed? No one knew.

The amount of ammonia I was planning to add was extremely small. Aqueous solutions of ammonia are often prepared from soluble salts. In my laboratory at the University of Connecticut I had weighed five tiny batches of ammonium chloride and sealed them in polyethylene vials. I now opened one vial, emptied the contents into a volumetric flask, and carefully brought the volume to 1 liter with filtered river water. The finished stock solution contained roughly a thousand times the amount of ammonia-nitrogen that might be excreted in 1 hour by a fish weighing 30 grams.[9] I reasoned that candirus can distinguish trace concentrations of attractants from the numerous odors around them. Adding 1 milliliter of this stock solution to 1 liter of unfiltered river water (approximately a thousandfold dilution) containing a candiru would yield a concentration very close to the desired value.[10]

Ammonia has a duality problem. In certain cases it might be an attractant, but even small amounts are toxic to fishes. We hoped the candirus would respond positively by rising off the bottom of their aquariums and entering a search pattern, as if seeking a nearby ammonia-excreting fish. However, any unusual activity might also be an aversive response induced by ammonia toxicity.

Still another problem had to do with design of the experiment. It involved the small number of available fish and my intention of using the same fish to test more than one attractant. Suppose they suffered "olfactory shock" or became habituated to one attractant and unable to detect the other. These concerns were genuine, but in real science, as in real life, you go with what you have. Sloshing around in the river had produced

FIG. 49 The four small aquariums used in experiments on the bank of the Rio Jauaperi, 1 November 1999. The candirus are in the plastic tray on the left. Source: Stephen Spotte.

nine specimens, and one was already dead. My computer model had specified a minimum sample size of 31 candirus *for each attractant*, tested one fish at a time. Catching so many seemed unlikely.

Finally, should the experiments be conducted at night? Candirus appear to be nocturnal. Paulo had taken several specimens from the Rio Jauaperi back to Manaus, kept them in an aquarium, and videotaped them entering the gills of goldfish to feed on blood. He first offered them a goldfish during the day. They ignored it until nightfall, then attacked it. The second time was also during daylight hours, and they attacked without hesitation.

The other stock solution was prepared by adding 1 milliliter of amino acid solution to a graduated cylinder and bringing the volume to 50 milliliters with filtered river water. When I added 100 microliters to 1 liter of unfiltered river water containing a candiru, the final concentration of amino acids in solution would be a mere 10^{-4}, or approximately one part in ten thousand parts water. However, this tiny amount elicits a response in certain other catfishes.[11]

We unpacked four handmade glass boxes (actually, tiny aquariums) measuring 15 by 19 by 14 centimeters. Paulo wrapped three of their sides in black paper to cut down the extraneous light, and we set them in the shade underneath the tarp (Fig. 49). To each I added 1 liter of unfiltered river water and one candiru.

The fish in each trial were given 30 minutes to acclimate to their new conditions. If within 3 minutes of receiving either the attractant or the placebo a candiru rose off the bottom and entered a vigorous search pattern, I would record "1" in my notebook. No response received "0." We crept under the tarp and conducted three trials, one with ammonia and two with amino acids, emptying and refilling the aquariums after each. There was not a single positive response. Nothing but zeroes. Usually the candirus rested quietly on the bottom or rose to swim lazily around before settling back down.

When the trials were finished, we put a candiru into a small "photography" aquarium belonging to Paulo and took several photographs of it in lateral view (Fig. 50). Kodak ruined this roll of film, which also contained photographs of the rapids and campsite. Some slides were salvaged in black and white by scanning them. Many months later, illustrations were prepared from preserved specimens (Fig. 51).

We returned all the fish to their tray and went off to make a few daytime sweeps of the upper rapids, concentrating on places where we caught candirus the previous night. We didn't catch any. Success for a second

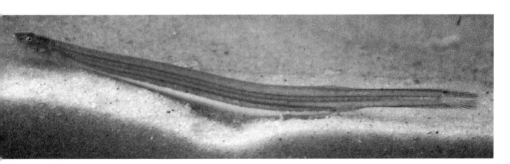

FIG. 50   Candiru (*Vandellia* cf. *plazai*) photographed on the bank on the Rio Jauaperi, 1 November 1999. Source: Stephen Spotte.

consecutive night would be tentative evidence that at least this species of candiru is mainly nocturnal. We tried swimming across the river, but the current was too strong: we were carrying nets and wearing sneakers. Our only choice was to fish along the south bank.

Paulo had befriended some *caboclos* camped beside the rapids, and they promised a fish of suitable size to tether in the river after dark. Later in the day Paulo returned from their camp with a catfish weighing about 3 kilograms. It was one of the beautifully marked tiger catfishes (*Pseudoplatystoma* sp.). The *caboclos* had tied a line to its tail, and we tethered it in a quiet pool until nightfall.

Just before sunset fish started rising where the current swept around a large rock near the shore, making little rings on the surface. I assembled my fly rod, tied on a dry fly resembling an ant, and cast it into the current several times, letting it drift past the rock, but nothing happened. Paulo examined my modest collection of flies and suggested switching to one that was bigger and more colorful.

The new fly elicited a few curious nibbles, but only one half-hearted strike. When it got too dark to see, I cut off the fly and threw it away. Paulo rigged a handline and baited a hook with strips of fish obtained from the *caboclos*. He soon caught three tiger catfish. We ran a line through the mouth and gills of the largest and tied it off with the other. The two smallest were left in a cloth bag immersed in the river.

At seven-thirty we took the two biggest catfish down to the rapids and tied them to a shrub overhanging the river. The location was about 4 meters downstream from the place where we had caught candirus the previous night. Any candiru attacking our tethered catfish would have navigated the swift waters of the rapids after detecting some sort of signal.

Meanwhile, we slogged around with my dip net, catching several candirus. At eight fifteen, we picked up the tethered fish and shook them over the dip net. From the gills of one a candiru fell out. We swept the substratum around both fish and caught several more. Two that Paulo caught regurgitated blood, and in the light of my flashlight his hands looked as if they were bleeding from deep cuts.[12]

While Paulo walked over to the next camp to chat, I caught seven candirus using the dip net. Then I turned off the flashlight and lay down in the river. I wedged myself among the weedy rocks, feeling the blood-warm water course over my shoulders.

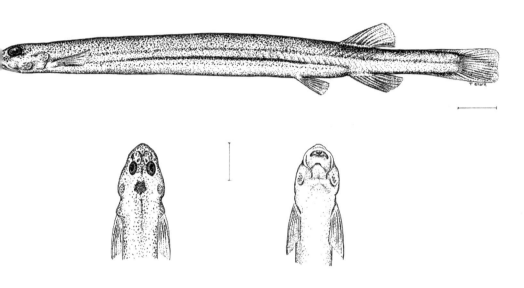

FIG.51   Illustration of a candiru (*Vandellia* cf. *plazai*) from the Rio Jauaperi. *Top:* Lateral view. *Bottom left:* Dorsal view of head and upper body. *Bottom right:* Ventral view of head and upper body. Scale bar = 5 millimeters. Illustrations by Tamara L. Clark. Source: Stephen Spotte.

"Come on, you little peckerworms!" I shouted. *"Here's a vacant urethra!"* I urinated mightily, straining until my eardrums popped and the noise of the Cachoeira do Travessão grew deafening. I pissed until I swelled the volume of the Rio Jauaperi, raised the temperature of the Rio Negro, lightened the muddy currents of the Rio Solimões, and raised the salt content of the mighty Amazon itself. Millions of candirus stopped what they were doing, turned, and started swimming upstream. I tensed for the attack that never came. Of course, I was wearing tight underwear.

The candirus at this single location were up and moving, no doubt about it, then suddenly they vanished. Paulo returned, and we fished with my net another half-hour before quitting with 21 specimens. I collected sand samples from the bottom for reference.

We had also caught a small electric eel, several more knifefishes, and an odd catfish that resembled a pipefish. We released the eel, but Paulo kept the other specimens for his aquariums. We gave the big catfish to the *caboclos*, one of which was theirs anyway, and showed them the candirus. They wondered aloud why we kept the little ones and gave away those of edible size.

At our campsite we released the other two catfish from the bag and dried off on dirty t-shirts. I was too excited to sleep and sat in one of the camp chairs. Above my head the black shoulders of the Universe sloped away, flecked with white lint that passed as stars. Our first objective had been achieved: we had captured, observed, and photographed candirus, and conducted a preliminary experiment on the riverbank. Someday their feeding patterns would be known, the factors that stimulate them identified and measured. It made me a little sad. Later, as I climbed into my hammock, I thought of Niels Bohr's dictum that the real function of science is to render all mysteries trivial.

In the beginning was the thing. And one thing led to another.

—Tom Robbins, *Half Asleep in Frog Pajamas*[1]

10.

Hora do Amor

Brazil is a very sensual country. When last I visited the evidence was everywhere. Beside the roads leading into Manaus were billboards depicting a handsome dark-haired man lying atop a handsome dark-haired woman, both dressed in evening clothes. The man is nuzzling the woman's neck. In his hand is a bottle of Antarctica beer dripping with condensation. "It's easy," the ad seems to say. "Drink lots of Antarctica beer and you too can make love to gorgeous Brazilian women."

Other billboards screamed, "Hora do Amor!" Motels offering rooms by the hour rent these spaces. The cost of a room is about $8 U.S., a little more with a Jacuzzi. Competition is fierce. Some establishments have a special weekday price that includes lunch; others throw in a ceiling mirror at no extra cost, silk sheets, or hidden entrances so your wife or husband can't find you.

According to Paulo, Brazilian women are very aggressive. "If one likes you," he explained, "you don't have much choice except to submit. Of course, you might play dead." I wasn't worried. Beautiful young women seldom pounce on an older guy like me unless he's in the movies or related to someone who once knew someone who was in the movies.

The alternative to playing dead was the aloof, worldly approach, and I thought of quoting Isaac Babel, the Russian writer who disappeared into the Gulag in 1939:[2] "Thus does a girl who thirsts for the inconveniences of conception look at a professor who is devoted to learning." My only problem was figuring how to say it in Portuguese. Not that it mattered. After two days and nights of wading in a stinking river catching stinking fish, we smelled worse than dead. No woman would dare come near us.

In Manaus, Paulo shared a house with Ning Labbish Chao, an ichthyologist and professor at Universidade do Amazonas. On the veranda were several aquariums and plastic holding trays. Paulo and I debated whether to transfer the candirus to city water or leave them in their original water from the Rio Jauaperi. They looked fine, and I saw no reason for a transfer. Paulo insisted that the tap water pumped from the Rio Negro through the city's treatment facility was only lightly chlorinated and, in addition, had a long residence time in the cistern on the roof. No chlorine remained by the time it reached the taps. He had never experienced problems with transferring fishes directly into it. Reluctantly, I relented.

By the next morning most of the candirus were dead and looking oddly lumpy. I got out forceps and a magnifying glass and examined several specimens. All had produced copious amounts of mucus before dying, probably in response to an irritant in the water. Paulo and I both deserved delation. True, his procedure had always worked in the past, but keeping fishes in municipal water is never a good idea. I felt stupid, as if all my years spent peering into aquariums had been mindless ones. Emollient words seemed pointless. We silently mixed formalin for the 23 dead specimens, then slumped into chairs on the veranda.

By afternoon more candirus had died, and the situation now seemed desperate. The day was sultry and damp. If you stood in one place, sweat dripped from your limbs forming little puddles on the floor. My right leg from the top of the ankle to the toes was swollen grotesquely from infected insect bites. A dog whined in the distance, and the pitch of its voice rose and fell, at times holding to a steady hum like the stridulations of an insect. I heard *boi bumbá* music and wondered if it came from the tall apartment building with the leaning silhouette. The previous year the government had condemned the structure and evicted everyone, but the former tenants grew homesick and moved back. This time no one intervened.

The next morning only four candirus remained alive, survivors from the previous day having been transferred to well water obtained at INPA. They seemed in good condition and dashed wildly around in their tray when they sensed our presence. We could confidently lay blame on the municipal water. Never go against your better judgement, I reminded myself, even if your judgement is usually no better than anyone else's.

Paulo and I went to INPA where we examined our dead candirus under a microscope and tried to identify them using ichthyological keys. Paulo's was written in Portuguese; I used a photocopy of Burgess' key I had brought along. After working through our respective documents we concluded that the fish belonged in one of two genera, depending on whether a patch of tiny teeth is absent from each mandibular ramus (*Vandellia*) or present (*Plectrochilus*). I discuss this situation in Chapter 3.

We cranked the microscopes to high power and looked in vain for these structures. Jansen joined us, and we put him to work at a microscope. Lúcia Rapp Py-Daniel, INPA's curator of fishes, wandered over from her office across the hall. Jansen was certain he saw patches of teeth, Lúcia and I were certain he hadn't, and Paulo was noncommittal. Knowing such issues can't be decided by vote, we kept looking. Our tentative *Plectrochilus* could just as easily be tentative *Vandellia*. From there the trail grew cold. Some specimens would have to be cleared and stained, a lengthy procedure that often reveals hard tissue not otherwise visible.[3]

A colleague of Jansen's had caught some very small catfish near Barcelos, a town up the Rio Negro. They were swimming around in a tray in Jansen's lab. We were ecstatic. Maybe now the experiment could be completed, but first we needed to identify the fish. We killed one in formalin and put it under a microscope. It was a trichomycterid, but not a candiru. The fish had all been captured in a stream under leaf litter, where they probably fed on insects.

The next morning Paulo and I ate a quick breakfast and packed up the minimal collecting equipment: three plastic trays, some large plastic bags and rubber bands, a bucket, and my dip net. A seine net we needed was at INPA. The net measured 6 by 3 meters and had a mesh of 5 millimeters. We were ready for a day on the Rio Solimões.

We loaded the Lada and meandered through a maze of back roads to Jansen's house, where his two snarling dogs met us at the gate. Jansen was ready. After picking up the net we drove to the riverfront, parked, lugged our stuff down the hill to the beach, and hired a boat. It was an open wooden skiff about 5 meters long with a 40-horsepower Yamaha outboard of recent vintage. Boat and motor seemed well maintained. Their owner wanted the equivalent of $40 U.S. for the day, which included $15 for gas. We accepted, tossed everything on board, and cast off.

The first stop was a refueling barge anchored in the Rio Negro, where I had a chance to examine the water closely. The color of the river really *is* black, or at least a deep reddish brown, stained by humic and fulvic acids originating from plant materials that after decomposition are percolated through shallow podzolic soils.[4]

The English naturalist Alfred Russel Wallace first saw the Rio Negro on the last day of the year 1849:[5]

> We might have fancied ourselves on the river Styx, for it was black as ink in every direction, except where the white sand, seen at a depth of a few feet through its dusky wave, appeared of a golden hue. The water itself is of a pale brown colour, the tinge being just perceptible in a glass, while in deep water it appears jet black, and well deserves its name of Rio Negro—"black river."

Wallace classified South American rivers on the basis of color and clarity:[6] "They may be divided into three groups, —the white-water rivers, the blue-water rivers, and the black-water rivers." He correctly tells us that[7] ". . . the difference of colour between the white- and blue-water rivers, is evidently owing to the nature of the country they flow through: a rocky and sandy district will always have clear-water rivers; an alluvial or clayey one, will have yellow or olive-coloured streams."

Of the blackwater streams Wallace writes,[8] "The causes of the peculiar colour of these rivers are not, I think, very obscure; it appears to me to be produced by the solution of decaying leaves, roots, and other vegetable matter." Again he assesses the situation correctly. The American zoologist James Orton agreed:[9] "When seen in a tumbler, the water of the Negro is clear, but of a light-red color; due, undoubtedly, to vegetable matter." Gordon MacCreagh, pragmatic as always, adds:[10]

> One of the first observable things about this Rio Negro is that it is really "black water," a clear thin ink when dipped up in the hand, and black night at a depth of ten feet. This last is a scientific observation made by myself, when I went over after the frying-pan.

At the junction with the Rio Solimões the color of the water changes abruptly to *café au lait*. The two rivers flow this way, side by side—the Manaus side blackwater, the opposite bank whitewater—until merging far downstream to become the Rio Amazonas, itself a whitewater river.

Upon crossing the boundary separating the waters of the two rivers, we entered the Rio Solimões and came upon a pod of pink dolphins (*Inia geoffrensis*), or *botos*, chasing fish near the shore. These animals were very pink. The captive pink dolphins with which I was familiar are never this brightly colored. Baby *botos* are gray at birth, gradually turning pink with maturity. The oldest *botos* are the most colorful. *Botos* are portrayed as sirens in South American legends. Wallace's friend, the English naturalist Henry Walter Bates, writes:[11]

> One [legend] was to the effect that a Bouto once had the habit of assuming the shape of a beautiful woman, with hair hanging loose to her heels, and walking ashore at night in the streets of Ega, to entice the young men down to the water. If any one was so much smitten as to follow her to the water-side, she grasped her victim round the waist and plunged beneath the waves with a triumphant cry. No animal in the Amazons region is the subject of so many fables as the Bouto . . .

We also have Woodroffe's ridiculous report. According to him, several species of *botos* exist in the Amazon, but the most common are those he designates "red" and "white." He says:[12]

> They are ugly-looking creatures, and when they come up to breathe they throw off a very offensive smell. . . . The white species is inoffensive, but the red one is greatly feared, for although both are carnivorous, the red one is exceptionally voracious. The writer has seen them fighting both the boa-constrictor [anaconda] and alligator.

F. Bruce Lamb recounts other *boto* legends, such as their sinister reputation for snatching paddles from canoeists leaving them drifting helplessly. On the other hand, Lamb writes, *botos* look kindly on people whose boats have capsized and push them to shore. A *boto* in the area means the water is safe from piranhas. When feeling mischievous, *botos* turn up at fiestas disguised as men, where they dance with the girls and later impregnate them. According to Lamb, more than one pregnant girl without a husband has blamed her situation on a charming *boto*.

At ten-thirty we pulled up on a broad sandbank along the river's edge, barren except for a few rotting aquatic plants brought by the swash, mainly water hyacinths (*Eichhornia crassipes*). This place was to be our hunting ground. By now the sky had descended in a hazy wash that hung gray and motionless as smoke. Distant riverboats faded to wriggling mirages, rose blue and vaporous above the river, and evaporated. Farther west, black vultures (*Coragyps atratus*) squabbled on the beach over some delicacy we couldn't see. We waded in and started seining, working westward along the submerged edge of the sand.[13] The water felt deceptively thick and oily, and its extraordinary warmth had an unsettling, preternatural quality. It was like stepping into the circulating fluids of some massive, homeothermic beast.

Pulling the net took two people, so we rotated. Although the area was free of submerged tree limbs, large rocks, and other obstacles, mud and sand quickly occluded the small mesh of the net and made dragging it ashore difficult. We trudged forward, often sinking into thigh-deep mud. Jansen proved himself a tireless seiner, easily outworking Paulo and me despite his smaller stature. Somehow, Jansen always found himself pulling the deep end of the net, and on occasion only his hat was visible above the surface. Paulo and I wore sneakers, but Jansen was barefooted despite the presence of stingrays.

I had forgotten to bring a thermometer, but the temperature of the river was at least 30°C and several degrees higher in some of the tiny scalloped bays. Even in these locations, which were nearly as hot as a bath, we caught fishes with every pull of the net. Along the edge of the sandbank were tetras, large hatchetfishes (*Thoracocharax* spp.) that can "fly" for short distances above the water, a few needlefish (*Pseudotylosaurus* sp.), and various loricariid catfishes. We caught specimens of *Charax gibbosus*, a characin with a black lateral spot that makes its living by stripping scales off other fishes and then swallowing them, and another closely related scale-stripper of smaller size. And there were candirus. In 3 hours of seining we caught 25 specimens (Fig. 52). Two died, but the rest made it to Labbish's house alive.

These candirus (Plate 7) looked like the specimens Paulo and I had caught in the Rio Jauaperi. If they proved to be the same, their presence in such different habitats showed evidence of impressive adaptability. The Rio Jauaperi is a fast-moving blackwater river with a bed of clean sand and stones. In contrast, this section of the Rio Solimões is sluggish, silty, and its bottom consists of mud and sand. No doubt the water chemistry of the two rivers also differs in important respects.

Back at the house we sluiced off with a garden hose, put the fish into holding trays, ate a roasted chicken, and preserved two dead candirus from the day's catch. Paulo then drove Jansen home. We were set to conduct a feeding trial the next day using the four surviving candirus from the Rio Jauaperi. They had been starved for nearly a week. All we needed were some live fish to use as prey.

FIG. 52   Paulo Petry (left) and Jansen Zuanon (right) picking candirus from a seine net on a sandbank of the Rio Solimões, 6 November 1999. Source: Stephen Spotte.

Rain fell hard just before dawn, breaking the intense heat. There was nothing to do in the morning except read, a welcome change especially because Labbish was out of town and I could commandeer one of his halogen reading lamps. The radio reported 27°C and 92 percent humidity. The rain had awakened armies of mosquitoes, but the air at least was cooler.

Paulo walked to the bakery down the street for croissants and bread. Three candirus from the previous day's catch had died overnight, and by the end of the day 10 more were dead. Seining is a much cruder technique than dip netting. Candirus are delicate, and dragging them through the mud and sand no doubt caused fatal injuries. The skin of these specimens showed evidence of abrasion.

I spent time watching the denizens of the several aquariums inside the house and outside on the veranda. I was learning new things about freshwater aquarium keeping. These aquariums received only indirect light, which helped control algal growth. The presence of one or more loricariids in each aquarium was the ultimate control because they feed almost exclusively on algae. Paulo also kept the water moving by the use of filters equipped with mechanical pumps. Tropical rivers and streams often flow rapidly, and the indigenous fishes have adapted to such habitats. Strong currents in the aquarium seemed to help, perhaps because at higher temperatures (these aquariums were 30°C) water holds less oxygen. Paulo's fishes were fed only twice weekly and seemed in good condition. Tropical marine fishes would quickly starve on such a restricted regimen. The fare of the algae-eating catfishes was supplemented weekly with slices of zucchini, scalded first so they sank. Finally, the water was kept very soft, like tropical river water. "Blackwater" conditions had been mimicked by the addition of peat moss to the filter compartments.

Most of Paulo's specimens were from the Rio Negro. Wallace was the first to note its incredible diversity of fishes:[14] "I am convinced that the number of species in the Rio Negro and its tributaries alone would be found to amount to five or six hundred." He later repeats this conviction:[15] "From the number of new fishes constantly found in every fresh locality and in every fisherman's basket, we may estimate that at least five hundred species exist in the Rio Negro and its tributary streams." Labbish and Paulo estimate the number of species at about 750.

The rain stopped by late morning, but the slate-gray sky persisted. We bought gas for Labbish's car and went to catch cichlids for a candiru feeding trial. Cichlids are the Southern Hemisphere's answer to panfishes. They inhabit all types of waters and can be caught easily with hook and line, but we took dip nets and buckets. In addition, we would fill the jugs with well water at a convenience store near the house and make partial water changes in all the aquariums.

Cichlids are wary. The rain had raised the level of the artificial stream that meanders through Bosque da Ciência, a small zoo and nature center on the grounds of INPA, and all the fishes avoided us easily. We followed the stream to where it emptied into a big pond, but the grass at the water's edge had been cut down. The cichlids ordinarily found hiding there were cruising in loose, straggling schools just out of reach. At a smaller pond nearby we caught two specimens of *Cichlosoma amazonarum*. We then drove to another INPA campus that has an aquaculture facility. In one of the ponds we caught four more cichlids of this species. Our method was to creep slowly along the edge of the pond and suddenly plunge a dip net into the tangle of aquatic vegetation. Six specimens were enough. After filling the bottles with well water, it was time to return to the house and set up the first trial using live fish.

Before doing anything, we got a large drinking glass from the kitchen, scooped up some water from the bucket containing the cichlids, and poured it into the aquarium with the four candirus from the Rio Jauaperi. This would serve as a crude test of whether the cichlids had excreted some substance that might be an attractant. When nothing happened after 1 minute, we added another glassful. Still nothing.

We put the two largest cichlids into the aquarium. After 4 minutes one candiru slipped under the right operculum of a cichlid and attached to its gills. The candiru fed for almost 2 minutes, its belly swelling noticeably, then it detached and dropped to the bottom. This episode was videotaped. The cichlids were removed after a few minutes.

We repeated the procedure 4 hours later with negative results, and again after waiting 45 minutes. During the third trial there were two unsuccessful attacks, meaning the attacking candiru attached to the gills only briefly, not long enough to ingest blood. A subsequent attack was successful, and the candiru stayed attached long enough to feed

Over the following days we introduced a cichlid and a goldfish simultaneously, giving the candirus a choice of victims. We were interested to know whether the candirus preferred an otophysan (the goldfish) or a perciform fish (the cichlid).[16] If they showed a clear preference, we could devise hypotheses for future tests.[17]

The next day, 8 November, was Monday. No more candirus had died overnight, and the original four now looked in excellent condition. As candirus ingest blood their abdomens swell noticeably and, in this species, become more reflective. The abdomen is always silvery, but the swelling appears to push more abdominal skin into lateral view. Three candirus had swollen bellies; the belly of the fourth looked the same as before. Possibly only three had fed. When homing in on a fish's gills the candiru became very active, and keeping track of each individual was difficult.

Over the next few days Paulo filled out reams of paperwork necessary to get our preserved fishes out of Brazil. I was hoping to take some of the dead candirus home for further study, and Paulo had preserved specimens of other species he was studying at Oregon State. There was the additional chore of delivering letters all over town to be signed by various authorities. Meanwhile, I conducted more trials using the purported chemical attractants. I filled the four little aquariums Paulo and I had used on the bank of the Rio Jauaperi and placed a candiru in each. As before, I added a tiny volume of plain water to the control aquariums and an equal volume of a premixed chemical solution to the test aquariums. To retard their decay, I kept my solutions in a refrigerator next to Labbish's beer and Chinese vegetables. There were two control aquariums and two that were treated. When the ammonium chloride stock solution turned brown, I replaced it. Neither the ammonia nor the amino acid solution ever induced a positive response. If the candirus sensed either, they gave no sign. I considered why this was so and came up with several possibilities.

(1) The concentrations of the attractants were too low. I had done a literature search on what levels of different compounds attract catfishes of other species. The concentration of the amino acid solution (10^{-4}) was known to be easily detected by captive channel catfish. To my knowledge, ammonia had never been demonstrated to attract fishes or elicit from them any sort of feeding response. I had simply based the concentration I was using on the amount excreted by a fish weighing 30 grams over 1 hour.[18]

(2) The candirus weren't hungry. Like the first possibility, this one was unlikely. The fishes used in the first few trials at Labbish's house had not been fed in 4 days.

(3) There *is* no discernible prey-search response, or the response is too subtle for our crude method of observation, which was simply watching for something to happen. Maybe things *were* happening, or maybe I was looking for a chimera. Even when feeding on live fishes, some of the candirus were almost languid in their approach. Rapid movement was occasionally not apparent until the end of the appetitive response when they darted into the gill openings and attached. I had anticipated a marked quickening of activity in the presence of the attractants.

(4) I was testing the wrong attractants. Possibly true. My selections were nothing but guesses. Perhaps the attractant—if indeed there is such a thing—is a skin component of the prey (e.g., sloughing mucus).

(5) Candirus find their prey by means other than chemical attraction. Possibilities include sensing electromagnetic fields around prey fishes, following their exhalent gill currents, homing in on sounds generated by the prey species or following in its wake, or vision (see Chapter 5). If so, a chemical alone would not elicit a response. In future experiments I hoped to anesthetize some candirus and blind them surgically. After a suitable recovery period, I could then test their prey-finding ability against a group with normal vision.

(6) The candirus seemed more active at night. Their activity picked up noticeably after dark, when they swam rapidly for long periods. During the day they mostly rested on the bottom or swam lazily. Maybe running the tests at night was the answer, although the problem would be detecting differences in the response. No doubt the control candirus would also be moving. And besides, they fed readily on live fish during the day.

(7) The ambient concentrations of ammonia and amino acids were too great for the candirus to detect the trace amounts we were adding. We didn't know the concentrations of these compounds already present in the water, and they might have masked our additions.

(8) A natural response is impossible in the restricted confinement of the test aquariums because the required stimuli, which we had not identified, are absent or attenuated. Perhaps the nuances and repertoire of responses are more intricate than I thought.

I increased the dosages of ammonia to twice and then three times the original concentration, and still there was no response. I increased the amino acid solution by factors of five and 10, but nothing happened. In desperation I caught one of the goldfish and scraped slime and a few scales from its sides with my pocketknife. I shook this material in a flask with a little water and poured it in with the test candirus using equal volumes of

FIG. 53 Aquarium set up on the veranda of Ning Labbish Chao's house in Manaus where candiru feeding experiments were conducted. Source: Stephen Spotte.

well water for the controls. The candirus were unimpressed. I took gill tissues and surface mucus from a freshly killed cichlid, mashed it to a bloody pulp, and poured this disgusting mess on top of the test candirus. Nothing.

Using candirus that had been starved for 7 days, we tried human urine with Paulo serving as donor. I felt momentarily sorry for our subjects, but when they ignored this offering I reconsidered. We were stymied. What did they want? Was our urine inferior? *How could they do this to us, the rotten little bastards!*

We now had 12 healthy, active candirus, four from the Rio Jauaperi and eight from the Rio Solimões. I divided the last into two permanent groups of four each, giving us three groups in all. That afternoon I drained an 80-liter aquarium, cleaned it, and set it up on the picnic table on the veranda for feeding trials using live goldfish and cichlids (Fig. 53). This would allow us to view and videotape proceedings from every angle.

In the failing light Paulo, Jansen, and I rigged bedside lamps around the aquarium in preparation to film. Paulo stood on a bench of the picnic table and used his camcorder to film straight down; Jansen used his camcorder to film through the side of the aquarium. I was assigned the job of goldfish tender. I tossed in a goldfish and within 15 seconds three candirus attacked almost simultaneously (Fig. 54). One candiru did not feed, but the others were very aggressive. The action was too fast to record with handwritten notes; fortunately real-time intervals could be obtained from the video.

The bright lights had no apparent effect on the behavior of the candirus, which was not unexpected. Before coming to Brazil, I had watched a video transferred from an 8-millimeter film made in 1959 by Richard M. Segedi of the Cleveland Aquarium. The scene shows candirus feeding on a goldfish. After watching it several times, I telephoned Rick and asked if the studio lights had been a deterrent. He laughed. Only to the goldfish,

FIG. 54   Candiru (*Vandellia* cf. *plazai*) feeding on a captive goldfish. Manaus, Brazil, 12 November 1999. Courtesy of Stephen Spotte and Kluwer Academic Publishers. Source: Spotte et al. (2001).

he said. The bright lights set up to film the event had not affected the candirus at all. A photograph taken from a frame of that film was later published with a journal article (Fig. 55).[19]

Paulo switched batches of candirus the next morning in preparation for another feeding trial. By rotating the three groups through the test aquarium, we could keep them hungry. We wondered why the candirus seemed to prefer goldfish to cichlids and discussed several possibilities, including the "alarm substance" hypothesis (see endnote 17). Statistical analysis of the data would explain the extent of any actual disparity.

Maybe it was the different behavior of cichlids that made them less palatable. When a goldfish was put into the aquarium with candirus, it swam back and forth and up and down the glass as if seeking to escape. A cichlid behaved differently. Instead of swimming it went immediately to the bottom, ordinarily wedging itself into a corner. This was a good strategy. Maybe it was the wake left by the swimming goldfish that attracted the candirus.

In addition, they seemed to notice movement, following with their eyes a goldfish swimming above, even turning their heads slightly towards it. Their eyes, unlike those of many fishes, are located near the top of the

FIG. 55   Candirus (*Vandellia cirrhosa*) feeding on a captive goldfish. Cleveland Aquarium, 18 May 1959. Courtesy of Richard M. Segedi and American Society of Ichthyologists and Herpetologists. Source: Kelley and Atz (1964).

head, which would make looking up relatively efficient. How their vision might fare in a turbid environment like the Rio Solimões is another matter.

A goldfish had died 20 minutes after a trial the previous day, sucked dry by the candirus. At INPA, Jansen and I examined its gills under a microscope looking for evidence of damaged tissue. The candirus often fed so violently that blood and bits of tissue appeared in the water. Surely this damage would be apparent, but it wasn't. The gills looked perfectly normal, no different than those of a fish on which no candiru had fed. Histological sections made from the gill filaments might have revealed subtle injuries.

Paulo and I bought more goldfish at a pet shop and refilled the water bottles with well water. Later the three of us conducted more feeding trials. After finishing, I gave Jansen my dip net so he could catch candirus after Paulo and I were gone. The preserved specimens from the Rio Solimões examined earlier in the day had torn fins, indicative of physical trauma. These were the fish that had died soon after capture. In contrast, the fins of specimens captured in the Rio Jauaperi with my dip net were all in excellent condition. Jansen decided to leave the net with Labbish temporarily in case Paulo and I made a last-minute dash into the field to catch more specimens.

The feeding trials continued in days that followed, and the three groups of candirus assumed personalities. Paulo called the group from the Rio Jauaperi the "A-Team" because of their voracity, although later statistical analysis showed the feeding patterns of the groups to be indistinguishable.

Often a candiru would detach and the others would begin circling the victim. By then the unfortunate fish was often lying quietly—and helplessly—on the bottom. Instead of attacking, the candirus sometimes lost interest and swam away despite blood and other fluids leaking from underneath the victim's gill covers. Such behavior, and the fact that cichlids were attacked less often than goldfish, suggests that movement of the prey might trigger or sustain an attack, but this is conjecture. The feeding trials lasted 5 minutes, during which time a newly introduced cichlid rarely moved. Swimming candirus often bumped into fishes lying quietly on the bottom without attacking them. In contrast, swimming fishes usually acquired a trailing pack of hungry candirus.

Superficially, these observations point to the importance of vision in the feeding sequence, but to conclude this might spring a clever trap set to befuddle the unwary scientist. What appeared to be visual tracking of the prey could mask the activation of another sensory mode. A candiru could conceivably rise off the bottom and follow a prey fish without using vision at all. Maybe it detects near-field effects generated by its moving victim; perhaps it relies on electroreception (Chapter 5).

These were frenetic days. Paulo, in preparation for moving back to the U.S., was organizing his belongings in the middle of the living room. Labbish's time was consumed with teaching, preparing grant proposals, and writing scientific papers. We ate when hungry, not according to the clock. Paulo sometimes ordered huge greasy pizzas. They were delivered tepid and limp, looking like remnants of an agouti or anteater killed during a collision with a vegetable truck. Often the remaining slices greeted us at lunch the next day. They seemed resentful, resilient, as if interrupted in the middle of growing hair.

When not working with the candirus or helping edit Labbish's manuscripts, I sat outside on the veranda sniffing in the sticky-sweet odor of dog shit from next door and feeling mosquitoes beating their tiny wings against my hot bare feet. Sometimes we went out to dinner and Labbish drove, shifting gears only when we seemed about to stall and depressing the clutch absently, as someone might step on the head of a small dog that had hold of his pants leg.

One time Labbish and I found ourselves in a Korean restaurant, deserted except for two old Korean men who sat picking their teeth. The only wall art was a poster of a hand holding a newborn baby by one of its ankles. We sat at a table covered with oilcloth in a bleak room illuminated by greenish fluorescent lamps. A Korean woman came out of the kitchen and gave us menus. The items in the pictures were unrecognizable, like the contents of a seine dragged through a muddy swamp.

In Portuguese, Labbish asked the woman to bring us beef. I took another look at the baby in the picture. The woman returned with slices of frozen beef and a gas-fired metal grill. I glanced up at the baby, although this meat was too red to be human flesh, which has the color and consistency of pork. I knew about such things from having once read a book on Maori cannibalism during a trip to New Zealand. Truly, no information sifted from life's roadside litter is ever useless.

Monday the 15th was a national holiday. Paulo said we would have to start packing up everything soon. The specimens going with us were to be wrapped in formalin-soaked cheesecloth and sealed inside plastic bags. In addition to the candirus there were the victims. I planned to take home all the dead goldfish and cichlids so they could be measured, weighed, and examined. Maybe today would be the last for collecting data.

The trials were proceeding rapidly. The candirus needed very little time to acclimate to the aquarium after being netted out of their holding trays. In 15 minutes they were ready to attack prey. Once again I was struck by the possibilities of vision. During trial 23 I noticed again that when a prey fish swam above a candiru lying on the bottom, the candiru moved its head and seemed to follow the other fish's movement. With eyes placed near the top of the head, candirus might even have bilateral vision, which many other fishes lack. As mentioned before, their sight appears to be directed upwards, not laterally. In the wild, candirus perhaps stay on the bottom or just above it. There they might scull in place headed into the current, waiting for a larger fish to swim overhead. Of course, without data this is merely speculation.

Paulo was getting nervous. Time was short, and he had lots to do. He stood looking at his belongings piled on the floor. "I can leave lots of this crap here," he said. "Labbish will look after it. Maybe I'll move back someday, who knows?"

"Don't leave anything!" Labbish shouted from his office in the next room. "I'll throw it away. And I don't want you back."

The next day was sunny and already 33°C by seven o'clock. I pulled on shorts, made some coffee, and started more feeding trials. As usual, the cichlids were ignored, the goldfish attacked. With practice, I had become adept at timing and recording the attacks and could conduct the feeding trials alone. The camcorder was no longer necessary. Paulo had left before I got up. He returned at midmorning and asked if I wanted to go to INPA where he had some projects to finish. I chose to stay behind and collect more data.

I was between feeding trials when Paulo telephoned. He needed my passport number and the date when the passport was issued. He was filling out another form. The bureaucratic nonsense involved in the export of a few dozen dead fishes from Brazil is truly ridiculous. If I wanted to set up a packing plant to export catfish filets from Manaus, no problem. About 20 million live ornamental fishes are exported each year officially from Amazonas for the home aquarium trade. At least that many more leave the country illegally. Of the sanctioned exports, 80 percent are cardinal tetras (*Paracheirodon axelrodi*). Paulo had hoped to take a few dozen preserved cardinal tetras home to study their morphology, but there could be no avoiding more excruciating paperwork.

During feeding trial 29 the goldfish was attacked, but the cichlid, upon being put into the aquarium, immediately went to the bottom and lay on its side. A candiru moved over its body, apparently unable to find the gill opening. Meanwhile, the cichlid remained motionless, its skin paling. This activity continued for perhaps 2 minutes before the candiru gave up.

When I checked the holding trays at noon, both remaining goldfish were dead. The trials would proceed with only cichlids. At trial 30 I dropped in two of them, including the one used in the previous trial. As before, it lay quietly in a corner tipped onto one side. The candirus approached, nosing up and down its length. One candiru waited patiently with its nose against the edge of the gill cover. When the cichlid breathed, it darted inside and attached. Such behavioral adjustments indicate some plasticity.

Paulo came back with disheartening news. We would not be allowed to take our specimens out of Brazil by air on the 18th. The bureaucrats had decreed we would have to *mail* them. I said I wanted to send the candirus to Connecticut by FedEx. At least we would have a tracking number. Putting them in the mail was like sticking a note in a bottle and tossing it into the Rio Negro. Today would be the last of the feeding trials. Tomorrow the fishes would have to be packed.

Paulo decided to leave his cardinal tetras behind. These were specimens preserved in alcohol. He and a colleague at the University of Alabama were doing DNA analyses to identify different populations throughout the Rio Negro region. They even had some fish from Colombia. Paulo stuffed the bottles into a large plastic bag, which he put in a vegetable drawer of a refrigerator. He would try to obtain a special permit to carry out the specimens in January. They were too valuable to ship, the risk too great. He had spent 4 years obtaining them.

On our last full day in Brazil we got up at six o'clock. At INPA we stood my dip net against Jansen's office door and returned the four little test aquariums used in the attractant experiments to someone else. Then we went to a workroom near the fish collections to prepare the candirus for shipment. This involved emptying the sample bottles and wrapping the fish and their labels in formalin-soaked cheesecloth. The fumes were terrible, even with a window open over the sink, and our eyes watered badly. These individual packets were put inside heavy plastic bags and sealed shut on a bag sealer. We put the bags together in a small box, printed a label with my name, stuffed a copy of the invoice inside, and taped it shut.

Paulo dropped me at the house and went to close his bank account. He returned thoroughly pissed off, having stood in a wrong line for more than an hour. He had given the clerks hell and stormed out. Now he had to go back to turn in his credit card. To cancel a credit card in the U.S. you call a toll-free number. Then you cut the card in half and throw the pieces away. In Brazil you must appear in person at the bank that issued the card and watch while someone else cuts it in half and throws the pieces away.

We choked down some warmed-over pizza and headed to the airport where the FedEx office was located; that is, where it used to be located. No, a cargo handler said, FedEx had moved across town. We got directions and went to the address. Over the door was a sign saying Federal Express, but the office was empty. We asked someone on the street. Go to that office over there, he said, the one that doesn't say Federal Express.

Inside, arctic air blew from a large window air conditioner and a surly woman with carefully stacked hair sat at a desk reading the Manaus daily, *A Critica.* I noticed her mouthing the words, never a good omen. Paulo asked her in Portuguese if this was the FedEx office. She furrowed her brow and pursed her lips, considering his question carefully. Yes, she answered after a time, this was the FedEx office. The matter decided, she went back to her newspaper.

Paulo told her that we wanted to ship a box. What kind of box? This kind. I held it up, turning it in my fingers like a rare jewel on display. She eyed it warily. What's in it? Fishes from INPA. Dead fishes. She shook her head. No, FedEx never ships dead fishes, even from INPA. What was INPA, anyway? The name didn't sound familiar.

Get someone else, Paulo instructed her. She turned and addressed an invisible presence in the inner office. After a few minutes a young man with sandy hair came out, a FedEx necktie dangling like a turkey wattle from his thin neck. We explained everything again. No, sorry. No chance. Under any circumstances we would still need an invoice. This is an invoice, Paulo told him, pointing to the invoice. The man examined it. The woman glanced up from *A Critica* and pursed her lips. It couldn't be an invoice, the man concluded. For dead fishes? Impossible! Anyway, he continued, he couldn't accept something like this without approval from São Paulo. The box was no doubt filled with water and would probably leak. No water? Then how did the fishes live? Ah, they were dead. Why hadn't we said so in the first place? And they were in . . . what? For-ma-*lin*? Was it explosive? No, eh?

There's a phone, Paulo suggested. Why not call São Paulo? What for? the man asked. To get permission to ship our box, Paulo said. It's a wasted call, you know. Do it anyway. Sure. Uh, where do you want it shipped? The U.S. The States? Oh, that's a big problem. Everything to the States goes through São Paulo. You're about to call São Paulo, remember? Yes, but the plane to the States won't go until Saturday, and that's a big problem. Not for us, Paulo answered. And not for these fishes, which are dead and don't care.

The clerk called São Paulo. There was no problem. Take the box, his boss told him. Charge the client 117 reals, or $58 U.S., for a package weighing less than half a kilogram. Would it ever arrive? Farewell candirus, I mumbled in English. The woman's lips stopped moving. She glanced up from her newspaper and looked at me strangely. Had I become an unwitting character in a Franz Kafka story? I counted out the money. No one had change for a 10 real note. I let them shortchange me 2 reals. I didn't care. Even Kafka's stories have endings. "Let's get the hell out of here," Paulo said, and we did.

I showered at six o'clock. The water gave out just as I finished lathering up. "Water!" I yelled.

"Son of a bitch, not again." Labbish slammed out of his office. He went outside and turned on the pump.

"We considered leaving you like that," Paulo said later.

"I considered rinsing off in your favorite aquarium, the one with the rare catfishes and two undescribed tetras."

Paulo grimaced. Labbish turned to him. "Why not?" he said. "They'll be dead soon anyway. You're leaving, remember?"

We went to a restaurant specializing in Brazilian food and ordered *pirarucú* cooked in a spicy sauce. The *pirarucú* (*Arapaima gigas*), the largest fish in the Amazon basin, is on the worldwide threatened species list, which means nothing in a biological context. What it means politically is that someone didn't want *pirarucú* meat sold for human consumption and lobbied to get a law passed. Nobody can realistically know how many *pirarucús* there are. In a place of such splendid remoteness as this, biological surveys have only limited quantitative value. Most of the Amazon region can't be sampled at all. Brazilians not only eat *pirarucús*, they do so openly.

Ceiling fans groaned in slow revolutions through the swollen air. Well-fed flies perched on the vacant chair at our table looking like bored waiters. The air smelled exotic, a mingled sharpness of spices, old cooking grease, exhaust fumes and cigarette smoke, the growth and rot of vegetation clamoring endlessly for light in the stagnant heat beside a black river.

"Maybe it's true," I said.

Labbish looked up from his plate. "Maybe what's true?" he asked.

"That threatened species taste the best."

Nothing is ever as you have explained it. Everybody is better off and worse than you could know in your furthest dreams.

—Barry Hannah, *Boomerang*[1]

11.

The Smoking Gun

Could a candiru actually fit inside a human urethra? Boulenger wondered about this:[2]

> In order that I might satisfy myself as to the possibility of the small fish *Vandellia cirrhosa* penetrating into the human urethra . . . Prof. C. Steward kindly took me to St. Thomas's Hospital on the 7th inst., when I was able to introduce without difficulty a no. 12 catheter, 5½ millim. in diameter, into the urethra of a male subject lying for post-mortem examination. The calibre of the fish being only 3 to 4 millim., no doubt can be raised as to its being able to enter the orifice of the urethra in the manner that has been described by various travellers in Brazil.

Herman describes the diameter of the candiru *Vandellia cirrhosa* as 4–6 millimeters, or comparable to a No. 12 French catheter.[3] But this was secondhand information. I obtained a catheter from a local hospital and took a photograph (Fig. 56). From the image it appears that if a catheter can fit inside a human urethra, so can a candiru.

However, the problem of proof lingered in Boulenger's day, and in Herman's. Halstead laments that[4] ". . . the species identity of the candirú continues to elude scientists because no specimen [*sic*] removed from the urogenital or rectal orifices of humans have ever found their way to a reputable ichthyological museum for scientific identification." This situation held true until 1999, when Paulo and I got our hands on a candiru that had been removed from a human being and kept for 2 years in a jar of formalin.

I had come to Manaus in October to capture candirus and conduct experiments on which factors attracted them, but also to meet Dr. Anoar Samad, the Manaus urologist, who, on 28 October 1997, removed a candiru from a male victim. I had as proof of this event a news clipping from *A Critica* faxed to me by Paulo when he had been in California on leave from INPA.[5] The photographs depict a young man of Middle Eastern ancestry (Samad) and what appears to be the ventral aspect of the offending fish. Titled "Doctor Removes a Patient's Candiru in Manaus," the article reads:[6]

Recorded as an "unbelievable case of *uretrorragia*" (hemorrhage of urethral origin), the unpublished surgery performed on the patient FBC, 23, last week in Manaus by the doctor, urologist Anoar Samad, 33, will be presented at the American Congress of Urology early next year in the United States.[7]

The doctor removed from the urethral canal of FBC a candiru of 12 centimeters in length and one [centimeter] in thickness. The candiru is a fish with small spines on its external sides.

"It was something incredible, and at the same time impressive. I only believe it because I went through the whole process, otherwise I think I would need to see all the evidence to believe it", admitted Anoar. "Many think I am kidding", he affirmed.

The history of FBC, according to Anoar, began during a bath in the [Amazon] river at Itacoatiara, 175 kilometers from Manaus. The boy, who was bathing in the river, was injured when he removed his swim trunks to

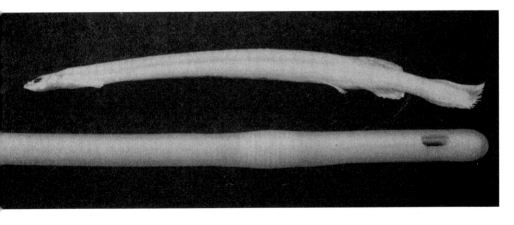

FIG. 56 Candiru (*Vandellia* cf. *plazai*) photographed beside a number 12 catheter. The specimen, captured in the Rio Solimões, measures 60.4 mm SL. Source: Stephen Spotte.

urinate. The fish, according to the doctor, entered in the boy's urethral canal through the penis.

"He said that he felt the candiru enter and from the first moment he knew what it was", according to the doctor, observing that, in agreement with the patient, when the fish enters there is no pain, only an indisposition. "The pain comes later", he said.

Despite the prompt diagnosis, FBS [*sic*] still had to be detained for three days at a hospital in Manaus under medical observation. "What represented a risk was [the fact] that the fish was dead and in a state of decomposition", Anoar affirmed.

After hearing the details of the boy's history, the doctor said that he got in touch with a researcher at the National Institute of Amazonian Research (Inpa) to learn a little more about the fish.

"He wanted to know things like its form and appearance."

"Before surgery I made an ultrasonograph to find out where the fish was and to document the fact, because it was something undocumented", recounted the doctor. The equipment used in the operation, which lasted between one and two hours, included endoscopes (to avoid cutting). After having located the fish and seeing what it was, Anoar used scissors to cut the spines of the candiru and pulled it out with forceps from the urethral canal.

Five days after the surgery FBC was discharged. He is being treated with anti-inflammatories and antibiotics, and [doing] well. "I should see him within two weeks", affirmed the doctor, adding that FBC does not have, nor should he have, lasting effects. "The one thing he has at present is a narrowing of the urethra, because of the lesion caused by the fish. But we still need to wait", concluded the doctor, who was trained at the University of Amazonas and specialized in urology in Boston, in the United States. [S. Spotte, transl.]

On the morning of 3 November—the same morning we discovered most of our candirus from the Rio Jauaperi had died—Paulo telephoned Samad's office and asked the receptionist if he could see us in the afternoon. Samad had supposedly videotaped the procedure by which he extracted the fish from FBC's urethra using an endoscope fitted with alligator-clip forceps. I wanted to interview him for more details, but he had not answered my faxes from Connecticut written in both Portuguese and English. Maybe he would meet with us now. The fish was still in a jar at his house, and he had promised Paulo we could examine it.

Paulo made telephone contact that afternoon. Samad was preparing to open a new kidney transplant clinic and had very little time. He could see us briefly in his office the next evening at seven o'clock. He would bring the fish. We hoped he might let us borrow it long enough to take photographs and perhaps identify it.

Realizing that first impressions are important, I showered late in the afternoon the next day and put on a clean shirt. Paulo also showered, but hadn't shaved. To his credit he was wearing long pants. On the negative side, there were his sandals. Although clean-shaven and shod in socks and shoes, I wore shorts. When combined, the favorable attributes of our attire were enough for only one. It would have to do.

We wedged into a parking space and made it to Samad's office at exactly seven o'clock. The waiting room was empty except for a couple of receptionists watching a soap opera on TV. The hallways were quiet, the air clean and cold. After 15 minutes we were ushered into the inner office and shook hands with the only man in recorded history known with certainty to have removed a candiru from a living human being. It had been almost 2 years to the day since the article had appeared in *A Critica.*

Anoar Abdul Samad is a darkly handsome man, slightly portly. He was dressed in white trousers and a white short-sleeved shirt. Transported to a different setting he might have passed for a short-order cook. He understood English, having spent a year at Boston's Lahey Clinic, but seemed uncomfortable speaking it. He and Paulo conversed in Portuguese while I tried to understand what they were saying. Samad had never received my faxes, which explained the lack of a response.

We shifted quickly to first names, and Paulo began by showing Anoar our preserved specimens of candirus from the Rio Jauaperi. He held the sample bottle briefly to the light before handing it back. No, he indicated, the candiru he had removed from the victim was much longer and thicker. The fish was at his house. We could see it later.

Then he told us the victim's story. Evidently, FBC's penis had *not* been submerged in the river at the time of the attack. According to FBC, he was standing in the river and had taken his penis out of his swimsuit to urinate. The water level reached to his upper thighs, but not to his scrotum or penis. *The fish had darted out of the water, up the urine stream, and into his urethra.* Startled, FBC grabbed the fish and tried to pull it out, but its body was too slippery. He had only one chance—a fleeting chance—then it was completely inside.

The victim might have been hospitalized for 3 days in Manaus as *A Critica* reported; prior to that he had spent 3 days in a clinic at Itacoatiara, his hometown on the Rio Amazonas east of Manaus. That's where he went just after the attack. Two local urologists had examined him without doing anything. Time passed. Finally they called Anoar, who at first thought he was being baited by some of his friends. Convinced at last the calls were genuine, he went to Itacoatiara. Unable to urinate because of the blockage, FBC's abdomen had become greatly distended, swollen like a soccer ball. The adult bladder ordinarily holds about 300 milliliters of urine, at full capacity perhaps 750 milliliters. The volume retained by this unfortunate man was not measured.

The patient was transferred to Manaus where Anoar, using the endoscope, removed the fish and videotaped the procedure. After FBC had been anesthetized, Anoar began by perfusing his urethra with distilled water while simultaneously inserting the end of the instrument. Almost at once FBC's scrotum began to swell, indicating a perforation between the urethra and scrotum. The candiru's forward progress had probably been blocked by the isthmus separating the penile urethra from the bulbous urethra at Cowper's gland just before the prostate (Fig. 57). Subsequently, according to Anoar, the fish had bitten through adjacent tissues into the scrotum. Some coagulated material was removed revealing a wound on the bulbous urethra 1 centimeter in diameter and associated with a small amount of local bleeding. Had the fish's progress not been impeded, Anoar told us, the candiru would have reached the urinary bladder and perhaps found its way into the intestine.

Fortunately, more invasive surgery was not required. Anoar had manipulated the forceps of the endoscope until they gripped the tail of the candiru, then pulled it out. The fish, long since dead, had begun to disintegrate. The patient recovered completely and suffered no lasting effects. To put a fitting end to this unusual story, the urologists in Itacoatiara had never reimbursed Anoar for his services.

Some of Anoar's observations require additional discussion. For a candiru to make an opening between the urethra and scrotum would require penetrating several layers of tissue (refer to Fig. 57). Starting from inside the urethra these are, sequentially, the membranous urethra itself, corpus spongiosum, Buck's fascia, deep layer of Colles' fascia, bulbospongiosus muscle, and major leaf of Colles' fascia. A candiru might make a hole with its opercular or interopercular spines or chew a hole using its toothless (or nearly toothless) jaws and vomerine teeth.

A candiru's teeth are needlelike, adapted for puncturing delicate tissue and holding on, not crushing or chewing. The fish that slipped into FBC's urethra had rapidly disappeared. How had it managed to chew a hole completely through to the scrotum before its head moved well past the point where this was least difficult? Gnawing through the bulbospongiosus muscle would be especially difficult for a fish with weak dentition. The perforation could be made most easily where the penis starts to curve; in other words, where it first attaches to the scrotum. However,

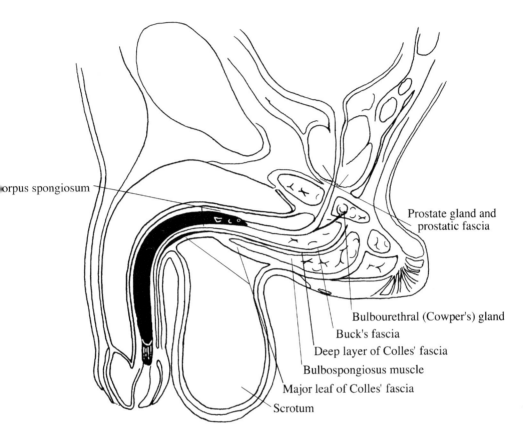

Corpus spongiosum

Prostate gland and prostatic fascia

Bulbourethral (Cowper's) gland
Buck's fascia
Deep layer of Colles' fascia
Bulbospongiosus muscle
Major leaf of Colles' fascia
Scrotum

FIG. 57   Diagrammatic illustration of a candiru lodged in the human male urethra. The effect on various tissues is explained in the text. Various sources.

once inside the urethra the fish would not have been able to return to this location because its spines might not have allowed it to back up. The head of this candiru would already have arrived at a place where the bulbospongiosus muscle is thickest.

Could this candiru have backed out anyway, even if it had no spines? I doubt it. The spaces between the gill arches of even a small prey fish are flexible; perhaps only the candiru's head is wedged between them as it feeds. In water, the loose and nearly weightless lamellae offer no resistance. In contrast, a human urethra is tighter, more muscular, considerably less flexible, and encircles the fish's whole body severely restricting any movement. A fish inside a human urethra has even fewer options than a fish out of water. Candirus are not known to swim backwards.

If, as Anoar claimed, the fish's forward progress stopped at the isthmus just before Cowper's gland, it had penetrated nearly to the level of the prostate, and the neck of the bladder would certainly have been next. Could a fish survive long enough to get there? We have only Ammerman's indirect account of surgery on a man's bladder to remove a candiru (see Chapter 1). Penetration of the intestine seems improbable, even that portion that lies atop the distended bladder.

I was stunned at the news that FBC had been urinating *above* the surface of the water when attacked. Lots of people stand and piss in the Rio Amazonas. Has de Castelnau been redeemed after almost 150 years? Can candirus indeed swim up urine streams directly into the penis? Several authors have mentioned this phenomenon. Whether the tales originate with de Castelnau and are simply repeated can't be known, but they might be more truthful than we think. Eigenmann and Allen discredit such accounts,[8] and although skeptical of how much real danger the candiru presents, von den Steinen tells us:[9]

> The fear of the Brazilians of this really harmless little fish might so be correct; it is best characterized by a tall story, which we were told seriously by a military officer: in the waters of Villa Caceres the Kandirú is so vicious and passionately voracious that it will climb quickly up the jet of water from somebody urinating from the river bank. [E. Muschaweck, transl.]

Breault gives little credence to de Calstenau's story about candirus and urine streams:[10] "The myth of the danger they pose sometimes exceeds common sense." To refute these statements, we have only FBC's story filtered through Anoar Samad.

Anoar gave us directions to his house on Rua Rio Purus, saying he would be home after eight o'clock. The Brazilian method of numbering houses is somewhat arbitrary, and both odd and even numbers often occur on the same side of the street. Alternatively, odd numbers can be on one side and even numbers on the other, although they still might not correspond. For example, on Rua Rio Purus number 14 was directly across the street from number 651. When we found number 17, supposedly Anoar's address, it turned out to be a beauty parlor. Paulo suggested continuing on. We passed numbers in the thousands when suddenly the system began again.

The second number 17 was a gated condominium complex. Anoar arrived just behind us and instructed the guards to let us through. We took an elevator to the third floor. Anoar knocked on one of the apartment doors, and his wife greeted us. She was dark-haired and pretty and dressed in a short skirt and sandals. Behind her was a child of about two. Anoar, Paulo, and I went into the living room and sat on couches. After a few minutes Anoar disappeared into another room and returned with the fish. It was floating in a brownish liquid inside an olive jar. Paulo and I exchanged glances. This was it, the smoking gun.

The candiru was bigger and more robust than any of our specimens. How it had entered a man's urethra so quickly and easily was difficult to imagine. Was it a species of *Vandellia*? We could not be certain. This fish had been through tough times, and its poor condition was hardly surprising. Moreover, Anoar had fixed it in a formalin solution of unknown strength. We held the jar to a lamp for a better view, and then Paulo placed it reverentially in his briefcase. Anoar had decided to donate the specimen to INPA, reserving the right to use it if needed. He was especially concerned that photographs of his fish not get into the tabloids.

We went into another room. It was smaller and contained a large armchair and a small couch. At one end was a huge Sony TV; lining the walls were VCRs and other audiovisual equipment. Mrs. Samad brought us glasses of Coke and left. We watched the black and white video of the extraction procedure, then watched it again. The trip into the urethra was like being in the engineer's seat on a subway train, nothing except gray walls all around and ahead, then suddenly, the candiru. The alligator clips clasped the tail and started to move in reverse. Anoar showed us photographs of the freshly extracted fish and of the victim's scrotum looking like a balloon from having filled with water during the surgery.

We moved into the study. Cooking odors filtered through from the kitchen. Time passed. Eventually the odors dissipated and the kitchen lights went out. Anoar showed me his letter of acceptance into the American Urological Association. He switched on his computer and tried repeatedly to log onto the Internet, but the server was malfunctioning. He finally connected and promptly sent the still photographs taken after surgery and scanned into his hard drive to Paulo's and my e-mail addresses. He and Paulo then composed a letter to INPA outlining terms of the donation. They printed the letter and Anoar signed it.

Anoar was presenting an abstract describing the incident at a Brazilian congress on urology within the next week and needed to know the candiru's identity. We promised a name as soon as possible, maybe even tomorrow. Anoar pulled up his text on the screen and typed our names as coauthors of his abstract. He looked forward to submitting a note to *American*

Journal of Urology or perhaps *Urology*, but felt uncomfortable writing in English. I said I would write the text, emphasizing the need for more details. No problem, Anoar said. He agreed to make a copy of his video for us; we could pick it up the next week. We got home at eleven-fifteen.

The next morning Paulo, Jansen, Lúcia, and I examined Anoar's fish at INPA, and Paulo logged it into the collections.[11] Paulo and Janssen made careful measurements. The fish was 133.5 millimeters SL, or 5.26 inches, the width of its head at the widest place 11.5 millimeters (0.45 inches). The length of the urethra of adult human females is 2.5–3.8 centimeters (1–1.5 inches); of adult males 6.4–7.6 centimeters (2.5–3.0 inches).[12] The urethra of both sexes is distensible, limited in adult males by the length of the penis when erect. A candiru 13.3 centimeters long and 11.5 millimeters wide can obviously fit inside a man's urethra.

Jansen, Paulo, and I took the candiru outside to photograph it in daylight. We placed it on the back of a lab report, which in turn was placed on a stool. Jansen pinned out the tail with a specimen pin, put a white centimeter scale beside the fish, and we took turns with our cameras (Plate 8). The specimen conformed with most characters of the genus *Plectrochilus*. As mentioned in Chapter 3, *Plectrochilus* and *Vandellia* might be synonyms, in which case *Plectrochilus* will be merged eventually into *Vandellia*.[13]

Paulo made photomicrographs of the fish's odontodes in one of the labs. According to the *A Critica* article, Anoar had clipped off some of the candiru's spines before removing it. This seemed unlikely. The only spines present—those on the operculum and interoperculum—were intact. Anoar had told Paulo and me that the fish slid out of FBC's urethra easily, far more easily than he would have guessed, undoubtedly because it was dead.

Paulo had written an official letter to Anoar from INPA accepting the fish for its collections. Lúcia, as head of the ichthyology section, needed to sign it, but she was not in her office. Paulo wanted to view the photomicrographs on his computer at the house, edit a few of the best ones, and make copies for Anoar to use in his upcoming presentation. We got in the car and weaved into the midday traffic.

The intention had been to drop off the photos and letter with Anoar, but the letter had yet to be signed. We decided to leave it anyway; Paulo would mail him a signed copy. We would also leave Anoar a copy on floppy disk of the images Paulo had made of the candiru's odontodes, the probable genus name (*Plectrochilus* or *Vandellia*), and photocopies of ichthyological descriptions of the genera. Afterwards, we would stop at the office of Brazil's equivalent of the Internal Revenue Service, which owed Paulo money.

While Paulo was arguing with the tax vultures, I climbed down a ladder to the beach and watched quarrelsome vultures of the feathered kind hissing over scraps of garbage, hopping like clumsy sparrows and lunging ineptly at each other with outstretched necks. Dressed in funereal black with beady eyes and bald heads, they lacked only eyeshades, desks, and neckties. A whistle blew signaling a riverboat's impending departure.

The air was sweltering and absolutely still, and the beach stank of decomposition. People swam in the fetid water. I took photographs, and in the span of a few minutes was approached by a scrofulous man who was obviously crazy, local citizens who interrupted while I was taking photographs to ask if I was taking photographs, a bored prostitute, a sweating water taxi driver, and a dozen or so street vendors selling iced drinks. I climbed back up the ladder to find Paulo waiting by the car. We got in. Before nosing into the traffic he turned to me and grinned: "Make any new friends?"

Across the street directly before me was the Customs House designed in England, shipped to Brazil in pieces, assembled, and opened in 1909. This was at the end of the rubber boom (1880 to 1910),[14] when women were imported from Europe. It was said that two of every three houses in the city of 30,000 were brothels. Cobblestones were shipped in to build streets, slabs of marble to beautify houses of the newly rich. Steamers brought automobiles from North America, wines from France, chandeliers, pianos, pearls, potatoes, caviar, champagne. Ladies sent their linens to Portugal to be starched.

When Eduardo Gonçalves Ribeiro became governor of Amazonas, he imported electric street lights and 25 kilometers of tramway. He built parks, gardens, bandstands, a racetrack, and an opera house that could accommodate 1600 people. Its ironwork came from Glasgow, the external tiles from Alsace-Lorraine, the chandeliers from Italy, the marble pillars from Carrara.

On my closet shelf back home in Connecticut was a white Panama hat with a black band. I had considered bringing it, but figured people would think I was a gringo trying to imitate a Brazilian. Seeing Paulo in his, I realized how wrong I was. "You look like a real Brazilian in that Panama," I remarked.

"That's funny," Paulo replied, swerving to avoid hitting a pushcart filled with melons. "When I wear it around here they tell me I look like a gringo."

12.

Candiru World

Why not a candiru exhibit as William E. Kelley, my former mentor, once suggested? For precedent, I point to an article by the American zoo director William G. Conway urging the exhibition of bullfrogs on a grand scale.[2] Conway's exhibit would be a protean sortie of the mind and senses into all things moist and froggy, a croaking tribute to the perspicuity of froghood. Its effect on society might be profound. Why drive a pickup when you can hop to work? I see us in recapitulated phylogeny turning green on the knees and long in the toes, addressing each other in Anglicized Amphibian.

Candirus ought to outrank mere frogs. Think about it. We already have Artichoke World, Disney World, Onion World, Safari World, Sea World, and Shell World, not to mention Hollywood and Dollywood. I now propose Candiru World.

Any exhibit logically begins with the star attractions. Because candirus have not been bred in captivity, ours must be obtained from the wild. Here an ugly philosophical problem goes humping across our path. I can summarize it this way: when you net a candiru and lift it out of a tropical river, something important is left behind, namely, everything. Minus its unique presence in space and time, this candiru, the specimen struggling under your gaze, loses all reality. From beneath nature's thin membrane, symbolized by the surface of the river, a vital element has been extracted. How vital? Spare any desultory piety. The effect I speak of is *syncretistic*, not simply ecological. An undulating candiru leaves a fleeting signature. Soon after the echoes of its wake disperse, all physical remnants of the real candiru will have disappeared. That netted object is a simulation.

Suppose the candiru we just caught, along with many others, is flown by air cargo to California and placed in this new facility called Candiru World. The developers of Candiru World hope to make a profit. At the same time they want their exhibits to be thought of as educational. Because the main show will consist simply of watching candirus suck blood from larger fishes, some didactic embellishment is needed. In public exhibits this is usually achieved by adding lots of heuristic noise to mask the faintness of the signal.

After queuing up out front, visitors pay admission and enter a darkened exhibit hall where the recorded chants of Jívaro warriors are piped over hidden speakers. The fidelity is excellent. If the crowd isn't too big you can even hear bare feet shuffling monotonously in the dust. Early on in the planning a film crew was sent deep into the Ecuadorian rainforest to record one tribe's rituals, including the preparation of *tsantsa*, or human heads shrunken to the size of an orange with hair and a moustache.

Later, a live enactment will be staged in one of the outdoor pavilions. The *tsantsa*, of course, are not human; they're the heads of puppies obtained from an animal shelter up the road. Still, the technique is the same, and children in particular are fascinated by how the facial features are kept intact after the skull has been carefully removed and the head reduced to a brown golf ball with a nose and two tiny, floppy ears. The Education Department even offers classes in *tsantsa*-making as part of its Rainforest Crafts Curriculum. For now, the chanting alone is sufficient to establish a mood conducive to learning and to flush from memory any residue of heavy metal or your last high school reunion.

Blinking greenly, the sinuous shapes of fiberoptic candirus glide in eerie contrast along the nearest wall, meandering among painted outlines of boulders and drowned trees, gathering in schools before dissolving and reforming once again at the end of the wall nearest the entrance. Whether candirus actually school isn't known, but the effect is striking.

Just around the corner the atonal chanting of Jívaros is replaced by an actor's voice. He is, he informs us, Carl Freidrich Phillipp von Martius, born 17 April 1794 in Erlangen, Bavaria. After a suitable pause he tells us he died 13 December 1868 in Munich. In lieu of flowers, donations can be made to Candiru World. Personal checks, credit cards, and cash are all accepted. Contributions are tax deductible.

According to von Martius, he was the first to describe purported candiru attacks on human beings. This, of course, makes him a celebrity to candiruphiles everywhere. Some visitors have even brought along digital voice recorders. The words of von Martius tumble out in thick, German-accented English seasoned with a smattering of Portuguese, no doubt a remnant of the years 1817–1820 when he tramped through Brazil in search of botanical specimens. His observations on the candiru were published in Latin about 1829, and he now reads from his text: "De alio pisce hominibus infesto nonnulla afferre debeo, quem Brasilienses *Candirú* . . ." He sounds like an American who doesn't know German impersonating a German just learning English trying to imitate a Brazilian speaking Latin for the first time. There's also the problem of a lisp. Except for a few Catholic priests in the crowd, nobody understands a word, but it doesn't matter. Everyone from babies sucking on federally certified carcinogen-free teething rings to deaf senior citizens leaning on candiru canes ($18.95 at the Gifte Shoppe) appreciates Candiru World taking the time to educate hell out of them.

The corridor ends at a wall partition serving as a light barrier. On the other side, visitors are blasted by the rays of a simulated tropical sun. Speakers crackle. Not to worry, says a pleasing feminine voice: to prevent sunburn, all ultraviolet rays have been filtered out. However, for those still concerned, we have lots of SPF 30 available at the Gifte Shoppe. The voice sounds calm, concerned, nurturing.

The air is warm and thick, redolent of vegetable lust and the sticky, subterranean embrace of simulated tubers. Holograms of tropical birds flit among simulated trees festooned with simulated epiphytes. From tiny speakers comes the buzzing of flies and the dripping of water, the distant factory roar of leaf-cutter ants crunching grimly through simulated undergrowth, the simulated floral anguish of pistils in heat. In front of you flows a simulated muddy river. Everyone queues up at a simulated dock in preparation for their next adventure.

While life vests are being handed out, you wander to a nearby Jungle Fruit Stand and order a glass of *jagua* juice, freshly squeezed from the fruit of a certain tropical tree and served piping hot. As a student of candiru lore you already know about this stuff and have been dying to try it. When some unfortunate member of the tribe gets a candiru jammed up his pecker, the witch doctor brews a tisane of *jagua* juice, which supposedly knocks the offender dead right there in the urinary tract. Nobody has any advice if a candiru becomes stuck in your asshole or maybe your ear. Then it's off to the witch doctor and his rusty knife.

There's also the bath in hot *jagua* juice. Having given this lots of thought, you can picture a hot bath working for every orifice except the nose, where breath-holding might be a problem. Your choice, the guide smirks, drink it or sit in it because if you fall overboard, well . . . he points out emergency *jagua* stands and hot baths along both sides of the simulated river, each bathtub heated by its own little gas flame. You chuckle along with everyone else and take a sip from your paper cup. It tastes like that smectic drain cleaner they make you drink before a colonoscopy. You glance uneasily at the restrooms hoping they aren't holograms.

A moment of your time, please, before embarking. This is me speaking, not the guide. What we have here are simulations, lots of them, which calls for a brief taxonomy. The French philosopher Jean Baudrillard places simulations into three levels of increasing complexity.[3] His "first-order" simulations are simply counterfeit reproductions of the original. The copies are generally crude, and close examination quickly reveals the distinctions between them and the original model. An example is a rainforest exhibit like this. Although the components were produced and assembled by experts, nobody is actually fooled into believing the result is genuine. What we have is a one-of-a-kind counterfeit rainforest. This is because the duplication of any large complex object is impossible. Despite superficial similarities, no rainforest exhibit can duplicate a rainforest, and no rainforest exhibit can be an exact copy of another.

In "second-order" simulation items roll off an assembly line, each an exact facsimile. The model on which they are based might be a binary code or a sculpted object from which a mold was taken. Where the original exists—and in what form—is irrelevant. It might not even look like the final product. What matters is that each unit matches every other unit as closely as possible.

We come then to "third-order" simulation, best represented by an inverted image of Disneyland. In Baudrillard's view, Disneyland represents what's real in America. Outside its admission gates stretches an imaginary landscape linked by countless islands of Walkmans, TV sets, movie theaters, lesser theme parks, museums (including public aquariums and zoos), shopping malls—distractions without substance or permanent memory leading us subtly away from reality. This is a simulation of the highest caliber. We could wander in and out of it without ever knowing the difference. Stop and look around. Is a large mouse wearing short pants trying to shake your hand? Don't worry, Baudrillard says it's real.

Baudrillard also gave us the "hyperreal," a dimension beyond simulation where reality has been produced from models devoid of any tactile substance or origin. No one can recall why such a thing happened or whether it ought to matter. The real is predictable in advance, rendering it indistinguishable from its simulation. In the hyperreal, deviation from either the real or the imagined is itself a simulation.

Consider this example. Early editors of the *Farmer's Almanac* predicted the weather using such quaint factors as width of the markings on caterpillars when measured in autumn. The distinction between the basis of the prediction and the prediction itself was clear enough. Computer models have since blurred these lines. As their accuracy and precision improve, encryptions in binary code and the predictions such models generate will merge. Near perfection having been attained, weather prediction and the weather will be hard to tell apart. A computer-generated snowstorm predicted to start at eleven-thirty tomorrow night can be viewed in advance tonight by logging onto the Internet and accessing the local weather. I zoom in on a simulation of my driveway after the simulated storm passes and see there's no need to get out the snow shovel, so the next night I go to bed as usual instead of watching the real storm. Having seen the movie, why read the book?[4]

The best literary examples I know of third-order simulation are the stories of the American writer George Saunders, in which fantasy and reality are so intertwined that separating them becomes impossible. The ghosts inside his theme parks are no less real than the visitors waiting in line, just more disoriented. His mostly unnamed protagonists, usually theme park employees, act out their bizarre lives in a simulated Hell of someone else's making. Nobody, it seems, is in control. The Universe has constricted to the dimensions of a soldier's uniform or a butter churn. Only other "Staff" seem real, but this too might be delusional. Everyone else—often families included—is an outsider, a faceless figure not "in-Park." In Saunders' theme parks, people are murdered or killed accidentally and reappear as apparitions. One, the ghost of a little kid ground to bits in the machinery of a water slide, now haunts the machine's operator, blaming him for missing his future prom.

The simulations devised by Saunders are third-order because the polarity of the real and the imaginary have been reversed. We can't tell which dimension we're in at a given moment. Saunders' theme park exhibits have evolved well beyond counterfeit reproductions of reality (first-order), nor are they products of an assembly line (second-order); rather, they are propelled forward by an unpredictable momentum, collapsing eventually into hallucinatory juxtapositions of time and shady pockets of cruelty, pathos, and guilt. In some cases the protagonists *are* the exhibit.[5]

The Polish writer Stanislaw Lem is also adept at inventing third-order simulations. In a story titled "Tale of the Three Storytelling Machines of King Genius," a wizard has simulated the beautiful Princess Ineffabelle, who ruled the Kingdom of Dandelia in the Middle Ages. Zipperupus, a present-day king, learns of this. In a dream he falls in love with Ineffabelle's image and seeks the wizard, who lives in the middle of a gold-plated desert. The wizard lifts the lid of his Black Box and allows the king a peek:[6]

> The King leaned over, looked and saw, yes, the Middle Ages simulated to a T, all digital, binary and nonlinear, and there was the land of Dandelia, the Icicle Forest, the palace with the Helical Tower, the Aviary That Neighed, and the Treasury with a Hundred Eyes as well; and there was Ineffabelle herself, taking a slow, stochastic stroll through her simulated garden, and her circuits glowed red and gold as she picked simulated daisies and hummed a simulated song.[7]

In Lem's world everything appears superficially to be first-order. The king isn't fooled, nor is the wizard trying to fool him. It isn't a case of attempting to pry reality and imagination apart. Both men know the Princess Ineffabelle to be a simulation, perhaps a cyborg or hologram. Quite simply, the king has gone daffy, the result of having selected this particular dream from his Cabinet That Dreamed. He fell in love with a dream, then a simulation, and, in the end, nearly sacrifices everything to join Ineffabelle's image inside the wizard's Black Box.

The Argentine writer Jorge Luis Borges ranks as all-time master of the hyperreal. In his stories, certain characters and scenes might be discussed in the context of a book review, except the book has never existed. Whole countries arise fully formed without palpable origin, participate on Borges' stage, then disappear. In "The Circular Ruins," a stranger's canoe sinks in the sacred mud near some ancient ruins. This being his destination anyway, the stranger scrambles ashore. Once inside the circle of toppled columns, he falls asleep. His purpose is to dream another man into reality, and so he sleeps almost continuously, dreaming of himself stand-ing among ruins similar to these and lecturing to his disciples, souls waiting (some for centuries) for an opportunity to become real. After sev-eral nights he chooses a rebellious young man and begins to teach him. One morning he awakens, realizing he had not dreamed the previous night. His work has come to nothing.

After weeks of struggling he finally sleeps and dreams of a beating heart. In the ensuing weeks he dreams of the skeleton, other organs, each indi-vidual hair, finally dreaming a whole man. After numerous trials, he dreams the image to life—a young man he calls his son—and begins to teach him, preparing him for reality. Simultaneously, his own conscious-ness begins to dim, having served to nourish this other being. Time passes; he grows old. His son, still a simulation, advances slowly towards reality.

Then one day encroaching fire destroys the circular ruins. He fears for his son because only fire can recognize a phantom, but he can do nothing. The fire approaches. He welcomes it and walks into the flames, astonished that his flesh does not burn. He feels no heat; the flames instead caress him:[8] "In relief, in humiliation, in terror, he understood that he, too, was an appearance, that someone else was dreaming him."

You drop your empty cup into the smiling mouth painted on the Recycle Here bin. Everyone on the simulated dock has been issued identical life jackets. These are second-order, having been mass produced. After-wards, all of you are helped into identical canoes, also second-order simu-lations. As I've mentioned, the exhibit itself—the plastic trees, the thunder and lightning storm every afternoon at three o'clock, the holograms of hummingbirds and kingfishers—is, of course, a first-order simulation.

Your guide, dressed to simulate a nineteenth-century South American explorer, paddles you down (or maybe up) the simulated river. Suddenly, he puts forefinger to lips. Listen! From all around, the simulated calls of birds and howler monkeys. Along the simulated riverbank *live* alligators bask on simulated mud under a simulated sun. *Live* anacondas hang in knotty loops from simulated tree limbs (you pass close enough to see their yellow eyes). And in a shallow, glass-fronted "eddy" nestled against the bank is a school of *live* piranhas. From behind the gigantic simulated but-tress of a simulated tree several hands flick out, and a *live* sloth lands with a splash. Being near the bow, you can see everything. The piranhas attack, ripping the sloth to pieces and staining the water red. From your canoe rises a collective gasp, then a cheer. Cruel, certainly, but nature at work. Relax, everything is in context.

Actually, nothing is in context, not the plastic logs and tree limbs, not the animal calls, and definitely not the live animals, including the sloth. Everything has either been manufactured or obtained pre-made to second-order specifications. The fact that some of the animals are alive is not evidence of their reality. Once placed inside a simulation, they too become simulations. Functionally, Baudrillard tell us,[9] "The confinement of the scientific object is the same as that of the insane and the dead." Out of sight, out of mind, out of the natural milieu— and out of circulation. When zoo animals reproduce, the offspring are second-order simulations. Change—that is, *natural* change—is out of the question. Assembly lines can be re-tooled when necessary, but in biology we call this evolution.

Keep your camera handy, the guide says. Never know when we might see a simulated ruby-topaz hummingbird. They're all around, hiding. You dutifully check the film counter on your camera and make sure the lens cap is off. The guide gives thumbs-up and winks approvingly. To be sure you'll recognize a ruby-topaz hummingbird, you open your brand new copy of *A Field Guide to Tropical Bird Holograms of Candiru World* ($29.95 at the Gifte Shoppe, plus tax).

The river is shorter than it seems. It actually comprises a series of loops thrown back on themselves like fairways of a golf course. Between each loop is a sound barrier made to look like rainforest vegetation. Visitors in canoes on the other side can't hear you, and you can't hear them.

The guide looks at his watch. Rain gear! he shouts. You struggle into your new Rainforest Monsooner. The thing has been on a closet shelf for how long now, 2 years? Thank god, at last a chance to use it! The guy beside you glances at the shoulder patch and looks away. He's jealous, no question. Thunder growls overhead, bolts of lightning flash. The rain begins gently to give seniors and kids time to get into their gear. Then everything breaks loose.

The image of a simulated tapir looms out of the deluge. Camera shutters click in unison. Look! The guide points towards the far bank. Barely visible is a hologram of a jaguar. This is terrific! exults the guide. We almost never get to see a jaguar. When we do, everyone wins a prize. He hands out soggy coupons for 20 percent off at the Candiru World Fried Catfish Grille.

I don't think these pictures will turn out, a woman in the stern remarks. It was raining so hard and all . . . . The guide nods sympathetically. Not to worry, he says, wildlife photography is an art requiring considerable patience and skill. Nobody can expect results the first time. Better buy an annual membership in Candiru World, then you can come back every day until you get just the right picture.

But we live in Vermont, the woman complains. You can still enjoy all the benefits of membership, ma'am, the guide replies. The woman turns on him. I'll bet if this was a real rainforest that goddamn jaguar would be posing right over there, and in better light than this. We're not in a real rainforest, replies the guide. Not really. But Candiru World's designers took everything the real rainforest could throw at them and went back for more. Staminawise and painwise and even humiditywise, I'd rate our River Trek Tour about four on a scale of, like, five.

Stop complaining, the woman's husband says. The guy's right. This is plenty hard enough. The woman turns sideways on her seat. Whose team are you on, you son of a bitch? The marriage counselor said you're supposed to be supportive, remember? The husband looks away and shrugs. Hey, take a floater, he mutters.

The guide knows when to interject. Folks, we can't get through this hellish experience without teamwork. The Conquistadors had it, Bolivar's ragtag army had it, the Brazilian national soccer team has it. Without pulling together, I'll be honest, our chances, like, border on suck. Those mosquito holograms? The ones you're slapping at every few seconds? Hey, they carry simulated malaria. That's why the ticket package we mailed out included Lariam placebos. You can't be too careful.

The guide turns cheerful. One thing you get free with a new membership, he says, is a video made by professionals that shows the tapir *and* the jaguar. It's all part of the package.

The woman in the stern brightens. That sounds like a really sweet deal, she says, and everyone in the canoe applauds. The guide holds his hand up for quiet. Not only that, he continues, in the Gifte Shoppe we sell individual photographs of every single hologram. Some of the images have even been transferred to our very own brand of personal shower clogs. And finally, every image is also in our book called *Official Guide to Candiru World: The Flora, Fauna, and You.* In my opinion, he says confidentially, an official Candiru World photograph of a hologram looks more real than the real thing.

You drift under a canopy of steaming simulated vegetation, hearing in the background the sound of a simulated stream sliding over simulated stones. The air looks fulvous against the simulated sky.

Ye gods, what's that terrible smell? It's the guy on the seat behind you. Tapirs sir, answers the guide. You mean you put tapir shit in here? the man asks. No sir, only the odor of tapir shit. We get an air-shipment out of Bolivia every week. The stuff comes in canisters like propane gas, part of our Candiru World Rainforest Restoration program to help the indigenous people use their natural products instead of sawing down trees. Same idea as Ben and Jerry's. They import Brazil nuts to make Rainforest Crunch, we import bottled tapir farts for your personal enjoyment.

Most people have shucked their rain gear because of the heat, the storm having lasted only a few minutes. Now they complain mildly about water dripping onto their backs and shoulders. The guide chuckles. It's a jungle in here, he says, and that gets everyone back in a good mood.

Okay, he barks, camera alert. Candiru photo op coming up on starboard. Ahead you can see a wide expanse of clear acrylic, the front of a large aquarium built into a simulated bluff above the simulated river. Within its confines is a live carp tied to a piece of driftwood to keep it immobile. Its left gill cover has been cut away to reveal the gills. Scurrying over the gill filaments, pausing to suck blood, are dozens of candirus. This carp is nearly done for.

Well, folks, says the guide. There they are—candirus. Cute little frackers, eh? This is like you going to a blood bank, except our friend the carp is about to donate all he's got. This gets a laugh.

I thought they'd be bigger, a little kid whines. You know, like piranhas. They look bigger in the pictures.

Those are closeup pictures, honey, the guide explains patiently. You let the camera lens zoom up close. Like this. He pretends to zoom in on her face with a circle made from his thumb and index finger. She squirms away. See? he says. If this was a camera I could get a picture of your whole eyeball, and it would look gigantic. He sits upright again. For you shutter-bugs, we can get closer. Put your lens right near the window and click away, no problem. And if you're afraid your shots won't turn out, remember what we've got waiting at the Gifte Shoppe in the way of images. Stills and videos both. And trust me, the price is a steal.

After letting everyone snap away, he backs the canoe out of the cul-de-sac into the main channel. Over there, he says, is one of our scenic spots. I'll stop so everyone can take a picture. Before you is a panoramic view of a rainforest framed by a couple of gigantic simulated mahogany trees. On one, a hologram of a column of ants is racing single-file up the trunk. On the other, a hologram of a troupe of spider monkeys climbs up and down lianas that extend out of sight into the canopy. Between the trees hangs a reddish appliqué, a sinking equatorial sun flattened on top and bottom as if squeezed between Heavenly palms.

You take in the scene. Thinking it looks more like a photograph in *National Geographic* magazine than a real rainforest, you decide not to waste any film. Nothing lost. The one real rainforest you've seen proved to be a letdown. It looked better on the Discovery Channel.

Another little side discussion, just between us. Photography is the most pervasive simulation of the second-order yet invented. Anyone can take a photograph then reproduce numerous copies from that single image. Photographs trivialize by dulling the senses, creating false beauty, making the exotic vulgar. At its most elemental, a photograph is an image of something. By extension, a photograph in a book is an image of an image.

The American writer Susan Sontag tells us in *On Photography*,[10] "To possess the world in the form of images is, precisely, to reexperience the unreality and remoteness of the real." You went to a theme park called Candiru World knowing it to be a simulation, yet you took along a camera. Had you seen that hologram of a ruby-topaz hummingbird and managed to take its picture, the result would have been the simulation of a real image, which itself was a simulation. Do photographs qualify as heuristic objects? Not if attempting to understand nature begins by delving beneath its surface.

This is the end of the River Trek Tour, the guide announces. He ties up the canoe at the simulated dock and starts helping people ashore. You've been a great group, he says. I wouldn't mind having you again sometime. Everyone joins in a unified cheer. There's nothing like adversity to promote solidarity.

What a day! Too bad the vacation is almost over. Back to reality tomorrow, or whatever. If you've learned anything it's that nature can be fun *and* educational. The proof is in the pictures, although even this notion totes some philosophical baggage. In future years, your photos from Candiru World won't evoke memories. Only you can evoke memories by looking at them.

See? you say to your grandchildren. Those are candirus. I wonder if that place, Candiru World, is still in business. Talk about excitement! I watched them suck a carp dry. Would you like to go see it? Naw, they answer, you're a dried up old fart, Grampa. Mom already bought us the hologram. It was boring. We'd rather go to that new theme park, Elephantiasis World. They run downstairs to play video games, leaving you alone with your photo album.

Real nostalgia sure isn't what it used to be.

Endnotes

Introduction

[1] It was mainly the American ichthyologist Carl H. Eigenmann who insisted on using Pygidiidae (e.g., Eigenmann 1918a). He was criticized for this by Tchernavin (1944), who argued for the taxonomic precedence of Trichomycteridae, the name used today. Also see Baskin (1973) and de Pinna (1998).

[2] The sharp-beaked ground finch (*Geospiza difficilis septentrionalis*) on Wenman Island in the Galápagos Islands feeds often—perhaps principally—on the blood of other birds (Bowman and Billeb 1965). It does this by perching on the tail or wing of a resting booby (*Sula* spp.), probes with its beak at the base of the larger bird's feathers to induce bleeding, then drinks the blood.

[3] According to Gudger (1930c: 1–2, footnote), "An effort has been made to ascertain the origin and meaning of the word *Candirú* (also spelled *Kandiroo*) but to little purpose. C. F. von Martius in his 'Wörtersammlung Brasilianischer Sprachen' (Leipzig, 1867) on p. 37 says that it is a Tupi word, and on p. 422 gives *Canderú* as a variant spelling."

1. Culmination of Evils

[1] Singer (1965: 150).

[2] James W. Atz (letter, 5 June 2000), Smith (1994). For brief accounts of Gudger's life and work, see Bernstein (1956), Nichols (1954), and Smith (1994). I am indebted to James W. Atz for drawing these references to my attention.

[3] Gudger (1930a, 1930b).

[4] Gudger (1930c).

[5] Gudger (1930c: viii).

[6] Alfred (1987: 2).

[7] See Eigenmann (1918a: 262–267), Eigenmann and Allen (1942: 142–148), Nomura (1996), Pellegrin (1909b), and Vinton and Stickler (1941).

[8] The phylogenetic relationships are illustrated in Fig. 2 as a cladogram. Forey et al. (1992: 3) say: "In biology, cladistics is a method of systematics . . . which is used to reconstruct genealogies of organisms and to construct classifications." More broadly, cladistics is a method of organizing information. Its first of four axioms states that the hierarchy of nature is knowable and can be represented by branching diagrams. The classic text is Hennig (1966). For a brief and elegant refutation of cladistics in biology, see Dodson (2000).

   The species *Nematogenys inermis* has mental (i.e., chin) barbels, a single barbel at the corner of the mouth, and lacks opercular and interopercular spines (Eigenmann

1918a: 278). Once considered a trichomycterid, it now occupies its own family, Nematogenyidae (see de Pinna 1998). More will be said about loricariids (also shown in Fig. 2) in later chapters.

9 The term *candiru* is a continuum without boundaries, a basket into which nearly anything can be tossed. My decision to restrict its use more or less follows a loose convention set by others (e.g., de Pinna and Vari 1995, Myers 1944). One author (Lowe-McConnell 1975: 43) refers to "the candiru" as a single species (*Vandellia cirrhosa*) believed to attack humans. I've taken the additional liberty of assuming those species I call "true" candirus are obligate bloodsuckers, although the existence of exclusively sanguinivorous fishes requires confirmation. Some ichthyologists include as candirus those trichomycterids that feed on the mucus or scales of other fishes (Baskin et al. 1980, Machado and Sazima 1983, Roberts 1972).

10 According to de Pinna and Vari (1995: 1): "The flesh-eating cetopsids, notorious for their voracious habits . . . are often inappropriately lumped with some semi-parasitic [*sic*] trichomycterids under the common name of 'candiru.'"

11 Baskin et al. (1980), de Pinna (1998).

12 Baskin et al. (1980).

13 de Pinna and Britski (1991).

14 Roberts (1972), Winemiller and Yan (1989).

15 Baskin et al. (1980), de Pinna and Britski (1991), Roberts (1972).

16 Baskin et al. (1980).

17 Reinhardt (1858) described *Stegophilus insidiosus*. Eigenmann (1918a: 267–268) provides a translation of key passages from Reinhardt's Danish.

18 Outro facto. Contaram-me que, certa vez, em uma volta do rio Purús, nas proximidades do grande lago Ayapuá, um pescador foi ao lugar onde se faziam ouvir repetidas rabanadas de peixe grande, ao pé de um *matupá*. Levado mais pela curiosidade que pela necessidade do pescado, o caboclo approximou-se mansamente e, de pé na prôa da montaria, arremeçou a tarrafa sobre as derradeiras bôlhas que o peixe deixára.

Recolhida a rêde, um só tambaquy vinha nella, o que causou extranheza ao pescador, que procurou descobrir a causa de tão anormal inquietação do peixe. Examinando-o, viu que apresentava o orifício anal corroído e, dentro do rectum, encontrou quatro candirús que justificavam o incommodo em que o tambaquy se achava.

Ha tempos, registou-se nas immediações do salto do rio Mogy-Guassú, em Pirassununga, S. Paulo, o seguinte: appareciam, á miude, dourados boiando mortos e com grande numero de peixinhos extranhos mettidos nas guelras. Esses desconhecidos inimigos dos dourados atacavam, de preferencia, o orgão mais sensivel do peixe inutilisando-o em pouco minutos; não me foi possivel obter nenhum desses peixinhos hematophagos, mas, disseram-me que eram elles como um pequenino cascudinho, de uma pollegada, com a bocca igual á do mandy e de côr escura; ficou conhecido na localidade com o nome de "Mata-dourado"; penso ser uma variedade dos Stegophilus insidiosus. (Couto de Magalhães 1931: 105).

[19] *Caboclos* are rural Brazilians of mostly Indian ancestry.

[20] The *tambaquí* (*Colossoma macropomum*) is a fruit-eating characin that grows to large size and is a valuable food fish throughout the Amazon basin (see Araujo-Lima and Goulding 1997).

[21] Characins of the genus *Salminus* (Barthem and Goulding 1997: 94).

[22] A loricariid catfish presently named *Isbrueckerichthys duseni*, but listed by Couto de Magalhães (1931: 238) as *Hemipsilichthys duseni*.

[23] Listed as the pimelodid catfish *Pimelodus valenciennes* by Couto de Magalhães (1931: 244). Now called *P. blochi*?

[24] Burgess (1989: 314).

[25] Este pequeño pez aparece en las redes que se tienden en la orilla del río, donde hay fondo arenoso, en busca de pececillos para carnada; así como también prendido al lomo de los silúridos grandes como el surubí, el patí y los armados, preferentemente en los meses de marzo y abril. De la referencia que tenemos de pescadores experimentados los peces atacados salen moribundos, semidesangrados y con la piel raída de arriba hacia abajo en dirección longitudinal.

Dada la pequeñez de los dientes anteriores y su situación un poco retirada del borde labial cómo se explican estas lesiones tan extensas? El doctor Couto de Magalhaes, en su "Monographia Brazileira de Peixes Fluviaes", cuenta que al introducir algunos ejemplares vivos de *Trichomycterus brasiliensis* en una acuario en al fondo del cual había una capa de arena, notó que éstos, para ocultarse, se introducían completamente en la arena, impartiendo al cuerpo con gran facilidad un movimiento vibratorio y propulsor. Recién hemos tenido oportunidad para observar los hábitos de otro pygidido (*Pygidium angustirostris*) y notamos también que éste, después de breve salida en busca de diminutas presas, vuelve a enterrarse rápidamente en la arena, impartiendo a la cabeza, a ese efecto, un movimiento oscilatorio. Postulamos, por lo tanto que el Chupa-chupa, al posarse sobre el lomo de su víctima lo roe con el propósito de hacerle sangrar con las espinas eréctiles del opérculo por medio del movimiento vibratorio aludido. Es difícil atribuir las lesiones a la acción de las espinas interoperculares por cuanto éstas se dirigen hacia atrás y son cóncavas hacia adentro. Para hacer entrar en juego a éstas el *Homodiaetus* tendría que impartir a su cuerpo un fuerte movimiento de retroceso. Posiblemente el examen del cuerpo de un pez lesionado aclarará este punto oscuro. (Devincenzi and Vaz Ferreira 1926–1940: 32)

[26] *Surubim, Pseudoplatystoma fasciatum.*

[27] The pimelodid catfish *Luciopimelodus pati.*

[28] Burgess (1989: 316).

[29] Assim, foi que apuramos, que o peixinho predador não atacava os peixes maiores em estado de hygidez, como afirmavam os pescadores, mas, apenas

áquelles que ficando presos entre as pedras, se debatiam, sangravam e estavam sem resistencia, quasi mortos.

Atacavam tambem os peixes grandes, presos em viveiros, facto ja observado por von Ihering, mas não apresentavam preferencia para determinada localisação (ano) adherindo sobertudo ás guelras, nadadeiras e lugares descamados . . . onde lhes fosse facil encontrar sangue em abundancia. (Alves Guimarães 1935a: 273).

[30] Observamos que este pequeno *Nematognata* ataca peixes mortos ha varias horas, os quaes sugam avidamente.

Corumbatás tirados do frigorifico dos Srs. Bianchini e Quilici, foram por nós collocados em um remanço, onde eram abundantes os parasitos que promptamente os atacaram.

Igual ataque fazem estes peixinhos ás pernas das crianças . . . que brincam dentro dagua, nellas se fixando sem causar lesões.

Esta fixação sobre suas victimas só é persistente dentro do rio.

Retirado da agua o hospedador, os parasitos se despregam e tombam quasi immediatamente, o que muito nos dificultou photographal-os.

Parece que a pressão da agua auxilia intensamente a manutenção do animal sobre sua presa nos momentos de sucção.

Notamos que o pequeno peixe náda em geral com o ventre para cima a procura do seu hospedador. Este facto, parace-nos ligado á grande quantidade de ar existente no interior do seu curto tubo intestinal quando falta o alimento, o qual é composto apenas de sangue sugado aos peixes maiores o que verificamos por exame microscopico.

O intestino quando repleto, apresenta-se como um tubo negro, occupando toda a parte ventral do animal e é facilmente observavel atravez da delgada parede do ventre. (Alves Guimarães 1935a: 274–275).

[31] According to Santos (1981: 36–38), about two dozen fishes of the genus *Prochilodus* (which he labels *Prochilodon* in his figure legends) go by the names *corimbatá, curimatã, corumbatá, grumatã*, and so forth. He illustrates *Prochilodon* [*sic*] *corumbata* on p. 36 and calls it the *curumbatá*.

[32] de Pinna (1998: 297).

[33] de Pinna and Vari (1995).

[34] See de [von] Spix and Agassiz (1829 [-1831]).

[35] See de Pinna and Vari (1995).

[36] Cândido de Melo Carvalho (1955), Goulding (1980), Roberts (1972).

[37] Baskin et al. (1980), Lundberg and Rapp Py-Daniel (1994), Santos (1962), Saul (1975).

[38] Santos (1962), Stradelli (1929).

[39] Goulding (1989: 184–185).

[40] Candirú—Calopsis candirú—Pequeno peixe muito voraz . . . que acode ao cheiro do sangue. Vão em cardumes, e desgraçado o ferido, homem eu animal,

que caïr no meio delles. Em poucos momentos é devorado vivo, só ficando o esqueleto perfeitamente limpo. Felizmente só atacam os feridos; si assim não fosse, em muitos logares seria impossivel banhar-se. (Stradelli 1929: 394–395).

41 de Pinna (1998: 292).

42 Santos (1962).

43 Voltando a falar do Candirú-y, lembro-me de ter ouvido de alguem, que a presença delles se faz sentir quando os rios baixam, pouco antes de começar o tempo das aguas. Apparecem, então, nesta época, em cardumes enormes, approximando-se das margens dos grandes rios e subindo pelos riachos que lá chamam de igarapés. A' bocca da noite, com fachos ou lanternas, pódem-se verificar os cordões que elles formam demandando, quasi á tona d'agua os mencionados cursos d'agua que vêm ter aos grandes rios; os pescadores interpretam a subida dos Candirús atravéz dos ribeirões, assim como a de outros peixes menores, como prenuncio de enchente proxima. Avisinham-se os Candirús, á noite, das margens dos grandes rios ou dos lagos que habitam. (Couto de Magalhães 1931: 105).

44 Jansen A. S. Zuanon (conversation, 5 November 1999).

45 Von Spix died at age 46 from infirmities contracted in Brazil between 1817 and 1820, leaving to Agassiz the task of organizing and describing his collection of fishes. Von Martius, von Spix's colleague and companion during the Brazil years, contributed the preface to the finished publication.

46 De alio pisce hominibus infesto nonnulla afferre debeo, quem Brasilienses *Candirú*, Hispani in provincia Maynas degentes *Canero* nuncupant. Singulari enim instinctu incitatur in ostia excretoria corporis humani intrandi, quae quum igitur in iis, qui in flumine lavant, attingit, summa cum violentia irrepit, ibique carnem morsu appetens, dolores, imo vitae periculum affert. Urinae odore hi pisciculi valde allici-untur, quam ob causam accolae intraturi flumen amazonum, cujus sinus hac peste abundant, praeputium ligula constringunt, et a mingendo abstinent. Pertinet hic piscis ad Cetopseos, quod dipinximus, genus; at nescio, an descriptarum specierum (C. Candiru et C. coecutientis) individua juniora, an tertiae cujusdam speciei minoris individua crudeli hoc instinctu a natura sint donata. (von Martius in de [von] Spix and Agassiz 1829 [–1831], p. viii).

47 Nicht selten hörten wir in *Pará* auch von den Gefahren reden, welchen die im Flusse Badenden durch den kleinen Fisch *Candirú* ausgesetzt seyen, und das, was von demselben erzählt wird, klingt so abentheurerlich, dass ich mich fast scheue, es hier zu wiederholen. *Cetopsis* ist eine zu den Salmen gehörige Gattung, die sich sowohl durch die einfache Reihe von Zähnen, als durch die abgestutzte Form des Kopfes und die kleinen, unter der Haut liegenden und kaum durchscheinenden, Augen auszeichnet. Eine Art dieser Gattung, die *Candirú* der Einwohner, ein Fis-chchen von der Länge und Dicke eines Fingers, — ob die jüngeren Individuen einer der beiden von uns abgebildeten Arten (*Cetopsis Candirú Pisc. t.* 10. *f.* 1., und *C. coe-cutiens t.* 10. *f.* 2.) oder ob eine dritte, noch unbeschriebene, kann ich leider nicht angeben, weil die von uns gesammelten Stücke verloren gegangen sind, — hat die

Gewohnheit, mit grosser Heftigkeit und sehr schnell in die äusseren Höhlungen des menschlichen Körpers hineinzuschlüpfen. Sie erregt hier die schmerzhaftesten und gefährlichsten Zufälle, und kann, weil sie die Flossen ausspreitzt, nur mit grosser Mühe wieder herausgebracht werden. Der Geruch menschlicher Excretionen scheint das Fischchen anzulocken, und die Indianer rathen desshalb sich im Bade der Befriedigung eines gewissen Bedürfnisses zu enthalten, oder einen gewissen Theil sorgfältig zu bedecken, Die Indianer, deren wir uns als Ruderer bedienten, bekräftigten ihre Erzählung von dieser seltsamen Eigenschaft durch mehrere Beispiele, da wir aber überhaupt die Bemerkung gemacht hatten, dass der Glaube an Unwahrscheinliches und Ausserordentliches, zugleich mit einer lächerlichen Gespensterfurcht, einen eigenthümlichen Zug im Character jener Menschen ausmache, so fanden ihre Berichte nicht eher Eingang, als bis wir durch unsern Freund Dr. Lacerda, als Augenzeugen, von der Wahrheit der Sache unterrichtet wurden. (von Spix and von Martius 1823–1831[?]: 955–956).

[48] Er ist in Maynas unter den Namen *Canero*, am Solimoēs als *Candirú* sehr bekannt und gefürchtet. Der Angriff eines Fisches auf diese Weise hat etwas so Abenteuerliches, dase man anfangs kaum an denselben glauben mag. Auch Hr. von Martius (Reise III. 965.) gesteht diese Erzählung der Indier sehr skeptisch betrachtet zu haben, bis sie der bekannte Naturforscher und Arzt zu Pará, Dr. Lacerda, in der Wahrheit begründet erklärt hatte. Ich selbst bin in Yurimaguas Augenzeuge eines solchen Falles gewesen, indem eine Indierin nach dem Einschlüpfen eines Canero in die Vagina auf einmal einen so furchtbaren Schmerz und Blutverlust erlitt, dass man sie verloren gab. Nach der innerlichen und äussern Anwendung der Xagua war das Fischchen, sogleich abgegangen, und die Frau entkam mit dem Leben. Der grosse Aberglaube der Indier verhinderte mich an seiner Erlangung, allein ich habe Caneros, in grosser Menge besessen, die um Yurimaguas gefangen alle kaum 2 Zoll lang, und so ausgebildet waren, dass sie nicht für junge Individuen gelten durften. Leider verdarben sie in dem schlechten Branntwein des Landes. Soviel aus Erinnerung sich urtheilen lässt, scheint keine der Abbildungen von *Cetopsis* (Martius *Pisces*. tab. 10. f. 1.2.) auf den Canero von Maynas zu passen. In einigen Gegenden des Marañon, besonders bei Pebas, waren die Caneros so ausserordentlich häufig, dass es genügte nur ein Paar Blutstropfen geschossener Vögel in das Wasser fallen zu lassen, um Schwärme dieser sehr kleinen und höchst gefährlichen Raubthiere herbeizulocken. (Poeppig 1836: 395, footnote).

[49] One of many common names for the fruit of the tropical tree *Genipa americana*. For a list of some of these, see Chapter 8, endnote 44.

[50] Schomburgk (1841: 18, No. 379, col. 72). I did not reproduce the German text because it contains nothing that isn't in the English version.

[51] I couldn't find a listing for the Rio Bremeo, and Schomburgk neglected to mention which country he was visiting.

[52] Schomburgk (1840: 396).

[53] Cette espèce est, de la part des pêcheurs de l'Araguay, l'objet d'un préjugé des plus singuliers: ils prétendent qu'il est fort dangereux d'uriner dans la rivière, car,

disent-ils, ce petit animal s'élance hors de l'eau et pénètre dans l'urètre en remontant le long de la colonne liquide. (de Castelnau 1855: 50).

[54] Eigenmann (1918a: 344).

[55] Günther (1864: 276–277)

[56] In diesen noch so wenig bekannten Gewässern, namentlich im Huallága, beobachtete der Reisende einen Fisch, den ich der Aufmerksamkeit der Wissenschaft ganz besonders empfehlen will. Man nennt ihn dort den Candirú und fürchtet ihn mit Recht ebenso sehr für das Gebiet des Wassers, wie man für das des Landes die Moskitos und Ameisen fürchtet. An sich selbst ist er nur ein kleines, kaum 3/4 Spannen langes Ding von welsartigem Körperbau, mit breitem, abgerundetem Kopf, auf dem die beiden kleinen Augen ziemlich dicht neben einander liegen, während die beiden Brustflossen flügelartig dicht unter ihm sich ausbreiten, und der übrige Körperteil keilförmig zuläuft. Den Rücken ziert eine dunklere Färbung mit undeutlich verlaufenden Flecken, sodaß das Geschöpfchen an sich selbst kaum irgendwie durch eine hervorragende Eigentümlichkeit ausgezeichnet ist. Eine um so schrecklichere Plage ist er für den Badenden, eine Art Blutegel nämlich, der mit unglaublicher Schwimmfertigkeit jenem zu Leibe geht, ihm überall schröpfkopfähnliche Wunden beibringt und, wenn es ihm gelungen, sich dadurch an dem Körper festzusetzen, in der Wunde ein Nadelbündel ausspreizt, an dem er wie an Widerhaken sich derart festklammert, daß er nur durch eine schmerzhafte Operation aus dem Körper entfernt werden kann. Diese Unart des Fisches ist um so größer und gehfährlicher, da er am liebsten die geheimsten Körperteile aufsucht; man erzählt sich Fälle, die bei der Operation mit dem Tode endeten. Ich werde dafür Sorge tragen, daß dieser seltsame Fisch, den ich in Spiritus vor mir habe, in die rechten wissenschaftlichen Hände gelangt und seinen wissenschaftlichen Namen empfängt, den er noch nicht hat. (Müller 1870: 180).

[57] A span is a unit of measure equal to 9 inches (about 22.9 centimeters).

[58] Burgess (1989: 316).

[59] Keller (1874: v).

[60] Marcoy (1875: 184). Marcoy's specimen could be a species of *Pseudocetopsis*. To Eigenmann and Allen (1942: 147), Marcoy's fish resembles *Hemicetopsis*.

[61] On recueillit aussi, par milliers, de ces "candirus", sortes de petits silures, dont quelques-uns sont microscopiques, et qui ont bientôt fait une pelote des mollets du baigneur, imprudemment aventuré dans leurs parages. (Verne 1881, in third paragraph of Chapter 11). I made a direct translation from an original French version of the novel then available on the Internet (http://jv.gilead.org.il/selva/jangada/html).

[62] Boulenger (1897a: 901).

[63] Je n'étais pas dans l'eau depuis cinq minutes, que je ressentis à la région lombaire, au ventre, sur les côtés de la poitrine, comme de légers coups de griffe qui se succédaient rapidement. Voyant l'eau se teinter en rouge autour de moi, je me

hâtai de regagner le rivage et je constatai que, dans les régions où j'avais éprouvé la sensation de ces coups de griffe, le sang s'échappait de blessures en scarification parallèles, qui eussent pu être attribuées à un instrument, tant elles étaient régulières; elles constituaient des groupes de cinq à six lignes, longues d'un centimètre au plus et très rapprochées; je n'ai pas cherché à apprécier la profondeur, mais ces blessures très étroites saignaient abondamment. (Jobert 1898: 497).

[64] Beim Baden werden wir vorsichtig. Es wurden Candirús gefunden, ein hier 2 cm langes transparentes Fischchen mit gelber Iris, das gern in die ihm zugänglichen Körperhöhlen eindringt. Wenn dasselbe, wie häufig vorkommen soll, in die Urethra schlüpft, ist die Lage wegen der gleich Haken sich in die Schleimhaut einbohrenden Flossen sehr kritisch; gelingt es nicht, durch ein warmes Bad den Störenfried herauszuschaffen, bleibt nur die Operation übrig. Es soll sich der Sertanejo alsdann auch nicht besinnen, die Urethrotomie auszuführen und in vielen Fällen an diesem heroischen Verfahren zu Grunde gehen. (von den Steinen 1886: 178–179). This paragraph was reproduced by Blanchard (1903).

[65] The word *escrivão* means clerk in Portuguese. I don't know what *candirooescrivão* means, nor have I seen the term used elsewhere.

[66] Lange (1912: 214).

[67] Gudger (1930c: 24).

[68] According to Lange (1912: 19), the rivers ". . . are occupied by river creatures, alligators, water-snakes, and malignant, repulsive fish, of which persons outside South America know nothing." Among the many examples of hairy-chested South American adventure: Barros Prado (1959), Davis (1952), and Duguid (1931).

[69] Lang (1912: 77).

[70] Eigenmann (1918a: 265).

[71] Eigenmann (1918a: 266–267).

[72] Eigenmann (1920: 441).

[73] Gudger (1930c: 29).

[74] Gudger (1930c: 30).

[75] Très petit, mais uniquement préoccupé à mal faire, est le "candiru" (Cetopsis), qui ne dépasse pas 5 à 8 centimètres de long. Il vient souvent accroché aux mailles de l'épervier et l'on se fait de mauvaises blessures aux éperons aigus de ses nageoires: réunis en légion ils luttent de savoir-faire avec les "piranhas" pour dépouiller un cadavre de ses chairs, ou même pour dévorer tout vivant un animal blessé qui cherche refuge dans le cours d'eau. Le pis est qu'il pénètre parfois dans les cavités anales ou vaginales des baigneurs ou des baigneuses et là, hérissant ses terribles éperons qui s'opposent à tout recul, peut causer de graves désordres s'il n'est extrait aussitôt avec les précautions nécessaires. Personnellement, nous connaissons déjà trois cas de ce curieux accident. (Le Cointe 1922: 365).

[76] Gudger (1930c: 105–106).

[77] Prodgers (1925: 210).

[78] Gudger (1930c: 107). The date of Starks' letter to Gudger is not mentioned.

[79] Gudger (1930c: 108–109).

2. Urinary Misconduct

[1] Telles Ribeiro (1994: 99).

[2] Doctorow (1994: 11).

[3] Muito se tem escripto sobre a extranha particularidade que têm esses peixinhos, de penetrar, com incrivel facilidade, pela uretra, vagina e mesmo pelo anus das pessôas que se banham nos rios onde elles abundam. Offerece sério perigo ás mulheres, principalmente, quando entram n'agua menstruadas e desprotegidas de tangas; os cardumes consideraveis de candirús, chamados pelo sangue, alvoroçamse e, ordinariamente, immiscuem-se pela mucosa a dentro. E' voz corrente que o candirú penetra pela uretra do homem, quando este, inadvertidamente, urina dentro d'agua onde elles enxameiam. Com o jacto da micção, o canal se abre e elles, que acodem pelo cheiro da urina ou por outra qualquer razão, mettem-se pela fenda a dentro. Mesmo quando não conseguem de todo entrar, a operação para os retirar é difficilima e muito dolorosa, pois, como é sabido, os seus operculos se dilatam no interior da uretra e os pequeninos espinhos que os guarnecem cravam-se na mucosa. (Couto de Magalhães 1931: 104).

[4] Esta denominação vulgar, amazônica, compreende dois gêneros de pequenos peixes de couro, uns da fam. *Trichomycterideos*, gên. *Vandellia* e *Stegophilus*, que, como as "Cambevas" da mesma família, têm o opérculo e o preopérculo providos de acículos; outros, da fam. *Cetopsídeos*, não têm êsses acúleos; os barbilhões, pequenos, são em número de 6. Êstes últimos peixes (gên. *Cetopsis* e *Hemicetopsis*) atingem 30 cms. de comprimento e daí o nome mais adequado de "Candiru-assú" .... Aos representantes da primeira família mencionada, *Vandellia cirrhosa* e *Stegophilus intermedius* e *insidiosus* (êste último do Rio S. Francisco) são da há muito imputados vários malefícios, os quais, porém, sempre haviam sido postos em dúvida ...

Das espécies de um gênero da mesma família, e também conhecidas por "Candirus", constam iguais façanhas. Já Castelnau relatara, do Araguaia, que *Pareiodon pusillus* é temido pelos pescadores, a ponto de êstes não se atreverem a urinar diretamente na água, porque receiam que o pequeno peixe, subindo o curso da coluna líquida, penetre na uretra. Miranda Ribeiro, em Manaus, verificou que *Pareiodon microps* é peixe carnívoro, que arranca pedaços circulares da pele de bagres vivos. A tanto de fato o habilita a dentição, que fica escondida numa prega da mucosa; mas, desnudando os maxilares, tem-se a impressão de uma miniatura dos dentes de tubarão (*Galeocerdus maculatus*), simplificados e com a ponta maior muito curvada para fora.

Reunidos em legião, como se fossem pequenas piranhas, descarnam não só os animais mortos, como também a caça ferida, que venha procurar refúgio na água.

Muito mais perigosa é a mania do candiru *Vandellia cirrhosa* que procura penetrar na abertura urogenital dos banhistas. O tamanho máximo que êste peixinho atinge é 70–80 mms. mas os exemplares de 40 mms. têm apenas 4 mms. de diâmetro e dêste modo lhes é fácil insinuar-se, de forma a penetrar completamente na cavidade. E o pior é que os peixes desta família, como também se nota nas "Cambevas", seus parentes próximos, têm numerosos espinhos na região opercular e êstes, ao se tentar a extração, cada vez mais se encravam nas carnes, provocando grande hemorragia. Não só êste fato foi várias vezes testemunhado por médicos amazonenses, chamados para proceder à difícil extração, como também a população ribeirinha, temendo o candirú, toma providências para evitar acidentes desta natureza, aos quais principalmente as mulheres estão mais sujeitas. Com evidente exagero os homens temem, até, verter água em jato direto nos rios habitados por candirús, porque êstes, dizem êles, poderiam mesmo dêste modo subir e penetrar. (von Ihering 1940: 201–202).

5 Siluriforms are sometimes called "skin fishes."

6 Correctly called *Trichomycterus brasiliensis* by Couto de Magalhães (1931: 237) and (Burgess 1989: 321). Santos (1981: 104) still calls it *Pygidium brasiliensis*.

7 Big candiru.

8 The correct name of this shark, the tiger shark, is *Galeocerdo cuvieri*. I can't tell from von Ihering's Portuguese whether de Miranda Ribeiro meant that the teeth of the *candiru-açu* are shaped like the tiger shark's teeth, or if von Ihering is simply using the tiger shark as representative of sharks generally.

9 Vinton and Stickler (1941: 511).

10 Vinton and Stickler (1941: 511).

11 Vinton and Stickler (1941: 512).

12 Gudger (1930c: 27–28).

13 Miles (1943b: 367).

14 Cotlow (1953: 137). Except for the omission of a few sentences, this account is repeated exactly in a later book (Cotlow 1966: 224–225).

15 Burroughs (1959: 41).

16 Chegou-se mesmo a dizer que não era preciso fazer tal dentro da água, pois bastava urinar, no rio mesmo a certa distância, pois o *candiru* subia pelo jato.

Isso ainda não se acha provado e até parece pouco provável. (Santos 1962: 115).

17 Lowe-McConnell (1975: 43).

18 Schreider and Schreider (1970: 68–70).

19 I think Armbrust got this idea from reading the account of Lüling (1965). I quote a section of Lüling's report in Chapter 7 (see endnote 4).

[20] Herman (1973: 266).

[21] Grzimek (1973: 381).

[22] Goulding (1980: 34).

[23] Goulding (1989: 185).

[24] Burgess (1989: 318).

[25] Burgess doesn't credit them, but it was Vinton and Stickler (1941) who caught candirus using a bloody piece of a cow's lung. The fish were later identified by John S. Robas of the American Museum of Natural History as specimens of *Vandellia plaizae* [*sic*]. They aren't listed in the museum's collections.

[26] Burgess (1989: 318).

[27] Halstead (1992: 223–228).

[28] Begossi and Manoel de Souza Braga (1992: 105).

[29] Homewood (1994).

[30] Paulo Petry, then at Instituto Nacional de Pesquisas da Amazônia (INPA), Manaus, Brazil (e-mail to Gene S. Helfman, 21 January 1998).

[31] John W. Fitzpatrick, Cornell Laboratory of Ornithology, Ithaca, New York (e-mail, 24 November 1998).

[32] Linnea Smith, physician, eastern Peru (e-mail, 22 January 2000).

[33] En cuanto a estos Trichomycteridae, fueron agarrados con red y sangro de pecari en Ecuador durante al mes de 1995, haciendo una expedición por el río Curaray y afluencia. Un soldado ecuatoriano murió un año antes en el río Curaray debido a la penetración de un "canero" (o "candirú) en el oido. (undated letter written by Jean-Luc Sanchez).

[34] Before renovation of the waterfront, this was a staircase in downtown Manaus that led directly to the Rio Negro. Because it was beside the PanAm office, it was known as *na escadaria da Panair*. This was when Panair do Brasil maintained a private floating port. Aerial transport (cargo, mail, people) was by float plane. Boats filled with produce stopped nearby and off-loaded to a street market called *feira da Panair*. This market still exists, but has been moved slightly east to the mouth of the first *igarapé* downstream from the city. It's a chaotic setup on stilts that resembles the main market. (e-mails, Paulo Petry and Jansen A. S. Zuanon, 30 August 2000).

[35] von Humboldt (1852?, Vol. 1: 197).

[36] See Robert L. Usinger's foreword in the reprint of Bates (1876).

[37] Agassiz and Agassiz (1868: 236–237).

[38] MacCreagh (1926: 5).

[39] MacCreagh (1926: 198).

3. A Very Singular Fish

[1] Calvino (1968: 71).

[2] Baskin (1973), Burgess (1989: 305–325), de Pinna (1998), Eigenmann (1918a), and Tchernavin (1944) discuss the trichomycterid catfishes in detail, and Burgess provides a recent key to the genera.

[3] The operculum, or gill cover, consists of four separate bones. These are the preopercle, opercle, interopercle, and subopercle.

[4] Median vomer according to Baskin (1973). The vomer is the anterior (i.e., frontmost) bone of the roof of the mouth and often contains teeth. The premaxillae (sometimes called the premaxillaries or intermaxillaries) lie on either side of the vomer and constitute the front of the upper jaw. Behind the two premaxillae (i.e., attached to the premaxillae by the anterior end) are the two maxillae (sometimes called the maxillaries). Both the premaxillae and maxillae can bear teeth.

[5] The ethmoid is a bone located on the top front part of the skull, or neurocranium.

[6] The premaxilla of Baskin (1973). These characters are not listed as such in any of Eigenmann's 1918 publications. Schmidt assembled his list of characters piecemeal from the text and key to the genera in Eigenmann (1918a), the text of Baskin (1973), and his own observations on *Paracanthopoma* (Robert E. Schmidt, letter, 18 October 2000). Although Eigenmann's key (Eigenmann 1918a: 278–279) indicates "claw-teeth" as diagnostic only of *Branchioica*, he mentions (p. 359) *Vandellia* has having ". . . from two to four comparatively large and very peculiar 'claw-teeth,' arranged like overlapping shingles, the outermost one being next the bone [*sic*], the second from the end overlapping this and so on to the proximal one."

[7] For hypotheses on the evolution of these and related fishes, see Baskin (1973), de Pinna (1998), and Schmidt (1993).

[8] Cuvier and Valenciennes (1846). Two of the three type specimens are listed in the collections of the Muséum National d'Histoire Naturelle, Paris (MNHN A.6308).

[9] Este muito certamente os obteve de Alexandre Rodrigues Ferreira que desta especie dá uma boa figura nos seus desenhos de Peixes e a qual reproduzimos aqui. (de Miranda Ribeiro 1911: 229, footnote 2). Alípio de Miranda Ribeiro (1874–1939) is considered the father of Brazilian ichthyology.

[10] . . . un très-singulier poisson, qui est probablement originaire d'Amérique. (Cuvier and Valenciennes 1846: 386).

[11] From Valenciennes' French, "est échancrée dans le milieu." This evidently refers to the shape of the lower jaw as seen superficially. The jawbones are actually separated.

[12] La longueur de nos exemplaires est de deux pouces neuf lignes. (Cuvier and Valenciennes 1846: 387). The pouce (French inch) = 1.066 English inches; 1 ligne (line) = 1/12 pouce. The candirus measured by Valenciennes were 2 pouce 9 lignes = 2.70 English inches = 6.87 centimeters = 68.7 millimeters.

[13] Pellegrin (1909b) claims that the hooked teeth, which Valenciennes says are on the vomer, could just as well be on the premaxilla, although others have since disagreed: in all species of *Vandellia*, these teeth indeed appear to be on the vomer. Descriptions and names of the bones with teeth have been used inconsistently in describing the vandelliines. This is understandable because the positioning of these structures is malleable, depending on developmental stages of the fish and other factors. To keep my own narrative consistent, I have followed Baskin's terminology. According to Baskin (1973: 83), "The single set of teeth on the vomer in the middle of the upper jaw has been often called premaxillary teeth [*sic*], while those on the premaxilla were thought to be maxillary teeth . . ." Based on Baskin's interpretation, Eigenmann (1912, 1918a) routinely confuses these structures. So does Mahnert (1985: 9), evidently unaware of Baskin's work, who writes, "The dentition is very peculiar: one set of five to ten very pointed, hooked teeth fits into the middle of the upper jaw (premaxillary . . .) [La dentition est très particulière: un série de cinq à dix dents très pointues et recourbées s'insèrent au milieu de la mâchoire supérieure (prémaxillaire . . .)"] As Schmidt (1993: 188) points out, de Pinna and Britski (1991) consider the vomer ". . . homologous to the stegophiline median premaxilla." The stegophilines are trichomycterid catfishes related to the vandelliines (Chapter 1).

[14] Je sais que cette description est incomplète, mais telle qu'elle est, on y trouve la preuve que ce poisson ne rentre dans aucun des genres connus. (Cuvier and Valenciennes 1846: 387–388).

[15] de Miranda Ribeiro (1912: 30).

[16] Eigenmann (1918a: 361), Eigenmann and Allen (1942: 161). Also see Lauzanne and Loubens (1985: 114).

[17] NEODAT, from the website http://www.neodat.org: "The Inter-Institutional database of Fish Biodiversity in the Neotropics is an international cooperative effort to make available systematic and geographic data on neotropical freshwater fish specimens deposited in natural history collections in the New World and Europe." NEODAT's listings are incomplete, and specimens exist in collections not yet logged into its database.

[18] Let's hope de Castelnau's aptitude for natural history exceeded his ineptitude as an ethnologist. The American zoologist James Orton tells us: "Near the sources of this river [the Rio Teffé, Brazil] Castelnau [*sic*] locates the [tribes] Canamas and Uginas; the former dwarfs, the latter having tails a palm and a half long—a hybrid from an Indian and Barigudo monkey." (Orton 1870: 319, footnote).

[19]   Genre *Vandellia*

Ce curieux genre a été établi par M. Valenciennes (*Hist. des Poissons*, t. XVIII, p. 386); il le place provisoirement dans la famille des *Ésoces*, mais il me semble avoir de grands rapports avec les *Trichomycterus*, que l'on place parmi les *Siluroïdes*, et je me suis décidé à lui faire suivre ces poissons.

On n'avait encore décrit qu'une espèce, le *Vandellia cirrhosa*, dont on ne connaît pas exactement la patrie, mais qui vient certainement d'un des fleuves du Brésil, et probablement de l'Amazone. Nous allons en faire connaître une seconde.

N° 4. VANDELLIA PLAZAII, nov. sp.
(Planche XXVIII, fig. 1.)

Cette espèce diffère de celle qui était connue jusqu'ici par son corps beaucoup plus allongé, et dont la hauteur est contenue treize l'ois dans la longeur, tandis qu'elle ne se trouve que de dix dans la *cirrhosa*. La tête est plus élargie, plus arrondie en avant; la queue est tronquée obliquement. Le corps est entièrement d'un blanc bleuâtre, uniforme, devenant un peu jaune en dessous; la tête est de couleur terre de Sienne; la nageoire caudale a sa moitié supérieure rouge et l'inférieure noire.

J'ai pris cette espèce dans le rio Ucayale (Pérou), le 13 septembre 1846.

Je dédie cette espèce au vénérable père Plaza, préfet des missions de la Pampa del Sacramento, qui nous recut avec autant de bienveillance que d'humanité, lorsque après des souffrances inouïes, nous parvînmes enfin à Sarayacu, dans un état qui fit verser des larmes à ce digne missionnaire.

Nota.—Comme point de comparaison, j'ai fait figurer, pl. 28, fig. 2, le *Vandellia cirrhosa*. (de Castelnau 1855: 51).

[20] Earlier ichthyologists sometimes described anatomical structures in terms of caliper widths instead of relative proportions. When the height of a fish's body is contained 13 times in the length, this means that the height, as determined by a caliper width, fits into the length 13 times. Authors writing in other languages did this too. I find it confusing and give the relative proportions in brackets.

[21] Sienna is an earth containing iron oxides and usually manganese. In the raw state it is brownish yellow, but turns orange or reddish orange after being burned.

[22] This is probably an error. If a species is named after a man (i.e., is given a masculine name), and the man's name ends in *i*, previous rules of nomenclature dictated the addition of another *i*. De Castelnau named his fish *V. plazaii* (this name also appears on the color plate shown here as Plate 2), but in his text gives the priest's name as Plaza. Either the man's name was Plazai or de Castelnau erred in naming this species.

[23] Cette espèce se distingue facilement de la précédente par ses formes plus allongées, la hauteur du corps étant contenue environ 13 fois dans la longueur totale; la tête est plus arrondie, le barbillon fait moins de la moitié de la longueur de la tête, la pectorale est aussi longue que la tête. La caudale est échancrée à lobes pointus. (Pellegrin 1909b: 198).

[24] The standard length of a fish is its length from the tip of the snout to the end of the vertebral column. Total length (tip of the snout to end of the tail fin) and fork length (tip of the snout to the fork of the tail in species with forked tails) are less reliable standards because the tail fin is sometimes damaged or even missing.

[25] Un autre très beau spécimen de cette espèce pêché par le Dr. [C.] Jobert au Calderão, dans le rio Solimoens (Haut-Amazone), existe également dans les collections du Muséum de Paris. (Pellegrin 1909b: 198). Jobert's specimen is MNHN A1987, collected in 1879.

[26] Eigenmann (1918a: 362).

[27] Dahl (1960: 315).

[28] Baskin et al. (1980), de Pinna and Britski (1991).

[29] Em ferimento em jacaré. (de Miranda Ribeiro 1947: 2). These specimens are probably MNRJ 1158 in the collections of the Museu Nacional, Rio de Janeiro. The collection date is not recorded.

[30] Specimens of *P.* cf. *plazai* caught the Rio Jauaperi (P. Petry and S. Spotte, coll.) on the nights of 31 October and 1 November 1999 were combined and logged into the collections of Instituto Nacional de Pesquisas da Amazônia, Manaus (INPA 15599). Those caught at midday in the Rio Solimões near Manaus (P. Petry, J. A. S. Zuanon, S. Spotte) on 6 November 1999 were archived as INPA 15600.

[31] Eigenmann (1912: 66, unnumbered Table).

[32] Eigenmann (1918a: 362).

[33] de Miranda Ribeiro (1912: 30).

[34] Academy of Natural Sciences of Philadelphia (number of specimens in parentheses): ANSP 175843 (2), ANSP 175844 (1).

[35] Robert E. Schmidt (letter, 18 October 2000).

[36] A single specimen collected in 1859 might be next in the chronology, but we know too little about it. The fish is deposited in the Museum of Comparative Zoology, Harvard University, Cambridge (Massachusetts) (MCZ 27572). Caleb Cooke, at Pará (now Belém), collected it from a stingray on 25 October 1859. He doesn't state the species of stingray, but notes that both freshwater and marine fishes were collected. The person who labeled it *V. gracilicauda* is unknown; the name is not valid at this time. I examined this fish. I think it looks like *V. cirrhosa*.

To my knowledge, this specimen is the first vandelliine recorded as having been obtained from an elasmobranch. A specimen of *V.* cf. *wieneri* deposited at the Royal Ontario Museum, Ottawa (ROM 50260), was taken from the gill chambers of a large stingray. G. Holeton caught it during October 1976 in the Rio Solimões, 30 kilometers west of the mouth of the Rio Negro.

[37] Capo molto appiattito, largo quanto lungo, poco più lungo dell' altezza del corpo, che (caudale esclusa) è contenuta 14 volte nella lunghezza totale. L' occhio rotondo a orlo libero, è situato verso l'estremità del muso; il suo diametro è contenuto 5 volte nella lunghezza del capo e $2^{1}/_{3}$ nello spazio interorbitale. L' angolo opercolare è armato da uncini relativamente robusti poco curvi, che sono situati in due gruppi, uno al subopercolo ed uno più numeroso all' angolo superiore dell'

opercolo. I barbigli sono grossi e brevi, lunghi la metà del capo. Le pettorali piccole, lunghe poco meno del capo, hanno 8 raggi. Le narici sono ovali e molto vicine all'orlo anteriore dell'occhio; esse misurano la metà del suo diametro. La bocca ci presenta forma particolare, ben rappresentata nella figura data da Cuv. e Val. a Tav. 547 per la *Vandellia cirrhosa*; essa è inferiore, totalmente priva di denti, il labbro inferiore presenta un' insenatura al suo orlo anteriore. Sul vomere spinto molto innanzi si vedono 8 denti ricurvi verso l' interno, dei quali i due mediani sono i più lunghi e robusti, misurando circa 1 mm. e gli altri decrescono gradatamente, i due esterni essendo molto piccoli. L' apertura branchiale è stretta e si apre immediatamente innanzi alle pettorali. Il corpo depresso verso il capo, si arrotonda fino davanti alla dorsale ed alla anale per terminare poi appiattito fino alla base della caudale. Le ventrali sono più brevi e strette delle pettorali, situate al terzo posteriore del corpo poco distanti dall' anale. Questa comincia sotto la metà della dorsale, conta 8 raggi distintamente articolati, alti come quelli della dorsale e due terzi della lunghezza del capo. La caudale è incavata, con i raggi esterni leggermente prolungati ed eguali tra loro.

Il colore generale (nell' alcool) è bruno sul dorso e giallastro sul ventre. Sul dorso si vede una minutissima punteggiatura nera che si estende anche sui raggi di tutte le pinne. La caudale è gialla.

Rio Beni. Missioni Mosetenes.

Secondo quanto dice il Günther nella Introduction to the study of Fishes, questi pesci vivrebbero parassiti nella cavità branchiale dei grandi siluridi. (Perugia 1897: 23–24).

[38] The reference is to Günther (1880: 581).

[39] Pellegrin (1909a).

[40] La coloration générale est olivâtre, les nageoires grisâtres. (Pellegrin 1911: B₁.11).

[41] La bouche est petite, infère, aplatie. La mâchoire supérieure est très proéminente; en avant se trouve une demi-couronne composée de neuf dents aiguës, en forme de crochets, à pointe dirigée vers l'intérieur; ces dents sont normalement couchées, mais susceptibles d'un certain degré d'érection; les médianes sont beaucoup plus longues que les latérales. (Pellegrin 1909a: 1017).

[42] The key presented here is from Pellegrin (1909b: 200), but nearly identical versions occur in Pellegrin (1909a: 1017, 1911: B₁.11). The key of Eigenmann (1918a: 360) contains the same information as these.

Hauteur de corps 7 fois dans la longueur sans la caudale. Barbillon faisant le tiers de la longueur de la tête. Pectorales plus courtes que la tête. Caudale fourchue, à lobes pointus.   *Vandellia Wieneri*, nov. sp.

Hauteur du corps 9 fois dans la longueur sans la caudale. Barbillon faisant la moitié de la longueur de la tête. Pectorales plus longues que la tête. Caudale très légèrement échancrée, à lobes arrondis, égaux.   *Vandellia cirrhosa* C. V.

Hauteur du corps 12 fois dans la longueur sans la caudale. Barbillon faisant moins de la moitié de la longueurde la tête. Pectorales aussi longues que la tête. Caudale énchancrée, à lobes poinus. *Vandellia Plazai* Castelnau

[43] C'est une croyance répandue depuis longtemps parmi les Indiens du Brésil que les baigneurs peuvent être attaqués par un petit Poisson du nom de *Candiru* qui, attiré par l'odeur de l'urine, pénètre dans l'urèthre et y détermine des désordres graves, suivis généralement de mort. (Pellegrin 1909b: 201).

[44] Les Poissons qui ont attaqué ainsi le Dr Jobert appartiennent suivant moi, incontestablement au genre Vandellie, peut-être même à l'espèce *Vandellia Wieneri*... Si l'on se reporte à la description donnée plus haut de la bouche et de l'appareil operculaire, on s'expliquera ainsi facilement le fonctionnement de ces divers organes; on comprendra aisément que la demi-couronne de dents en crochet placée en avant de la bouche, dents *susceptibles d'un certain degré d'érection et au nombre de 5 à 6 principales* produit ces *scarifications parallèles, régulières et an groupe de 5 à 6 lignes.* Les épines interoperculaires du dessous de la tête, aussi un peu érectiles, peuvent également, dans une certaine mesure, déchirer les téguments, mais elles doivent surtout servir à la fixation. Quant aux épines operculaires... elles me semblent plutôt, étant donnée la direction de leur pointe, destinées à faciliter la progression de l'animal et à empêcher tout recul lorsqu'il s'engage dans un conduit étroit, par exemple entre les lamelles branchiales des Platystomes. (Pellegrin 1909b: 203–204).

[45] Estes peixinhos, por vezes, também se agarram como as sanguessugas às pernas de quem penetra no rio, mas sem causar dano.

Quando se agarram nas pernas basta sair fora da água para que logo caiam e morram. (Santos 1981: 107).

[46] L'ensemble de ces divers appareils indique une grande spécialisation: les dents et les épines operculaires et interoperculaires permettent la fixation sur un hôte et l'érosion des téguments; la disposition de la cavité buccale semble destinée à faciliter l'ingurgitation des liquides sanguins épanchés des plaies ainsi obtenues. (Pellegrin (1909a: 1017)

[47] La disposition très particulière des appareils buccal et operculaire nettement visible sur le *Vandellia Wieneri* indique une grande spécialisation et paraît établir un parasitisme fort avancé. (Pellegrin 1909b: 201)

[48] En arrière des dents, la cavité buccale est tappissée de nombreuses papilles, puis limitée par un repli assez prononcé. Sur les côtés les lèvres sont assez épaisses. La machoire inférieure, fortement échancrée en son milieu, est complètement dépourvue de dents; en arrière s'élève un vaste voile membraneux, percé en son centre d'une petite ouverture qui ne paraît pas accidentelle; ce voile, en se rapprochant du repli supérieur, ferme ainsi toute la partie antérieure de la cavité buccale; à l'état de repos il se rabat postérieurement. (Pellegrin 1909b: 199). Pellegrin (1909a: 1017) gives nearly the same description.

[49] ... à l'état de repos il se rabat postérieurement. (Pellegrin 1909a: 1017).

[50] Eigenmann (1918a: 363–365).

[51] Haseman never said where he collected these specimens. It might have been Bolivia or possibly Mato Grosso, Brazil. If Brazil, the likely collection site is now in Rondônia. Also see Lauzanne and Loubens (1985: 114).

[52] Muséum National d'Histoire Naturelle, Paris (MNHN 1988, 1984, 85 millimeters total length) collected by Lauzanne and Loubens in 1983 in the Rio Mamoré, Bolivia. The specimen was obtained from a characin (parasite de *Colossoma*).

[53] Les yeux sont petits, ovalaires, leur grand diamètre est un peu inférieur à l'espace interorbitaire et à 2 fois leur distance du bout du museau. (Pellegrin 1909b: 199).

[54] di Caporiacco (1935: 59–60).

[55] Corporis totius longitudo (sine cauda) mm. 57; corporis altitudo maxima mm. 5,5; capitis longitudo mm. 6; capitis amplitudo maxima mm. 5,5.

Longitudo capitis fere decies, altitudo corporis plus quam decries in longitudine corporis continentur.

Rostrum rotundatum. Spatium præorbitale tertia parte oculo maius; spatium interorbitale oculi diametrum (mm. 1,5) adæquat. Barbæ maxillaris long. mm. 2,5, ita ut dimidiam capitis longitudinem non attingit. (di Caporiacco 1935: 59).

[56] Præmaxillaria dentibus 9 robustis, longissimis munita; mandibula denticulis minutissimis munita. (di Caporiacco 1935: 59–60).

[57] Mandibula dentibus minutis armata a *V. plazai* Castelnau et a *V. hasemani* Eigenm. (an quoque a *V. cirrhosa* C. V. et a *V. wieneri* Pellegrin?) distinguitur; præmaxillaribus novem dentibus instructis et numero radiorum pinnæ dorsalis et analis a. *V. sanguinea* Eigenm.; numero radiorum pinnae dorsalis et analis et pinna caudali non furcata a *V. wieneri* Pellegrin; numero radiorum pinnæ analis et pectorali capite breviore a *V. cirrhosa* C. V. distinguitur. (di Caporiacco 1935: 60).

[58] Personal communication in Schmidt (1987).

[59] Operculum aculeis 10 biseriatis; interoperculum aculeis 9. . .

Pinnæ dorsalis initium ad 42 dum mm. ab apice rostri; basis eius longitudo mm. 3,5; pinnæ analis initium paullo post initium pinnæ dorsalis, ad 44 tum mm. ab apice rostri; basis eius longitudo mm. 3,5. Pinnæ pectoralis longitudo mm. 5,75. Pinnæ ventralis initium ad 36 tum mm. ab apice rostri, longitudo eius mm. 5. Pinna caudalis vix emarginata. (di Caporiacco 1935: 60).

[60] Colore albo: parte superiore adsunt cromatophora, maculas obscuras parvas parum distinctas designantia, præsertim capite et parte superiore pedunculi caudalis visibiles; maculæ quoque adsunt apud anum et parte inferiore pedunculi caudalis. Pinna caudalis infuscata. (di Caporiacco 1935: 60).

[61] Schmidt (1987: 236).

[62] The holotype is the principal specimen on which a taxonomic description is based.

[63] I thank Robert E. Schmidt (letter, 18 October 2000) for pointing this out. Böhlke (1953: 45) writes: "*Lecto-holotype*: SU 16766; Rio Tietê, Salto, São Paulo, Brazil. No types were designated in the original description and no indication was given as to the deposition of the specimens. The above specimen which was obtained directly from the author of the species is here designated lectotype of the species." A lectotype is a specimen designated as the holotype if the person who described the species fails to designate one.

[64] According to Barthem and Goulding (1997: 94), the *dourados* are large predatory characins (e.g., *Salminus* spp.); *douradas* are predatory catfishes.

[65] Alves Guimarães (1935b) also refers to this genus of characins as *Bricon*.

[66] Altura do corpo 6 vezes no comprimento (sem caudal). Olhos 1/4 do tamanho da cabeça. Barbilhão partindo de uma prega da commissura do labio superior com 1/3 do comprimento da cabeça. Peitoraes pouco mais curtas que a cabeça, com 6 a 7 raios. Caudal truncata de terminação ligeiramente obliquada com os raios superiores um pouco mais longos . . . . Operculo e preoperculo com bordos recobertos por cerdas rijas. Escudo occipital com forma de cunha, de ponta anterior e com uma serie de espiculos de cada lado do, terço para a base. Focinho com extremidade terminada inferiormente em labio espesso. Bocca inferior.

Tamanho médio de 6 exemplares medidos:

Cabeça: 4 m/m comprimento
Occipital: 4 m/m altura (mx. do corpo)
Corpo: 24 m/m (sem caudal)
Olhos: 1,1 m/m
Peitoral: 3,³/₄ m/m com 6–7 raios
Dorsal: 20 m/m da base da cabeça
Ventral: 21 m/m da base da cabeça
(Alves Guimarães 1935b: 302).

[67] A especie por nós descripta é parasita de grandes *Characidae*. Não ataca peixes sãos e livres, mas apenas aquelles que ficam amarrados em viveiros. Por esta razão os nossos informantes julgam na especifica como parasita de *Salminus* sp. e *Brycon* sp., unicos peixes que em Salto costumam ser conservados presos.

Suspensos estes peixes por um cordel passando pela cavidade branchial são immergidos no rio e ahí ficam a espera de compradores eventuaes. Os candirús, nome vulgar da especie, nadam ao longo do lombo dos peixes captivos e vão collocar-se nas proximidades dos operculos. Quando estes se abrem em um movimento respiratorio, penetram os parasitos rapidamente na cavidade branchial indo se alojar sobre as guelras onde se fixam, sugando de tal forma que, quando abandonam a presa têm o seu corpo augmentado de 3 a 5 vezes na espessura, pelo volume de sangue ingerido. Vê-se então o intestino rectilineo e curto do animal corado em vermelho escuro, através da tenue parede abdominal muito distendida.

Atacam aos cardumes as suas victimas e produzem hemorrhagias fataes. Parasitam porém exclusivamente a região branchial, o que os differe biologicamente do peixe descripto por von Ihering, que parasita de preferencia a região anal e o intestino terminal do hospedador, segundo o referido autor.

Estes peixinhos foram observados em Salto pela primeira vez este anno e no fim de quinze a vinte dias tinham desapparecido tão subitamente como haviam surgido. (Alves Guimarães 1935b: 303–304).

[68] The single exception could be *P. machadoi*, described on the basis of one specimen. It apparently differs from species of *Vandellia* in certain morphological features, and placing it in a different genus might be justified (Jansen A. S. Zuanon, e-mail, 28 November 2000). Further evaluation is necessary.

[69] This specimen is probably MNRJ 978 in the collections of the Museu Nacional, Rio de Janeiro. The fish was caught in the Rio Solimões by Alte. Machado da Silva (date not recorded).

[70] This river also flows through Ecuador and Mato Grosso, Brazil. Allen wasn't specific about the country where he caught the fish. However, he caught specimens of *Plectrochilus erythrurus* in the Rio Morona, Peru.

[71] Eigenmann (1922).

[72] Eigenmann (1918a: 365).

[73] Je ne crois pas qu'il y ait de dents aux mâchoires, mais sur le chevron du vomer, qui avance . . . jusqu'au bord des intermaxillaires, il y a un petit groupe de cinq dents pointues et en crochets, dont la mitoyenne est la plus longue; puis viennent les deux latérales, un peu plus courtes, et enfin l'externe, qui est la plus petite. (Cuvier and Valenciennes 1846: 386–387).

[74] La machoire inférieure, fortement échancrée en son milieu, est complètement dépourvue de dents . . . (Pellegrin 1909b: 199).

[75] Eigenmann (1918b: 64).

[76] Eigenmann (1920: 441).

[77] Burgess (1989: 317).

[78] . . . mandíbula inferior sin dientes, o con algunos dientes excesivamente pequeños en el extremo de las ramas . . . (Devincenzi and Vaz-Ferreira 1939: 173).

[79] Perhaps de Miranda Ribeiro should have stuck to Portuguese. This is a strange and disjointed description with an even odder vocabulary. Some words aren't even Latin. For example, what in hell does *symphyse* mean? After translating the text I consulted three Latin scholars to no avail. Later, in desperation, I put my problem before a class of high school students. No one could fill in the blanks. De Miranda Ribeiro's original effort:

Plectrochilus gen. nov.

In faciem *Stegophilorum*. Capot parvum depresum, antice cuneatum, ore infra posita, ex hiatu transversa, symphyse [?] incurvata dentibusque autem corona vomerina irradiante uniseriatis *Vandellarum* modo; intermaxillaribus stylis tribus, erectibilibus, subtriangularibus, base crossaeformi [?] incurvatis, e mar-supio labiale ad barbulæ basin exeuntibus; barbula singula, masillare, naribus in fossula antiocuiare; oculis subcutaneis, supra versis; operculis preoperculisque dense aculeatis, opertura branchiali ampla, membrana branchiostega isthmum superante. Corpus compressum; pinnis dorsali analique subsequentibus, postice positis; pectoralibus ventralibusque liberis. Linea laterali adest.

Plectrochilus machadoi, sp. nov.

Capitis long. 7,5; maxima altitudine 6,3. Ore ut supra, barbula dimidium pre-operculum attingenti. Oculis parvis, ante mediam capitis longitudinem positis. Pinna pectoris capitis longitudinem subæquante, primo radio subproducio, cæteris truncatis; ventralibus dimidio longitudine a pectoraiium fimbria usque ad caudalis basin orientibus, parvis, anum attingentibus. Dorsali post ventralis ori-ente. Anait [Anail?] sub tertio dorsali radio, postice subtruncata, parce planum post dorsalem superante. Pedunculus gracilis. Cauda bifida, lobis subæquantibus, radiis accessoriis numerosis. Color est badia punctulis nigris adspersa dorso. Longit. maxima—65 millim. Ab incolis "*Candirú-Pequeno*" vocatur. (de Miranda Ribeiro 1917: 50–51).

[80] Eigenmann (1918a: 365–366, Plate LIII).

[81] Eigenmann (1918a, 1918c, 1920) called this location San Antonio de Rio Madeira. The specimen is probably FMNH 58086 listed by NEODAT as collected 3 November 1909 and archived at the Field Museum of Natural History, Chicago.

[82] The description of *V. sanguinea* is repeated in Eigenmann (1918c: 701–702).

[83] Eigenmann (1922). These specimens seem to be in the collections of the California Academy of Sciences, San Francisco. I found 14 listed in NEODAT collected by Allen in Peru in 1920: CAS 64602 (3), 64603 (1), 64599 (1), 64600 (6), 64601 (1), 64604 (2). Another (CAS 76964) was collected by N. E. Pearson (W. E. Pearson?) in 1921.

[84] Eigenmann (1918b).

[85] Eigenmann (1922: 114).

[86] Baskin (1973).

[87] Burgess (1989: 638, Plate 156, Fig. 1).

[88] Eigenmann (1922, Plate IV, Fig. 16). I show this as Fig. 21.

[89] Eigenmann (1922: 114).

[90] Eigenmann and Allen (1942: 162).

4. And Four Not So Singular

[1] Cortázar (1966: 34).

[2] What, for example, can *facho* mean within the context of a fish description? The term refers to flashlight, torch, or beam. And to what can we attribute "larval characteristics?" As noted by Robert E. Schmidt (e-mail, 9 November 2000), probably the fish's appearance: small, transparent, elongate. In modern Portuguese dictionaries of biology and medicine, *entalhado* means dentate, in which case de Miranda Ribeiro is describing a jaw that is dentate but doesn't contain teeth. Paulo Petry interprets *entalhado* to mean "carved," as in "carved mandible (dentary) and without teeth." That was my first interpretation too. "Carved" might refer to shape of the jaw. And de Miranda Ribeiro describes the dorsal as beginning "a little behind the distance between the base of the pectorals and the tip of the caudal." Where exactly would this be? The ventrals (pelvic fins) are located "anteriorly," presumably to some other structure, but we aren't told which one. Finally, we're informed that the anal fin is lower than the dorsal fin. I suppose this is always true, except perhaps in the case of upside-down catfishes. According to Schmidt (e-mail, 9 November 2000), ". . . 'lower' probably refers to the *height* of the fin, not its position on the body. Another way of saying this . . . might be, 'distance from anal fin base to tip of anal rays smaller than distance from dorsal fin base to tip of dorsal rays.'" He could be right. However, "are located" (a passive verb) is the last verb used by de Miranda Ribeiro in the previous sentence. Because no new verb is introduced, the same thought must continue, and the phrase says clearly, "under the anal . . ."

[3]   Paravandellia, *gen. nov.*

Entre *Stegophilus* e *Vandellia* deve ser considerado este genero cujos facies geral é o do primeiro grupo. Dorsal posterior ás ventraes e semi-anterior á anal; ambas posteriores ao meio do corpo. Cabeça triangular, narinas separadas, sem barbilhão, olhos sem margem livre; boca inferior, dentes n'uma serie nos maxillares e n'um facho nos intermaxillares; um barbilhão no angulo da bocca; preoperculo e operculo separados, providos de facho acicular.

Paravandellia oxyptera, *sp. nov.*

D. *12; Ps. 1 + 6; Vs. 6; A. 10* [D. 12, A. 10, P. 7]

Facies lavar; corpo anteriormente deprimido, posteriormente comprimido. Cabeça triangular, ou melhor cordiforme, 1/8 do comprimento total, incl. a caudal que lhe é egual em comprimento; olhos grandes (porque se vê todo o globo devido a transparencia dos tegumentos), aproximadamente 2 e 1/2 vezes na cabeça e á 1 diametro da ponta do focinho; bocca inferior, com o mandibular entalhado e desprovido de dentes, o barbilhão mal attiugindo á meia distancia do extremo do facho acicular preopercular. Peitoraes grandes, falcadas, 1/4 maiores que a cabeça, com o primeiro raio aculeiforme, rijo e o maior em extensão; d'ahi decrescem os outros bruscamente até o quarto para augmentarem de novo até o ultimo interno. Dorsal iniciando-se um pouco atraz da distancia entre a base das peitoraes e a ponta da caudal. As ventraes são muito pequenas e ficam-lhe anteriores; a anal sob os ultimos raios da dorsal e é da mesma forma que ella, porém mais baixa; caudal furcada, com o lobo superior um peuco maior. Branco uniforme, retina negra. Um exemplar medindo 0,m022. (de Miranda Ribeiro 1912: 28–29).

[4] Eigenmann (1918a: 366).

[5] Eigenmann (1918a: 367). This is a sloppy translation. Eigenmann omits any mention of the fish's shape, probably because he couldn't understand de Miranda Ribeiro's Portuguese either. Eigenmann's statement about the length of the maxillary barbel reaching at most to the tips of the interopercular spines (or preopercular spines of de Miranda Ribeiro) isn't what the original description says. Nor does it say that the origin of the dorsal is closer to the tip of the caudal than to the base of the pectorals.

[6] Encontrei este curioso peixe egualmente nos pseudo-rhyzomas do Agua-pé, em Caceres, margens do Rio Paraguay, em Outubro de 1908. (de Miranda Ribeiro 1912: 29). This specimen is probably MNRJ 790 in the Museu Nacional, Rio de Janeiro. No collection date is listed for NEODAT's entry.

[7] Eigenmann (1918a: 269).

[8] Eigenmann (1918a: 367).

[9] Shirley Keel, The Nature Conservancy (e-mail, 13 March 2000).

[10] de Miranda Ribeiro (1947: 2).

[11] Burgess (1989: 318).

[12] Winemiller and Yan (1989). Burgess' source might have been Paulo de Miranda Ribeiro's report (see endnote 14). Otto Schubart's fish was indeed collected from a characin (*Prochilodus* sp.), but no mention is made of an electric eel. Moreover, de Miranda Ribeiro provides an ichthyological description of Schubart's fish but never actually identifies it as a specimen of *P. oxyptera*.

[13] de Miranda Ribeiro (1947).

[14] O exemplar enviado pelo Dr. Otto Schubart No. 4684 da coleção ictiológica do Museu Nacional, oferece as seguintes características: — Comprimento total — 0,m023 e standart 0,m020; cabeça — até a abertura opercular — 0,m003; olhos relativamente grandes; espaço interorbital — 0,m001; maior altura — 0,m002; bôca inferior, mostrando duas barbelas em cada canto sendo que as internas são minimas; um agrupamento de dentes maiores que os demais, arrumados em três séries, tendo de cada lado uma série de dentes bem menores, na parte anterior do maxilar superior; dentes em forma de garra "claw-teeth" presentes; mandibula com dentes nas extremidades dos seus ramos. Não possui barbelas nasais, nem no mento. Membrana opercular estreitamente ligada ao istmo, sem contudo formar prega sôbre o mesmo. Acúleos operculares e preoperculares relativamente fortes e curvos — 12–13; distância do primeiro raio dorsal à ponta do focinho, 0,m014 e daquele mesmo ponto a base dos raios caudais medianos — 0,m007. O primeiro raio anal implanta-se correspondendo, mais ou menos ao meio da base da dorsal. Distância do primeiro raio ventral à ponta do focinho — 0,m014 e daquele mesmo ponto à base dos raios caudais medianos — 0,m065. Peitorais — 6, truncadas; anal — 7; dorsal, 8; caudal subtruncada com poucos raios acessórios evi-

dentes. O colorido é isabelino com leve pontilhado esparso, disposto em séries paralelas ao longo da linha mediana dorsal para os lados — como pode ser visto na estampa — pontilhado que se repete sôbre os raios das nadadeiras. (Material conservado em álcool). Segundo informe do Dr. Otto Schubart — êste exemplar foi coligido entre as escamas de um *Prochilodus* pescado no rio Mogi-Guaçu. (de Miranda Ribeiro 1947: 4–5).

[15] Não passa hoje de velha relíquia; exemplar de diminutas dimensões, está transformado em verdadeira múmia. (de Miranda Ribeiro 1947: 3).

[16] Eigenmann (1918a: 367).

[17] O exemplar, motivo da presente nota é, a nosso vêr, *Paravandellia oxyptera*.

Apesar de não termos podido constatar — dado o mau estado do exemplar, a presença dos dentes em "forma de garra" no tipo de *Paravandellia oxyptera*, — a verificação de dentes na mandíbula não deixa que tenhamos dúvidas em concordar com o Professor Eigenmann quanto à possibilidade de sinonímia de seu gênero com *Paravandellia*. (de Miranda Ribeiro 1947: 5).

[18] A caudal do tipo dêste último gênero, dita "furcada" (enquanto a de *Branchioica* é descrita como subtruncada) — pode assim ter sido julgada em virtude de, pelo ressecamento de seus raios, não ter permitido com a abertura dos mesmos, um perfeito julgamento do seu corte . . . (de Miranda Ribeiro 1947: 5).

[19] Baskin (1973: 81).

[20] Eigenmann (1918a: 367).

[21] de Miranda Ribeiro (1947).

[22] Baskin (1973).

[23] Eigenmann (1918a: 269).

[24] de Miranda Ribeiro (1922: 15).

[25] Eigenmann (1918a: 368–369, 1918b, 1918c: 702–703). Eigenmann (1918c) gives de W. Bertoni's residence as Asuncion [*sic*].

[26] Eigenmann (1918a: 269). This species is given as *Pyaractus brachypomus* by Devincenzi and Vaz-Ferreira (1939: 173). *Piaractus* is considered a co-subgenus with *Colossoma* (i.e., the *pacus*) by Géry (1977: 254–255).

[27] Eigenmann (1918c: 702–703).

[28] Egenmann (1918a, Plate XLIII). Later, de Miranda Ribeiro (1947, Plate II) incorrectly cites this as Plate XLVIII.

[29] In his key, Burgess (1989: 308) states that the genus *Branchioica* can be distinguished in the subfamily Vandelliinae by, among other characters, the "Large claw-like tooth at the end of each maxillary bone." Burgess took this statement directly from Myers (1944), thereby repeating his mistake. Baskin (1973: 82) had written, "Myers' (1944, [p. 598]) key . . . states that *Branchioica* is the only vandelliine with

'A large claw-like tooth at the end of each maxillary . . ', and that all other genera (other than *Paracanthopoma*) lack this tooth. The bone in question is the pre-maxilla, not the maxilla, and in all of the Vandelliinae examined here this bone bears claw-like teeth . . ." Whatever characters might serve to distinguish *Branchioica*, this isn't one of them.

[30] Eigenmann (1918a: 369).

[31] Burgess (1989: 639, Plate 157).

[32] A atividade alimentar de *B. bertonii* ocorria em fluxo de dezenas a centenas de indivíduos, que se deslocavam ao longo do corpo do hospedeiro, no sentido da cauda para a cabeça . . . Os seus movimentos eram anguiliformes, podendo o deslo-camento ser interrompido de quanto em vez, com paradas de 2 a 3 segundos. Nestas interrupções, o animal adotava posição oblíqua, com sua boca tocando o parecendo raspar a superfície do hospedeiro, ondulando a porção posterior do corpo. A con-centração de hematófagos era maior na região branquial do hospedeiro, onde numerosos indivíduos entravam na câmara branquial e outros saíam, quando os opérculos ficavam abduzidos durante os movimentos respiratórios do bagre. O período de permanência dos hematófagos na câmara branquial foi de 1 a 3 minutos no máximo, saindo os animais com o abdômen de cor avermelhada, grandemente dilatado . . . . Os indivíduos assim dilatados geralmente abandonavam o hospedeiro e nadavam em direção ao fundo (alguns destes indivíduos alimentados deslocavam-se sem direção definida pelo corpo da presa sem, entretanto, voltarem à câmara branquial). Numa ocasião, foi observada intensa atividade de *B. bertonii* próximo à abertura anal de um dos *Pseudoplatystoma fasciatum*, sem ter sido possível afirmar se penetraram na cavidade intestinal.

A sucessão de numerosos indivíduos de *B. bertonii*, pela câmara branquial de um mesmo hospedeiro, foi observada uma vez por um período de até 6 h seguidas, envolvendo milhares dos hematófagos. Quando o hospedeiro era reti-rado da água, os hematófagos abandonavam, com presteza, a câmara branquial. Contudo, em duas ocasiões, alguns espécimes foram retirados diretamente da câmara . . . estando o hospedeiro exposto ao ar. Morte de um *P. fasciatum* cativo foi observada uma vez, cerca de 1 h após o início da atividade de *B. bertonii*. Após a morte deste exemplar, a atividade dos hematófagos cessou. As brânquias dos peixes atacados por *B. bertonii* apresentaram diversos pontos sangrando, princi-palmente na região proximal e mediana dos filamentos do primeiro arco bran-quial. (Machado and Sazima 1983: 345–346).

[33] Weitzman and Vari (1988: 448, Table 1).

[34] Eigenmann (1918a: 367).

[35]   *Branchioica phaneronema*, nueva especie.

Altura, 6 a 7, cabeza 5.33–6.0, ojo 4 en la cabeza, 1 a 1.5 en la distancia interor-bitaria. Un grupo ovalado de espinas en el opérculo, dirigidas hacia arriba, y otro en el interopérculo en sentido posteroinferior. Dos series de dientes largos delgados en el premaxilar, con una serie irregular de dientes más cortos a lado y lado. Un pequeño grupo de dientes en la terminación interior de cada elemento mandibular, ocultos en la carne del labio inferior, sus puntas curvas en ángulo recto.

Distancia entre el origen de la aleta dorsal y la de la cola es algo menor que la distancia predorsal. Distancia entre anal y caudal, 6 en la talla esqueletal. El origen de las ventrales, es más cerca a la punta de la caudal que al origen de las pectorales. El anal nace bajo los últimos radios dorsales, y el primer radio dorsal está encima de un punto adelante de las ventrales. Caudal emarginada, su lóbulo superior el mayor. Pedúnculo caudal con pocos radios accesorios. Aletas pectorales 1,6, el primer radio curvo, más grueso y largo que los restantes, su longitud, medida desde la terminación de las espinas operculares, más larga que la cabeza. Proceso humeral prominente.

Se diferencia del genotipo *Br. bertonii* en que la barbilla maxilar superior es más corta, y termina al nivel del centro del ojo, mientras que la inferior es más grande y visible —de ahí el nombre específico, del griego, *phaneros*, visible, y *nema* hilo. También difiere en la forma de la boca y en los dientes mandibulares curvos. Se distingue de *Br. magdalenae* Miles en el color, en las aletas pectorales, en el tamaño de las barbillas, en el proceso humeral más prominente y en los radios accesorios menos destacados.

Color en la vida translúcido, la parte inferior roja, una banda lateral oscura que naciendo tras el opérculo se hace sucesivamente más oscura y se extiende sobre los radios centrales de la aleta caudal. El labio superior y las barbillas pigmentados.

Typus. Un ejemplar que mide 27 mm. Escuela Superior de Agricultura Tropical, Cali. Colectores, Miles y Olaya.

Paratypus. Tres ejemplares de 24 mm., 25 mm. y 26 mm. distribuidos así: Museo de Zoología Comparada, Cambridge, Mass., EE. UU., Museo Nacional, Washington, EE. UU., e Instituto de Ciencias Naturales, Bogotá, Colombia. (Miles 1943a: 32–33).

[36] Miles (1943b: 367).

[37] see Eigenmann (1918a: 368–369).

[38] Román-Valencia (1998).

[39] Román-Valencia (1998: 301, Table 1).

[40] Miles (1943b).

[41] Miles (1943b: 369).

[42] *Branchioica magdalenæ*, especie nueva. El Branchioica del Magdalena es muy parecido a la forma del Alto Cauca, pero cada uno de los muchos ejemplares estudiados son más pequeños que los del Valle, carecen de pigmentación, con excepción de una banda lateral poco definida, y que no se extiende sobre los radios de la aleta caudal. El primer radio de la aleta pectoral no es notablemente más fuerte que los demás y es más corto que la longitud cefálica. La barbilla superior se extiende al borde posterior del ojo, mientras que la inferior es insignificante; en este detalle se asemeja al genotipo, pero los dientes maxilares son similares a los

de *Br. phaneronema*. Todos los ejemplares de *Br. magdalenæ* fueron encontrados en las agallas del Bagre Tigre, *Pseudoplatystoma fasciatum*, mientras que los de *Br. phaneronema* fueron descubiertos enterrados en el lodo del fondo. *Typus*, 1 ejemplar de talla esqueletal 22 mm., colectado en Honda por Luis Olaya, que reposa en el Instituto de Ciencias Naturales, en Bogotá, Colombia. También fueron despachados paratipos a la M. C. Z. en Harvard y al Museo Nacional en Washington. (Miles 1943a: 33, footnote).

[43] Weitzman and Vari (1988: 448, Table 1).

[44] Dahl (1971: 72).

[45] Róman-Vanencia (1993).

[46] This fish, a piranha (family Characidae: subfamily Serrasalminae), has been renamed *Pygocentrus nattereri* (see Fink 1993). In NEODAT's entry the prey species is listed as *Salminus maxillosus*.

[47] . . . ilustrado amateur en Ciencias Naturales y colaborador honorario del Museo de Historia Natural —a la vez que gran aficionado a la pesca —trajo al Museo un lote de peces que le parecían de interés, llamando especialmente la atención sobre un pequeño ejemplar que había encontrado adherido a las branquias de una "palometa de río" (*Rooseveltiella nattereri Kner*). (Devincenzi and Vaz-Ferreira 1939: 165).

[48] Al pretender desprenderlo, encontró una gran resistencia, viéndose obligado a emplear el lomo de un cuchillo para conseguirlo; observando entonces que el pequeño pez tenía el estómago lleno de sangre y que las agallas de la palometa seguían sangrando. (Devincenzi and Vaz-Ferreira 1939: 165).

[49] Allí nos fué dado averiguar que este pez, conocido con el nombre vulgar de "sanguijuela", es considerado por los pescadores como una verdadera plaga, ya que, según ellos, en ciertas épocas del año, "desangran" al pescado, dejándolo "descolorido" e inapto para el consumo. (Devincenzi and Vaz-Ferreira 1939: 166).

[50] Las informaciones que se nos suministran sobre los hábitos fueron en todo contradictorias, pues mientras unos aseguran que vive fijo sobre su huésped en forma permanente, según otros la fijación es accidental, abandonando al huésped una vez satisfechas sus necesidades; no obstante, todos los ejemplares obtenidos —oche hasta ahora —fueron extraídos de las branquias de dos especies distintas, inclinándonos el hecho de que no se hayan desprendido del huésped al ser éste sacado fuera de agua a la primera hipótesis. (Devincenzi and Vaz-Ferreira 1939: 166).

[51] Longitud total, mm. 19.9; longitud sin caudal, 17.7; cabeza, 6.7 en long. sin caudal; ojo, 3.8 en cabeza; hocico, 3.3.

Hocico a origen de la dorsal, mm. 12.05; hocico a origen de la anal, mm. 12.85. D. 8. A. 7. (Devincenzi and Vaz Ferreira 1939: 174).

[52] Burgess (1989: 317).

[53] El "sanguijuela" se alimenta exclusivamente de sangre de otros peces, que obtiene introduciéndose en las cavidades branquiales y provocándoles laceraciones de las laminillas; después de saciarse, su tubo digestivo, casi recto, aparece dilatado, globuloso y rojo, similar al de una verdadera "sanguijuela". (Vaz-Ferreira 1969: 42).

[54] Devincenzi and Teague (1942: 33).

[55] This is MZUSP 3431 in the collections of the Museu de Zoologia, Universidade de São Paulo.

[56] A specimen in the collections of the California Academy of Sciences (CAS 76896).

[57] Baskin (1973), Schmidt (1993).

[58] Schmidt (1993) is referring to couplet *f* in the key to subfamilies and genera of the Trichomycteridae (=Pygidiidae) in Eigenmann (1918a: 278).

[59] Burgess (1989: 308).

[60] Devincenzi and Vaz Ferreira (1939: 173–174) start with couplet *hh* of Eigenmann's key (Eigenmann 1918a: 279):

Clave de los Géneros de la Subfam. Vandelliinae

Boca más estrecha; ramas mandibulares débiles, no reunidas en la línea media; dientes escasos, débiles, puntiagudos (*Vandelliinae*).

m.—Algunos dientes depresibles en una serie simple en el medio de la mandíbula superior; mandíbula inferior sin dientes, o con algunos dientes excesivamente pequeños en el extremo de las ramas; caucal redondeada o emarginada.
                                                                    Vandellia Cuv. & Val.
mm.—Una banda de dientes depresibles en el medio de la mandíbula superior; una serie simple de dientes mucho más pequeños a los lados de la banda mediana; sin dientes en la mandíbula inferior, caudal ahorquillada, con el lóbulo superior más largo.   *Paravandellia* Mir. Rib.
mmm.—Dos series de dientes depresibles en el medio de la mandíbula superior; una serie simple de dientes mucho menores al lado de la serie mediana y un diente en garra (*claw-like tooth*) en el extremo de la serie mediana; dos cortas series de dientes en el extremo de las ramas mandibulares; caudal subtruncada.
                                                                    Branchioca Eigenmann.
mmmm.—Varias series de dientes, numerosos en la serie frontal, en el medio de la mandíbula superior; serie simple de dientes laterales, sin diente en garra intermedio; una pequeña serie de dientes en cada extremo de las ramas mandibulares; caudal emarginada.   *Parabranchioica* Devincenzi

[61] These situations no doubt frustrate taxonomists, but pigeon holes will always outnumber pigeons. Individuals possess ontological autonomy except for their membership in the class of individuals (Ghiselin 1997). This paradox, pointed out

by the nineteenth-century set theorist Georg Cantor, is recognized in a slightly different form as Russell's paradox after Bertrand Russell, the English mathematician and philosopher. As Smart (1963: 4) puts it, "The class of all classes not members of themselves is a member of itself."

[62] Alves Guimarães (1935b) did not state how many specimens were used in his description of *Vandellia hematophaga*, but implied more than one. If *V. hematophaga* is excluded from the list of species, the number of known specimens of all the other species used in the original descriptions totals 30.

5. Good Smells, Good Vibrations

[1] Calvino, I. (1988: 67).

[2] Calvino (1988: 71).

[3] In terms of aphrodisiacs, the most effective perfume of all might be our own pheromones. These are volatile hormonelike substances excreted into the air, ordinarily serving as sexual attractants. Androstenol in human underarm sweat is a sexual attractant to both swine and humans, and college coeds are demonstrably attracted to male students wearing necklaces impregnated with androstenol (Cowley and Brooksbank 1991).

[4] The yellow bullhead (*Ictalurus natalis*), a siluriform catfish, is indigenous to North America. Specimens 25 centimeters (10 inches) long have more than 175,000 taste buds (Caprio 1988). Whether trichomycterid catfishes (including candirus) are equipped similarly is unknown.

[5] The channel catfish is also a freshwater siluriform from North America. Other organic compounds that fishes can taste in tiny amounts include small peptides, nucleotides, quaternary ammonium compounds, and organic acids. Compounds they can smell include amino acids, bile acids, gonadal steroids and derivatives, and prostaglandins. See the review of Sorensen and Caprio (1998).

[6] Weissburg and Zimmer-Faust (1993) studied the interaction between the hard clam (*Mercenaria mercenaria*) and the blue crab (*Callinectes sapidus*), one of its principal predators. The clams lie buried in the sand with only their siphons exposed. One siphon (the incurrent) pumps water in; the other (the excurrent) pumps water out. Crabs foraging along the substratum downcurrent can detect odorants in a clam's excurrent siphon, in part because the odorant plume spills onto the substratum and attaches to the sediment. A crab's respiratory current draws water upward from this same sublayer. Having detected the plume, the crab simply follows it upcurrent to its source. In this way a hidden clam divulges its location.

[7] For example, see Weissburg et al. (1998).

[8] Weissburg and Zimmer-Faust (1993).

9 Weissburg and Zimmer-Faust (1993).

10 Hawkins (1993), Schellart and Wubbels (1998).

11 Rogers and Cox (1988), Schellart and Wubbels (1998).

12 Hawkins (1993).

13 Schellart (1992).

14 All swimming animals generate mainly dipole fields (Kalmijn 1988a).

15 Hawkins (1993).

16 Kalmijn (1989).

17 Hanke et al. (2000).

18 Müller et al. (1997).

19 Kalmijn (1989).

20 Kalmijn (1988b).

21 Hawkins (1993), Schellart and Wubbels (1998).

22 Hawkins (1993). This phenomenon was first reported by von Frisch (1938).

23 At the mechanistic level, activating appropriate sections of the inner ear involves acceleration, not displacement (Rogers and Cox 1988).

24 Although true, this statement is misleading. More accurately, the lateral line detects variation in fluid accelerations, and explanations in this context involve more physics than needed in a book about catfishes. As Kalmijn (1989) noted, thinking of the lateral line solely in terms of displacement obscures its function as a detector of velocity and acceleration. Plotting sound frequency (i.e., "physiological tuning curves") against displacement gives artificially higher frequencies than those to which fishes appear most sensitive. Plotting frequency against acceleration yields lower curves within the range at which most fishes *behave* as if they hear. For a review of how fishes and other animals receive hydrodynamic stimuli, see Bleckmann (1994).

Dijkgraaf (1963) used the neologism *Ferntastsinn,* or "distant touch," to describe this phenomenon. His interpretation is unfortunate. Dijkgraaf's "distant touch" metaphor has the same undefined, fuzzy quality as the telephone company's advertisement to "reach out and touch someone." In neither case is anything actually being touched. Those who would justify retention of this term by arguing that a fish's sensory perception might differ profoundly from ours miss the point. "Touch" has a specific connotation quite different from the idiomatic "get in touch," used when placing a phone call. Consider the telephone analogy. In a fish, hearing is augmented by the swimbladder, which serves as a transducer specifically, "a pressure-to-motion converter" in the words of Kalmijn (1989: 211). Similarly, a telephone receiver, which is actuated by electric power, supplies acoustic power to the surrounding air. If a fish's lateral line is an organ of "touch," then so is the human ear.

[25] Enger et al. (1989), Kalmijn (1988a, 1989). According to Kalmijn (1988a, 1989), this is because the acceleration about a local dipole falls off steeply with the third power of the distance. The differences in acceleration along the lateral line disintegrate even faster, with approximately the fourth power of the distance from the source.

[26] Kalmijn (1988a).

[27] Kalmijn (1989: 207).

[28] Enger et al. (1989).

[29] Kalmijn (1988a, 1989).

[30] Kalmijn (1989: 212–213) writes: "After all, the acoustic wave equation not only governs the propagating sound wave but also demands the local-flow field for its solution. When the local flow, as an essential part of the acoustic field, is detected by the inner ear, it is certainly proper to speak of hearing. When the local flow, in its guise of an incompressible flow, is detected by the lateral line, it is equally proper to speak of hydrodynamic detection."

Kalmijn (1988a: 106) states: "Moreover, I see no reason to exclude the near field from the definition of 'sound,' neither do I feel inclined to apply the term 'hearing' to the function of the lateral line."

[31] Also see Schuijf and Buwalda (1980) for a discussion of underwater sound localization by fishes.

[32] Kalmijn (1988a, 1989).

[33] See reviews of Bullock (1982), Heiligenberg (1993), Kalmijn (1974, 1988b, 1989), and von der Emde (1998).

[34] Peters and Buwalda (1972), Peters et al. (1974), von der Emde (1998).

[35] Peters and Bretschneider (1972), Kalmijn (1972), Peters et al. (1974), Roth (1972).

[36] Roth (1972).

[37] Kalmijn (1988b, 1989). The DC electric field of an injured animal is said to exceed 1 millivolt per centimeter (Hawkins 1993). If so, this response exceeds by more than 3,000 times the sensitivity threshold of 0.3 microvolts per centimeter stated by Knudsen (1974).

[38] Bullock (1982).

[39] The actual conduits of the transmitted signal are afferents entering the brain by means of the anterior lateral line nerve (Bullock 1982).

[40] Asano and Hanyu (1986), Kalmijn (1988b), Peters and Meek (1973), Roth (1972).

[41] Kalmijn (1988b).

[42] Because of the canal, the voltage gradient is actually defined as the space between the receptor pore (external environment) and the cellular location (internal environment) where the signal is received (von der Emde 1998).

[43] Human hair follicles can be stimulated by alternating current (AC) electric fields (Kato et al. 1989). Men ordinarily are more hairy than women and therefore have lower thresholds of sensation. Not surprisingly, sensitivity is greatest in humid weather.

[44] About 1 milliampere.

[45] Brown et al. (1984), Heiligenberg (1993), Kalmijn (1988b).

[46] The ionic strength of water exerts control over bioelectric fields. Because freshwater has greater resistivity, a freshwater catfish usually has stronger voltage but weaker current fields than a catfish living in seawater and carries a lesser electric "load" (Kalmijn 1988b). Waters of exceptionally low ionic concentrations, such as South American lowland rivers and streams, are especially resistive. As a result of their greater resistivity, freshwater fishes "load" uniform electric fields, which causes diminished electric potentials at the skin (Kalmijn 1974). The consequence is that freshwater fishes are less efficient than seawater fishes from the standpoint of voltage sensitivity (Kalmijn 1974).

[47] Bretschneider et al. (1991), Butsuk and Bessonov (1981), Zhadan and Zhadan (1976).

[48] A. J. Kalmijn, unpublished, in Bullock (1982); Peters and Bretschneider (1972).

[49] The electric fields of siluriforms are thought to be involved in communication (Peters and Bretschneider 1972).

[50] Tricas et al. (1995). Orientation by males ordinarily occurs at distances of less than 1 meter.

[51] Kalmijn (1972, 1974), Peters and Bretschneider (1972).

[52] Haseman (1911b: 315).

[53] Asano and Hanyu (1986) studied electroreception in the *namazu* (*Parasilurus asotus*), a Japanese siluriform. They suggest that the *namazu* might track its prey from a distance using olfaction and gustation. When within the range of the prey's electric field, the *namazu* might determine its exact location using electroreception. The same situation might also apply to how candirus find their prey, but this is speculation.

[54] The muskellunge (*Esox masquinongy*) is a North American freshwater fish related to the pikes and pickerels. "Muskies" are ambush predators. A muskie uses vision to identify and stalk a smaller prey fish, which it then captures with an explosive burst of speed. This last part of the capture sequence probably involves the lateral line more than vision (New et al. 2001).

[55] Fernald (1990).

[56] Nilson and Modlin (1994: 226–227) explain it this way: "Diffraction, which is inversely proportional to the diameter of the imaging lens, allows more fine detail to be reproduced behind a larger lens. Light capture, which determines photon shot noise, is also improved by a larger lens." See references in their report.

[57] Fernald (1988).

[58] Lythgoe (1988).

[59] Lythgoe (1988).

[60] Lythgoe (1988).

[61] Leenheer (1980).

[62] The use of a shark's image in this example is not anomalous. Sharks are commonly found far up the Amazon, Orinoco, and other large South American rivers that drain into the Atlantic Ocean (e.g., Smith 1981).

[63] Protasov (1968).

[64] Lythgoe (1988).

[65] Loew and McFarland (1990: 5–6) write: "It must be remembered that neither the presence of multiple visual pigments nor the ability to generate electrophysiological or behavioural spectral-sensitivity curves proves that an animal has colour vision in the human meaning of the term."

[66] Leenheer (1980).

[67] Einige der von mir gefangenen Vandellia-Welse konnte ich bis zu drei Tagen in kleinen Aquarien mit Schlammboden halten. Die Tierchen gruben sich dort oberflächig ein, und zwar so, daß die durch intensive Guaninflimmer stark glänzenden, rückenseitigen Partien der Augenkugel deutlich auf der Schlammoberfläche zu sehen waren. Wenn die Fische schnell umherschwammen, blitzten ihre Augenbulbi auf. Sie werden wahrscheinlich in der Lage sein, selbst im trüben Wasser diese für sie charakteristischen "Leuchtspuren" zu orten und so — besonders zur Laichzeit — Kontakt miteinander halten können. (Lüling 1969: 576).

[68] Muntz (1982).

6. A Bloodsucking Life

[1] Stoker (1897: 205).

[2] Stoker (1897: 20).

[3] Campbell (1991), Mommsen and Walsh (1992), Randall et al. (1981), Walsh (1998).

[4] Ammonia is excreted primarily by the gills, but little of it is produced there. Most is generated in the liver, although the kidney and lateral body musculature also

contribute (Wood 1993). For a review of the functional morphology of fish gills, see Hughes (1980); for a review of the fish kidney, see Hickman and Trump (1969).

[5] Eckert and Randall (1983).

[6] Forman (1972), Huxley (1865).

[7] Mitchell and Tignor (1970).

[8] Wimsatt and Guerriere (1962).

[9] Randall et al. (1981).

[10] McFarland and Wimsatt (1969).

[11] McFarland and Wimsatt (1969).

[12] McFarland and Wimsatt (1969)

[13] The process of urea formation must indeed be rapid for the osmolarity of the plasma not to decline initially from the heavy load of water. McFarland and Wimsatt (1969: 993) saw just an increase: "The source of the increased blood urea is unknown, but most likely it represents an enhanced synthesis of urea in response to the nitrogenous load that results from feeding. Body fluid osmotic concentration, therefore, at least as indicated by plasma values, is somewhat labile in vampire bats showing an increase of about 8–9 per cent with feeding." Osmole is defined in endnote 29.

[14] At peak flow, urination is 4.0 milliliters per kilogram of body mass per minute, the highest rate observed in any mammal (McFarland and Wimsatt 1969).

[15] McFarland and Wimsatt (1969: 1004).

[16] Reading about vampire bats started me thinking about the "living dead" embodied by Dracula and Lestat. Dressing in black and wearing a black cape is very batish, and vampires do lots of skulking about in cemeteries and dark alleys and outside the open bedroom windows of innocent young women who have flowing hair and sleep in white negligées. The wings of vampire bats give them a similar rakish look that never goes out of style. Like vampires, vampire bats come out only at night when they frequent pastures and enter unprotected human habitations, being less particular about the sex or appearance of their victims.

Some vampires, as we know from the movies, are solitary, but others are social. Anne Rice's novels depict in exhaustive detail their petty bickering, backbiting (mostly figurative), jockeying for political dominance, and other revolting behavior obviously learned when they were human and serving on faculty committees. No one knows much about the diurnal habits of vampires, but some evidently nap in moldy coffins or in shabby Victorian rooms with the shades drawn. Vampire bats are social too. During the day they hang upside-down together in caves, abandoned buildings, and hollow trees.

Long before current fads, vampires in the Middle Ages had embraced the high-protein, low-carbohydrate diet, no doubt complaining bitterly about its side effects. Vampires don't drink daintily from their victims. They guzzle, preferring larger vessels like the jugular veins. An adult human contains about 5.5 liters of blood. If a vampire sucks its victim dry, which is usually the case, this is equivalent to chugging 15.5 bottles of beer without pause (12 US fluid ounces = 355 milliliters). The sudden fluid load is considerable. What does it weigh? The weight of blood is affected mainly by its hematocrit concentration, which is variable. (To estimate of the weight of your blood, multiply your body weight by the constant 0.08.) After sucking all the blood from a 67-kilogram (150-pound) person, a vampire will have increased its weight by 5.34 kilograms (12 pounds). Having been acquired suddenly, all this extra weight will be concentrated in the stomach and intestine. Instant potbelly. What became of the svelte figure?

Without quickly ridding itself of the immense nitrogen load, renal failure and brain poisoning would be imminent. I therefore believe vampires must have a digestive system similar to a vampire bat's. If so, copious urination commences even as a vampire feeds on its victim. Unlike its early predecessors, the modern vampire can wear diapers (perhaps stealing them by the case after attacking the night pharmacist). The fully distended adult bladder holds perhaps 750 milliliters, or about 770 grams of urine assuming a density similar to that of full-strength seawater. Based on one manufacturer's specifications, I calculate that a diaper for incontinent adults might hold 1270 grams of urine. These products are clearly heavy-duty. Assuming a vampire ingests no water or nutrients other than blood, and that its stomach, intestines, and kidneys function similarly to those of vampire bats, we can make the following projections, with the caveat that we know nothing about vampire digestive efficiency or defecation patterns.

Having ingested 5.5 liters of blood, the amount of fluid discharged as urine (roughly 40 percent of the total volume in vampire bats) will be almost 2.25 liters weighing 2.3 kilograms, or about 5 pounds. If the average diaper holds 1270 grams, a vampire needs to wear three of them to be socially secure. We're told vampires cut striking figures, but I doubt it. As for their lightning speed, imagine sprinting down a dark alley while 5 pounds of soggy diapers slap coldly against your loins. They say vampires have lots of fun, but I'm not so sure. What fun can it be to start pissing your pants every time you sit down to dinner?

[17] See the reviews of Mommsen and Walsh (1992), Spotte (1992), Walsh (1998), Wilkie (1997), and Wood (1993).

[18] Wood (1993).

[19] See references in Wright (1993).

[20] Mangum et al. (1978), Wilson and Snellgrove (1999, not peer reviewed).

[21] One interesting example is the tilapia Oreochromis alcalicus, which lives in Lake Magadi in the southern Rift Valley of Kenya. According to Wood et al. (1994: 14), "Most of the lake's surface is covered with a solid crust of crystalline 'trona' which is up to five meters in depth. . . . The trona is composed largely of Na_2CO_3 and $NaHCO_3$; these salts enter the lake in an alkaline liquor flowing from volcanic hot

springs around the margin of the lake and form a floating precipitate as the water evaporates and cools." Here the pH is 10 and the temperature often reaches 42°C. Also see Randall et al. (1989).

[22] Evans (1993), Schmidt-Nielsen (1975), Spotte (1992).

[23] For comments on the vampire bat, see Greenhall et al. (1969) and Wimsatt (1969).

[24] Dalquest (1955).

[25] In a captive colony of six vampire bats, the weight of dry feces per bat ranged from 0.1–3.8 grams (McFarland and Wimsatt 1969).

[26] Rouk and Glass (1970: 470) state: "The tunica propria appears to be an almost continuous vascular channel resulting in each acinus being bathed on all sides by blood." Oddly, the walls of the stomach apparently lack elastic tissue.

[27] Morton (1986), who then adds on p. 89A: "The intercellular spaces in the mucosal epithelium, lamina propria, submucosa and blood vessels were distended with absorbed fluid." He goes on to describe other features of the fundic cecum. McFarland and Wimsatt (1969: 998) mention the result of rapid absorption of fluid from the stomach, noting that the simultaneous increase in a bat's body weight must reflect an increase in extracellular space: "Since all of the red-blood cells remain in the stomach of the bat for a time, this increase in extracellular space may approximate 20–25 per cent of the bats' body volume (assume Ht [hematocrit] of blood of prey of 50%)."

[28] McFarland and Wimsatt (1969).

[29] An osmole is the amount of solute that when dissolved and brought to 1 liter has the same osmotic pressure as 1 mole of a nonelectrolyte. An osmole is determined by the number of particles in solution. Physiologists use it because osmosis (the movement of water across a membrane) is affected by the concentration of particles in solution. 1 milliosmole = 0.001 osmole. See Evans (1993: 316, Table 1) and Schmidt-Nielsen (1975: 385, Table 9.5).

[30] Evans (1993: 316, Table 1). Seawater is about 1050 milliosmoles per liter.

[31] . . . des Zusammenlebens ungleichnamiger Organismen. (de Bary 1879: 5). De Bary had used the term symbiosis as early as 1873 in attempting to describe the association between the algal and fungal components of lichens.

[32] Saffo (1992: 18).

[33] An example of mutualism is the association between the hermit crab *Eupagurus prideauxi* and the sea anemone *Adamsia palliata*. These species, which live in British waters, are never found apart. With time, the anemone expands to completely cover the borrowed mollusk shell and extend some distance beyond, eliminating the crab's need to find larger shells as it grows. The crab, which is immune to the anemone's toxins, presumably gains protection from predators, and the two

share food discovered by the crab during its travels. Without the crab to carry it around, the anemone's range would be severely restricted. See Gotto (1969) for other examples.

[34] van Beneden (1876). An example of commensalism is the polychaete worm *Nereis fucata* that lives in association with various hermit crabs (notably *Eupagurus bernhardus* in the Irish Sea). As the crab feeds, the worm glides forward and steals food from the crab's mandibles, then hastily retreats into the shell. See Gotto (1969) for other examples.

[35] Croll (1966: 8, footnote).

[36] Whitfield (1979: 8).

[37] For example, see Riffkin et al. (1996).

[38] Askonas (1984: 633). To appreciate just how complex host-parasite interactions can be, see Wyler (1990).

[39] Medawar (1953). The fetal-placental unit ordinarily survives despite the maternal immune system's potential recognition of the father's complement and antigens (Herrera-Gonzales and Dresser 1993).

[40] Croll (1966).

[41] Crofton (1971: 192).

[42] In statistical terms, overdispersion (i.e., a clumped pattern) refers to counts of something, such as fleas on dogs, in which the variance is greater than the mean. The other possibilities are a random pattern (variance equal to the mean) or a uniform pattern (variance less than the mean). In any group of dogs some have more fleas than others, and the variance derived from flea counts per dog is likely to exceed the mean. Clumping is the expected pattern in nature; randomness and uniformity are rare (Ludwig and Reynolds 1988). In my opinion, Crofton's criterion of clumping is therefore superfluous.

[43] Uma das características mais notáveis, observada no comportamento alimentar de *B. bertonii*, é o grande número de indivíduos reunidos num mesmo peixe hospedeiro, podendo suceder-se e assim atingir a milhares de indivíduos. Este número provavelmente está relacionado ao fato do hospedeiro estar cativo, não podendo se deslocar e assim evitar o fluxo de hematófagos. Não acreditamos que um indivíduo sadio, de espécie ativa como *P. fasciatum*, seja atacado com tal intensidade em circunstâncias habituais. É provável que *B. bertonii*, outros Vandelliinae e mesmo Stegophilinae, percebam as ocasiões em que um hospedeiro potencial esteja ferido, cativo ou em outra condição desvantajosa. . . . Em circunstâncias habituais, o número de hematófagos explorando uma mesma presa deve ser consideravelmente menor, embora isto seja difícil de observar devido aos hábitos dos peixes usados como hospedeiros. (Machado and Sazima 1983: 347–348).

[44] Whitfield (1979) discusses the snail kite (*Rostrhamus sociabilis*) as an exception.

Unlike other hawks the snail kite has evolved a slender, downcurving beak specialized to cut the columnella muscle connecting the body of its prey (snails of the genus *Pomacea*) to its shell. The kite lives exclusively on these snails.

[45] Some biologists extend this definition even to parasitoid relationships in which one organism deposits its egg or larva on the prey. At a later time the prey serves as a living source of food. Whitfield (1979: 13) writes: "In most examples this utilization ultimately kills the host. This fatal end-result means that in reality the association is a temporally elongate predator-prey relationship. The long period of association and the controlled feeding, however, show some similarity to host-parasite relationships."

[46] Saul (1975).

[47] Croll (1966: 11) writes: "Some authors choose to define blood-sucking ectoparasites as 'micropredators'; this merely illustrates the great confusion about exact definitions."

[48] The dexterity with which *Plasmodium* spp. avoid the human immune response is legendary. By going through four stages in its life cycle, the malaria parasite gives the immune system only a shifting look before changing form. Its sporozoites don't stay in the bloodstream long enough for antibodies to find them, and its merozoites are in the liver too briefly for killer T cells to mobilize and attack. Even spending part of the life cycle in a mosquito seems to be an evolutionary means of shortening contact with the human immune system. See Taube (2000).

[49] Fernandez et al. (1998).

[50] See the discussion in Trager (1986).

[51] Die ganze Gruppe dieser winzigen, schwachpigmentierten Kleinwelse ist in ihrem Bestreben, in Bauch- und Kiemenhöhlen von anderen großen Fischen einzudringen, und in ihrem Verhalten der Urinophilie stammesgeschichtlich sehr auffallend: Sie sind "Gelegenheits- und Halbparasiten", soweit sie aber wirklich Bauchwände, kiemenfäden und die Wandungen der Harn- und Geschlechtsorgane von Säugern und Menschen aktiv verletzen und Blut aufnehmen, echte parasitische Wirbeltiere. (Lüling 1969: 575–576).

[52] Les Vandellies représentent donc, chez les Siluridés, le dernier terme de la spécialisation en vue d'un parasitisme de plus caractérisés. (Pellegrin 1909b: 204).

[53] Lagler et al. (1977: 420).

[54] Nelson (1994: 168–169).

[55] Grzimek (1973: 381).

[56] Günther (1880: 581).

[57] Les Vandellies, ainsi que l'indiquent le développement des épines operculaires et interoperculaires, la spécialisation de l'appareil buccal du *Vandellia Wieneri*, ne

sont pas de simples commensaux, mais des parasites, vivant certainement aux dépens de leur hôte. (Pellegrin 1909b: 202)

[58] Pellegrin (1909b).

[59] Eigenmann (1918a: 265–266).

[60] Eigenmann (1918a: 267–269).

[61] Il y a lieu en terminant de noter que les dents volumineuses peu nombreuses, en forme de crochets acérés de la mâchoire supérieur, sont particulières au genre *Vandellia*, qu'elles sont absentes dans les genres voisins *Stegophilus* Reinhardt et *Acanthopoma* Lütken, où elles sont remplacées par une bande de très nombreuses petites dents acérées. (Pellegrin 1909b: 204).

[62] Curtis (1949: 255).

[63] Burgess (1989: 305).

[64] Halstead (1992: 224).

[65] Warthin (1930; foreword in Gudger 1930c: xi-xii).

7. Embracing Urine

[1] Joyce (1916: 7).

[2] Darnton (1984: 23).

[3] Spotte et al. (2001). Such efforts aren't entirely worthless. A scientist's objective in designing an experiment is to test the null hypothesis, not to "prove" that the alternative hypothesis is correct. Acceptance of the null is merely one of the possible conclusions. For a discussion of negative results, see Browman (1999).

[4] Ich wundere mich ein wenig, daß die beiden Fischer bei dieser Hitze mit, wie mir scheint, recht dicken und enganliegenden Badehosen ins Wasser steigen, und ich wende mich an meine Begleiter. Man versucht, mir das zu erklären, doch ich verstehe sie kaum in ihrem breiten, fast singenden Zungenschlag und höre nur das Wort "canero" mehrfach heraus. Da kann ich mir den Zusammenhang denken, denn ich weiß, daß hier im lehmigen Schlamm hochinteressante, winzige Fischchen leben, die so heißen. Es sind das die zu den Schmerlenwelsen gehörigen *Plectrochilus*- und *Vandellia*-Arten. Sie sind nur wenige Zentimeter lang, bandförmig schmal, ganz weißlich, da sie bis auf einige Pigmentstreifen fast farblos sind. Am Kiemendeckel haben diese Kerlchen ein winziges Feld spitzer Dornen. Diese Welszwerg (in Brasilien "candiru" genannt) sollen durch Urinspuren angezogen werden und so, wenn auch nur gelegentlich, in die Urinorgane amphibisch lebender Säuger und höchst selten in die Harn- und Geschlechtsorgane badender Menschen kommen. Das gibt sekundär häßliche Entzündungen. So nennt sich sinnigerweise eine dieser Arten *Urinophilus diabolicus* . . . was soviel wie der "teuflische Urinfreund" heißt. Es soll im weiten Amazonien Indianerstämme geben, bei denen bei bestimmten Mannbarkeitsriten die Glans penis bzw. die Vagina

durch Bastschnüre gewissermaßen als Mutprobe kräftig abgebunden bzw. geschlossen wird. Man führt dieses Ritual ursprünglich auf die Furcht vor diesen urinophilen Kleinwelsen zurück. Daher also die Scheu der Fischer, unbekleidet oder nur mit leichter, nicht genügend deckender Badehose ins Wasser zu gehen!

Mit einer Pinzette klaube ich die winzigen Fischchen aus den Schlammresten im Netz und betrachte sie eingehend. Dann werden einige in Alkohol konserviert, und andere kommen lebend in eine separate kleine Kanne. 3–4 Tage kann ich die zarten Fischzwerge in kleinen Vollglasbecken mit ein wenig Schlammboden halten, in den sie sich sofort oberflüchig einbuddeln. Als ich dann an der einen Seite etwas Urin ins Aquariuim gebe, kommen zwei von ihnen tatsächlich hervor und Schwimmen aufgeregt umher. (Lüling 1965: 159–160).

[5] Brachte ich mit einer Pinzette etwas Urin in eine Seite des Beckens, so konnte wohl eine Aktivitätssteigerung festgestellt werden, aber es kam in der Enge des Beckens nur zu einem richtungslosen Umherschwimmen nach allen Seiten. (Lüling 1969: 576).

[6] Die meisten *Vandellia*- und *Plectrochilus*-Arten sind ganz sicher stark urinophil, während das bei dem "klangvollen Namen" "*Urinophilus diabolicus*", wie gesagt, noch keineswegs sicher ist. (Lüling 1969: 575).

[7] Allen (1921: 379). Exactly the same statement is repeated in Eigenmann and Allen (1942: 10).

[8] Eigenmann and Allen (1942: 142–143). I wonder: did Eigenmann really label urinophilic behavior by a catfish as "opprobrious" or is Allen exaggerating? This depends on whether you think a candiru can disgrace itself in public.

[9] Eigenmann and Allen (1942: 147).

[10] Comment les candirus trouvent-ils leurs hôtes humains? Longtemps on a parlé d'une attraction par la présence d'urine dans l'eau et ce n'est qu'après les expériences d'un chercheur américain que l'on commença à douter prétendu comportement urophile de ces poissons. Mais ce problème n'est pas encore résolu d'une manière satisfaisante: le chercheur en question n'avait apparemment pas vérifié la présence de candirus dans la rivière où il avait immergé son piège contenant un chiffon imprégné d'urine. Plus probablement, les vandellies sont attirées par la transpiration des baigneurs ou par la présence de sang dans l'eau. (Mahnert 1985: 12).

[11] At the end of September 1998 I was staying temporarily at the Estación Científica Yasuní on the Rio Tiputini (an affluent of the Rio Napo), working under auspices of Pontificia Universidad Católica del Ecuador in Quito. The field station monitors wildlife and conducts research in the 1.5 million hectare (3.75 million acres) Parque Nacional Yasuní. Ovchynnyk (1968: 255) and Stewart et al. (1987: 33) list *Vandellia wieneri* from the Rio Napo. This river is also the type location of the species (Pellegrin 1909a; see Chapter 3). A checklist of the fishes of Parque Nacional Yasuní (Barriga 1994: 31) includes *V. wieneri*, but doesn't mention the Rio Tiputini.

[12] Vinton and Stickler (1941: 513). Also see Jobert (1898).

[13] Eigenmann (1918a: 266–267).

[14] Eigenmann (1920: 441).

[15] Anonymous (1982), Shmaefsky (1990). Specific gravity is the ratio of densities of the solution being tested to distilled water (specific gravity = 1.000 at 4°C), both solutions at the reference temperature, or after being corrected to the reference temperature (Spotte 1992: 7–8).

[16] This assumes that reference and standard temperature have been calibrated beforehand, typically at 15.56°C (Spotte 1992: 26–35).

[17] The human blood fluke, Schistosoma haematobium.

[18] Se os candirus atacam o homem, e os animais domésticos, animas de "sangue quente" digamos assim, não atacarão o peixe-boi e o bôto tão comuns na Amazônia? (Santos 1962: 115).

[19] Henry (1811: 147).

[20] Mr. F.'s beetles could have entered through his urethra, although whether as larvae, pupae, or adults is impossible to say. Alternatively, they might have been swallowed and afterwards penetrated to a part of the intestine lying against the bladder. The American physician Hugh Cabot (1936) noted that several objects swallowed weeks or even years earlier had been removed from the bladders of children and adults, including a darning needle, a whale-bone mouthpiece of a pipe, and a pencil.

[21] Could Mr. F. have swallowed his beetle larvae while eating hazelnuts? What follows came from several sources. The hazelnut weevil, or beetle, Curculio (=Balaninus) nucum, is widespread. Adults feed on several fruits (e.g., hazelnuts, pears, peaches, rarely apples, plums, or cherries), but the larvae feed only on hazelnuts. Adult females bore into the husks of embryonic hazelnuts and lay their eggs. Upon hatching, the larvae feed on the developing nuts and fall to the ground in autumn. They burrow 10–15 centimeters into the earth and enter diapause for 1–3 years before pupating and metamorphosing into adults.

[22] Taneja and Guerin (1977).

[23] Hribar et al. (1992).

[24] Mumcuoglu et al. (1986).

[25] Larson et al. (1979), Norwood et al. (1992).

[26] Yardley (1958). Some of my references are old, but not outdated. Much of the earlier work in urine chemistry is valid today and unchallenged by later studies. This is largely because ever-shfting states of dilution render the solute concentrations of urine unstable. The measurement of any solute is therefore a snapshot in time, its value depending on the state of hydration of the subject. Because of the wide range, "average" values of typical solutes in urine often have little meaning.

[27] Gudger (1930: 73). Gudger doesn't mention the date of Starks' letter.

[28] I cite Stradelli (1929) in this regard (see Chapter 1). Cândido de Melo Carvalho (1955: 69) briefly mentions how schools of the species *Hemicetopsis candiru* are attracted to blood.

[29] Yardley (1958).

[30] Yardley (1958).

[31] King and Boyce (1963: 40–41) write: "While the medical literature has long referred to urinary 'albumin,' this was a term of convenience rather than a statement of established fact. 'Urinary protein' would be a more appropriate term. . . . Many recent biochemistry and pathology texts state that normal urine contains no protein, while some authors have given estimates up to 13 mg per cent . . . most of this protein is said to be 'albumin.'"

[32] Lippman (1957).

[33] King and Boyce (1963).

[34] Eigenmann and Allen (1942).

[35] Hara (1994), Sorensen and Caprio (1998).

[36] Caprio (1975). See Marui and Caprio (1994) for a review of gustation in fishes.

[37] King and Boyce (1963: 39–61).

[38] Eigenmann and Allen (1942: 10).

[39] Gudger (1930c: 38). Gudger does not reveal the date of the letter.

[40] Eigenmann and Allen (1942: 143).

[41] Myers (1927: 132).

[42] These specimens are listed in the collections of the California Academy of Sciences, San Francisco (CAS 65912). They were collected in 1958 by Jerrold D. Conners in the Rio Yaguas at Santa Maria (state of Loreto, Peru).

[43] Vinton and Stickler (1941: 518).

[44] Shirreffs and Maughan (1997).

[45] For the sources of these concentrations, see references in Geier et al. (1999). The actual amount of nitrogen lost by sweating depends on several factors, including level of exercise and percentage of protein in the diet (Bourges et al. 1968).

[46] Braks and Takken (1999), Haustein (1989).

[47] See references in Geier et al. (1999). Cork and Park (1996) reported L-lactic acid concentrations of 1–5 milligrams per liter.

[48] Geier et al. (1999).

[49] Van der Goes van Naters and den Otter (1998), Van der Goes van Naters and Rinkes (1993).

[50] de Jong and Knols (1995).

[51] Nicolaides (1974).

[52] Knols et al. (1997).

[53] Der Kopf der Tiere ist mit feinen Sinneszellen bedeckt, die auf Wasserströmung reagieren. In das Maul der großen Fische zu schwimmen, wagen sie nicht, das ist ihnen zu gefährlich, denn sie könnten verschluckt werden. Sie nehmen den Weg durch den Seitenausgang, den sie als Eingang benutzen. Im Augenblick, wenn der große Fisch das Atemwasser über die Kiemen ausstößt, nimmt der Wels den Wasserstrom wahr, schwimmt blitzschnell dagegen und setzt sich in den Kiemen fest. Dieser Wasserstrom ist es, der ken kleinen Kerl irreführt, wenn ein Säugetier im Wasser uriniert. Er spürt den Wasserstrom, schwimmt ihm entgegen und ist in eine tödliche Falle gegangen. Natürlich nur, wenn die Menschen keine Badehose tragen. (Armbrust 1971: 83).

[54] Norman and Greenwood (1975: 236).

[55] Curtis (1949: 255).

[56] Breault (1991: 309).

[57] Schultz and Stern (1948: 66).

[58] Die Sonderlinge haben sich anscheinend ein ganz besonderes Hobby ausgedacht, das normalerweise mit ihrem eigenen Tod endet. Es kann also nicht gut Vorsatz, sondern nur ein Irrtum sein, der sie so handeln läßt. (Armbrust 1971: 82).

8. On Dressing Down

[1] Belloc (1931: 6).

[2] Urinae odore hi pisciculi valde alliciuntur, quam ob causam accolae intraturi flumen amazonum, cujus sinus hac peste abundant, praeputium ligula constringunt, et a mingendo abstinent. (von Martius in de [von] Spix and Agassiz (1829 [–1831], p. viii). [Translation in Eigenmann (1918a: 263); the translation given by Gudger (1930c: 3) follows this one closely.]

[3] Je n'étais pas depuis vingt-quatre heures au Pará, que j'avais déjà été mis en garde contre les Candirûs: "*Cuidado com o Candirû, ô homen!*" faites bien attention "*com este bicho temivel*"; ne vous baignez pas ou bien n'urinez jamais dans l'eau, ou encor imitez les Tapuyos et usez de la ligature protectrice, qu'on vous apprendra à appliquer au lieu d'élection.

Je crus d'abord qu'il s'agissait là de ces récits et de ces recommandations fantaisistes que l'on aime à faire au nouveau-venu; plus tard, je dus reconnaître qu'il fallait tenir un certain compte de ce que je qualifiais de racontars. Quand je vis mes Tapuyos appliquer, avec cette gravité triste que possède l'Indien, la ligature préventive, je crus alors sinon à la possibilité de l'attaque du Candirŭ, mais au moins à la crainte sérieuse de l'attaque. Certes, le spectacle de ces pêcheurs se livrant, sur le bord de l'eau, à l'acte précautionnel ne manquait pas d'originalité: l'application de cette ligature ne pouvait avoir rien de bien agréable, mais la conviction profonde du danger évité, l'étonnement de la part de ces braves gens devant mon refus de les imiter, donnait à cette opération bizarre un cachet sérieux qui excluait toute hilarité. Ils durent attribuer mon immunité à quelque préparation, à quelque manœuvre mystérieuse dont les blancs sont pour eux coutumiers.

Du reste, la frayeur qu'inspire le Candirŭ n'est pas aussi générale qu'on pourrait le croire; et si la croyance à son existence, aux désordres qu'il peut causer, est ancrée dans tous les esprits, beaucoup de pêcheurs oublient cependant les précautions fondamentales et ne pratiquent nullement la constriction. Malgré cela, je n'ai jamais entendu parler d'accident. (Jobert 1898: 495–496).

[4] Gudger (1930c: 19).

[5] Boulenger (1897a: 901).

[6] Sur la menace de semblable péril, on ne saurait prendre trop de précautions: aussi les indigênes du Jurua ont-ils soin, avant d'entrer dans l'eau, de loger de précieux organe dans une petite noix de coco percée à son extrémité d'un trou permettant tout juste le passage de l'urine. La noix de coco est maintenue en place par un petit filet en fibres de palmier, attaché à une ceinture de même tissu. (Jobert 1898: 493).

[7] In merkwürdigster und primitivster Weise schützen sie sich gegen eindringende Insekten, — präputium filo gossypii rubro ante gladem farciminis instar constringunt. Auch dürfte diese Vorrichtung im Wasser gegen das vorwitzige Kandirú-fischchen von Nutzen sein. (von den Steinen 1886: 195).

[8] Yurunae peni imponunt "pileolum" (eine Hülse von der Form eines oben wagerecht, unten schräg abgeschnittenen Kegels) aridis palmae foliis factum, qui altitudinem et diametrum duarum inferiorum phalangum digiti minimi fere aequat. Quo pileolo directe e scroto urgente corpora cavernosa in scrotum reprimuntur, ita ut tumoris instar infletur. Penis autem externi plane nihil extra pileolum apparet. Atque cum urethra prorsus conclusa sit, insecta intrare non possunt. (von den Steinen 1886: 239, footnote).

[9] Könnte für die heranwachsenden Männer, wenn die Glans durch Erektionen und sexuellen Verkehr dauernd frei zu werden droht, der Wunsch entstehen, sie zum Schutz bedeckt zu erhalten? Es lässt sich Vieles dafür anführen. Zwar möchte sich dieses Schutzbedürfnis noch am wenigsten auf Gestrüpp und Dornen beziehen. Ernsthafter sind die Insulte der Tierwelt zu nehmen. Wenn die Trumaí, wie von ihnen behauptet wurde, Tiere wären, die im Wasser lebten und auf dem Boden des Flusses schliefen, wären sie sogar in die dringende Notwendigkeit versetzt, die Urethralöffnung dem Kandirúfischchen (*Cetopsis Candiru*) zu verschliessen. Dies transparente, spannenlange kleine Scheusal, dessen Vorkommen im Batovy wir 1884 festgestellt haben, hat die eigentümliche Neigung, in die ihm zugänglichen Körperöffnungen des im Wasser befindlichen Menschen einzu-

dringen; es schlüpft in die Urethra, kann wegen der Flossen nicht zurück und verursacht leicht den Tod des Unglüchlichen, dem Nichts übrig bleibt, als schlecht und recht mit seinem Messer die Urethrotomia externa zu vollziehen. (von den Steinen 1894: 195).

[10] See de Pinna and Vari (1995).

[11] Da die Amphibiennatur der Trumaí aber auf gerechte Zweifel stösst, und der Aufenthalt im Wasser selbst für den Fischer oder den sein Kanu durch die Katarakte bugsierenden Ruderer nur eine nebensächliche Rolle spielt, so ist es nicht notwendig, auf die von dem Kandirú ausgehende, nur gelegentliche Gefahr zurückzugreifen. Dagegen macht allerdings das Gesindel der "Carapatos" (Ixo-didae), der beim Durchwandern des Waldes zahlreich von den Blättern abgestreiften und herabgeschüttelten Zecken, den Schutz der Glans den Waldbe-wohnern im höchsten Grade wünschenswert. Die zum Teil winzig kleinen Schmarotzer saugen sich auf der Haut fest, pumpen sich voller Blut, bei ihrer dehnbaren Körperwandung bis zu Erbsengrösse anschwellend, und haften mit den in die Haut scharf eindringenden Hakenspitzen ihrer Kieferfühler so fest, dass man sie zerreisst, wenn man sie abpflücken will, und durch die zurückbleibenden Teile schmerzhafte Entzündungsstellen hervorgerufen werden. Der Brasilier, der häufig mit Karapaten wie besät aus dem Walde kommt, entledigt sich schleunigst seiner Kleidung und schüttelt Hemd und Beinkleid über dem Lagerfeuer aus; hat sich einer der Schmarotzer in die Glans eingebohrt, so pflegt er ihm mit einer brennenden Zigarette so nahe auf den Leib zu rücken, als seine eigene Empfind-lichkeit nur eben gestattet, damit das Tierchen, durch die Hitze bedrängt, frei-willig seinen Aufenthalt aufgibt und sich aus der Schleimhaut zurückzieht, ohne zerissen zu werden. Wir Alle haben trotz unserer Kleidung das eine oder andere Mal dieses Verfahren einschlagen müssen und die Situation, bevor die Erlösung erreicht ist, als eine der peinlichsten gekostet. Ich bin auch der Ansicht, dass der Schutz, dessen sich die Indianer erfreuen, sicherer ist, als der einer verhüllenden Bekleidung. (von den Steinen 1894: 195–196).

[12] Kleidung ift kaum vorhanden. Die frauen gehen vollkommen nackt von klein auf. Die Männer tragen von der Reifezeit an den aus Blattstreifen geflochtenen Penisstulp (imudjé) . . . . Er wird meist so über die Eichel gezogen, daß die Dorhaut norn wurstzipfelartig hervorschaut; die Kante des Stulpes liegt an der Unterseite . . . . Als sonstige Kleidung kommen noch an Stricken befestigte Leder-sandalen und geflochtene Strohhüte nor, beide auf Einfluß der Brasilianer zurückgehend. (Krause 1911: 376).

[13] Gudger (1930c: xi).

[14] O fato é que os etnógrafos têm assinalado que em várias regiões amazônicas e das Guianas, os índios protegem as partes pudendas, de forma a evitar acidentes, entre os quais os mais temidos são os provocados pelas piranhas e pelos candirús. (von Ihering 1940: 202).

[15] Gudger (1930c: Fig. 14, p. 85; Fig. 15, p. 87; Fig. 16, p. 91).

[16] Schutzvorrichtungen brasilianischer Indianerstämme vor dem Eindringen urinophiler Welse in die Geschlechtsorgane ... (Lüling 1969: 576, legend to Fig. 4).

[17] Im flachen Wasser jagt das Candiru-fischchen umher, das nur zu gern in alle Körperöffnungen eindringt. (Krause 1911: 50).

[18] Estellita Lins (1945: 705–706).

[19] Malgrado a insignificância de seu tamanho, quando muito uns três centímetros, são bastante temidos os candirus, com o hábito singular de se intrometer pelos pertuitos naturais das pessoas que se banham nas águas por êles infestadas. Já houve quem daí tirasse a ilação de que não era por outro motivo que os Parintintins e mais alguns índios usavam trazer a ponta do prepúcio constantemente amarrada. (Cruls 1958: 130).

[20] Anonymous (1969: 9).

[21] Grzimek (1973: 381).

[22] Ein ungewöhnliches Verhalten zeigt der bis 9 cm lange Pygidiide *Vandellia cirrhosa* Cuv. & Val. Er ist in seinem Vorkommen auf den Amazonas beschränkt und wird von den dort einheimischen Indianern Candirú genannt. (Der Name Candirú wird von den Indianern des Amazonengebietes aber auch auf ähnliche Gattungen und Arten angewandt.) Dieser Wels hat die höchst unangenehme Eigenart, badenden Menschen oder auch Tieren in die Harnröhre einzudringen, wogegen sich die Indianer durch verschiedene Schutzbedeckungen aus Kokosschalen und Palmfasern zu sichern versuchen. (Kinzer 1959: 13).

[23] Norman and Greenwood (1975: 236).

[24] Burgess (1989: 318).

[25] Halstead (1992: 224).

[26] Lutwick and Chapnick (1996).

[27] Boyle (1979: 155).

[28] Nous avons attiré déjà l'attention sur le Candiru, petit Poisson des eaux douces du Brésil, qui a la réputation évidemment peu fondée de s'introduire dans l'urêthre des baigneurs. Le long des cours d'eau qu'il habite, les indigènes et souvent les individus de race blanche se gardent d'entrer dans l'eau sans avoir apposé sur leur prépuce une ligature protectrice ou sans s'être coiffé la verge d'un préservatif en sparterie. (Blanchard 1904: 153).

[29] Here Blanchard is referring to his article published the previous year (Blanchard 1903). It had no coauthor, nor did the 1904 article.

[30] Une croyance et une pratique toutes semblables sont répandues dans l'Afrique australe, là ou existe l'hématurie bilharzienne. On admet que cette maladie est causée par un parasite qui vit dans l'eau et qui pénètre par l'urèthre, au moment du bain. Aussi les indigènes ont-ils l'habitude de se coiffer le gland ou de se lier la verge, quand ils entrent dans l'eau ...

Nous représentions ci-contre le préservatif dont tout usage les Zulus de la Rhodesia. Cet intéressant objet, très habilement tressé, a été rapporté récemment de Buluwayo par le Dr A. Loir, a la libéralité duquel nous en sommes redevable. (Blanchard 1904: 153).

[31] Gudger (1930c: 96).

[32] In humans, schistosomiasis includes diseases caused by three species of blood flukes: *Schistosoma mansoni*, *S. japonicum*, and *S. haematobium*. Their life cycles are similar, although *S. haematobium* principally infests the urogenital system; the other two flukes are intestinal.

[33] For further information on the life cycle of *S. haematobium* and the pathological changes it causes, see Chandler (1955), Hunter et al. (1960), or another text on parasitology or tropical medicine. Possible entry of cercariae directly into the urethra is believed to occur in Egypt and other Muslim countries as a result of the custom of rinsing the genitals after urination. See Bitschai and Brodny (1956).

[34] Bitschai and Brodny (1956).

[35] A brief review of the life cycle of *Schistosoma haematobium* will aid in evaluating this information. Microscopic eggs produced by adult worms are shed with the urine and hatch soon after entering a more dilute body of water. The hatchlings—actually swimming embryos called miricidia—can survive 6–8 hours until finding a suitable host, which must be a snail of the family Physidae (=Bulinidae). The miricidium burrows into the snail's tissues and becomes a mother sporocyst. In this form it produces many daughter sporocysts that migrate to the gonad and digestive gland of the snail and metamorphose into thousands of cercariae. This is the infective stage. The cercariae burrow out of the snail's tissues and into the water. If a human is encountered they burrow into the skin, producing a mild itching sensation. Penetration occurs in less than 5 minutes. Within 24 hours the larvae will have worked into the peripheral blood vessels, where they are carried by the blood to the right side of the heart and from there into the pulmonary capillaries. They next enter the veins and are carried through the left side of the heart into the systemic circulation. If they survive this intricate journey they wind up in the portal circulation, where they develop by feeding on portal blood, eventually crawling into the larger portal veins.

[36] The ureters are the cylindrical excretory ducts from 30–36 centimeters long extending from the pelvis of the kidney to the base of the bladder. Schistosome eggs deposited in the ureters cause hydronephrosis or pyonephrosis.

[37] Butterworth (1990).

[38] Bitschai and Brodny (1956: 5-6).

[39] Als ich für die Folia Urologica auf Auftrag des Herausgebers derselben . . . über die letzten zehn Jahre der Bilharziaforschung einen kurzen Überblick zu verfassen hatte, stieß ich auf eine Notiz von R. Blanchard, daß die Zulus von Rhodesia gegen die Haematuria parasitaria, d. h. Bilharzia, eine Art von Kondom als Prophy-

lacticum anzuwenden pflegen und zwar immer dann, wenn sie in den Fluß sich begeben, in welchem nach ihrer Annahme die Distomen [cercariae] in die Harnröhre einschlüpfen sollen, was eben diese Kondoms verhindern sollen. R. Blanchard bildet auch ein solches, von Dr. Loir aus Buluwayo mitgebrachtes Instrument ab: es besteht aus dicht geflochtenem Stroh und hat die Form eines Flaschenkürbis — und wird bezeichnet als: "Préservatif contre la Bilharzie, utilisé par les Zulus de la Rhodesia." (Pfister 1913: 59).

[40] Zugleich wird darauf aufmerksam gemacht, daß auch die Indianer von Zentralbrasilien aus einem ähnlichen Gedankengange, nämlich gegen das Eindringen der Candirus, transparenter Fischchen von 2 ccm Länge mit gelber Iris solche Futterale verwenden. Diese Tierchen sollen gern in ihnen zugängliche Körperhöhlen eindringen und sich auch in die Urethralschleimhaut mit ihren Flossen einbohren. Ein solches Futteral — es handelt sich um eine Hülse von der Form eines oben wagrecht, unten schräg abgeschnittenen Kegels aus Palmblättern — ist bei K. von den Steinen abgebildet. (Pfister 1913: 59).

[41] Ruffer (1910).

[42] Chandler (1955: 281).

[43] Read (1970: 12).

[44] Coetzee (1974: 82).

[45] *Genipa americana* (coffee family, Rubiaceae) is widely planted in tropical America for shade, fruit, and timber. Throughout its range (West Indies and México to Argentina) the fruit has dozens of common names in different Indian languages, Creole, Spanish, English, and Portuguese. A few of these are *jagua, huitoc, brir, angelina, caruto, arasaloe, tapoeripa, palo colorado*, buitach apple, huitach apple, *maluco, guatil, genipap*, marmalade-box, ibo-ink, juniper, genip, lana, geniptree, *genipa, genipapo, jenipapo, jenipapeiro* (or *genipapeiro*), and *genipapinho*.

Lange (1912: 145) knew that the fruit of *Genipa americana* produces a rich black dye that is glossy, waterproof, and stable. Fernández de Oviedo (1526: 90–91) mentions that Indians use the dye to stain their skin and also for bathing. A later author (Anonymous 1668: 634–635), attempting to verify some of these properties, writes: "Whether the Juice of the Fruit of the Tree Junipa, being as clear as any Rock-water, yields a brown Violet-dye, and being put twice upon the same place, maketh it look black. And whether this Tincture cannot be got out with any Soap, yet disappears of it self in 9 or 10 days. And whether certain Animals, and particularly Hogs and Parrots, eating of this Fruit, have their Flesh and Fat altogether tinged of a Violet colour."

[46] Der frische Saft der Xagua gilt mit allem Recht für das sicherste Mittel jenen zwei Zoll langen Fisch zu tödten und abzutreibem, der bei unvorsichtigem Baden in die äusseren Höhlungen des menschlichen Körpers schlüpft und die furchtbarsten Zufälle erregen kann. . . . Ich selbst bin in Yurimaguas Augenzeuge eines solchen Falles gewesen, indem eine Indierin nach dem Einschlüpfen eines Canero

in die Vagina auf einmal einen so furchtbaren Schmerz und Blutverlust erlitt, dass man sie verloren gab. Nach der innerlichen und äussern Anwendung der Xagua war das Fischchen, sogleich abgegangen, und die Frau entkam mit dem Leben. (Poeppig 1836: 395, footnote).

[47] Anonymous (1969: 9).

[48] Vinton and Stickler (1941: 518–519).

[49] Vinton and Stickler (1941: 514) quoting Gudger (1930c: 11).

[50] I compared the English translation of Marcoy's work with the original French edition, published in Paris in 1869. Marcoy clearly meant dissolve, not expel. The quoted sentence appears on p. 146 of the French edition. With emphasis added, the last clause reads ". . . sur les voies urinaires et *dissout* l'animal qui les obstruait."

[51] Vinton and Stickler (1941: 515).

[52] Vinton and Stickler (1941: 516).

[53] Estellita Lins (1945: 706).

[54] Suby et al. (1943).

9. Down by the Riverside

[1] O'Hanlon (1988: 139).

[2] Coordinates of the campsite: 00°28.784'N 060°29.802'W.

[3] Haseman (1911a: 297).

[4] Haseman (1911a: 297).

[5] The net I use has a heavy wooden handle that screws together in two sections. The net attaches to a stainless steel frame measuring 46 by 23 centimeters. It's a "Bottom Aquatic Kick Net #425–A50" from Wildlife Supply Co. (Wildco), 95 Botsford Place, Buffalo NY 14216; (800) 799-8301.

[6] Barnes (1985: 31).

[7] von Humboldt (1852?, Vol. 1: 177).

[8] von Humboldt (1852?, Vol. 1: 178).

[9] The "correct" amount can only be a guess. The amount of ammonia excreted by fishes is highly variable, affected by composition of the diet (protein concentration), interval since the last feeding, pH of the water, the difference in partial pressure between ammonia on both sides of the gill, relative permeability of the gill, and other factors (see reviews of Mommsen and Walsh 1992, and Wood 1993).

Based loosely on information in Leung et al. (1999), I estimated that a fish of 30 grams might excrete 0.742 milligram per liter of ammonia-nitrogen per hour. The ordinary "comet" goldfish sold in pet stores are about 30 grams. The stock solution was prepared by dissolving 2.838 grams of ammonium chloride (NH_4Cl) and bringing the final volume to 1 liter.

[10] I say "approximately" and "very close to" because the concentrations weren't volumetric. To be completely accurate, 1 milliliter of stock solution would be added to 999 milliliters of untreated river water, not to 1 liter, or 1000 milliliters.

[11] Hara (1994).

[12] Baskin et al. (1980) and Roberts (1972) have also reported newly captured candirus regurgitating blood.

10. Hora Do Amor

[1] Robbins (1994: 298).

[2] Babel (1994: 168).

[3] In the summer of 2000, Robert E. Schmidt stained and cleared some of our specimens and saw these tiny structures. I later found them using a scanning electron microscope (Plate 5). Jansen had been right.

[4] Leenheer (1980).

[5] Wallace (1889: 112).

[6] Wallace (1889: 281).

[7] Wallace (1889: 282).

[8] Wallace (1889: 283).

[9] Orton (1870: 242).

[10] MacCreagh (1926: 267).

[11] Bates (1876: 357).

[12] Woodroffe (1914: 244).

[13] Coordinates of the site: 03°09.102'S 059°54.443'W.

[14] Wallace (1889: 187).

[15] Wallace (1889: 325).

[16] These are two very large groups of fishes. The otophysans, or ostariophysans (characins, carps and minnows, siluriform catfishes), comprise about 5000 species and perhaps 70 percent of all species of freshwater fishes. Their first four or five vertebrae have been modified (the Weberian ossicles) and connect the swimbladder with the inner ear. Perciforms, or perchlike fishes, lack this modification. Unlike the otophysans, the first rays of their dorsal and anal fins are thickened, unjointed, and often sharp. The pelvic fins ordinarily have one spiny ray. Perciforms comprise perhaps 8000 species and include the cichlids, perches, and seabasses.

[17] If the preference was for goldfish, we might later investigate the possibility of "alarm," or "fright," substances." Certain fishes, mainly some otophysans, reputedly excrete these compounds into the environment. Released from damaged skin during attack by a predator, they serve as chemical warning signals to other members of the species (Smith 1992). They might also attract more predators, giving the victim a chance to escape in the heightened confusion (Mathis et al. 1995). Evidence that "alarm substances" exist is indirect, having been based almost entirely on behavioral studies using European and North American minnows and their predators. Until these compounds can be identified, chemically defined, and tested for effect, their existence remains doubtful.

[18] Leung et al. (1999).

[19] Kelley and Atz (1964: 702, Fig. 1).

11. The Smoking Gun

[1] Hannah (1989: 94).

[2] Boulenger (1897b).

[3] Herman (1973: 265).

[4] Halstead (1992: 223).

[5] The literature citation is Queiroz (1997). Also see Samad's website: http://www.internext.com.br/urologia/Casoclinicos.htm.

[6] Registrada como "caso inacreditável de uretrorragia" (hemorragia de origem uretral), a cirurgia inédita, feita no paciente FBC, 23, na semana passada, em Manaus, pelo médico, urologista Anoar Samad, 33, vai ser apresentada no Congresso Americano de Urologia, no início do próximo ano, nos Estados Unidos.

O médico retirou do canal da uretra de FBC um candiru de 12 centímetros de comprimento por um de espessura. O candiru é um peixe com pequenos espinhos do lado externo.

"É algo incrível, impressionante mesmo. Só acredito porque fui eu que fiz todo o processo, senão, acho que precisaria ver todas as provas para crer", confessou, Anoar. "Muitos acham que estou brincando", afirmou.

A história de FBC, segundo Anoar, começou durante um banho de rio em Itacoatiara, a 175 quilômetros de Manaus. O rapaz, que tomava banho no rio, foi ferido no momento em que tirou a sunga para urinar. O peixe, segundo o médico, entrou no canal uretral do rapaz através do pênis.

"Ele disse que sentiu o candiru entrando e desde o primeiro momento sabia o que era", contou o médico, observando que, de acordo com o paciente, quando o peixe entra não há dor, somente um incômodo. "A dor vem depois", disse.

Com o diagnóstico pronto, FBS ainda teve que ficar três dias internado num hospital de Manaus, sob observação médica. "O que representou um risco, porque o peixe estava morto e em estado de decomposição", afirmou Anoar.

Depois de ouvir os detalhes da história do rapaz, o médico disse que entrou em contato com um pesquisador do Instituto Nacional de Pesquisas da Amazônica [*sic*] (Inpa) para saber um pouco mais sobre o peixe.

"Queria saber qual era sua forma, sua aparência, coisas assim".

"Antes da cirurgia fiz uma ultrasonografia para saber como o peixe estava e para documentar o fato, já que era algo inédito", contou o médico. Os aparelhos utilizados na operação, que durou entre uma e duas horas, foram para cirurgias endoscópicas (que não precisam cortar). Depois de ter localizado o peixe e visto como ele estava, Anoar utilizou uma tesoura para cortar as harbatanas do candiru é o puxou com uma pinça pelo canal da uretra.

Cinco dias após a cirurgia FBC recebeu alta. Ele está sendo tratado com anti-inflamatórios e antibióticos, e passa bem. "Deverei vê-lo dentro de duas semanas", afirmou o médico, destacando que FBC não tem e nem deverá ter seqüelas. "O que ele pode apresentar é um estreitamento de uretra, devido à lesão que o peixe causou. Mas ainda precisamos esperar", concluiu o médico, que foi formado pela Universidade do Amazonas e fez especialização em urologia em Boston, nos Estado Unidos. (Queiroz 1997).

[7] Samad didn't attend the conference.

[8] Eigenmann and Allen (1942: 146).

[9] Die Angst der Brasilier vor dem an und für sich so harmlosen Fischchen ist somit wohl gerechtfertigt; sie wird am besten durch eine Münchhauseniade charakterisiert, die uns ein Offizier mit ernsthafter Mien für wahr berichtete: in den Gewässern bei Villa Cáceres ist der Kandirú so bösartig und so auf seine Passion versessen, das er sogar, wenn Jemand vom Ufer aus ein Bedürfnis befriedigt, eilfertig in den Wasserstrahl empordringt. (von den Steinen 1894: 195, footnote).

[10] Breault (1991: 307). Goulding (1989: 185) is another skeptic. His comments are quoted in Chapter 2.

[11] Instituto Nacional de Pesquisas da Amazônia, Manaus (INPA 15590).

[12] Anonymous (1982).

[13] The next year I received a note from Jansen in Manaus (e-mail, 28 November 2000) stating that de Pinna had examined the fish and believed it to be similar to *V. plazai* (i.e., *V.* cf. *plazai*). Most of our specimens obtained from the Rio Jauaperi and Rio Solimões were less than half as long (approximately 60 millimeters), but otherwise similar. In an e-mail to Paulo on 23 February 2001, de Pinna states with apparent certainty that the fish is a specimen of *Vandellia erythrurus*. Evidently, de Pinna doesn't consider *Plectrochilus* a valid genus, although it has yet to be formally discarded and merged into *Vandellia*. The 10 type specimens of *Plectrochilus* (=*Urinophilus*) *erythrurus* described by Eigenmann (1918a) ranged in length from 120–145 millimeters (see Chapter 3).

[14] Information on the history of Manaus in this paragraph and the next is from Smith (1990: 291–295) and a handout on the Customs House I picked up in Manaus in November 1999.

12. Candiru World

[1] Roethke (1964: 79).

[2] Conway (1968).

[3] Baudrillard (1983).

[4] I've taken considerable liberty by implying that models can someday be fault-lessly predictive. A model is, by definition, quantitatively incorrect. Were this not true there would be no need for them. Models are nothing but simulations.

[5] See Saunders' story "Pastoralia" (Saunders 2000: 1–66).

[6] Lem (1974: 226).

[7] The American computer scientist Douglas R. Hofstadter has a point when he wonders about the difference between a simulated song and a real song (Hofstadter and Dennett 1981: 99). I don't care. I love the notion of the Princess Ineffabelle's "stochastic stroll."

[8] Borges (1968: 62).

[9] Baudrillard (1983: 17).

[10] Sontag (1973: 164).

Literature Cited

Page numbers of longer works in which the candiru is mentioned are given in brackets.

Agassiz, L. and Mrs. L. Agassiz. 1868. *A Journey in Brazil.* Ticknor and Fields, Boston, xix + 540 pp.

Alfred, B. M. 1987. *Elements of Statistics for the Life and Social Sciences.* Springer-Verlag, New York, xiii + 190 pp.

Allen, W. R. 1921. The centennial expedition of Indiana University to Peru. Science (N. S.) (Washington, D.C.) 53: 377–379.

Alves Guimarães, J. R. 1935a. Notas sobre a biologia do *Pseudostegophilus scarificator* Ihering. Revista de Industria Animal (São Paulo) 2(3): 273–275.

Alves Guimarães, J. R. 1935b. Contribuição para o conhecimento de uma nova especie de peixe hematophago, ecto-parasita de "Characidae", encontrado em São Paulo (Rio Tietê): *Vandellia Hematophaga* sp. n. Revista de Industria Animal (São Paulo) 2(3): 300–304.

Anonymous. 1668. Of vegetables. Philosophical Transactions of the Royal Society of London 3: 634–635.

Anonymous. 1969. Discovery. Environment Southwest (San Diego), No. 414, p. 9.

Anonymous. 1982. *Implementing Urologic Procedures.* Intermed Communications, Springhouse, 160 pp.

Araujo-Lima, C. and M. Goulding. 1997. *So Fruitful a Fish: Ecology, Conservation, and Aquaculture of the Amazon's Tambaqui.* Columbia University Press, New York, xii + 191 pp.

Armbrust, W. 1971. Schmerlenwelse. Aquarien und Terrarien (Stuttgart) 24(3): 82–84.

Asano, M. and I. Hanyu. 1986. Biological significance of electroreception for a Japanese catfish. Bulletin of the Japanese Society of Scientific Fisheries (Tokyo) 52: 795–800.

Askonas, B. A. 1984. Interference in general immune function by parasite infections; African trypanosomiasis as a model system. Parasitology (New York) 88: 633–638.

Babel, I. 1994. Red cavalry: evening. In *Collected Stories.* Penguin Books, New York, pp. 167–170.

Barnes, J. 1985. *Flaubert's Parrot.* McGraw-Hill Paperback, New York, 216 pp.

Barriga, R. 1994. Pesces del Parque Nacional Yasuni. Politecnica (Quito) 19(2): 9–41.

Barros Prado, E. 1959. *The Lure of the Amazon.* The Adventurers Club, London, 175 pp.

Barthem, R. and M. Goulding. 1997. *The Catfish Connection: Ecology, Migration, and Conservation of Amazon Predators.* Columbia University Press, New York, xvi + 144 pp.

Baskin, J. N. 1973. Structure and relationships of the Trichomycteridae. Ph.D. dissertation, City University of New York, xxi + 389 pp.

Baskin, J. N., T. M. Zaret, and F. Mago-Leccia. 1980. Feeding of reportedly parasitic catfishes (Trichomycteridae and Cetopsidae) in the Rio Portuguesa Basin, Venezuela. Biotropica (Lawrence) 12: 182–186.

Bates, H. W. 1876. *The Naturalist on the River Amazons.* University of California Press, Berkeley, viii + 465 pp., maps. (1962 facsimile edition, probably of the 4th edition, John Murray, London, 1876.)

Baudrillard, J. 1983. *Simulations.* Semiotext(e), New York, 159 pp.

Begossi, A. and F. Manoel de Souza Braga. 1992. Food taboos and folk medicine among fishermen from the Tocantins River (Brazil). Amazoniana (Plön and Rio de Janeiro) 12: 101–119.

Belloc, H. 1931. On dressing up. In *A Conversation with a Cat and Others.* Books for Libraries Press, Freeport, pp. 6–11. (1969 facsimile edition.)

Bernstein, J. 1956. Dr. E. W. Gudger—"Fish Detective." Audubon magazine (New York) 58(1): 29–31.

Bitschai, J. and M. L. Brodny. 1956. *A History of Urology in Egypt.* Riverside Press, New York, vi + 122 pp.

Blanchard, R. 1903. Piranhas et candirus. Archives de Parasitologie (Paris) 7: 168–169.

Blanchard, R. 1904. Candiru et Bilharzie. Archives de Parasitologie (Paris) 8: 153.

Bleckmann, H. 1994. *Reception of Hydrodynamic Stimuli in Aquatic and Semi-aquatic Animals.* Gustav Fischer Verlag, Stuttgart, viii + 115 pp.

Böhlke, J. 1953. A catalog of the type specimens of recent fishes in the natural history museum of Stanford University. Stanford Ichthyological Bulletin (Palo Alto) 5: 1–168. [p. 45]

Borges, J. L. 1968. The circular ruins. In *The Aleph and Other Stories, 1933–1969.* E. P. Dutton, New York, pp. 55–62.

Boulenger, G. A. 1897a. Exhibition of specimens, and remarks upon the habits, of the siluroid fish *Vandellia cirrhosa.* Proceedings of the Zoological Society of London 1897: 901.

Boulenger, G. A. 1897b. Further remarks on the habits of the siluroid fish *Vandellia cirrhosa.* Proceedings of the Zoological Society of London 1897: 920–921.

Bourges, H., N. S. Scrimshaw, and V. R. Young. 1968. Exercise and protein requirements in man. Federation Proceedings (Washington, D.C.) 27: 485. [Abstract]

Bowman, R. I. and S. L. Billeb. 1965. Blood-eating in a Galápagos finch. The living bird (fourth annual edition), Cornell Laboratory of Ornithology, Ithaca, pp. 29–44.

Boyle, T. C. 1979. Green hell. In *Decent of Man*. Penguin Books, New York, pp. 139–157.

Braks, M. A. H. and W. Takken. 1999. Incubated human sweat but not fresh sweat attracts the malaria mosquito *Anopheles gambiae* sensu stricto. Journal of Chemical Ecology (New York) 25: 663–672.

Breault, J. L. 1991. Candirú: Amazonian parasitic catfish. Journal of Wilderness Medicine (New York) 2: 304–312.

Bretschneider, F., J. Vervey, and P. Heuts. 1991. Functioning of catfish electrore-ceptors: input impedance and stimulus efficiency. Comparative Biochemistry and Physiology (Amsterdam) 99A: 295–299.

Browman, H. I. 1999. Negative results. Marine Ecology Progress Series (Hamburg) 191: 301–309.

Brown, H. R., G. N. Andrianov, and A. Mamadaliev. 1984. Electroreception in the Turkistan catfish. Experientia (Basel) 40: 1366–1367.

Bullock, T. H. 1982. Electroreception. Annual Review of Neuroscience (Palo Alto) 5: 121–170.

Burgess, W. E. 1989. *An Atlas of Freshwater and Marine Catfishes: A Preliminary Survey of the Siluriformes*. T. F. H. Publications, Neptune City, 784 pp. [pp. 305–325, plates 148, 154–157]

Burroughs, W. S. 1959. [*The*] *Naked Lunch*. Grove Weidenfeld, New York, xix + 232 pp. [p. 41]

Butsuk, S. V. and B. I. Bessonov. 1981. Direct current electric field in some teleost species: effect of medium salinity. Journal of Comparative Physiology (Heidelberg) 141: 277–282.

Butterworth, A. E. 1990. Immunology of schistosomiasis. In *Modern Parasite Biology: Cellular, Immunological, and Molecular Aspects*. W. H. Freeman, New York, pp. 262–288.

Cabot, H. 1936. Foreign bodies in the bladder. In *Modern Urology*, 3rd edition, Vol. 2, H. Cabot (editor). Lea and Febiger, Philadelphia, pp. 174–179.

Calvino, I. 1968. The aquatic uncle. In *Cosmicomics*. Harcourt Brace Jovanovich, Orlando, pp. 70–82.

Calvino, I. 1988. The name, the nose. In *Under the Jaguar Sun*. Harcourt Brace Jovanovich, San Diego, pp. 67–83.

Campbell, J. W. 1991. Excretory nitrogen metabolism. In *Environmental and Metabolic Animal Physiology* [*Comparative Animal Physiology*, fourth edition], C. L. Prosser (editor). Wiley-Liss, New York, pp. 277–324.

Cândido de Melo Carvalho, J. 1955. Notas de viagem ao Javari—Itacoaí—Juruá. Publicações Avulsas do Museu Nacional (Rio de Janeiro), No. 13, 81 pp. + 8 figs., 4 endmaps. [p. 69, cetopsids]

Caprio, J. 1975. High sensitivity of catfish taste receptors to amino acids. Comparative Biochemistry and Physiology (Amsterdam) 52A: 247–251.

Caprio, J. 1988. Peripheral filters and chemoreceptor cells in fishes. In *Sensory Biology of Aquatic Animals*, J. Atema, R. R. Fay, A. N. Popper, and W. N. Tavolga (editors). Springer-Verlag, New York, pp. 313–338.

Chandler, A. C. 1955. *Introduction to Parasitology, with Special Reference to the Parasites of Man*, 9th edition. John Wiley and Sons, New York, xiv + 799 pp.

Coetzee, J. M. 1974. The narrative of Jacobus Coetzee. In *Dusklands*. Penguin Books, New York, pp. 57–121.

Conway, W. G. 1968. How to exhibit a bullfrog: a bed-time story for zoo men. Curator (New York) 11: 310–318.

Cork, A. and K. C. Park. 1996. Identification of electrophysiologically-active compounds for the malaria mosquito, *Anopheles gambiae*, in human sweat extracts. Medical and Veterinary Entomology (Oxford) 10: 269–276.

Cortázar, J. 1966. *Hopscotch*. Random House, New York, 564 pp. (English edition of *Rayuela*, Editorial Sudamericana Sociedad Anónima, Buenas Aires, 1963.)

Cotlow, L. 1953. *Amazon Head-hunters*. Henry Holt and Company, New York, vi + 245 pp. [pp. 135–137]

Cotlow, L. 1966. *In Search of the Primitive*. Little, Brown, Boston, xxii + 454 pp. [pp. 224–225]

Couto de Magalhães, A. 1931. *Monographia Brazileira de Peixes Fluviaes*. Graphicars (Romiti, Lanzara e Zanin), São Paulo, 263 pp. [pp. 104–105, 237, Fig. 42]

Cowley, J. J. and B. W. L. Brooksbank. 1991. Human exposure to putative pheromones and changes in aspects of social behaviour. Journal of Steroid Biochemistry and Molecular Biology (Oxford) 39B: 647–659.

Crofton, H. S. 1971. A quantitative approach to parasitism. Parasitology (New York) 62: 179–193.

Croll, N. A. 1966. *Ecology of Parasites*. Harvard University Press, Cambridge (Massachusetts), 136 pp.

Cruls, G. 1958. *Hiléia Amazônica: Aspectos da Flora, Fauna, Arqueologia e Etnografia Indígenas*, 3.ª edição. Coleção Documentos Brasileiros 101, Livraria José Olympio Editôra, Rio de Janeiro, xvi + 447 pp. [p. 130]

Curtis, B. 1949. *The Life Story of the Fish: His Morals and Manners.* Harcourt, Brace, New York, xii + 284 pp. [p. 255]

Cuvier, G. and A. Valenciennes. 1846. Des Vandellies (*Vandellia*, nob.), et en particulier du *Vanellia cirrhosa*, nob. In *Histoire naturelle des Poissons*, Vol. 18. F. G. Levrault (Paris), xix + 505 pp., plates 520–553. [pp. 386–388, Plate 547]

Dahl, G. 1960. Nematognathous fishes collected during the Macarena expedition, 1959. Novedades Colombianas (Popayán) 1(5): 302–317.

Dahl, G. 1971. *Los Peces del Norte de Colombia.* Inderena, Bogotá, xvii + 391 pp. [p. 72]

Dalquest, W. W. 1955. Natural history of the vampire bats of eastern Mexico. American Midland Naturalist (Notre Dame) 53: 79–87.

Darnton, R. 1984. *The Great Cat Massacre.* Basic Books, New York, xi + 298 pp.

Davis, H. 1952. *The Jungle and the Damned.* Duell, Sloan and Pearce, New York, 306 pp.

de Bary, A. 1879. *Die Erscheinung der Symbiose.* Karl J. Trübner, Strassburg, 30 pp.

de Castelnau, F. 1855. *Animaux nouveaux ou rares recueillis pendant l'Expédition dans les parties centrales de l'Amérique du Sud, de Rio de Janeiro a Lima, et de Lima au Para; exécutée par ordre du gouvernement Français pendant les années 1843 a 1847, sous la direction du comte Francis de Castelnau. II, Poissons.* Chez P. Bertrand, Libraire-Éditeur, Paris, 12 and xii + 112 pp., 50 plates. [p. 51, Plate 28]

de Jong, R., and B. G. J. Knols. 1995. Selection of biting sites on man by two malaria mosquito species. Experientia (Basel) 51: 80–94.

de Miranda Ribeiro, A. 1911. *Fauna Brasiliense,* Vol. 4, *Peixes.* Archivos do Museu Nacional (Rio de Janeiro) 16: 228–229.

de Miranda Ribeiro, A. 1912. Loricariidae, Callichthyidae, Doradiidae e Trichomycteridae. Historica Natural (Zoologica), Annexo No. 5. Comissão do Linhas Telegráphicas Estratégicas de Matto-Grosso [*sic*] ao Amazonas (Rio de Janeiro), Septembro, pp. 27–32.

de Miranda Ribeiro, A. 1917. De Scleracanthis fluvio "Solimões" anno MCMVIII a cl. F. Machado da Silva duce brasiliense inventis et in Museo Urbis "Rio de Janeiro" servantis per classis dispositis val descriptis. Revista da Sociedade Brasileira de Ciencias (Rio de Janeiro), No. 1, pp. 49–52.

de Miranda Ribeiro, A. 1922. Critical notes on Brazilian zoology. Archivos da Escola Superior de Agricultura e Medicina Veterinária de Nictheroy (Pinheiro) 6(1/2): 11–15.

de Miranda Ribeiro, P. 1947. Notas para o estudo dos *Pygidiidae brasileiros* (Pisces — Pygidiidae — Vandelliinae). II. Boletim do Museu Nacional — Zoologia (N. S.) (Rio de Janeiro), No. 78, pp. 1–8 + 2 plates.

de Pinna, M. C. C. 1998. Phylogenetic relationships of neotropical Siluriformes (Teleostei: Ostariophysi): historical overview and synthesis of hypotheses. In *Phylogeny and Classification of Neotropical Fishes*, L. R. Malabarba, R. E. Reis, R. P. Vari, Z. M. S. Lucena, and C. A. S. Lecena (editors). EDIPUCRS, Porto Alegre, pp. 279–330. (Some pages printed twice.)

de Pinna, M. C. C. and H. A. Britski. 1991. *Megalocentor*, a new genus of parasitic catfish from the Amazon basin: the sister group of *Apomatoceros* (Trichomycteridae: Stegophilinae). Ichthyological Exploration of Freshwaters (Munich) 2: 113–128.

de Pinna, M. C. C. and R. P. Vari. 1995. Monophyly and phylogenetic diagnosis of the family Cetopsidae, with synonymization of the Helogenidae (Teleostei: Siluriformes). Smithsonian Contributions to Zoology, No. 571, Smithsonian Institution Press, Washington (D.C.), iii + 26 pp.

de Spix, J. B. and L. Agassiz. 1829 [–1831]. *Selecta genera et species piscium quos in itinere per Brasiliam annis MDCCCXVII—MDCCCXX*. C. Wolf, Munich, 3 p. l., ii, [2], xvi, 6, 138, frontis, 97 plates included with text. [p. viii, introduction of von Martius]

Devincenzi, G. J. and R. Vaz-Ferreira. 1926–1940. Álbum Ictiológico del Uruguay. Anales del Museu de Historia Natural, Montevideo, 8 pp, 48 plates.

Devincenzi, G. J. and R. Vaz-Ferreira. 1939. Nota preliminar sobre un pygidido hematofago del rio Uruguay. Archivos de la Sociedad de Biología de Montevideo 9: 165–178.

Devincenzi, G. J. and G. W. Teague. 1942. Ictiofauna del Rio Uruguay medio. Anales del Museu de Historia Natural de Montevideo, Series 2a, Vol. 5, No. 4. Imprenta ROSGAL, Montevideo, 100 pp., indices, 6 plates. [p. 33]

di Caporiacco, L. 1935. Spedizione Nello Beccari nella Guiana Britannica. Monitore Zoologico Italiano (Firenze) 46: 55–70.

Dijkgraaf, S. 1952. Bau und Funktionen der Seitenorgane und des Ohrlabyrinths bei Fischen. Experientia (Basel) 8: 205–216.

Dijkgraaf, S. 1963. The functioning and significance of the lateral-line organs. Biological Reviews (New York) 38: 51–105.

Doctorow, E. L. 1994. *The Waterworks*. Random House, New York, 253 pp.

Dodson, P. 2000. Origin of birds: the final solution. American Zoologist (McLean) 40: 504–512.

Dolan, T. 1960. *Sports Afield Collection of Know Your Fish*. Hearst, New York, unpaginated.

Duguid, J. 1931. *Green Hell*. Century, New York, x + 339 pp.

Dyott, G. M. 1922. *Silent Highways of the Jungle: Being the Record of an Adventurous Journey Across Peru to the Amazon*. Chapman and Dodd, London, x + 320 pp.

Eckert, R. and D. Randall. 1983. *Animal Physiology: Mechanisms and Adaptations.* W. H. Freeman, New York, xviii + 830 pp.

Eigenmann, C. H. 1912. *The Freshwater Fishes of British Guiana, Including a Study of the Ecological Grouping of Species and the Relation of the Fauna of the Plateau to that of the Lowlands.* Memoirs of the Carnegie Museum (Pittsburgh), Vol. 5, No. 1, xvii + 554 pp., frontis, 50 plates. (Also cited as Publications of the Carnegie Museum, Serial No. 67.)

Eigenmann, C. H. 1918a. The Pygidiidae, a family of South American catfishes. Memoirs of the Carnegie Museum (Pittsburgh) 7(5): 259–398 + 21 plates. [pp. 261–270, 273, 277, 279, 344, 358–369, plates 38, 43, 53]

Eigenmann, C. H. 1918b. The Pygidiidae. Proceedings of the Indiana Academy of Science (Indianapolis) 1917: 59–66.

Eigenmann, C. H. 1918c. Descriptions of sixteen new species of Pygidiidae. Proceedings of the American Philosophical Society (Philadelphia) 56: 690–703. [pp. 690, 702–703]

Eigenmann, C. H. 1920. Limits of the genera *Vandellia* and *Urinophilus*. Science (N. S.) (Washington, D.C.) 51: 441.

Eigenmann, C. H. 1922. On a new genus and two new species of Pygidiidae, a family of South American nematognaths. Bijdragen tot de Dierkunde (Amsterdam) 22: 113–114 + 2 plates.

Eigenmann, C. H. and W. R. Allen. 1942. *Fishes of Western South America.* The University of Kentucky, Lexington, xv + 494 pp., endmap. [pp. 10, 142–149, 190]

Enger, P. S., A. J. Kalmijn, and O. Sand. 1989. Behavioral investigations on the functions of the lateral line and inner ear in predation. In *The Mechanosensory Lateral Line: Neurobiology and Evolution*, S. Coombs, P. Görner, and H. Münz (editors). Springer-Verlag, New York, pp. 575–587.

Estellita Lins, E. 1945. The solution of incrustations in the urinary bladder by a new method. Journal of Urology (Philadelphia) 53: 702–711.

Evans, D. H. 1993. Osmotic and ionic regulation. In *The Physiology of Fishes*, D. H. Evans (editor). CRC Press, Boca Raton, pp. 315–341.

Fernald, R. D. 1988. Aquatic adaptations in fish eyes. In *Sensory Biology of Aquatic Animals*, J. Atema, R. R. Fay, A. N. Popper, and W. N. Tavolga (editors). Springer-Verlag, New York, pp. 435–466.

Fernald, R. D. 1990. The optical system of fishes. In *The Visual System of Fish*, R. Douglas and M. Djamgoz (editors). Chapman and Hall, London, pp. 45–61.

Fernandez, A. Z., A. Tablante, F. Bartoli, S. Beguin, H. C. Hemker, and R. Aptiz-Castro. 1998. Expression of biological activity of draculin, the anticoagulant factor from vampire bat saliva, is strictly dependent on the appropriate glycosylation of the native molecule. Biochimica et Biophysica Acta (Amsterdam) 1425: 291–299.

Fernández de Oviedo, G. 1526. [*Natural History of the West Indies.*] Studies in the Romance Languages and Literature, No. 32. University of North Carolina Press, Chapel Hill, xvii + 140 pp. [Translation by S. A. Stoudemire, 1959.]

Fink, W. L. 1993. Revision of the piranha genus *Pygocentrus* (Teleostei, Characiformes). Copeia (Lawrence) 1993: 665–687.

Forey, P. L., C. J. Humphries, I. L. Kitching, R. W. Scotland, D. J. Siebert, and D. M. Williams. 1992. *Cladistics: A Practical Course in Systematics.* Clarendon Press, Oxford, x + 191 pp.

Forman, G. L. 1972. Comparative morphological and histochemical studies of stomachs of selected American bats. University of Kansas Science Bulletin (Lawrence) 49: 591–729.

Geier, M., O. J. Bosch, and J. Boeckh. 1999. Ammonia as an attractive component of host odour for the yellow fever mosquito, *Aedes aegypti.* Chemical Senses (Oxford) 24: 647–653.

Géry, F. 1977. *Characoids of the World.* T. F. H. Publications, Neptune City, 672 pp.

Ghiselin, M. T. 1997. *Metaphysics and the Origin of Species.* State University of New York Press, Albany, xi + 377 pp.

Giltay, L. 1935. Notes ichthyologiques. X—Description d'une espèce nouvelle de Trichomycteridae. Bulletin du Musée Royal d'Histoire Naturelle de Belgique (Brussels) 11(27): 1–3.

Good, K. (with D. Chanoff). 1991. *Into the Heart: One Man's Pursuit of Love and Knowledge Among the Yanomama.* Simon and Schuster, New York, 349 pp.

Gotto, R. V. 1969. *Marine Animals: Partnerships and Other Associations.* American Elsevier, New York, 96 pp.

Goulding, M. 1980. *The Fishes and the Forest: Explorations in Amazonian Natural History.* University of California Press, Berkeley, xii + 280 pp. [pp. 34–35, 192–195]

Goulding, M. 1989. *Amazon: The Flooded Forest.* Sterling, New York, 208 pp. [pp. 184–185]

Greenhall, A. M., U. Schmidt, and W. López-Forment C. 1969. Field observations on the mode of attack of the vampire bat (*Desmodus rotundus*) in Mexico. Anales del Instituto de Biología, Universidad Nacional Autónoma de México (Mexico City) 40: 245–252.

Grzimek, B. 1973. *Grzimek's Animal Life Encyclopedia,* Vol. 4, Fishes I. Van Nostrand Reinhold, New York, 531 pp. [p. 381]

Gudger, E. W. 1930a. On the alleged penetration of the human urethra by an Amazonian catfish called candiru with a review of the allied habits of other members of the family Pygidiidae. Part I. American Journal of Surgery (N. S.) (New York) 8: 170–188.

Gudger, E. W. 1930b. On the alleged penetration of the human urethra by an Amazonian catfish called candirú with a review of the allied habits of other members of the family Pygidiidae. Part II. American Journal of Surgery (N. S.) (New York) 8: 443–457.

Gudger, E. W. 1930c. *The Candirú.* Paul B. Hoeber, New York, xvii + 120 pp. (Reprint of Gudger 1930a and 1930b with frontis, preface, forward by A. S. Warthin.)

Guenther, K. 1931. *A Naturalist in Brazil.* George Allen and Unwin, London, 400 pp. [p. 176] (English edition of *Das Antlitz Brasiliens,* R. Voigtländers Verlag, Leipzig, 1927.)

Günther, A. 1864. *Catalogue of the Fishes in the British Museum.* Trustees of the British Museum, London, Vol. 5, xxii + 455 pp., appended list of catalogs (8 pp.). [pp. 276–277]

Günther, A. C. L. G. 1880. *An Introduction to the Study of Fishes.* Adam and Charles Black, Edinburgh, xvi + 720 pp. [p. 581]

Halstead, B. W. 1992. *Dangerous Aquatic Animals of the World: A Color Atlas.* Darwin Press, Princeton, xix + 264 pp. [pp. 223–228]

Hanke, W., C. Brücker, and H. Bleckmann. 2000. The ageing of the low-frequency water disturbances caused by swimming goldfish and its possible relevance to prey detection. Journal of Experimental Biology (Cambridge, U.K.) 203: 1193–1200.

Hannah, B. 1989. *Boomerang.* Houghton Mifflin, Boston, 150 pp.

Hannah, B. 1996. Get some young. In *High Lonesome.* Grove Press, New York, pp. 3–41.

Hara, T. 1994. The diversity of chemical stimulation in fish olfaction and gustation. Reviews in Fish Biology and Fisheries (Dordrecht) 4: 1–35.

Harvey, R. 1998. The judgement of urines. Canadian Medical Association Journal (Ottawa) 159: 1482–1484.

Haseman, J. D. 1911a. A brief report upon the expedition of the Carnegie Museum to central South America. Annals of the Carnegie Museum (Pittsburgh) 7: 287–314. [pp. 292–297]

Haseman, J. D. 1911b. Descriptions of some new species of fishes and miscellaneous notes on others obtained during the expedition of the Carnegie Museum to central South America. Annals of the Carnegie Museum (Pittsburgh) 7: 315–328 + 7 plates. [p. 315]

Haustein, U-F. 1989. Bakterielle Hautflora, Wirtsabwehr und Hautinfektionen. Dermatologische Monatsschrift (Leipzig) 175: 665–680.

Hawkins, A. D. 1993. Underwater sound and fish behaviour. In *Behaviour of Teleost Fishes,* 2nd edition. T. J. Pitcher (editor). Chapman and Hall, London, pp. 130–169.

Heiligenberg, W. 1993. Electrosensation. In *The Physiology of Fishes*, D. H. Evans (editor). CRC Press, Boca Raton, pp. 137–160.

Helfman, G. S., B. B. Collette, and D. E. Facey. 1997. *The Diversity of Fishes.* Blackwell Science, Malden, xii + 528 pp. [p. 231]

Hennig, W. 1966. *Phylogenetic Systematics.* University of Illinois Press, Urbana, 263 pp.

Henry, W. 1811. Case in which the larvae of an insect were voided in the urine. Edinburgh Medical Journal 7: 147–148.

Herman, J. R. 1973. Candirú: urinophilic catfish: its gift to urology. Urology (New York) 1: 265–267.

Herrera-Gonzalez, N. E. and D. W. Dresser. 1993. Fetal-maternal immune interaction: blocking antibody and survival of the fetus. Developmental and Comparative Immunology (Oxford) 17: 1–18.

Hickman, C. P. and B. F. Trump. 1969. The kidney. In *Fish Physiology*, Vol. 1, W. S. Hoar and D. J. Randall (editors). Academic Press, New York, pp. 91–239.

Hofstadter, D. R. and D. C. Dennett. 1981. *The Mind's I: Fantasies and Reflections on Self and Soul.* Bantam Books, Toronto, vii + 501 pp.

Homewood, B. 1994. Vampire fish show their teeth. New Scientist (London) 144(1954): 7.

Hribar, L. J., D. J. Leprince, and L. D. Foil. 1992. Ammonia as an attractant for adult *Hybomitra lasiophtalma* (Diptera: Tabanidae). Journal of Medical Entomology (Lanham) 29: 346–348.

Hughes, G. M. 1980. Functional morphology of fish gills. In *Epithelial Transport in the Lower Vertebrates*, B. Lahlou (editor). Cambridge University Press, Cambridge (U.K.), pp. 15–36.

Hunter, G. W. III, W. W. Frye, and J. C. Swartzwelder. 1960. *A Manual of Tropical Medicine*, 3rd edition. W. B. Saunders, Philadelphia, xxx + 892 pp.

Huxley, T. H. 1865. On the structure of the stomach in *Desmodus rufus*. Proceedings of the Zoological Society of London 1865: 386–390.

Jobert, C. 1898. Sur la prétendue pénétration de poissons dans l'urèthre. Archives de Parasitologie (Paris) 1: 493–502.

Joyce, J. 1916. *A Portrait of the Artist as a Young Man.* Viking, New York, 253 pp. (1976 facsimile edition with corrections.)

Kalmijn, A. J. 1972. Bioelectric fields in seawater and the function of the ampullae of Lorenzini in elasmobranch fishes. SIO Reference Series, Contribution No. 72–83, Scripps Institution of Oceanography, La Jolla, 21 pp.

Kalmijn, A. J. 1974. The detection of electric fields from inanimate and animate sources other than electric organs. In *Handbook of Sensory Physiology*, Vol. III/3, A. Fessard (editor). Springer-Verlag, Berlin, pp. 147–200.

Kalmijn, A. J. 1988a. Hydrodynamic and acoustic field detection. In *Sensory Biology of Aquatic Animals*, J. Atema, R. R. Fay, A. N. Popper, and W. N. Tavolga (editors). Springer-Verlag, New York, pp. 83–130.

Kalmijn, A. J. 1988b. Detection of weak electric fields. In *Sensory Biology of Aquatic Animals*, J. Atema, R. R. Fay, A. N. Popper, and W. N. Tavolga (editors). Springer-Verlag, New York, pp. 151–186.

Kalmijn, A. J. 1989. Functional evolution of lateral line and inner ear sensory systems. In *The Mechanosensory Lateral Line: Neurobiology and Evolution*, S. Coombs, P. Görner, and H. Münz (editors). Springer-Verlag, New York, pp. 187–215.

Kato, M., S. Ohta, K. Shimizu, Y. Tsuchida, and G. Matsumoto. 1989. Detection-threshold of 50 Hz electric fields by human subjects. Bioelectromagnetics (New York) 10: 319–327.

Keller, F. 1874. *The Amazon and Madeira Rivers: Sketches and Descriptions from the Note-Book of an Explorer*. Chapman and Hall, London, xvi + 177 pp. [p. 86]

Kelley, W. E. and J. W. Atz. 1964. A pygidiid catfish that can suck blood from goldfish. Copeia (Lawrence) 1964: 702–704.

King, J. S. Jr. and W. H. Boyce. 1963. *High Molecular Weight Substances in Human Urine*. Charles C Thomas, Springfield (Illinois), xiv + 165 pp.

Kinzer, J. 1959. Fische als Fischparasiten? Aquarien und Terrarien (Stuttgart) 6: 11–14.

Knols, B. G. J., J. J. A. van Loon, A. Cork, R. D. Robinson, W. Adam, J. Meijerink, R. de Jong, and W. Takken. 1997. Behavioural and electrophysiological responses of the female malaria mosquito *Anopheles gambiae* (Diptera: Culicidae) to Limburger cheese volatiles. Bulletin of Entomological Research (Wallingford) 87: 151–159.

Knudsen, E. I. 1974. Behavioral thresholds to electric signals in high frequency electric fish. Journal of Comparative Physiology (Heidelberg) 91A: 333–353.

Krause, F. 1911. *In den Wildnissen Brasiliens. Berichte und Ergebnisse der Leipziger Araguary-Expedition, 1908*. R. Voightländer, Leipzig, viii + 512 pp. [p. 50]

Lagler, K. R., J. E. Bardach, R. R. Miller, and D. R. M. Passino. 1977. *Ichthyology*, 2nd edition. John Wiley and Sons, New York, xv + 506 pp. [p. 420]

Lamb, B. 1954. The fisherman's porpoise. Natural History magazine (New York) 63: 231–232.

Lange, A. 1912. *In the Amazon Jungle: Adventures in Remote Parts of the Upper Amazon River, Including a Sojourn Among Cannibal Indians*. G. P. Putnam's Sons, New York, xx + 405 pp. [pp. 40, 214–217]

Larson, T. V., D. S. Covert, and R. Frank. 1979. A method for continuous measurement of ammonia in respiratory airways. Journal of Applied Physiology (Bethesda) 46: 603–607.

Lauzanne, L. and G. Loubens. 1985. *Peces del Rio Mamoré.* Éditions de l'ORSTOM, Institut Français de Recherche Scientifique pour le Développement en Coopération, Paris, 116 pp. [p. 114]

Le Cointe, P. 1922. *L'Amazonie Brésilienne: Le pays — Ses habitants, Ses ressources*[;] *Notes et statistiques jusqu'en 1920*, Vol. 2. Augustin Challamel, Paris, ii + 495 pp. [p. 365]

Leenheer, J. A. 1980. Origin and nature of humic substances in the waters of the Amazon River basin. Acta Amazonica (Manaus) 10: 513–526.

Lem, S. 1974. Tale of the three storytelling machines of King Genius. In *The Cyberiad: Fables for the Cybernetic Age.* The Seabury Press, New York, pp. 173–248.

Leung, K. M. Y., J. C. W. Chu, and R. S. S. Wu. 1999. Effects of body weight, water temperature and ration size on ammonia excretion by the areolated grouper (*Epinephelus areolatus*) and mangrove snapper (*Lutjanus argentimaculatus*). Aquaculture (Amsterdam) 170: 215–227.

Lippman, R. W. 1957. *Urine and the Urinary Sediment: A Practical Manual and Atlas,* 2nd edition. Charles C Thomas, Springfield (Illinois) ix + 140 pp.

Loew, E. R. and W. N. McFarland. 1990. The underwater visual environment. In *The Visual System of Fish*, R. Douglas and M. Djamgoz (editors). Chapman and Hall, London, pp. 1–43.

Lowe-McConnell, R. H. 1975. *Fish Communities in Tropical Freshwaters: Their Distribution, Ecology and Evolution.* Longman, London, xvii + 337 pp. [p. 43]

Ludwig, J. A. and J. F. Reynolds. 1988. *Statistical Ecology: A Primer on Methods and Computing.* John Wiley and Sons, New York, xviii + 337 pp.

Lüling, K. H. 1965. Jagd auf Fischriesen und Fischzwerge. Aquarien und Terrarien (Stuttgart) 12(5): 154–161.

Lüling, K. H. 1969. Seltsame Fischwelt in Amazonien. Natur und Museum (Frankfurt) 99: 571–579.

Lundberg, J. 2001. Freshwater riches of the Amazon. Natural History magazine (New York), September, pp. 36–43.

Lundberg, J. G. and L. Rapp Py-Daniel. 1994. *Bathycetopsis oliveirai*, gen. et sp. nov., a blind and depigmented catfish (Siluriformes: Cetopsidae) from the Brazilian Amazon. Copeia (Lawrence) 1994: 381–390.

Lütken, C. 1892. Om en med Stegophiler og Trichomycterer beslægtet sydamerikansk Mallefisk (*Acanthopoma annectens* Ltk. n. g. & sp.?). Videnskabelige Meddelelser Naturhistorisk Forening (Copenhagen) 5(3): 53–60.

Lutwick, L. I. And E. K. Chapnick. 1996. A whopper of a fish story. Infections in Medicine (New York) 13: 846, 854.

Lythgoe, J. N. 1988. Light and vision in the aquatic environment. In *Sensory Biology of Aquatic Animals*, J. Atema, R. Fay, A. N. Popper, and W. N. Tavolga (editors). Springer-Verlag, New York, pp. 57–82.

MacCreagh, G. 1926. *White Waters and Black.* Grosset and Dunlap, New York, viii + 404 pp.

Machado, F. A. and I. Sazima. 1983. Comportamento alimentar do peixe hematófago *Branchioica bertonii* (Siluriformes, Trichomycteridae). Ciência e Cultura (São Paulo) 35: 344–348.

Mahnert, V. 1985. Les candirus ou le danger des baignades exotiques. Musées de Genève 253: 8–12.

Mangum, C. P., M. S. Haswell, K. Johansen, and D. W. Towle. 1978. Inorganic ions and pH in the body fluids of Amazon animals. Canadian Journal of Zoology (Ottawa) 56: 907–916.

Marcoy, P. [L. Saint-Cricq] 1875. *Travels in South America: From the Pacific Ocean to the Atlantic Ocean*, Vol. 2: *Tumbuya—Sarayacu—Tierra Blanca—Nauta—Tabatinga—Santa Maria de Belem*. Scribner, Armstrong and Company, New York, viii + 496 pp., frontmaps. [pp. 184–187] (English edition of *Voyage à travers l'Amérique du Sud, de l'Océan Pacifique à l'Océan Atlantique*, Vol. 2. Librairie de L. Hachette et cie, Paris, pp. 145–146, 1869.)

Marui, T. and J. Caprio. 1994. Teleost gustation. In *Fish Chemoreception*, T. J. Hara (editor). Chapman and Hall, London, pp. 171–198.

Mathis, A., D. P. Chivers, and R. J. F. Smith. 1995. Chemical alarm signals: predator deterrents or predator attractants? American Naturalist (Chicago) 145: 994–1005.

McConnell, R. 1967. The fish fauna of the Rupununi district, Guyana. Timehri (Journal of the Guyana Museum and Zoo of the Royal Agricultural and Commercial Society) (Georgetown), No. 43, pp. 58–71.

McFarland, W. N. and W. A. Wimsatt. 1969. Renal function and its relation to the ecology of the vampire bat, *Desmodus rotundus*. Comparative Biochemistry and Physiology (Amsterdam) 28: 985–1006.

McMurtry, L. 1999. *Duane's Depressed.* Simon and Schuster, New York, 431 pp.

Medawar, P. B. 1953. Some immunological and endocrinological problems raised by the evolution of viviparity in vertebrates. Symposia of the Society for Experimental Biology (Cambridge, U.K.) 7: 320–338.

Miles, C. W. 1943a. *Estudio Economico y Ecologico de los Peces de Agua Dulce del Valle del Cauca.* Publicaciones de la Secretaría de Agricultura y Fomento del Departamento, Cali, 97 pp. [pp. 31–33]

Miles, C. 1943b. On three recently described species and a new genus of pygidiid fishes from Colombia. Revista de la Academia Colombiana de Ciencias

Exactas, Fisicas y Naturales (Bogotá) 5: 367–369.

Miller, L. E. 1921. *In the Wilds of South America.* T. Fisher Unwin, London, xiv + 428 pp.

Mitchell, G. C. and J. R. Tigner. 1970. The route of ingested blood in the vampire bat (*Desmodus rotundus*). Journal of Mammalogy (Lawrence) 51: 814–817.

Mommsen, T. P. and P. J. Walsh. 1992. Biochemical and environmental perspectives on nitrogen metabolism in fishes. Experientia (Basel) 48: 583–593.

Morton, D. 1986. The structure of the fundic caecum of the recently fed common vampire bat, *Desmodus rotundus.* Anatomical Record (New York) 114: 89A. [Abstract]

Müller, U. K., B. L. E. van den Heuvel, E. J. Stamhuis, and J. J. Videler. 1997. Fish foot prints: morphology and energetics of the wake behind a continuously swimming mullet (*Chelon labrosus* Risso). Journal of Experimental Biology (Cambridge, U.K.) 200: 2893–2906.

Mumcuoglu, Y., R. Galun, and R. Ikan. 1986. The aggregation response of human body louse [*sic*] (*Pediculus humanus*) (Insecta: Anoplura) to its excretory products. Insect Science and its Application (Nairobi) 7: 629–632.

Muntz, W. R. A. 1982. Visual adaptations to different environments in Amazonian fishes. Revue Canadienne de Biologie (Montreal) 41: 35–46.

Myers, G. S. 1927. Descriptions of new South American fresh-water fishes collected by Dr. Carl Ternetz. Bulletin of the Museum of Comparative Zoölogy (Cambridge, Massachusetts) 68: 106–135.

Myers, G. S. 1944. Two extraordinary new blind nematognath fishes from the Rio Negro, representing a new subfamily of Pygidiidae, with a rearrangement of the genera of the family, and illustrations of some previously described genera and species from Venezuela and Brazil. Proceedings of the California Academy of Sciences (San Francisco) 23: 591–602 + 5 plates.

Nagel, T. 1974. What is it like to be a bat? Philosophical Review (Ithaca) 83: 435–450.

Nelson, J. S. 1994. *Fishes of the World,* 3rd edition. John Wiley and Sons, New York, xvii + 600 pp. [pp. 168–169]

New, J. G., L. A. Fewkes, and A. N. Khan. 2001. Strike feeding behavior in the muskellunge, *Esox masquinongy:* contributions of the lateral line and visual sensory systems. Journal of Experimental Biology (Cambridge, U.K.) 204: 1207–1221.

Nichols, J. T. 1954. Retirement of E. W. Gudger. Copeia (Lawrence) 1954: 164–165.

Nicolaides, N. 1974. Skin lipids: their biochemical uniqueness. Science (Washington, D.C.) 186: 19–26.

Nilsson, D-E. and R. F. Modlin. 1994. A mysid shrimp carrying a pair of binoculars. Journal of Experimental Biology (Cambridge, U.K.) 189: 213–236.

Nomura, H. 1996. *Usos, Crendices e Lendas Sobre Peixes.* Fundação Vingt-Un Rolsado, Colção Mossoroense, Vol. 882 (Série C), Co-edição com ETFRN/UNED, Mossoró, 103 pp. [pp. 18–21]

Norman, J. R. and P. H. Greenwood. 1975. *A History of Fishes*, 3rd edition. Ernest Benn, London, xxv + 467 pp. [pp. 235–236]

Norwood, D. M., T. Wainman, P. J. Lioy, and J. M. Waldman. 1992. Breath ammonia depletion and its relevance to acidic aerosol exposure studies. Archives of Environmental Health (Washington, D.C.) 47: 309–313.

O'Hanlon, R. 1988. *In Trouble Again: A Journey Between the Orinoco and the Amazon.* Vintage Departures (1990 edition), New York, xi + 272 pp. [pp. 2–3, 66–68]

Orico, O. 1937. *Vocabulario de Crendices Amazonicas.* Companhia Editora Nacional, São Paulo, 283 pp. [p. 56]

Orton, J. 1870. *The Andes and the Amazon: Or, Across the Continent of South America.* Harper and Brothers, Philadelphia, xxiv + 356 pp.

Orton, J. 1876. *The Andes and the Amazon: Or, Across the Continent of South America*, 3rd edition. Harper and Brothers, Philadelphia, xxii + 645 pp., frontis, endmap. [pp. 482–483]

Ovchynnyk, M. M. 1968. Annotated list of the freshwater fish of Ecuador. Zoologischer Anzeiger (Leipzig) 181(3/4): 237–268.

Pellegrin, J. 1909a. Sur un poisson parasite nouveau de genre *Vandellia*. Comtes Rendus de l'Académie des Sciences (Paris) 149: 1016–1017.

Pellegrin, J. 1909b. Les poissons du genre *Vandellia* C. V. Bulletin de la Société Philomathique (N. S.) (Paris) 10: 197–204.

Pellegrin, J. 1911. Poissons de l'Equateur, Recueillis par M. le Dr. Rivet. In *Mission du Service Géographique de l'Armée pour la Mesure d'un Arc de Méridien Équatorial en Amérique du Sud, sous le Contrôle Scientifique de l'Académie des Sciences, 1899–1906*, Vol. 9—Zoologie, No. 2. Gauthier-Villars, Paris, pp. $B_1.1$–$B_1.15$ + plate.

Perugia, A. 1897. Di alcuni pesci raccolti in Bolicia dal Prof. Luigi Balzan. Annali del Museo Civico di Storia Naturale de Genova 18(Serie 2[a]): 16–27.

Peters, R. C. and F. Bretschneider. 1972. Electric phenomena in the habitat of the catfish *Ictalurus nebulosus* LeS. Journal of Comparative Physiology (Heidelberg) 81: 345–362.

Peters, R. C. and R. J. A. Buwalda. 1972. Frequency response of the electroreceptors ("small pit organs") of the catfish *Ictalurus nebulosus* LeS. Journal of Comparative Physiology (Heidelberg) 79: 113–135.

Peters, R. C. and J. Meek. 1973. Catfish and electric fields. Experientia (Basel) 29:

299–300.

Peters, R. C., W. J. G. Loos, and A. Gerritsen. 1974. Distribution of electroreceptors, bioelectric field patterns, and skin resistance in the catfish, *Ictalurus
nebulosus* LeS. Journal of Comparative Physiology (Heidelberg) 92: 11–32.

Pfister, E. 1913. Über das Penisfutteral des ägyptischen Gottes Bes. Archiv für
Geschichte der Medizin (Leipzig) 6: 59–64.

Prodgers, C. H. 1922. *Adventures in Bolivia.* Dodd, Mead and Company, New
York, xvi + 232 pp. [p. 115]

Prodgers, C. H. 1925. *Adventures in Peru.* E. P. Dutton and Company, New York,
xv + 250 pp. [p. 210]

Protasov, V. R. 1968. *Vision and Near Orientation of Fish.* Institute of Animal Evolution, Morphology, and Ecology, Academy of Sciences of the USSR,
Moscow, iv + 175 pp. (English edition, Israel Program for Scientific Translations, Jerusalem, 1970.)

Queiroz, E. 1997. Médico retira candiru de paciente em Manaus. A Critica
(Manaus), 6 November, p. A2.

Randall, D. J., W. W. Burggren, A. P. Farrell, and M. S. Haswell. 1981. *The Evolution of Air Breathing in Vertebrates.* Cambridge University Press, Cambridge
(U.K.), vii + 133 pp.

Randall, D. J., C. M. Wood, S. F. Perry, H. Bergman, G. M. O. Maloiy, T. P.
Mommsen, and P. A. Wright. 1989. Urea excretion as a strategy for survival in
a fish living in a very alkaline environment. Nature (London) 337: 165–166.

Read, C. P. 1970. *Parasitism and Symbiology: An Introductory Text.* Ronald Press,
New York, vii + 316 pp.

Reinhardt, J. 1858. Stegophilus insidiosus [*sic*], en ny Mallefisk fra Brasilien og
dens Levemaade. Videnskabelige Meddelelser fra Dansk Naturhistorisk
Forening (S. I.) (Copenhagen) 10: 79–97 + plate.

Riffkin, M., H-F. Seow, D. Jackson, L. Brown, and P. Wood. 1996. Defence against
the immune barrage: helminth survival strategies. Immunology and Cell
Biology (Carlton) 74: 564–574.

Robbins, T. 1994. *Half Asleep in Frog Pajamas.* Bantam Books, New York, 386 pp.

Roberts, T. R. 1972. Ecology of fishes in the Amazon and Congo basins. Bulletin
of the Museum of Comparative Zoology (Cambridge, Massachusetts) 143:
117–147. [pp. 136–138]

Roethke, T. 1964. In a dark time. In *The Far Field.* Doubleday, New York, p. 79.

Rogers, P. H. and M. Cox. 1988. Underwater sound as a biological stimulus. In
Sensory Biology of Aquatic Animals, J. Atema, R. R. Fay, A. N. Popper, and W.
N. Tavolga (editors). Springer-Verlag, New York, pp. 131–149.

Román-Valencia, C. 1993. Historia natural del jetudo, *Ichthyoelephas longirostris* (Steindachner 1879) (Pisces: Prochilodontidae) en la cuenca del Rio La Vieja, Alto Cauca, Colombia. Brenesia (San José) 39/40: 71–80.

Román-Valencia, C. 1998. Redescripcion de *Branchioica phaneronema* Miles, 1943 (Pisces: Trichomycteridae) de la cuenca del Rio Magdalena, Colombia. Revista de la Academia Colombiana de Ciencias Exactas, Fisicas y Naturales (Bogotá) 22(83): 299–303.

Roosevelt, T. 1920. *Through the Brazilian Wilderness*. Charles Scribner's Sons, New York, 410 pp. + frontmap.

Roth, A. 1972. Wozu dienen die Elektrorezeptoren der Welse? Journal of Comparative Physiology (Heidelberg) 79: 113–135.

Rouk, C. S. and B. P. Glass. 1970. Comparative gastric histology of five North and Central American bats. Journal of Mammalogy (Lawrence) 51: 455–472.

Ruffer, M. A. 1910. Note on the presence of "bilharzia haematobia" in Egyptian mummies of the twentieth dynasty (1250–1000 B.C.). British Medical Journal (London), No. 1, p. 16.

Saffo, M. B. 1992. Coming to terms with a field: words and concepts in symbiosis. Symbiosis (Rehovot) 14: 17–31.

Santos, E. 1962. *Peixes da Água Doce (Vida e costumes dos peixes do Brasil)*, 2nd edição, revista e aumentada. F. Briguiet e Cia., Editôres, Rio de Janeiro, 278 pp. [pp. 115–117]

Santos, E. 1981. *Peixes da Água Doce: (Vida e costumes dos peixes do Brasil)*. Editora Itatiaia, Belo Horizonte, 267 pp. [pp. 105–107]

Saul, W. G. 1975. An ecological study of fishes at a site in upper Amazonian Ecuador. Proceedings of the Academy of Natural Sciences of Philadelphia 127: 93–134. [pp. 117–118]

Saunders, G. 2000. Pastoralia. In *Pastoralia: Stories*. Riverhead Books, New York, pp. 1–66.

Schellart, N. A. M. 1992. Interrelations between the auditory, the visual and the lateral line systems of teleosts; a mini-review of modelling sensory capabilities. Netherlands Journal of Zoology (Leiden) 42: 459–477.

Schellart, N. A. M. and R. J. Wubbels.1998. The auditory and mechanosensory lateral line system. In *The Physiology of Fishes*, 2nd edition, D. H. Evans (editor). CRC Press, Boca Raton, pp. 283–312.

Schmidt, R. E. 1987. Redescription of *Vandellia beccarii* (Siluriformes: Trichomycteridae) from Guyana. Copeia (Lawrence) 1987: 234–237.

Schmidt, R. E. 1993. Relationships and notes on the biology of *Paracanthopoma parva* (Pisces: Trichomycteridae). Ichthyological Exploration of Freshwaters

(Munich) 4: 185–191.

Schmidt-Nielsen, K. 1975. *Animal Physiology: Adaptaton and Environment.* Cambridge University Press, New York, 699 pp.

Schomburgk [R. H.]. 1840. Remarkable habit in a fish. Annals and Magazine of Natural History (London) 6: 395–396.

Schomburgk [R. H.] 1841. Miscellen. Froriep's Neue Notizen aus dem Gebiete der Natur- und Heilkunde (Weimar) 18(379), col. 72. (German translation of Schomburgk's 1840 article.)

Schreider, H. and F. Schreider. 1970. *Exploring the Amazon.* National Geographic Society, Washington (D.C.), 207 pp. [pp. 68–70]

Schuijf, A. and R. J. A. Buwalda. 1980. Underwater localization—a major problem in fish acoustics. In *Comparative Studies of Hearing in Vertebrates,* A. N. Popper and R. R. Fay (editors). Springer-Verlag, New York, pp. 43–77.

Schultz, L. P. and E. M. Stern. 1948. *The Ways of Fishes.* D. Van Nostrand, Princeton, xii + 264 pp. [pp. 65–67]

Shea, C. 1999. Ask Audubon. Audubon magazine (New York) 101(1): 104.

Shirreffs, S. M. and R. J. Maughan. 1997. Whole body sweat collection in humans: an improved method with preliminary data on electrolyte content. Journal of Applied Physiology (Bethesda) 82: 336–341.

Shmaefsky, B. R. 1990. Artificial urine for laboratory testing. American Biology Teacher (Reston) 52: 170–173.

Sick, H. 1960. *Tukani.* Eriksson-Taplinger Company, New York, 240 pp. [p. 29]

Singer, I. B. 1965. Yentl the yeshiva boy. In *Short Friday and Other Stories.* Signet Books, New York, pp. 124–150.

Smart, J. J. C. 1963. *Philosophy and Scientific Realism.* Routledge and Kegan Paul, London, viii + 160 pp.

Smith, A. 1990. *Explorers of the Amazon.* Viking, New York, 344 pp.

Smith, C. L. 1994. Fish really are interesting! Friends of Fishes Newsletter (New York), June issue, pp. 2–4.

Smith, N. J. H. 1981. *Man, Fishes, and the Amazon.* Columbia University Press, New York, x + 180 pp. [pp. 68, 98]

Smith, R. J. F. 1992. Alarm signals in fishes. Reviews in Fish Biology and Fisheries (Dordrecht) 2: 33–63.

Sontag, S. 1973. *On Photography.* Farrar, Straus and Giroux, New York, 207 pp.

Sorensen, P. W. and J. Caprio. 1998. Chemoreception. In *The Physiology of Fishes*, 2nd edition, D. H. Evans (editor). CRC Press, Boca Raton, pp. 375–405.

Spotte, S. 1992. *Captive Seawater Fishes: Science and Technology*. John Wiley and Sons, New York, xxii + 942 pp.

Spotte, S., P. Petry, and J. A. S. Zuanon. 2001. Experiments on the feeding behavior of the hematophagous candiru, *Vandellia* cf. *plazaii*. Environmental Biology of Fishes (Guelph) 60: 459–464.

St. Clair, D. 1968. *The Mighty, Mighty Amazon*. Souvenir Press, London, xv + 304 pp. [p. 13]

Stewart, D., R. Barriga, and M. Ibarra. 1987. Ictiofauna de la cuenca del Río Napo, Ecuador oriental: lista anotada de especies. Politecnica (Quito) 12(4): 10–63. [pp. 33–34]

Stoker, B. 1897. *Dracula*. Barnes and Noble Books, New York, 404 pp. (1992 facsimile edition.)

Stradelli, E. 1929. *Vocabularios da lingua geral portuguez-nheêgatú e nheêgatú-portuguez, precedidos de um exboço de gramatica nheênga-umbuê-sauá-miri e seguidos de contos em lingua geral nheêngatú poranduua*. Revista do Instituto Histórico e Geográphico Brasileiro (Rio de Janeiro), Vol. 104, 158 (2° de 1928): 1–768. [pp. 394–395]

Suby, H. I., R. M. Suby, and F. Albright. 1943. Properties of organic acid solutions which determine their irritability to the bladder mucous membrane and the effect of magnesium ions in overcoming this irritability. Journal of Urology (Philadelphia) 48: 549–562.

Szabo, T. 1974. Anatomy of the specialized lateral line organs of electroreception. In *Handbook of Sensory Physiology*, Vol. III/3, A. Fessard (editor). Springer-Verlag, Berlin, pp. 13–58.

Taneja, J. and P. M. Guerin. 1997. Ammonia attracts the haematophagous bug *Triatoma infestans*: behavioural and neurophysiological data on nymphs. Journal of Comparative Physiology (Heidelberg) 181A: 21–34.

Taube, G. 2000. Searching for a parasite's weak spot. Science (Washington, D.C.) 290: 434–437.

Tchernavin, V. V. 1944. A revision of some Trichomycterinae based on material preserved in the British Museum (Natural History). Proceedings of the Zoological Society of London 114: 234–275.

Telles Ribeiro, E. 1994. *I Would Have Loved Him If I Had Not Killed Him*. St. Martin's Press, New York, vii + 199 pp. (English edition of *O Criado-Mudo*, Editora Brasiliense, São Paulo, 1990.)

Trager, W. 1986. *Living Together: The Biology of Animal Parasitism*. Plenum Press,

New York, xii + 467 pp.

Tricas, T. C., S. W. Michael, and J. A. Sisneros. 1995. Electrosensory optimization to conspecific phasic signals for mating. Neuroscience Letters (Coclare) 202: 129–132.

van Beneden, P-J. 1876. *Animal Parasites and Messmates*. D. Appleton and Company, New York, xxviii + 274 pp.

Van der Goes van Naters, W. M. and C. J. den Otter. 1998. Amino acids as taste stimuli for tsetse flies. Physiological Entomology (Oxford) 23: 278–284.

Van der Goes van Naters, W. M. and T. H. N. Rinkes. 1993. Taste stimuli for tsetse flies on the human skin. Chemical Senses (Oxford) 18: 437–444.

Vaz-Ferreira, R. 1969. *Peces del Uruguay*. Editorial Nuestra Tierra, Montevideo, 72 pp. [pp. 41–42]

Verne, J. 1881. *The Giant Raft. Eight Hundred Leagues on the Amazon*. Fredonia Books, Amsterdam, iv + 167 pp. (2001 English edition of *La Janagada. Huit cent lieues sur l'Amazone*, translator and date of translation unknown.)

Vinton, K. W. and W. H. Stickler. 1941. The carnero: a fish parasite of man and possibly other mammals. American Journal of Surgery (N. S.) (New York) 54: 511–519.

von den Steinen, K. 1886. *Durch Central-Brasilien Expedition zur Erforschung des Schingú im Jahre 1884*. F. A. Brockhaus, Leipzig, xii + 372 pp., frontis, endmap. [pp. 178–179]

von den Steinen, K. 1894. *Unter den Naturvölkern Zentral-Brasiliens. Reiseschilderung und Ergebnisse dur Zweiten Schingú-Expedition 1887–1888*. Verlagsbuchhandlung Dietrich Reimer (Berlin), xiv + 570 pp., endmap. [pp. 195–196, including footnote] (1968 facsimile edition, Johnson Reprint Company, New York.)

von der Emde, G. 1998. Electroreception. In *The Physiology of Fishes*, 2nd edition, D. H. Evans (editor). CRC Press, Boca Raton, pp. 313–343.

von Frisch, K. 1938. The sense of hearing in fish. Nature (London) 141: 8–11.

von Humboldt, A. 1852? *Personal Narrative of Travels to the Equinoctial Regions of America During the Years 1799–1804*, Vol. 1. George Routledge and Sons, London, xxii + 505 pp.

von Ihering, R. 1940. *Dicionario de Animais do Brasil*. Directoria de Publicidade Agrícola, São Paulo, 898 pp. [pp. 201–203]

von Müller, K. 1870. Gustav Wallis: Eine biographische-naturgeschichliche Skizze 14. Reise in dem Andengebirge. Die Natur (Halle) 19: 180–182.

von Poeppig, E. 1836. *Reise in Chile, Peru und auf dem Amazonenstrome, während der Jahre 1827–1832*. F. A. Brockhaus Kommentar und Gesetzestext GmbH.,

Stuttgart, xii + 464 pp., 16 plates, endmap. [p. 395, footnote] (1960 facsimile edition.)

von Spix, J. B. and C. F. P. von Martius. 1823 [–1831?]. *Reise in Brasilien in den Jahren 1817–1820*, Vol. 3. M. Lindauer, München, viii + pp. 885–1388. [pp. 955–956] (1966 facsimile edition, F. A. Brockhaus, Stuttgart.)

Wallace, A. R. 1889. *A Narrative of Travels on the Amazon and Rio Negro*, 2nd edition. Ward, Lock and Company, London, xxvi + 363 pp. (1972 facsimile edition, Dover Publications, New York.)

Walsh, P. J. 1998. Nitrogen excretion and metabolism. In *The Physiology of Fishes*, 2nd edition, D. H. Evans (editor). CRC Press, Boca Raton, pp. 199–214.

Weissburg, M. J., M. H. Doall, and J. Yen. 1998. Following the invisible trail: kinematic analysis of mate-tracking in the copepod *Temora longicornis*. Philosophical Transactions of the Royal Society of London 353B: 701–712.

Weissburg, M. J. and R. K. Zimmer-Faust. 1993. Life and death in moving fluids: hydrodynamic effects on chemosensory-mediated predation. Ecology (Washington, D.C.) 74: 1428–1443.

Weitzman, S. H. and R. P. Vari. 1988. Miniaturization in South American freshwater fishes: an overview and discussion. Proceedings of the Biological Society of Washington (Washington, D.C.) 10: 444–465.

Whitfield, P. J. 1979. *The Biology of Parasitism: An Introduction to the Study of Associating Organisms*. University Park Press, Baltimore, x + 277 pp.

Wilkie, M. P. 1997. Mechanisms of ammonia excretion across fish gills. Comparative Biochemistry and Physiology (Amsterdam) 118A: 39–50.

Wilson, R. W. and D. L. Snellgrove. 1999. Sodium and ammonia transport mechanisms in acidophilic Amazonian fish. In *Nitrogen Production and Excretion in Fish*. Physiology Section, American Fisheries Society, Madison, pp. 19–26.

Wimsatt, W. A. 1969. Transient behavior, nocturnal activity patterns, and feeding efficiency of vampire bats (*Desmodus rotundus*) under natural conditions. Journal of Mammalogy (Lawrence) 50: 233–244.

Wimsatt, W. A. and A. Guerriere. 1962. Observations on the feeding capacities and excretory functions of captive vampire bats. Journal of Mammalogy (Lawrence) 43: 17–27.

Winemiller, K. O. and H. Y. Yan. 1989. Obligate mucus-feeding in a South American trichomycterid catfish (Pisces: Ostariophysi). Copeia (Lawrence) 1989: 511–514.

Wood, C. M. 1993. Ammonia and urea metabolism and excretion. In *The Physiology of Fishes*, D. H. Evans (editor). CRC Press, Boca Raton, pp. 379–425.

Wood, C. M., H. L. Bergman, P. Laurent, J. N. Maina, A. Narahara, and P. J. Walsh. 1994. Urea production, acid-base regulation and their interactions in the Lake Magadi tilapia, a unique teleost adapted to a highly alkaline environment. Journal of Experimental Biology (Cambridge, U.K.) 189: 13–36.

Woodroffe, J. F. 1914. *The Upper Reaches of the Amazon.* Macmillan, New York, xvi + 304 pp. [pp. 95–96]

Wright, P. A. 1993. Nitrogen excretion and enzyme pathways for ureagenesis in freshwater tilapia (*Oreochromis niloticus*). Physiological Zoology (Chicago) 66: 881–901.

Wyler, D. J. 1990. *Modern Parasite Biology: Cellular, Immunological, and Molecular Aspects.* W. H. Freeman, New York, xvii + 428 pp.

Yardley, H. J. 1958. The composition of normal and pathological urine with an estimate of the concentration of unanalyzed substances. Clinica Chimica Acta (Amsterdam) 3: 280–287.

Zar, J. H. 1999. *Biostatistical Analysis,* 4th edition. Prentice Hall, Upper Saddle River, xii + 663 pp., appendices, index.

Zhadan, G. G., and P. M. Zhadan. 1976. Effect of sodium, potassium, and calcium ions on electroreceptor function in catfish. Neurophysiology (New York) 7: 312–318.

Index

Index entries have been excluded for figure and table legends and content, author's names in literature citations (endnotes), and foreign language endnotes (entries from their English translations in the main text have been included).

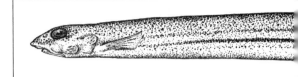

Photo by Lucia S. Spotte

STEPHEN SPOTTE, a marine scientist at Mote Marine Laboratory in Sarasota, Florida, was born and raised in West Virginia. He was formerly a research scientist at the Marine Sciences and Technology Center, the University of Connecticut. Spotte holds a bachelor's degree from Marshall University, a doctorate from the University of Southern Mississippi, and is author of eighty scientific articles, eight nonfiction books, and two works of fiction.